WRITERS AND PROTESTANTISM
IN THE NORTH OF IRELAND

And I, born to the purple passage
Was heir to all that Adamnation
And hand-me-down of doom, the late comer
To the worn-out womb.

W.R. Rodgers, from 'Epilogue' to
The Character of Ireland

Writers and Protestantism in the North of Ireland

Heirs to Adamnation?

BARRY SLOAN

IRISH ACADEMIC PRESS
DUBLIN • PORTLAND, OR

First published in 2000 by
IRISH ACADEMIC PRESS
44, Northumberland Road, Dublin 4, Ireland
and in the United States of America by
IRISH ACADEMIC PRESS
c/o ISBS, 5804 NE Hassalo Street,
Portland, OR 97213-3644

website: www.iap.ie

British Library Cataloguing in Publication Data
Sloan, Barry
Writers and Protestantism in the North of Ireland: heirs to adamnation
1. Protestantism and literature 2. Protestantism
I. Title
820. 9'382804

ISBN 0-7165-2636-0

Library of Congress Cataloging-in-Publication Data
Sloan, Barry.
Writers and Protestantism in the north of Ireland: heirs to adamnation/
Barry Sloan.
p. cm.
Includes bibliographical references and index.
ISBN 0-7165-2636-0 (hardcover)
1. English literature—Northern Ireland—History and criticism.
2. English literarure—Protestant authors—History and criticism. 3. English
literature— Irish authors—History and criticism. 4. English literature—
20th century—History and criticism. 5. Protestantism and literature—
History—20th century. 6. Northern Ireland—Intellectual life—20th
century. 7. Protestants—Northern Ireland—Intellectual life. 8. Northern
Ireland—In literature. 9. Protestants in literature.   I. Title.

PR8891.N67 S6 2000
820.9'9416–dc21   99–085975

Typeset in 11pt on 13pt Sabon by
Carrigboy Typesetting Services, County Cork
Printed by Creative Print and Design (Wales), Ebbw Vale

For Brendan and Liam

Contents

Preface

B ARRY SLOAN'S *Writers and Protestantism in the North of Ireland: Heirs to Adamnation* is a careful and ordered examination of a culture which has been, in academic and critical terms, frowned upon and more often than not, dismissed as a contradiction in terms.

I recall an intense and heated conversation in Galway in 1985 with several highly respected Irish writers and critics who were not at all amused by the fact that, along with the Belfast-based critic and academic, Edna Longley, I was editing *Across a Roaring Hill*, an anthology of essays which set out to examine the relationship between the terms 'Protestant', 'imagination' and 'modern Ireland'. This was giving some kind of literary and/or academic cover to the noxious sectarianism of unionism and amounted to political folly. Even the leopard's spots were mentioned in passing, half-jokingly.

It was, as we say now, all part of a learning curve.

Cultural stereotypes just don't happen: intellectuals and the media maintain them. It is generally the case that while ordinary folk get on with living their lives as best they can, ignoring (or defying) the typecasting, the civic and cultural moulds by which, for instance, literature is read, are mostly dependent on critical and historical assumptions fabricated by political will.

In *Writers and Protestantism in the North of Ireland*, Barry Sloan has traced some of the main roots of modern northern Irish Protestantism and its impact on the fiction, drama and poetry of a selective group of writers from Northern Ireland. Mindful of the extent to which religion in the form of Protestantism has its very own imaginative laws and structures, Barry Sloan reminds us in this important work of how unacceptable it is to overlook the nature of northern Protestantism and the cultural formations out of which radical Presbyterianism, as well as unionism, emerged over the last two centuries and more.

As he rightly states in the chapter dealing with 'The Legacy of John Calvin': 'In Ireland, and especially among the Protestants of Ulster, the Calvinistic inheritance is particularly complex, reaching deep into the spiritual lives of many generations, and also permeating the entire culture of the region in very particular ways'.

Bearing in mind the necessary strictures which many now feel need to be applied to the obsessive, essentializing politics (and literature) of identity, Barry Sloan's study is a powerful act of cultural self understanding and retrieval. He has furnished us with a coherent and concise illustration of how one of the key heterogeneous elements of literary and political culture in Ireland was formed.

From this complex base, the meshing of that culture – religious and political – can perhaps now be critically seen as precisely *that* – complex. An acknowledgement more easily said than done.

In the hothouse of Irish literary and critical debate, with so much taken as a foregone conclusion, Barry Sloan has written a clear-sighted and imaginative study. As a resource, it will point students of Irish literature to novels and drama and historical writing which they might not come in contact with in the ordinary run of events.

The argument which he presents is vindicated with extensive reading and yet it will also allow for divergent interpretations.

Barry Sloan cites E.R.Dodds' recollection of a comment by Louis MacNeice: 'I believe that as a human being it is my duty to make patterns and to contribute to order – good patterns and a good order'. The important thing is that Barry Sloan has brought in *Writers and Protestantism in the North of Ireland* an intensely focused range of work, for the first time, into a coherent and articulate critical shape. In his patient study, Barry Sloan has achieved 'good patterns and a good order'.

One can ask no more of any critic in this day and age.

GERALD DAWE
Trinity College Dublin
June 2000

Acknowledgements

THE ORIGINS OF this book lie ultimately in my own background and upbringing in the Protestant community in Northern Ireland and involve all kinds of indebtedness extending over three generations of family and friends which it would be impossible to catalogue. The book itself is an attempt to explore and explain the complexity of that background, particularly in respect of its significance for writers of various kinds. After long neglect, summary dismissal or marginalisation, the growing awareness of Northern Irish Protestant culture as distinctive and worthy of serious consideration owes much to the important work of critics and commentators such as Terence Brown, John Wilson Foster, Edna Longley, Norman Vance, Gerald Dawe and Peter McDonald, all of whom have given great stimulus to my own thinking and research.

More specifically, I am especially grateful for the encouragement and helpful suggestions I received from Norman Vance; for the interest shown in my work by Gerald Dawe, John Erskine, David Silvanus and Bernard Tucker, who, as my former Head of Department, also enabled me to have a sabbatical semester which was of invaluable practical help in enabling me to complete my writing; for the assistance of the staff in the University of Southampton New College library, and for the support given by Linda Longmore of the Irish Academic Press. I must also acknowledge the part played by some of my former students who shared in discussions about many of the writers and issues dealt with here and who were interested to know more and to ask why.

My final word, however, goes to my late dear wife, Diane, for her patience and backing from first to last, and to my sons for their sense of humour.

I wish to thank the following: Abbey Press for permission to quote from *The Rest is History* by Gerald Dawe; Arnold for permission to quote from Joel Hurstfield (ed.), *The Reformation Crisis*; Mrs C. Barkley and White Row Press for permission to quote from *Blackmouth and Dissenter* by John M. Barkley; B.T. Batsford Ltd. for permission to quote from *An Irish Portrait* by Paul Henry; Belcouver Press for permission to quote from *The Idea of the Union* edited by John Wilson Foster; Csilla Bertha, Donald E. Morse and Lajos Kossuth University for permission to quote from *Worlds Visible and Invisible: Essays on Irish Literature* by Csilla Bertha and Donald E. Morse; The Blackstaff Press for permission to quote from *A History of Ulster* by Jonathan Bardon; from *December Bride* by Sam Hanna Bell; from *Collected Plays 1* and *2*, from *Out of My Class* and *The Middle of My Journey* all by John Boyd; from *A Precarious Belonging: Presbyterians and the Conflict in Ireland* by John Dunlop; from *No Surrender: An Ulster Childhood* by Robert Harbinson; from *Ancestral Voices: The Selected Prose of John Hewitt* and *The Collected Poems of John Hewitt* both by John Hewitt; from *Images of Belfast* by Robert Johnstone and Bill Kirk; from *The Road to the Somme* by Philip Orr; Blackwell Publishers for permission to quote from *Irish Literature: A Social History* by Norman Vance; Bloodaxe Books for permission to quote from *Journey into Joy* by Brendan Kennelly, *Poetry in the Wars* and *The Living Stream: Literature and Revisionism in Ireland* both by Edna Longley, and *Ireland and the English Crisis* by Tom Paulin; D. George Boyce and *History Ireland* for permission to quote from 'Ireland in the First World War'; for permission to quote from *Proust and Three Dialogues with George Duthuit*, I thank The Samuel Beckett Estate and The Calder Educational Trust, London and Grove/Atlantic, Inc; Cambridge University Press for permission to quote from *Religion and Political Culture in Britain* by David Hempton, *The Christian Polity of John Calvin* by Harro Höpfl, *Varieties of Parable* by Louis MacNeice, *The Puritan-Provincial Vision (Scottish and American Literature in the Nineteenth Century)* by Susan Manning, *A Critical History of Modern Irish Drama 1891–1980* by D.E.S. Maxwell, *Scenes of Nature, Signs of Men* by Tony Tanner; Carcanet Press Ltd for permission to quote from *Collected Poems* by Iain Crichton Smith; Lucy Rodgers Cohen for permission to quote from *The Return Room* by W.R. Rodgers; Columba Press for permission to quote from *Where Do We Go From Here? Protestants and the Future of Northern Ireland* by Timothy Kinahan; Peter Coveney for permission to quote from *The Image of Childhood*; W. and B. Eerdmans Publishing Co. for permission to quote from the *Institutes of the Christian Religion* by John Calvin; Faber and Faber Ltd for permission to quote from *Apostate* by Forrest Reid; from *Observe the Sons of Ulster Marching Towards the Somme* by Frank McGuinness; from *Celtic Revivals: Essays in Modern Irish Literature* by Seamus Deane; from *The Redress of Poetry* by Seamus Heaney; from *A State of Justice, The Strange Museum, Liberty Tree,*

Fivemiletown, Walking a Line, Writing to the Moment: Selected Critical Essays and *Minotaur: Poetry and the Nation State* all by Tom Paulin; Field Day Publications for permission to quote from *The Whole Protestant Community: The Making of a Historical Myth* by Terence Brown, *Watchmen in Sion: The Protestant Ideal of Liberty* by Marianne Elliott, *Revising the Rising* edited by M. Ní Dhonnchadha and T. Dorgan, and *The Field Day Anthology of Irish Writing*; Four Courts Press for permission to quote from *The Siege of Derry in Ulster Protestant Mythology* by Ian McBride; The Gallery Press for permission to quote from *Courtyards in Delft, The Hudson Letter: Selected Poems* and *Journalism* all by Derek Mahon and from *Poems* by W.R. Rodgers; Gill and Macmillan for permission to quote from *Ulster Presbyterianism: The Historical Perspective 1610–1970* by Peter Brooke, *Louis MacNeice: Sceptical Vision* and *Northern Voices* both by Terence Brown, *Forces and Themes in Ulster Fiction* by John Wilson Foster, *Memory and Redemption: Church, Politics and Prophetic Theology in Ireland* by Terence P. McCaughey, *Queen's Rebels: Ulster Loyalism in Historical Perspective* by David W. Miller, *Contemporary Irish Drama (from Beckett to McGuinness)* by Anthony Roche, and *Over the Bridge* by Sam Thompson with introduction by Stewart Parker; HarperCollins Publishers Ltd for permission to quote from *Hope Against Hope* by Nadezhda Mandelstam; Hugh Haughton, Bernard O'Donoghue and Seren for permission to quote from *The Chosen Ground: Essays on Contemporary Poetry of Northern Ireland*, edited by Neil Corcoran; Nick Hern Books for permission to quote from *A Love Song for Ulster* by Bill Morrison; David Higham Associates for permission to quote from *Collected Poems* and *The Strings Are False* by Louis MacNeice, and to David Higham Associates and Oxford University Press for permission to quote from *Selected Plays of Louis MacNeice, Selected Literary Criticism of Louis MacNeice, Selected Prose of Louis MacNeice*; Finlay Holmes for permission to quote from his book, *Henry Cooke*; C. Hurst and Co. for permission to quote from *Loyal to King Billy: A Portrait of the Ulster Unionists* by Robert G. Crawford; *Irish University Review* for permission to quote from essays by Terence Brown, Kathleen Shields and Bill Tinley in *Special Issue: Derek Mahon*; Island Publications for permission to quote from *Beyond the Fife and Drum*; E. Kennedy-Andrews and Macmillan for permission to quote from *Contemporary Irish Poetry: A Collection of Critical Essays* edited by Elmer Andrews; Lapwing Publications for permission to quote from *Poverty Street and Other Poems* by Thomas Carnduff; The Lilliput Press for permission to quote from *Ireland's*

Literature: Selected Essays by Terence Brown, *Colonial Consequences* by John Wilson Foster, *The Battle of the Books* by W.J. McCormack, *Galway of the Races: Selected Essays by Robert Lynd* edited by Sean McMahon, and *A Citizen's Inquiry: The Opsahl Report on Northern Ireland* edited by A. Pollak; Belinda Loftus and Picture Press for permission to quote from *Mirrors: William III and Mother Ireland* and *Mirrors: Orange and Green* both by Belinda Loftus; Edna Longley and Faber and Faber Ltd for permission to quote from *Louis MacNeice: A Study* by Edna Longley, and Edna Longley and Blackstaff Press for permission to quote from *Across a Roaring Hill: The Protestant Imagination in Modern Ireland* edited by Gerald Dawe and Edna Longley; Manchester University Press, Manchester UK for permission to quote from *Mirror up to Nature: Twentieth-Century Irish Drama* by Christopher Murray; Methuen Publishing Ltd for permission to quote from *Tea in a China Cup* by Christina Reid; The Nonesuch Library for permission to quote from *Milton: Collected Poetry and Selected Prose* edited by E.H. Visiak; Oberon Books for permission to quote from *Three Plays for Ireland* by Stewart Parker; The O'Brien Press Ltd for permission to quote from *The Ferret Fancier* by Anthony C. West; Orion Publishing Group Ltd for permission to quote from *Collected Poems 1945–1990* by R.S. Thomas; Oxford University Press for permission to quote from *The Tragedy of Belief: Division, Politics and Religion in Ireland* by John Fulton, from *Culture and Anarchy in Ireland 1890–1939* by F.S.L. Lyons, from *Louis MacNeice: The Poet in His Contexts* and from *Mistaken Identities: Poetry and Northern Ireland* both by Peter McDonald, from *Apollo's Blended Dream: A Study of the Poetry of Louis MacNeice* by W.T. McKinnon, from *Night Crossing, Lives, The Snow Party, Poems 1962–1978* and *The Hunt by Night* all by Derek Mahon, from *The Cave of Making: The Poetry of Louis MacNeice* by Robyn Marsack, from *Improprieties: Politics and Sexuality in Northern Irish Poetry* by Clair Wills, and from an article by Kingsley Amis in *Essays in Criticism*; Oxford University Press (New York) for permission to quote from essays by Paul John Eakin and Linda Peterson in *Studies in Autobiography* edited by James Olney, and from *Theology of Culture* by Paul Tillich; The Presbyterian Church in Ireland for permission to quote from *God's River in Spate: The Story of the Religious Awakening of Ulster in 1859* by John T. Carson, *Our Irish Presbyterian Heritage* by R.F.G. Holmes, and *Presbyterian Principles and Political Witness*; Random House U.K. Ltd for permission to quote from *Inventing Ireland* by Declan Kiberd; Rodopi for permission to quote from *Politics and the Rhetoric of Poetry: Perspectives on Modern Anglo-Irish Poetry*, edited by Tjebbe A. Westendorp and Jane Mallinson; RKP for permission to quote from *A Gathered Church: The Literature of the English Dissenting Interest 1700–1930* by Donald Davie, and Routledge for permission to quote from *History and Ethnicity* edited by E. Tonkin, M. McDonald and M. Chapman, *Evangelical Protestantism in Ulster Society 1740–1890* by David Hempton and Myrtle Hill, and *Ireland's Field Day* edited by Seamus Deane; SCM Press for permission to quote from *The Long-Legged Fly* by Don Cupitt, *Metaphorical Language: Models of God in Religious Language* by Sallie McFague, and *The Go-Between God* by John V. Taylor; Secker and Warburg for permission to quote from *Gilchrist* by Maurice Leitch; The Society of Authors as the literary representative of the estate of St John Ervine for permission to quote from *John Ferguson, Mixed Marriage, The Orangeman, Boyd's Shop, Friends and Relations, The Foolish Lovers,* and *The Wayward Man*, all by St John Ervine; Norman Vance and *Religion and Literature* for permission to quote from 'Catholic and Protestant Literary Visions of 'Ulster': Now You See It, Now You Don't' by Norman Vance; A.P. Watt Ltd on behalf of Althea C. Harvey and Susan Harper for permission to quote from *An Irishman Looks at His World, The Northern Iron, The Red Hand of Ulster* and *Pleasant Places*, all by George Birmingham; A.P. Watt Ltd on behalf of David Alexander for permission to quote from *As Strangers Here* by Janet McNeill.

I also acknowledge brief specific references to the following publishers and works: Abacus (Little, Brown and Co.) for *Burning Your Own* by Glenn Patterson; W. and G. Baird for *Challenge and Conflict: Essays in Presbyterian History and Doctrine; The Bell*; Benham and Co. for *Essex Roundabout* by W.R. Rodgers; Blackstaff Press for *Further Reminiscences* by Paul Henry and for *From the Jungle of Belfast* by Denis Ireland; Bucknell University Press for *W.R. Rodgers* by Darcy O'Brien; *Causeway*; T. and T. Clark for *Calvinism* by Abraham Kuyper; Dorman for *An Ulster Protestant Looks at his World* by Denis Ireland; Douglas Dunn and Carcanet for *Two Decades of Irish Writing* edited by Douglas Dunn; Dolmen Press for *Time Was Away: The World of Louis MacNeice* edited by Terence Brown and Alec Reid, and for *Even Without Irene* by Robert Greacen; Duckworth for *Armour of Ballymoney* by W.S. Armour; *Folklife*; Fontana for *Reformation Europe 1517–1559* by G.R. Elton; *Fortnight*; Gaberbocchus for *Green Seacoast* by George Buchanan; Granta for *The Star Factory* by Ciaran Carson; Grant Richards for *Ireland A Nation* by Robert Lynd; Francis Griffiths for *Irish and English* by Robert Lynd; Robert Harbinson for *Up Spake the Cabin Boy* and *The*

Protégé; HarperCollins for *Home Life in Ireland* by Robert Lynd; Harrap for *The Arts in Ulster* edited by Sam Hanna Bell, Nessa A. Robb and John Hewitt; *Honest Ulsterman*; Institute of Irish Studies for *Cultural Traditions in Northern Ireland* edited by Maurna Crozier, *The Poet's Place: Ulster Literature and Society* edited by Gerald Dawe and John Wilson Foster, *Culture in Ireland: Division or Diversity?* edited by Edna Longley and *The Cultures of Europe: The Irish Contribution* edited by J.P. Mackey; *Irish Review*; Lagan Press for *Life and Writings* by Thomas Carnduff, *A Life Elsewhere* and *False Faces: Poetry, Politics and Place* by Gerald Dawe, *Even Without Irene* and *Collected Poems 1944–1994* by Robert Greacen, *Tuppenny Stung* by Michael Longley, *Returning to Ourselves: Second Volume of Papers from the John Hewitt International Summer School* edited by Eve Patten, and *Styles of Belonging: The Cultural Identities of Ulster* edited by Jean Lundy and Aodán Mac Póilin; Peter Lang for *History and the Shaping of Irish Protestantism* by Desmond Bowen; Maunsell for *If the Germans Conquered England, and other essays* by Robert Lynd; Julie Mitchell for *Sunday Afternoons*; Mullan and Son Ltd for *Planted by a River* by W.F. Marshall; New American Library for *Jonathan Edwards: Basic Writings* selected and edited by Ola Elizabeth Winslow; Presbyterian Reformed Publishing Co. for *The Calvinistic Concept of Culture* by Henry van Til; Pretani Press for *The Cruthin: The Ancient Kindred* by Ian Adamson; *Rann*; Rich and Cowan for *From the Irish Shore* by Denis Ireland; Colin Smythe for *The Irish Writer and the City* edited by Maurice Harmon, *Cultural Contexts and Literary Idioms in Contemporary Irish Literature* and *Poetry in Contemporary Irish Literature* both edited by Michael Kenneally, and *Irish Writers and Religion* edited by Robert Welch; University of Wales Press for *Peripheral Views* edited by I.A. Bell.

The full publishing details of all the works listed above are included in the bibliography. Every effort has been made to secure all necessary clearances and to trace copyright holders. Both the author and the publishers will be glad to recognise any holders of copyright not acknowledged above.

A version of some of the material included in chapter four has been published in *Irish Encounters: Poetry, Politics and Prose* (1998) edited by Alan Marshall and Neil Sammells; some of the issues raised in chapter six formed the basis of a paper given at a conference.

BARRY SLOAN
Salisbury 1999

Introduction

IN PART THIS IS a book about Protestants and Protestantism in the north of Ireland and about the impact of a particular kind of theology in shaping the history and culture of the region. Primarily, however, it is an exploration of how that theology and the culture related to it have influenced the thought and imagination of various kinds of writers – poets, novelists, dramatists, autobiographers and essayists. Curiously, although this is a connection that has been noticed in general terms, and occasionally developed with reference to specific works, it has not been systematically examined. To address this absence, therefore, the book's scope is broad: while there are substantial discussions of particular poets and of selected works of autobiography, fiction and drama, the opening three chapters concentrate on theology – on the history of Protestantism in the north of Ireland and the priorities it has espoused, especially since the late nineteenth century, and how these have driven it, and on the perceptions contemporary Protestants have of their church, society and culture. These explorations provide the context against which the literary writing is then read. For the same reason, the starting point is not Irish at all, but rather the theology of John Calvin and an examination of major emphases in his teaching and their implications both for the individual and for the social, political, cultural and artistic life of a community touched by them. The purpose here is to identify some of the theological dogma which underpins the history and development of the kind of Presbyterianism which, in particular, has been such a distinctive and potent force in the north-east of Ireland since the seventeenth century.

Beset by hostility from the episcopal church as much as from Catholics, legislated against because of their non-conformity and often insecure in their possession of lands and properties, many of which had been seized by force, the Presbyterians were also fortified by the discipline of a theology which prepared them to expect persecution and encouraged rugged resistance to it. They were strengthened by their belief in the rectitude of their faith and practices and their conviction that God would not abandon his own. Paradoxically, this

1

same faith left them balanced uneasily between radical individualism and acceptance of the need for obedience to their church and its statements of belief laid down in the *Westminster Confession of Faith* and catechisms. The tension between these opposing attitudes, the increasing domination of conservative, authoritarian influences during the course of the nineteenth century, and the complex reasons which energised this movement of events have been of enormous and lasting importance. Their influences have permeated every aspect of Northern Irish Protestant life, secular as well as religious, in ways that this book seeks to explain. They have had consequences for the relationships between the different Protestant denominations themselves, as well as with Catholics, and have affected perceptions of the activities of the British and Irish governments, particularly in the past quarter of a century. Conversely, they have also contributed significantly to negative impressions of Northern Irish Protestants as a monolithic group who are irrationally intolerant, blinkered, contentious, uncultured, dictatorial and lacking in compassion. Such views are represented, for example, by Declan Kiberd when he wrote of the 'curious blend of resolution and hysteria, of barbarous vulgarity and boot-faced sobriety, which lies beneath the emotions of Ulster Protestantism', while in some lines from 'In Belfast', the Scottish poet, Iain Crichton Smith, captures another familiar stereotype:

> The years' lessons are written on the walls –
> *No Surrender – Ulster Says No.*
> I see in the sky a Presbyterian rainbow
> orange and unforgiving, woven of fire.[1]

And at a popular level, the most visible and audible expressions of Northern Irish Protestantism are typically associated with men marching in idiosyncratic dress accompanied by bands belting out a repertoire of tunes to sectarian songs, with apparently incomprehensible confrontations between groups of angry people determined to assert – or resist – the right to parade down certain roads, or with the rhetorical style vividly represented by Ian Paisley.

Yet, whatever the less appealing attributes of Northern Irish Protestantism and however anachronistic these may seem in the modern world, it has always been a much more complex phenomenon both in form and influence than reductive summaries would have us believe. Very often the temptation to caricature and dismiss the Protestant community has proved too great – or too convenient – for critics, commentators and the media to resist, with consequences that have done little to advance an understanding of the people, their religion or their culture. Such reactions also ignore the multiple ways in which Protestant influences have been specifically operative upon many Irish writers or are reflected in their work, not least because there has been no adequate examination of their cultural background and of the kind of religion that has shaped it.

In his astute and thoughtful study of Northern Irish poetry, Peter McDonald warns against the disabling effects of employing the notion of Protestant or Catholic 'identity' 'as a usable concept in political or cultural discussion', because 'the term itself favours certain lines of development in reasoning, thus aligning the perspective in vital ways with certain determinist assumptions fundamental to nationalism.'[2] However, there is an important difference between the kind of 'identity-discourse' which McDonald finds so frustrating, and the effort to understand how priorities and preoccupations learnt or inherited from Protestant theology and cultural practices in Northern Ireland have affected and influenced particular poets and auto-biographers, and the representation of character and theme in fiction and drama, which is the undertaking here. The aim is not 'to identify and essentialize Protestants from Northern Ireland', but to highlight the diversity and individuality of writing that has its origins in this community, specifically through showing how it has been conditioned by Protestant influences, and to contest oversimple notions of the nature of Protestant culture.[3] Indeed, it is also to show how a culture, which has often been contemptuously dismissed as wholly inimical, or at best indifferent, to literary activity in particular and the products of the imagination in general, has either informed or stimulated a great deal of writing.

As is mentioned later, Calvin's attitude to art and artists is to a large degree a matter of inference, although his concern that the work of artists should never be confused with the unique creativity of God, and his hostility towards art that might encourage idolatry are apparent. It is certainly true historically that for theological reasons Protestant churches and forms of worship have remained simplest in design and form where Calvinist influences have continued strongest. It is also true that ornate decoration and the use of liturgy have often been regarded as dangerously Catholic in tendency, whereas austerity has been accounted a positive value in itself. This lies behind the bitter words of the narrator in R.S. Thomas's poem, 'The Minister', who dubs Protestantism:

> . . . the adroit castrator
> Of art; the bitter negation
> Of song and dance and the heart's innocent joy

an attitude that is reiterated in various ways by a number of the writers who grew up within the Northern Irish Protestant community.[4]

Such perceptions of Protestantism may also have affected the reception these writers' work has been given, as Robert McLiam Wilson suggests in a review of Maurice Leitch's novel, *Gilchrist*. Why, he asks, do Irish writers with Catholic backgrounds receive more critical notice and acclaim than their fellow artists born into the Protestant community? And he speculates that 'The Protestant vision, the Protestant version, isn't popular. It's got no rhythm. It's white South African. It's too complicated. The Catholic vision is familiar, *more Irish* somehow'.[5] The emphasis on complication here is particularly important and is central to the concern of this book, because while many of the refusals of Northern Irish Protestants this century have been construed merely as simple-minded stubbornness and reluctance – or inability – to adapt to the sophisticated political, religious and social circumstances of modern times, not all dissent is of this kind. The church Calvin was instrumental in establishing in Geneva was based upon a comprehensive act of dissent from the Catholic Church of the day. He set out to justify this in his *Institutes of the Christian Religion*, which not only spelt out the grounds of his disagreement with Catholicism, but also defined the beliefs and theological priorities of Protestantism, and their implications for every aspect, public and private, of the lives of the members of the new Church. Calvin was at one and the same time freeing people from what he saw as a tyranny and enfolding them in new, if different, codes and prescriptions. Crucially, however, the principle of dissent was established and the integrity of the individual's relationship with God affirmed. By definition in these circumstances, Calvin's *Institutes* could never hope to be the last word, the standard by which every individual would be bound. Further dissent was inevitable, as history has proved; and it has given Protestantism its multifaceted complexity.

This is reflected in the story of the Presbyterian Church in Ireland – for example, formerly in the disagreements between subscribers and non-subscribers to the *Westminster Confession* and more recently in the opposition of Paisley's independent Free Presbyterian Church to mainstream Presbyterianism. However dissent from within, separation and regrouping have been repeated features of Irish Presbyterianism and their effects have been far-reaching, enduring and variable not only inside churches and congregations, but in the wider community. At worst, the consequences have been weakening and damaging, while at best dissent has kept alive a sturdy individualism which is not afraid to articulate a particular vision or point of view.

It has been said that 'Puritanism is not a body of doctrine but a state of mind', and it is perhaps fair to reformulate this and observe that in the course of the twentieth century especially, Protestantism has become primarily a 'state of mind' for many people in Northern Ireland.[6] This is reflected in many of the cultural practices and attitudes discussed in chapter three, as are the psychological needs and insecurities these disclose. However, there is also the evidence of those who come from within the Protestant community and who have, willy-nilly, inherited that 'state of mind', yet who have examined, interrogated and represented it with the kind of individual self-consciousness that is a hallmark of dissenting thought. On the one hand, there has been the concern of individuals, including clergymen, to reinstate informed theological understanding in the social and political attitudes of Protestants. On the other, the autobiographies and essays considered in the fourth chapter not only highlight processes of critical examination, but show how for some writers a self-conscious evaluation of their Protestant background and of the 'state of mind' which characterised it, convinced them of the necessity of deliberately distancing themselves from it in order to develop as artists. In a different way again, the final two chapters, drawing upon selected novels and plays in which the writers have recreated particular Protestant preoccupations in their imaginative renderings of the lives of their characters, examine what they disclose and the means by which such disclosures are made.

Each of the other chapters (5–9) deals with the work of a poet – W.R. Rodgers, John Hewitt, Louis MacNeice, Derek Mahon and Tom Paulin respectively. Any such selection – like the choices made elsewhere – immediately invites questions: 'Why *x* and not *y*? What about *z*?' The criterion throughout has been to focus on writers in whose work the influences of Protestantism and of their own experience of coming from or continuing to live in the Protestant community in the North of Ireland are particularly strong. They are never apologists for Protestantism especially in its conservative and narrow theological and cultural forms – more often they are among its most searching and honest critics. Yet they share radical Protestantism's commitment to liberty of conscience; its preoccupation with the revealing power of words, even when this is subject to modernist or post-modernist uncertainties; its deep-seated moral awareness and its courage to challenge preferred opinions and shibboleths. Above all, they are essentially dissenters whose work is marked with evidence of their origins in a particular tradition of theology and thought. Brendan Kennelly has described 'a shrewd, reticent humanism' in much Northern Irish poetry since Hewitt and MacNeice, which he regards as 'Protestant', 'because it involves the habitual workings of a conscience and/or consciousness which seems interchangeable'.[7] The significance of self-consciousness in writers from this background has already been mentioned, but Kennelly's specific reference to conscience and to its active coexistence with consciousness, is pertinent. The claims of conscience have been prominent in Protestant dissent, whether within the church – as in the disputes between 'Old' and 'New Light' ministers – or in the work of post-Protestant writers and poets who have dissented from the Church itself and from its theology, yet still find themselves shadowed by them.

The Protestant emphasis on the accountability of the individual and on the role of conscience as a mentor can be by turns disabling and empowering – as so much of the writing considered in this book demonstrates. It can invoke despair or induce self-reliant courage and responsibility and it can encourage the kind of scrupulous self-examination which is capable of yielding up unexpected insights. Kennelly enumerates characteristics, many of which exist in paradoxical tensions with each other, that he associates with the 'Protestant humanist' writer:

> Intelligent, sensitive, tough, sceptical, cautious, ironic, romantic, witty, nostalgic, reticent yet capable of outbursts at moments, constantly thoughtful, fighting against his own capacity to expect or to anticipate, conscious of the fact that he did not ask to be born, fighting his own tendency to use, yet insisting on self-respect, showing concern for others yet not exploiting them if at all possible . . . , persisting relentlessly through the dullness of the days: this is the writer who is forced out to the edges of society. This is the writer who rejects the confusion of certain forms of involvement in the daily and nightly mess. This is the ironic romanticism of the person who knows how to refuse, the refuser who refuses to be forgiven except by himself. Never by a sacrament because he has no formula for self-forgiveness. He has not forced his God to exist because he himself never asked to exist, because existence was forced on him, not chosen by him and he has it now and he must endure it because he has nothing else.[8]

This projects an invitingly complex view of writers whose work commonly inclines to the pessimistic or sceptical, for whom the joys and beauties of life, real and felt as they are, can never wholly extinguish a counterawareness of their transience and of the inscrutability of life, and yet who resist self-indulgent or escapist strategies in their best writing. Such writers reveal the activity of restless critical intelligence and robust imaginative powers that are profoundly marked by the influence of the Protestant theology and culture of their Northern Irish backgrounds. Far from producing monolithic or indistinguishable responses – or no responses worth taking seriously – their individual dissenting voices show the 'great courage' admired by Iain Crichton Smith in another of his poems, 'A Note on Puritans', and avoid the 'singleness and loss of grace' which lead to the attitude of 'contempt and barrenness' that some have hastened to ascribe as Northern Irish Protestantism's pre-eminent, or only, cast of mind.[9] It is the purpose of the chapters that follow to show how this is so.

BARRY SLOAN
Salisbury, 1999

CHAPTER ONE

The Legacy of John Calvin

*'Calvinistic' is a catch-all bogey-word, possessing, often
enough, no strictly accountable meaning at all.*

Donald Davie, *A Gathered Church: The Literature
of the English Dissenting Interest 1700–1930.*

FOR MOST PEOPLE, John Calvin's name, like that of Martin Luther,
is inextricably linked with the sixteenth-century revolt against the
Church of Rome known to history as the Reformation. Likewise,
even for those with limited knowledge of the theological emphases of
the two reformers, the terms 'Calvinism' and 'Calvinistic' are commonly understood to imply narrowmindedness and austerity, a bleak
and judgemental view of human conduct and a cold religiosity more
concerned with discipline than with love or forgiveness. Lutheranism,
on the other hand, is conceived of as more appealing, humane and
warm-hearted. At a popular level, both sets of perceptions are probably coloured by what is generally known of the personalities of the
two men themselves as much as by what they declared and did. Yet,
however much they simplify affairs, these impressions are not wholly
without foundation, especially perhaps in the case of Calvin.

Although both Luther and Calvin wrote extensively, the enduring
strength of Calvin's influence was decisively reinforced by his
Institutes of the Christian Religion in which he systematically and
progressively spelt out and defended the principles of reformation
theology with their justification in scripture, or what may be deduced
from it. The comprehensiveness, logic, clarity of style and organisation
of this book gives it a special status among the writings of the
reformers and ensured that it continued to be a seminal source of
reference as the Protestant church expanded. Furthermore, the
dogmatic and uncompromising way in which Calvin expounded his
theology and the legalistic exactitude of his expositions of scripture,
themselves became characteristic of the practice of many of those
who claimed to follow him, often earning them a reputation for
confrontation and intolerance with dissenters within their own ranks

as well as in their dealings with members of other communions.[1] The very structure of the *Institutes*, with numbered sections and paragraphs, suggests a legal treatise and reflects the author's early training in law. Just as the text demonstrates a scrupulous care to cover every detail and eventuality of belief and religious conduct, so it invites, and has received, equally precise scrutiny and interpretation by others, often resulting in bitter disagreements and divisions over detail, even though Calvin's basic principles remain clear enough, as they did throughout the evolution of the book between its first and final editions in 1536 and 1559 respectively.

One of the most distinctive features of this theology is its attempt to embrace all aspects both of individual and of social life. Starting from a small number of central articles of belief, Calvin proceeded to deduce and elaborate a logically coherent world-view that addresses not only issues related to faith and to the practice and organisation of religion, but also to matters of conduct, morality, citizenship and government. This ambition is cast into sharper relief by Henry Van Til's comment on the difference between the undertakings of Luther and Calvin. He observes that:

> . . . whereas the German Reformation was primarily the restoration of true worship and the office of ministry, Calvin sought the restoration of the whole life, in home, school, state and society.[2]

Since Calvin's concerns embraced the entire range of activities that constitute human culture, this inevitably has implications for creative artists of all kinds and indeed for all who come into contact with their work. Likewise, the very role of the artist may become problematic within a world-view which recognises only one true creator, God himself, and where the purposes and ends of artistic creation will be adjudicated against the Calvinist's understanding of the appropriate focus for work and for worship. Finally, an artist's work will be valued in terms of its effects upon those who see, read, or hear it and whether or not these effects are held to be consistent with the obligations of all men and women to God as revealed in scripture.

Given the unique status and incontestable importance of scripture as the Word, it is not surprising that in a cultural environment influenced by Calvinism words more generally, and the uses and abuses to which they are put, have been a constant preoccupation in secular as well as in religious contexts. This has had particular significance for literature, where the potential and the adequacy of words to reveal, define, explore and articulate experience are both exploited and interrogated. Accordingly, within the work of the Irish writers which is considered in later chapters, the ambiguity, instability and limitations of words, as well as their capacity to convey meaning, are recurrent and pressing concerns which evoke a variety of individual responses. However, to understand such issues more clearly, they must first be placed in the context of the major beliefs and theological points in Calvin's teaching and of their interpretation by his successors.

I

THE PRINCIPLES OF CALVINISM

The starting point for Calvin in the *Institutes of the Christian Religion* is the conviction that God alone is the source of all truth, wisdom and virtue, and the creator of everything. Complementing this is the belief that as individuals acquire self-knowledge, which actually means awareness of their own ignorance, frailty and corruption, so they increasingly come to realise the primary fact, 'that in the Lord, and none but He, dwell the true light of wisdom, solid virtue, exuberant goodness'; and that

> ... not a particle of light, or wisdom, or justice, or power, or rectitude, or genuine truth, will anywhere be found, which does not flow from Him and of which He is not the cause.[3]

From the outset, this not only elevates God, but equally importantly it insists on human inferiority, dependence and lack of worth – a theme which recurs throughout Calvin's writings and motivates much of what he had to say. According to this view, sin not only divides humans from God and corrupts their perception of the divine in the natural world, but its implications also govern the very state of human existence itself. As Susan Manning writes:

> Division becomes the structuring principle of life. . . . Man and man are divided one from another by the absoluteness of the distinction between elect and reprobate. Man is, finally, divided from within himself; he becomes a battleground of warring faculties: the intellect against the will, the head against the heart, reason against faith.[4]

The intellectual and emotional consequences of this way of understanding have proved to be among the most resilient aspects of the

Calvinist legacy, often outlasting subscription to the beliefs which generated them.

And yet Calvin maintains that 'some sense of Deity' is engrained in everyone, although, whereas 'pure and genuine religion' is characterised by the voluntary obedience of the believer and is based on 'confidence in God coupled with serious fear', many are distracted by their own presumptuousness, wantonness and folly to seek and erect their own gods.[5] These Calvin describes as 'carnal dreams and depraved fictions'. Significantly, he also observes:

> The higher anyone was endued with genius, and the more he was polished by science and art, the more specious was the colouring which he gave to his opinions.[6]

This reveals a deep suspicion, perhaps even hostility, towards human cleverness, imagination and creativity which at best may tempt an individual into misplacing his trust, overestimating his own ability, and failing to see his own frailty. At worst they may seduce and betray him into what Henry Van Til calls 'apostate art' which presumes to attribute creativity to merely human powers, or which fails to refer itself back to God.[7] Such a view does not encourage unorthodox thought or the notion that there are different ways of seeing and expressing truth or of describing the world, both of which commonly underpin the activities of the creative imagination. Indeed, Calvin specifically warns against the 'variety of fictions' which have been set up as substitutes for the proper worship of God, and while it is true that in its context the term does not have a literary connotation, it reveals general scepticism towards anything that is held to be 'made' or 'devised' by men and women rather than emanating directly from God.[8]

There is also a potential tension between Calvin's unease with human cleverness and the long-standing association between dissenting religion and the enthusiastic promotion of education for all kinds of people. While this always had its major justification in equipping individuals to read the Bible, once basic literacy has been acquired it will inevitably give a freedom which can never afterwards be contained. Some of its less predictable consequences are eloquently illustrated in the poetry, prose, drama and autobiographies of dissenting writers.

Bible-reading itself was such a high priority because Calvinist confidence centred on the conviction that scripture is nothing less than God's revelation of himself through the Word. Furthermore, the

Word is the complete truth beyond which nothing else is required to direct the lives of humans and to enable them to find their proper relationship to God. (In this sense, all other books are unnecessary, and it is paradoxical that Calvin wrote a series of books to set out his theology, and that these themselves have been crucial in shaping further written codes of belief and practice such as the *Westminster Confession of Faith* [1646] and the *Larger and Shorter Catechisms* [1648]). Van Til summarises the indispensable importance of the Bible when he declares:

> The first principle of Calvinism is the acknowledgement of Scripture as the Word of God. This was the formal principle of the Protestant Reformation set forth in all Calvinistic creeds and the end of all contradiction in all of Calvin's own writings. Scripture was not only the authoritative guide for the way of salvation, but it furnished man with an authoritative interpretation of reality as a whole, and, more particularly, of man's existence *under the sun*.[9]

Here then is the affirmation of this book-based theology in which the Word occupies a privileged position – and in which exposition – though not interpretation – of it assumes primary significance. Indeed, part of Calvin's attack on Catholicism stems from what he sees as its failure to give due place to the exposition of the Word. Thus, in his criticism of the Roman Mass, he maintains that:

> Any utility which we may derive from the Supper requires the word. Whether we are to be confirmed in the faith, or exercised in confession, or aroused to duty, there is need of preaching. Nothing, therefore, can be more preposterous than to convert the Supper into a dumb action.[10]

Likewise, Calvin's abhorrence of religious images, statuary and ritual, flow from his view of the way in which these detract from or replace the primacy of the Word. Art, like ritual, must be the servant of the Word, inferior to it and of lesser importance; it should not draw attention to itself or become a focal point in its own right. This principle has proved particularly enduring in Irish Protestantism, where even the episcopal church has remained relatively 'low' in its ritual practices, despite occasional accusations of Romanist tendencies made by more extreme non-conformists – accusations which themselves pinpoint the sectarian basis of the criticism. Elsewhere, in literary contexts, plainness of style has both informed and been challenged in the work of writers as varied as John Hewitt, W.R. Rodgers, Louis MacNeice and Derek Mahon.

In his emphasis on reading scripture literally, Calvin was a man of his time, although even latter-day Calvinists have often remained antagonistic to the type of probing scholarship which has developed in the past century. The governing presumption remains that all meaning is contained in the Word and can be known from it. The role of the preacher as expositor is to direct the minds and hearts of the congregation or audience to that meaning.

Although this might seem to imply an entirely closed view of the world and the irrelevance of advances in human knowledge, science, art, history and other branches of learning since biblical times, such an interpretation is not sustainable. Rather, it is the case that the Calvinist maintains that the pursuit of all intellectual or cultural ends must take as its reference point the Word as it has been received in scripture, and which, as Van Til puts it, 'is normative and gives man the ultimate truth about every fact'.[11] The acceptability, relevance and value of the cultural activities of humans are thus entirely dependent upon how they are related to the Word, for, as Calvin understands it, nothing can be read truly without the spectacles of the Word of God.[12]

By insisting on the regulative role of scripture, which itself is beyond question and which includes matters that should not be speculated upon and cannot be understood, Calvinism may again be regarded as inimicable to the kind of imaginative and divergent thought that characterises most literary and artistic activity. It is likely to display suspicion of the new, the unfamiliar and the unconventional in both thought and action and it is possible to see how this may find expression in censoriousness, petty-mindedness and a strong sense both of propriety and of guilt – all of which have been seen by some commentators as defining traits of Irish Protestants. These attitudes may be further reinforced by Calvin's logical argument that whatever happens is foreseen by God and, however it may seem to us, is his will: 'What seems to us contingence, faith will recognise as the secret impulse of God', he asserts.[13]

The effect of such teaching might be to produce resignation and passivity in the face of an immutable and inscrutable divine plan, a reaction which might also seem to be endorsed by Calvin's cautionary warning that God will judge according to his penetrating insight into the deepest human motives. In this, as in other matters, Calvin refers approvingly to St Augustine, who, he says:

> . . . truly observes, that when God makes his scrutiny, he looks not to what men could do, or to what they did, but to what they wished to do, thus taking account of their will and purpose.[14]

But if these words serve to send men and women away to make an anxious examination of their inner motivation, they may also encourage a sense of sturdy independence and confidence in the justice of God, however the rest of the world may judge an individual's actions. The significance of this can scarcely be overstated. It must be related to Calvin's view on liberty of conscience and contributes to the fact that despite the gloomier and harsher elements in his theology, Calvinists have commonly played an active and assertive part in the world and have never shunned controversy. In so acting, they have, of course, also followed the exemplary figure of John Calvin himself.

Yet despite this, the worth of any human action is seen to rest wholly on the fact that it derives from God's grace, not from the exercise of free will, a notion of which Calvin was extremely wary because he sensed that here again men might be tempted into a misguided opinion of their own autonomy (see the *Institutes of Christian Religion*, Vol 1, Book 2, chapter 2, section 7, pp 228–229). Calvin does allow, however, that even when human effort has been erroneously directed, in, for example, the work of 'profane authors', 'the admirable light of truth' may still be found in them and should serve to remind us 'that the human mind, however much fallen and perverted from its original integrity, is still adorned and invested with admirable gifts from its Creator'.[15] Thus, truth may be accepted from any source, lest in rejecting the gift the giver himself is rejected; but the believer should not be deceived into thinking that the source of truth is other than God himself. In allowing this leeway, Calvin shows a greater generosity of thought than some of his successors have done.

Here and elsewhere, as has already been suggested, there is a seeming paradox that recurs in Calvin's teaching whereby the emphasis on the sinfulness and frailty of humans and their absolute dependence on God's grace appears to be juxtaposed with an equal insistence on the integrity of the individual's relationship with God. So it is that humans are at once worthless and also capable of receiving the infinitely precious gift of God's grace. Calvin does not undertake to explain why this should be so, any more than he tries to explain the doctrine of predestination which he follows Augustine in extrapolating from Pauline teaching. These matters are comprehensible only to God; humans must simply live their lives in the knowledge and faith that things are this way, although even the ability to do so constitutes in itself another mysterious gift from God:

Perseverance is the gift of God, which he does not lavish promiscu-
ously on all, but imparts to whom he pleases. If it is asked how the
difference arises – why some steadily persevere, and others prove
deficient in steadfastness – we can give no other reason than that the
Lord, by his mighty power, strengthens and sustains the former, so that
they perish not, while he does not furnish the same assistance to the
latter, but leaves them to be monuments of instability.[16]

Even here it is notable that those denied the gift of perseverence
become 'monuments' or signs, thereby serving God's purpose in their
own particular way. Tony Tanner has commented on Calvinists'
fixation with signs in a discussion of seventeenth-century American
Puritanism where he writes that:

> ... the Puritans were forever seeking to 'read' people, to find out or
> interpret signs or rather symptoms, not so much of their grace but of their
> sins. Thus the whole community lived in an atmosphere of sadistic
> semiology, everybody looking for the bad signs in everybody else. Once
> discerned, these could be translated into more enduring, more visible,
> signs, tokens, badges: as it were, extracting the sin *out of* the body and
> making it into a concrete sign which could be imposed *on* the body.[17]

Symbolism and its importance as a system of signs may be considered
in association with Calvin's teaching on the sacraments of the church.
Rejecting the seven sacraments of Catholicism, Calvin recognises only
baptism and the Lord's Supper as true sacraments, and even these, he
insists, are essentially *signs* used by God to 'announce and manifest'
his grace, although 'like earnests and badges, [they] give a ratification
of the gifts which the divine liberality has bestowed upon us'.[18] While
he upholds the close connection between the signs – water, bread,
wine – and the spiritual gifts they signify, Calvin regards it as nothing
less than a Satanic delusion for Catholics to claim the presence of
Christ in the bread in the doctrine of transubstantiation. As he sees
it, when Catholics prostrate themselves before the bread, they are
guilty of a form of idolatry by worshipping the gift rather than the
giver. Again, therefore, the issue of ritual and its proper subordinate
relationship to the Word is at stake.

This also provides further evidence of Calvin's design to cut away
what seemed to him to be the pernicious superstition and mysti-
fication of Catholicism and to restore to ordinary worshippers an
immediacy and directness in their relationship with God which he
believed had been usurped by the Pope, the priesthood, and the
institution and doctrines of the Catholic Church itself.

Yet while appearing to adopt a more rationalistic attitude towards the signs and symbols of faith, Calvin still defends their importance. He even maintains that humans may see further signs of God in natural phenomena, citing as examples the tree of life given to Adam and Eve and the rainbow revealed to Noah, and observing that:

> These were to Adam and Noah as sacraments: not that the tree could give Adam and Eve the immortality which it could not give to itself; or the bow (which is only a reflection of the solar rays on the opposite clouds) could have the effect of confining the waters; but they had a mark engraven on them by the word of God, to be proofs and seals of his covenant. The tree was previously a tree, and the bow a bow; but when they were inscribed with the word of God, a new form was given to them: they began to be what they previously were not.[19]

Such a view encourages the attempt to see in particular events and phenomena signs which have a larger or defining significance. It presupposes not only the ability to recognise such signs in the first place, but also to decode them accurately. And while Calvin is careful to distinguish between signs inscribed on natural phenomena or disclosed in miracles, and man-made rites and symbols which he condemns as impious and degenerate, it is easy to see how this distinction can become blurred or lost. Ulster Protestant thought has long been dominated by memory and celebration of events which have been given great symbolic importance, or interpreted as signs inscribed with meaning that has virtually the authority of scripture.[20] Furthermore, such signs can exercise a tyranny of their own, becoming a fixed code which pre-empts the possibility of other interpretations and alternative readings not only of the past, but also of present and future directions of history.

Calvin would have agreed with Mr Deasy, a character with explicitly Northern Irish Protestant forebears in Joyce's *Ulysses*, who understands history as movement towards the eventual disclosure of God; and it has often been pointed out that for centuries Western culture reflected confidence in the notion of history which is unfolding towards some higher and more orderly conclusion, despite conflict and disharmony on the way.[21] Don Cupitt has written that:

> The Bible, the Creed, the life of Christ, and the system of Christian doctrine has this shape. So did the sermon, the history-book, the symphony, the sonata, the drama, the epic and the novel. And so also, if less obviously and directly, did the ways of stating, discussing and solving a problem over a whole range of intellectual disciplines.[22]

But, as he also argues, people trusted in texts to copy and reflect the structures of reality: writers might be capable of a longer view than most of their readers, but that view would be a truthful image of an agreed version of reality and an affirmation of it. Here Cupitt points to the Calvinist sermon as 'a particularly vivid illustration of the principle':

> A great cosmic drama of Fall and Redemption was in process. Scripture epitomized it in text. The text of scripture was in every part the infallible Word of God; that is, it was a sign whose adequate mediation of the signified was guaranteed. Thus when the preacher expounded any text of scripture the entire cosmic Plan of salvation came into view; and because of the guaranteed hook-up between text and reality the preacher's audience were caught up into the objective process of cosmic Redemption.[23]

The confidence implicit in this perspective goes a long way towards explaining the robustness that characterises much Calvinist thought and action: meaning is there to be grasped and every individual is a participant in the universal outworking of God's design. (This underpins the Miltonic aspiration to 'assert Eternal Providence, / And justifie the wayes of God to men'.[24]) By the same token, when that confidence, both in the design itself and in the unquestionable adequacy of the Word, no longer exists as in the modern age, creative writers will be among the most sensitive to the consequences of its loss and the limitations of language, as the discussions in later chapters show.

In spite of his oft-repeated comments on human sinfulness and dependence, it is precisely because the individual is identified as a significant participant in the cosmic drama, involved in a direct relationship with God, and having access to all necessary truth in scripture, that Calvin is also able to argue the liberties available to him. While worldly ambition is wrong, and self-denial and obedience are upheld as real virtues, Calvin never repudiates the pleasures of the senses or the things of this world in themselves. Rather, he emphasises the individual's responsibility to indulge and use them rightly, moderately and in a spirit of stewardship. While these conditions might appear to impose serious constraint on human enjoyment of earthly goods and pleasures, and have often been interpreted in precisely this way, Calvin is careful to avoid being over-prescriptive:

> I indeed confess that here consciences neither can not ought to be bound by fixed and definite laws; but that Scripture having laid down

general rules for the legitimate use, we should keep within the rules which they prescribe.[25]

Thus, the onus rests upon the individual to apply the standard implicit in the Word and upheld by conscience.

The role assigned to conscience is closely linked with Calvin's understanding of Christian liberty. Indeed his theology avers the truth of the familiar paradox that in the service of Christ perfect freedom may be found. If conscience guides our actions, we will act in moderation and moderation is the keynote of Christian liberty. On this subject Calvin is both reassuring and encouraging, not only insisting that it was never forbidden

> . . . to laugh, or to be full, or to add new to old and hereditary possessions, or to be delighted with music, or to drink wine,

but criticising those who on the one hand feel bound by convention to act in certain ways, and on the other those who feel obliged to make a display of breaking it – for example, by eating fish on Fridays.[26] Such conduct is no true expression of liberty, Calvin argues; it fails to recognise that real liberty may mean refraining from doing something as much or more than doing it. The act of refusal is thus given a positive value and refusal has characterised the behaviour of Calvinists in many spheres of political, social and artistic life, without necessarily having the negative connotations sometimes ascribed to it.

In *The Calvinistic Concept of Culture*, Henry R. Van Til takes up this idea, pointing out that apart from the spheres of influence of the church and state, Calvin's identification of a third sphere, the adiaphora, or things indifferent – which include music, architecture, technical learning, social festivities and the choices of everyday life – where individual conscience alone holds sway, provides the cornerstone of his doctrine of Christian liberty.[27] It is ironic that later followers of Calvin have often shown themselves to be particularly intolerant in matters that relate to this third sphere, where legalism has commonly replaced liberty. Such restrictiveness is implicit in the connotations of the well-known Ulster Protestant expression of approbation whereby a person is said to be 'good living'.

Calvin is also in no doubt that the individual's exercise of conscience is the means by which he must be governed in spiritual matters. This is an inalienable and absolute right, purchased by Christ's own blood, and stands above any human authority.[28] At the same time there is a clear warning to those who would seek to exploit this freedom and to find in it an excuse or justification for the abolition of any kind of authority beyond that of individual self-determination. 'In man', he insists, 'government is twofold':

> ... the one spiritual, by which the conscience is trained to piety and divine worship; the other civil, by which the individual is instructed in those duties which as men and citizens, we are bound to perform.[29]

Ideally, these two jurisdictions, the spiritual and the temporal, as they are referred to in the *Institutes*, should exercise claims upon the individual that are consistent with one another. This is certainly the situation Calvin strove to create and uphold in the Genevan church and state, and the degree to which he succeeded made a deep impression upon contemporaries who visited it and also helped to make Calvinism such a potent force.[30]

However, there is a recognition that a harmony of claims may not always exist and in such circumstances the liberties which the individual rightfully possesses in spiritual matters do not extend to the domain of civil law. Calvin's treatment of this issue is indicative of the characteristic tension in his thought between the religious radical's affirmation of individual conscience and freedom in spiritual matters and the disciplinarian lawyer's fear of social breakdown and disorder deriving from human wickedness and frailty. Thus, he argues:

> Our consciences have not to do with men but with God only. Hence the common distinction between the earthly forum and the forum of conscience.[31]

Whereas he always reserves the right of conscience to reject authority in the spiritual sphere – as is perfectly consistent with his objections to Catholicism – he is equally firm in asserting the obligations of the citizen to the state. This is spelt out in particular detail in the fourth book of the *Institutes*, and its practical consequences are evident in the records of the punishments meted out to Genevan citizens who fell short of the conformity expected of them. One must add, however, that there is an unresolved tension between Calvin's insistence on obedience to secular rulers and the ferocity of some of his rhetoric towards them which others interpreted as an encouragement to violence. It has also been a particular feature of the situation in the north of Ireland where political and religious priorities are so intermeshed, that many Protestants there have justified defiance of the state as a legitimate exercise of conscience in defence of their spiritual beliefs – although it is not clear that Calvin's own teaching would approve such conduct.

The need for civil government is related directly to human imperfection. As the sole proper end of human life is to achieve greater knowledge of God and an improved relationship to him, so it is incumbent on those holding temporal power

> . . . to prevent the true religion, which is contained in the law of God, from being with impunity openly violated and polluted by public blasphemy.[32]

Magistrates are to mirror God himself in the performance of their duties by aspiring to exhibit 'in themselves . . . a kind of image of the Divine Providence, guardianship, goodness, benevolence, and justice'.[33] It is perfectly consistent with their role as images of Providence for them to order executions and other punishments, to wage war and to raise taxes, but each decision should follow the example adduced from scripture. Here, as Van Til says, Calvin overthrows the medieval idea of the state and its officers as servants of the church, presenting them instead as the servants of God.[34] However, it is not a system which envisages the state needing to afford equal respect to differing, and even opposing, beliefs and values and to tolerate their practice within agreed limits, which is the basis of modern democratic societies. This again has had specific significance in Northern Ireland.

The citizens themselves are required to honour the offices of their rulers 'as a delegated jurisdiction from God', and even when a corrupt or tyrannical individual is in power, they should be obedient to him.[35] As ever, Calvin cites scripture in support of his insistence on obedience, pointing out that all rulers are in position by divine decree. He continues:

> If we constantly keep before our eyes and minds the fact, that even the most iniquitous kings are appointed by the same decree which establishes all regal authority, we will never entertain the seditious thought, that a king is to be treated according to his deserts, and that we are not bound to act the part of good subjects to him who does not in his turn act the part of a king to us.[36]

While it may be relatively straightforward to grasp the idea that respect for the office is more important than respect for its holder, the question that arises is how a God credited with the qualities of wisdom, justice, truth and foresight could ever allow a tyrant to exercise power. In Calvin's theology, this must be understood in the context of his view of predestination. On this matter he teaches that:

> All are not created on equal terms, but some are preordained to eternal life, others to eternal damnation; and, accordingly, as each has been created for one or other of these ends, we say that he has been predestinated to life or to death.[37]

Why this is so is unknown, save to the mind of God, and is another instance of something that is to be accepted in faith rather than questioned. Since God knows everything that will happen, and permits it to do so, *even though it may not be his will*, events such as the rule of a tyrant occur with his permission and are therefore to be endured rather than resisted by true Christians who do not falter in their obedience.[38]

It also follows from this view that all instances of evil and apostasy occur within the scheme of God's foreknowledge. Although they are contrary to God's will and defy the Word of God as revealed in scripture, they may nonetheless be valuable as signs of God's purpose to his faithful people. This is consistent with the point made earlier that even art and cultural activities that fail to be God-centred, and are therefore 'apostate', may yet yield up truth to the believer.

Predestination is an essential part of Calvinist theology, and along with the related idea that those who are saved constitute the 'elect', it presents some of the biggest intellectual and emotional difficulties for many people. It is often and understandably viewed as the final denial of human freedom and choice, the terminal reduction of men and women to the puppets and playthings of an arbitrary and perverse God. Yet Calvin himself neither saw nor intended it this way. For him, predestination was a logical necessity if, as he believed, God is both omnipotent and omniscient. If all are unworthy because born in sin, then it is only because of God's grace and mercy that any can be saved and there is nothing either surprising or unjust in others being condemned. Furthermore, the drama of life lived according to Calvinist theology is heightened by virtue of the fact that no one can know whether he or she is predestined to election or reprobation. Therefore, the onus is permanently on every individual to live life according to God's will as revealed in scripture and to seek to know God through Christ, always in the hope of God's mercy, but never with final assurance of it until the hereafter. In this, the emphasis of Calvinism is very different from the conversionist theology of evangelical denominations and sects, and this too is significant in the context of the history of Protestantism in Ulster, as the next chapter shows.

All life is therefore lived against a background of radical suspense and urgency of conscience and there seems little doubt that this gave Calvinism much of its mobilising power in its early stages. However, as with other parts of Calvin's teaching, the emphasis shifted with the passage of time and with increasing belief that the elect could be recognised not least because of their material prosperity and worldly success. The possibility of hypocrisy and arrogance grew in ways that would have appalled Calvin himself. Once again, this development discloses how the carefully defined value Calvin placed upon signs could all too easily slip into arbitrary and self-serving interpretations detached from any scriptural basis.

II

CONSEQUENCES OF CALVINISM

As one looks at these central principles, it is possible to see how on the one hand Calvinism became such a potent force in the world and at the same time was darkened by its less attractive characteristics. Indeed, these features are intimately related. The historian, G.R. Elton, identifies two facts as the keys to the later success of Calvinism over Lutheranism. First, the theology of predestination served to give Calvinists a sense of assurance of their rightness and conviction in their ability to succeed even in the most unpromising circumstances, particularly after the emergence of the consoling modification of thought that the elect could be sure of their status. But there was also a negative aspect to this development. As Elton puts it:

> Under the pressure of persecution and resistance the Calvinists grew in self-reliance and contempt for all others; by no means sectarians in intent, they nevertheless acquired the sectarian's unshakable endurance in the face of adversity, an endurance born of their conviction that they were the Lord's elect.[39]

The experience, and indeed the expectation, of persecution seems to have been an integral part of the background of Calvinism. G.R. Potter observes that 'Geneva was treated as if it were a city in a state of siege; the religious morale of the garrison must be kept high, and so it was'.[40] The military image is apposite. Geneva was a refuge for thousands of people fleeing from persecution because of their beliefs. It sent back into the wider world men who had been further toughened by Calvin's discipline and who were ready to withstand siege in their own societies and to train others to do likewise. One thinks, for instance, of John Knox in Scotland, of the Pilgrim Fathers in New England, and of the Presbyterian planters and their descendants in Ulster. All faced situations which tested their resolution, and there might sometimes seem to be an inverse relationship between the persecution these groups faced and their sense of rightness and even superiority over others. Elements of this still survive in Northern Ireland, where the image of a Protestant city under siege from Catholics without its walls retains undiminished potency three centuries after the events from which it derives. As Ian McBride has commented:

> The basic themes of the siege myth – defiance, solidarity, sacrifice, deliverance – are obvious enough. The story serves to reinforce the social cohesion and political resolve of Ulster Protestants by recalling the unchanging threat to their faith and liberties posed by the Catholic majority in Ireland; 'No Surrender', the watchword of the defenders of Derry, has become the arch-slogan of loyalism. After 1689 the Relief of Derry was quickly assimilated to a providential reading of history which centred on the confrontation between the reformed religion and Rome.[41]

Thus, in a sense, Derry was for Northern Irish Protestants what Geneva had once been for Calvin's early followers. Meanwhile, the mythology that derives from the siege it withstood has assumed a variety of nuances reflecting directly upon the contemporary state of the relationship between the Protestant and Catholic communities, and indeed between Protestants and British administrations which have aspired to alter the terms of the Act of Union.[42]

The second feature of Calvinism noted by Elton was its extraordinarily well-conceived system of church government. This gave it a resilience and effectiveness that the much more loosely structured Lutheran church lacked. It drew together the clergy and the laity in mutual responsibility and dependence so that it had 'all the advantages of a subversive movement organised in cells and filled with a total faith in its future'.[43]

Again, however, there is another side to this. If Calvinism is democratic in the sense that it upholds the value of the individual's experience and the directness of his or her relationship to God, and in that the laity are deeply involved in and charged with responsibility in running the church, it is also autocratic and uncompromising in the demands it makes on people. It is because of this that Henry Van Til speaks of Calvinism as being both radical and totalitarian and Harro Höpfl shows that Calvin himself foresaw the risk endemic in too much emphasis being placed upon individual liberty:

> The danger was that this same individual right of separation from sin, heresy and tyranny might also be claimed as a ground for separating from evangelical churches, or disrupting them, in virtue of some deficiency or defect or other.[44]

The combination of absoluteness of view and respect for individual liberty has proved as paradoxical as it sounds and in the context of Ulster Protestantism often precipitated the factionalism and church splitting that have repeatedly taken place. Out of conviction of their own rightness, Protestants have, ironically, weakened their position by self-inflicted divisions. In doing so they have helped further to sustain their feelings of persecution and treachery – not only from enemies from without, but also from within their own ranks.

In its origins, Calvinism was uncompromisingly hostile towards Catholicism which is systematically and polemically attacked in the *Institutes of the Christian Religion*. This set a definitive precedent for Calvin's successors who not only continue to criticise the Catholic Church, but are equally ready to direct their energies against fellow members of the reformed churches who, in their view, risk the integrity of Protestantism by softening its sharper edges or modifying its confrontational posture. Calvin discouraged bridge-builders or those political leaders who sought accommodation with their Catholic counterparts and regarded any such moves as irresponsible backsliding. Furthermore, he did not believe one's convictions should be concealed either for reasons of personal safety or to advance one's own interests. Again, in his view, such tactics represented a weakening of resolve and commitment. This kind of intransigence has characterised religious, and by extension, political attitudes in Northern Irish Protestantism. If the outspoken assaults on Catholicism and ecumenism have most commonly been associated with Revd Ian Paisley and other ministers in his church in recent times, their views are by no means unique and have a significant history. Given the position of the Protestant community in the north-east of Ireland, living in close proximity to a much larger Catholic population which is believed to have expansionist ambitions in both the political and religious and cultural spheres, it is scarcely surprising that advocates of Calvinistic attitudes to the Roman church have retained a sympathetic following, or that residual suspicions of Catholicism are sometimes apparent even in the writing of an avowed secularist like John Hewitt.

However, in the Northern Irish context one might question whether self-confidence or fear is more influential in determining Protestant attitudes and whether aggressive self-righteousness may not be a defence mechanism as much or more than a display of assurance of salvation. This dilemma, too, seems implicit in Calvinism with its reiterated insistence on the need for obedience which can lead to timidity and a burdensome sense of duty accompanied by fear of being seen to fail. Höpfl comments:

> . . . given the ultimate unintelligibility of Calvin's God, nothing but unquestioning obedience makes much sense. It is scarcely surprising, therefore, that the notion of discipline should have spread outwards: the whole notion of Christian life is now conceived as a kind of training, under supervision and command, for immortality. The impetus towards the conversion of the evangelical understanding of the Christian life into an ethic of duty is apparent, and as a consequence the gap between the general and the political theology narrows perceptibly: both deal in duties, owed in both cases to God.[45]

Given the emphasis on an ethic of duty which embraces not only the religious but also the secular and political life of an individual, it is not hard to see that religious and political views will inevitably become conflated. It has long been a popular truism that religion and politics are inextricably mixed up in Northern Ireland in ways that they are not, for example, in England. What is perhaps less readily noticed is that right from its origins in Geneva, Calvinism engaged itself in politics, and it did so as part of its aim of embracing every aspect of human activity, and to sustain itself against opponents who might weaken or destroy it.

In Geneva, Calvin used the magistracy to uphold unity among the clergy and in the congregation and therefore the duty of political obedience which he enunciated was a logical necessity. It was also a strategy to avoid fragmentation and schisms, but while unity in obedience and political compliance may have been a high priority in Geneva, it does not follow that the same applies in all circumstances.

Höpfl points out that in other, and perhaps more complex situations, Calvinists came to place the demands of pietas above those of a magistracy which was not necessarily sympathetic to the ideals of the Reformation.[46] The notion of a covenantal relationship between a people and their rulers which the former are only bound to uphold for as long as the latter protect and advance the Protestant cause is one way in which Calvin's view was subsequently modified and it has particular relevance in Northern Ireland. There, the idea of the Protestants being God's chosen few, held by him in a covenantal relationship like the Israelites of Old Testament times, still exists and is apparent in scenes depicted on some of the banners paraded by members of the Orange Order and Black Preceptory.[47] Fired with this conviction, it is clear why their loyalty and commitment to the institutions of government are provisional upon them guarding Protestantism. Even where the religious belief has weakened or lapsed, the defiant attitude lingers on in well-known slogans such as 'No Surrender' and 'This We Will Maintain'. This also explains why in the Northern Irish context, as D.W. Miller puts it:

> Loyalty is quite different from nationality. Everyone, according to the myth of nationality by which our world is ordered, possesses a nationality. Not everyone, according to Irish loyalist thinking, is loyal. . . . Loyalty is moral principle translated from the realm of personal relationships into politics. It ought to override any pleas of nationality. It carries the connotation of lawfulness, which Protestants understood to be what distinguished them from their Catholic counterparts.[48]

Thus, Calvinism in society has been characterised at one extreme by radical defiance and at the other by conservative bigotry. Naturally given to disputatiousness and obsessed with fixed ideas of truth which may be garnered from scripture and applied to every facet of life, the strength it accrues from its assertive self-confidence, discipline and organisation and the totality of its claim on the whole of an individual's life, must be balanced against tendencies that are judgmental, self-destructive and disabling. What this has meant specifically for the Protestant community in the north-east of Ireland is explored further in the next two chapters.

III

ART IN A CALVINIST CULTURE

Although Calvin alludes to the arts in his writings and was an admirer of the *Psalms*, he does not develop any sustained teaching about them. Since, however, he did not regard the cultural activities of humans – including their artistic enterprises – as neutral or free of moral and religious significance, Calvinism clearly has implications for artists and their work. The Dutch Calvinist, Abraham Kuyper, maintained that

> . . . Calvin esteemed art, in all its ramifications, as a gift of God, or more especially as a gift of the Holy Ghost; that he fully grasped the profound effects worked by art upon the life of the emotions; that he appreciated the end for which it had been given, *viz.*, that by it we might glorify God, and ennoble human life, and drink at the fountain of higher pleasures, yea even of common sport; and finally, that so far from considering art a mere imitation of human nature, he attributed to it the noble vocation of disclosing to man a higher reality than was offered to us by this sinful and corrupted world.[49]

This is consistent with Calvin's central conviction that since humankind is wholly dependent on God, cultural or artistic activities that recognise and uphold that relationship are acceptable whereas those which ignore or deny it are forms of apostasy. The abilities of the artist are God-given and should be returned to God in work which honours and acknowledges him and which simultaneously bestows upon others insight into divine greatness. Thus, while cultural activities are an essential part of being human, they cannot humanise us of themselves, for that process can only be accomplished by religion.[50]

Where the religious foundation of life is neglected, human culture becomes materialistic and temporal, and self-interest and egoism prevail. Kuyper regards any call for a wholly secular art as absurd, insisting on the idealistic origins of all true art which draws its inspiration from 'an Eternal Beautiful which flows from the fountain of the Infinite'.[51] Writing in the late nineteenth century, he reacts with hostility to realism, seeing it as a by-product of the loosening of social and ethical ties begun by the French Revolution and furthered by the development of a scientific and evolutionary view of life which moves God from the central position, ascribed to him by Calvinism, and places humans there instead.[52] Any such art is diametrically opposed to the cultural focus of men and women who are true to their religious nature, and who act, in Van Til's words, as 'analogue[s] of the great Architect and Artist of the universe', and 'co-workers with God in bringing creation to its fulfilment'.[53] The notion of the involvement of humans as analogues of God is reinforced by the Calvinist emphasis on the covenantal relationship between God and man already noted and further helps to explain why cultural activities in general, and the activities of artists in particular, can never be a matter of indifference.

Calvinists are as distrustful of aestheticism as of realism, seeing it as a dangerous temptation. Quoting Emil Brunner, Van Til writes:

> The sad fact is that men no longer see the proper function of art as 'an imaginary elevation of life in the direction of the perfect', but art is taken as that one thing in life which gives men true joy and a detachment from misery.[54]

This view, he argues, is illusory, confounding imaginary with real perfection and unrealities with reality, whereas God alone is the creator of reality. Art should serve to remind us of this by pointing to the fact that we live in a fallen world and uplifting us with glimpses of future glory. The artist should not simply gratify our baser senses – one of the problems with realism – but, rightfully employed, 'can create a kind of cosmos in architecture' or 'embellish nature's forms in . . . sculpture and create the illusion of real life by lines and tints in . . . paintings, and probe the mystery of sound and feeling in music and poetry'.[55] However, to conflate these with the unique creativity of God is to fall into vain and fatal error. The truth of this is illustrated by reference to the misconceived aims of the builders of the Tower of Babel (see Genesis ch. 2, v. 1–9) whose hubris symbolises the human tendency to overreach, to aspire to too much, and which led to confusion and breakdown.

Such a sceptical view of the world and of human achievement has been described by Sallie McFague as a 'characteristic sensibility' of Protestantism, which was classically exemplified in the Reformation debate over what is meant by the assertions 'This is my body' and 'This is my blood' made during the Eucharist. Distinguishing between what in broad terms she calls the Catholic 'symbolic mentality' and the metaphorical view of Protestants, McFague observes:

> The Protestant sensibility tends to see dissimilarity, distinction, tension and hence to be skeptical and secular, stressing the transcendence of

God and the finitude of creation. The Catholic sensibility tends to see similarity, connection, harmony and, hence, to be believing and religious, stressing the continuity between God and creation.[56]

This judgement complements Paul Tillich's notion of the 'Protestant principle' which, he says, 'emphasises the infinite distance between God and man'.[57]

For the Calvinist, just as the bread and body of Christ are never one and the same, so a clear distinction remains between the fallen world we live in and artistic representations of it, and the world intended by God at which art may no more than hint, but which it should be concerned to illumine, albeit in a limited way. Art, however, can never be more than a handmaiden of religion, a permissible aid to spiritual development which, ideally, would become redundant:

> The more . . . Religion develops into spiritual maturity, the more it will extricate itself from art's bandages, because art always remains incapable of expressing the very essence of Religion.[58]

Art which transgresses these limits and makes claims for itself, or for which claims are made, divorced from acceptance of God as the source of all creation, perfection and truth, is idolatry, and therefore defies the second commandment. Calvin saw this as one of the great errors of Catholicism, where he deemed that art had become a distraction, contributing to the drift away from true worship. Thus, although he did not condemn religious art in itself, he was wary of its potential to mislead and the plainness of architecture, decor and ritual in Calvinist churches has remained a distinctive feature which derives from this view.

The Calvinist position, therefore, is that the more godlike the ambition of the artist and the more removed he becomes from a proper sense of subservient relationship to God, the more he forfeits a true sense of artistic harmony and proportion. In Van Til's words:

> Man has been blinded to the sight of beauty, and his sense of calling as king over God's universe has been dulled. Sin has separated man from his God, who is the source of created beauty, and who determines truth by his law and his interpretation, and, therefore, man in sin cannot attain to the harmony of the perfect paradise in his art creations; he can only reflect that which is mediated by his sin-corrupted consciousness.[59]

Here again the problem of human sinfulness occupies a central place and the permissible role for the artist which seems extremely circumscribed, is governed by consciousness of this belief.

One might contrast this with the well-known view of Joyce's Stephen Dedalus, who thinks of himself as a secular priest endowed with the imaginative power to transmute the transient elements of ordinary life so that they assume enduring significance – a notion which boldly ascribes to the artist the mystical transformative power which in the Catholic doctrine of transubstantiation is held to be mediated uniquely through the priest celebrating the Mass.[60] Stephen's representation of artistic activity as sacramental derives from an appropriation and subversion of Catholic doctrine and belief, just as the more sceptical and agnostic attitudes of many writers with Protestant backgrounds testify to the residual legacy of Calvinist teaching upon them.

Although Calvinist thought on art and the role of artists may seem essentially pessimistic, there is, as so often, a paradox within it. Thus, although Abraham Kuyper argues that Calvinism fails to develop a dominant art style of its own because its emphasis on spirituality was not sympathetic to 'the wedding of art-inspired worship, with worship-inspired art', at the same time he also credits it with freeing artists to celebrate and explore individual experience and every aspect of social life rather than being restricted by the demands of priests and princes.[61] This is again so because of the religious basis of every part of life and the value placed upon each individual in Calvinist theology. Ironically, therefore, in a very real sense Calvinism led indirectly to the greater secularisation of art, although clearly this was not the original intention. Kuyper even goes so far as to acknowledge that the logic of Calvinism's emphasis on the absolute importance of liberty of conscience is to allow freedom of speech and worship, and the spread of literature with which it could not sympathise, although he admits that in practice this has seldom been the attitude it has taken up.[62] And Van Til, following Kuyper, writes that art

> . . . took into its purview the body, not in the pagan sense of animal vitality and lust, but as instrument of the soul, since the Calvinist confesses belonging to his faithful Saviour with body and soul. Even the doctrine of election . . . has the practical effect of drawing attention to the little, the insignificant, and the lowly, for there is nothing that is worthless and without value, since the very hairs of our head are all numbered. But, on the other hand, there is no respect of persons with God. No longer did art exclusively direct its attention to Greek demigods, to heroes and saints, but the common man came into prominence and human personality as such took the centre of the stage. But also human suffering and misery, as part of God's all-wise providence, are

depicted sympathetically, and the more sombre tints and tones form a strong contrast to the central light.[63]

Nor is this all; for just as there are those who are predestined to damnation, who yet may display aspects of goodness and holiness in their lives, so, writes Kuyper:

> Calvinism . . . has taught us that all liberal arts are gifts which God imparts promiscuously to believers and to unbelievers, yea, that as history shows, these gifts have flourished even in a larger measure outside the holy circle.[64]

Put in another way, it was Cain's rather than Abel's descendants that received artistic gifts, '. . . not as if art were Cainitic, but in order that he who has sinned away the highest gifts, should at least, as Calvin so beautifully says, in the lesser gifts of art have some testimony of the Divine bounty'.[65] This may make the genius of artists sound rather like a consolation prize given by God to some of those whom he has not chosen to elect to salvation, and it clearly serves to sustain the underpinning belief that God alone is the only real creative artist as well as the bestower of limited creative gifts upon humans (Kuyper is insistent that art cannot 'originate from the Evil One; for Satan is destitute of every creative power'). It may also help to explain why creative artists have often felt marginalised by and antipathetic towards Calvinist religion. Yet it continues to restate the notion that art is capable of expressing important truths and insights even when it is produced by individuals whose lives do not conform to the strict standards of Calvinism.

So it is that in matters relating to art the legacy of Calvinism once again appears to be two-sided. On the one hand there is the sobriety and earnestness of Calvin's belief that art should be committed to and contained within the all-embracing purpose of life, which is to know God and to worship him. This is complemented by, at best, a cautious view of artists and their work as potentially blasphemous or idolatrous, while at the same time the artistic genius is acknowledged as the gift of God and art itself may be a blessing which enables the faithful to see more clearly the fallen nature of the world and reminds them of perfection yet to come. On the other hand, Calvinism may rightly be associated with encouraging and expanding the range of art and with a more generous view of the subjects which it is proper for it to address. In this sense at least it was a democratising influence. Kuyper observed how

> ... puritanic sobriety went hand in hand with the reconquest of the entire life of the world, and Calvinism gave the impulse to that new development which dared to face the world with the Roman thought: *nil humanum a me alienum puto*, although never allowing itself to be intoxicated by its poisonous cup.[66]

The emphasis on the common man in preference to demigods, heroes, prophets and saints also points the way to the growth of bourgeois art in the seventeenth century and beyond, although the question of remaining free from intoxicating external and secular influences is problematic. Unsurprisingly, in the sphere of art as much as in the practice of religion and politics, Calvinism has not been static in its attitudes, and the forms and intensity of its influence have been modified by other historical and cultural pressures. However, its abiding influence is well illustrated in various forms of literary production where Calvinism and its derivatives have been major forces.

Thus, in America, for example, Calvinism not only underpinned the seventeenth-century historical and devotional works of the puritan settlers, and was revived again in the preaching and writing of Jonathan Edwards, but it also coloured the Enlightenment, the secularism of Benjamin Franklin, and the religious scepticism of a succession of novelists and poets throughout the nineteenth and into the twentieth centuries. More generally, it is worth adding that the strength and impact of Calvinistic Protestantism in American life were hugely boosted by the sustained influx of emigrants from Ulster across much of the eighteenth century.[67]

In England, too, Calvinism has been a lasting influence, as Donald Davie demonstrated in his 1976 Clark Lectures, where he observed that 'Distinguished individuals from the ranks of Dissent have indeed enriched our culture in every generation since 1700 . . .'.[68] He also points out that Calvinist theology was not peculiar to the dissenting churches alone, but played its part in the development of the Church of England. In varying degrees, not only English hymnody, but poetry, fiction and autobiography all bear witness to non-conformist and Calvinistic theological influences in the formative years, if not always in the adult beliefs, of writers as diverse as Milton, Bunyan, Richard Baxter and Isaac Watts, or George Eliot, Mark Rutherford, Edmund Gosse and D.H. Lawrence. More predictably, perhaps, Scottish literature, too, provides important examples of writing strongly coloured by stern Protestant influences. It is clear, therefore, that Calvinism, far from defeating the literary imagination, has often stimulated it – albeit sometimes in a polemical or deeply critical vein. In Ireland, and especially among the Protestants of Ulster, the Calvinistic inheritance is particularly complex, reaching deep into the spiritual lives of many generations, and also permeating the entire culture of the region in very particular ways, as we will see.

Undoubtedly, the difficulty for artists in reconciling the conservative and the liberating features of Calvinist thought in their work is very real and has never been finally resolved. For those who accept the opportunity of inclusiveness but who are also conscious of the rival emphasis upon propriety of purpose, restraint and the claims of religion, and who observe the effects of these conflicting attitudes both in their own lives and in the lives of others, this typical Calvinist paradox generates tensions which are often overlaid with feelings of guilt. Furthermore, the tensions themselves may be so deeply embedded that even when the original religious ideas that generated them have softened or been rejected by the individual, they have commonly remained a potent and visible source of anxiety. It is the strategies whereby particular writers from the north of Ireland have negotiated and represented these dilemmas that provide the focus for the later chapters of this book.

CHAPTER TWO

Presbyterianism, Evangelicalism and Unionism

No other denomination in the Kingdom can produce a record of equal services rendered to the cause of civil liberty and Bible Christianity.

W.D. Killen on the Presbyterian Church in *Reminiscences of a Long Life*.

[Evangelical religion] contributed to the creation of an Ulster Protestant identity and ultimately to the rise of Unionism.

David Hempton and Myrtle Hill, *Evangelical Protestantism in Ulster Society 1740–1890*.

I

COMMENTATORS ON Irish affairs have often remarked on the degree to which religious and political issues are intermixed, and on how, for the Protestants of Ulster in particular, history itself appears to consist of the record of their triumphs over or betrayals at the hands of Roman Catholics. To some extent such observations are true, although they avoid the more difficult question of why this should be so. The complexity of the problem may be traced to the seventeenth century during which Ireland experienced a massive influx of population and underwent a radical alteration in the religious composition of its landowners. In Ulster especially, the arrival of numerous settlers with Anglican and Presbyterian backgrounds and the extensive expropriation of Catholic property ensured that:

Religion, landownership and ethnic identity were . . . at the centre of profound divisions in [the] society, which by the eighteenth century had a luxuriant tradition of historical conflict on which to draw. The fact the Church of Ireland was the Established Church of a landed minority, that Ulster Presbyterianism was virtually a state within a state, and that Roman Catholicism was the creed of a defeated race

34

ensured that the province's religious life would have more than its fair share of turbulence.[1]

Furthermore, it was inevitable that in such a fractured and confrontational situation this 'turbulence' would not be confined only to religious matters, but would permeate the entire cultural and social fabric of the community.

The Protestantism of the planters was strongly influenced by Calvinism, and again this was particularly pronounced in Ulster where many of those who arrived in the early 1600s came from the Scottish church which had been decisively shaped by the militant Calvinist, John Knox. This was profoundly influential in determining the future character of the region and its difference from the rest of the country. However, within the Anglican communion too, Calvinist principles are reflected in the Lambeth Articles (1596) and the Established Church was represented at the Calvinist Synod of Dort in 1618. In Ireland itself

> . . . the Convocation of the Church of Ireland in 1615 drew up 104 articles of faith that were decidedly Calvinist. In them the necessity of episcopal ordination was ignored, absolute predestination was taught, and the pope was affirmed as the anti-Christ.[2]

These articles in turn had a bearing upon the formulation of the *Westminster Confession of Faith* (1646) and were stoutly defended by the distinguished Archbishop of Armagh, James Ussher. He was 'a strong Calvinist', who insisted on their retention even when the Irish Convocation of 1635 was compelled to accept the Thirty-Nine Articles of the Church of England, which it had previously rejected in 1615 under Ussher's persuasion.[3] Although the strength of Calvinistic influences within the Church of Ireland varied over time, they never wholly disappeared and they have been important in preserving the relatively 'low' church forms of worship which are characteristic of much Irish Anglicanism.

The direct religious and cultural legacy of Calvinism in Ireland is, however, most directly reflected in the history of the Presbyterian Church which retained the potentially divisive Calvinist commitment to individual liberty of conscience and to democratic, non-prelatic church structures.[4] It also upheld the importance of scripture as the source of truth and knowledge and of the preaching of the Word over and above liturgy and ritual. Like Calvinism, Presbyterianism claimed the whole of life as the proper sphere of religion. This is an ideal which remains as valid at the close of the twentieth century as at any time in the past. As John Dunlop makes clear in his account of the contemporary Church's attitude:

> Everything matters.
>
> All of life is to be lived before God and everything ought to be influenced by God, whether it is formal worship, cleaning the house, ploughing a field, keeping a farmyard, riveting steel, applying for grants, from the giving of one's word to completing an undertaking or doing business of any kind. All must be done to the glory of God, since the whole earth belongs to God. The whole of life is integrated under the rubric of living in such a way that God is glorified.[5]

In matters of political activity, Presbyterianism upheld the citizen's duties to the monarch and to appointed governmental authorities, although always allowing that they might be superseded by the individual's ultimate duty to God in cases of conflict between religious and civil obligation.

The direct Scottish influence on the Protestant church in Ulster was crucial from the outset: some of the clergy who accompanied the planters joined the Church of Ireland but soon asserted their Calvinist beliefs and practices within it, while others were subsequently instrumental in the formation of the Presbyterian Church in the community.[6] Thereafter, for generations, until the establishment of the Queen's Colleges in the 1840s, prospective entrants to the Presbyterian ministry from Ulster almost invariably went to Scotland (usually to Glasgow) to receive higher education. And at various key moments in their troubled history, Presbyterians from Ulster, both lay and clerical, withdrew to Scotland to avoid persecution for their religious practices and beliefs, thereby further reinforcing the connections between the two communities. Likewise, the Ulster Presbyterians were always conscious of the difficulties and divisions that beset their mother church in Scotland, whether as a result of governmental pressures or internal divisions, and on occasion became involved in them.

If Calvin's Geneva was akin to a city under siege as well as being the source of a brand of theology that was to spread far afield, so too the position of the Presbyterians in Ireland has often seemed to be under threat. James Seaton Reid's mid-nineteenth-century history of the Irish Presbyterian Church reveals this perspective very clearly. He dates the identifiable history of Irish Presbyterianism from the accession of James I and the plantation of Ulster, although pointing out that many of the early settlers were anything but pious or godly and attributing the first real successes of Presbyterianism to the Scottish ministers who adopted a missionary approach to Ulster in the 1620s.[7] Then, he claims:

> Rarely has the church of Christ in any land experienced so sensible an increase in so limited a period, as under the ministry of these brethren.[8]

At this stage, the Presbyterian Church did not exist as a separate institution from the episcopal church but it was not long before Bishop Echlin, disliking the influence of the Scottish clergy over the people, refused to ordain further ministers unless they promised conformity to the English church. Here one is immediately confronted with the classic dilemma which has repeatedly presented itself in Irish Presbyterianism and, by extension, in the politics and other concerns of Presbyterians – whether or not agreement to conform to any type of legalistic requirement is an unwarrantable intrusion upon the individual's right of conscience which underpins Calvinistic theology.

Reid's history is in many ways a deliberate demonstration of the resilience of Presbyterianism despite repeated attempts to subjugate its independence and reduce it to particular versions of conformity. Equally, it presents history as the providential activity of God in preserving the Presbyterian Church even in the face of overwhelming odds. He perceives the real threat as coming from all those individuals whose efforts were directed – from the point of view of the Presbyterian historian – at reversing the progress of the Reformation and returning the church to 'Romish ritual' – Laud, Wentworth, Charles I, Charles II and James II. Oliver Cromwell, too, is seen as an enemy of Presbyterianism because of his treatment of the Irish parliament and his plan to reduce dissent in Ulster by forcibly removing leading Presbyterians from Down and Antrim to parts of Munster.

Faced with continuing opposition and persecution, Presbyterianism came to define itself increasingly sharply in Calvinistic terms. Thus, Charles I's attempts to introduce a new liturgy and book of canons led not only to the celebrated incident in St Giles' Church in Edinburgh in 1637, when Jenny Geddes disrupted the service by throwing a chair at the Dean, but also to the renewal of the National Covenant in Scotland, abjuring the errors of Catholicism and undertaking to defend civil and religious liberty. A year later the Scottish General Assembly approved the abolition of the prelacy, condemned the contentious liturgy and book of canons, and affirmed Presbyterian organisational practices and standards of piety. The influence of these events was felt in Ireland where Wentworth was seeking to impose conformity by making all northern Scots, under penalty of expulsion, subscribe to the 'Black Oath' whereby they were to promise never to oppose the King's commands and to refrain from taking any other binding oaths. This resulted not only in wide-spread resistance, especially in Ulster where the Presbyterian influence within the Church of Ireland was strongest in Down and Antrim, and where the Bishop of Derry, John Bramhall, who was a supporter of Laud's liturgical reforms, met fierce clerical opposition; but it also led to many Presbyterians going to Scotland and subscribing to the National Covenant instead.[9] Reid identifies Wentworth's design and the resistance it met as a critical moment in the history he records:

> Had this nefarious project succeeded, it would not only have over-turned the foundations on which the Presbyterian Church chiefly rested for support in Ireland, but it must have terminated in the ruin of protestantism, and the desolation of the northern province. Destitute of the powerful aid of the numerous and resolute presbyterian population, the few and scattered protestants who would have remained in the kingdom could never have withstood the exterminating fury of the Roman Catholics, during the rebellion which, in twelve months after, broke out in Ulster.[10]

It is notable that Reid attaches the greatest importance to the position and influence of the Presbyterian community, both as the authentic defenders of Protestantism and as the creators and upholders of civilised life in Ulster, thereby voicing a self-perception that has had a lengthy history, and is still evident. The significance of their resistance is further substantiated by reference to the 1641 rebellion which has its place in Protestant mythology as an exemplary instance of Catholic treachery and of the potentially apocalyptic dangers that have repeatedly beset Irish Protestantism in general and Ulster Presbyterianism in particular. Desmond Bowen has recently suggested that this uprising and its aftermath also initiated the Ulster Protestant sense of being a people under siege which is more commonly associated with the events at Derry in 1689. He comments:

When the Scots army of Robert Monro appeared to deliver the Protestants, many of them saw the arrival of his troops as an act of Providence;

and it was some of the chaplains and elders who accompanied these troops who established the first presbytery in Ulster at Carrickfergus in 1642.[11] This underpins Reid's presentation of the Presbyterians in particular as the crucial group in ensuring the survival of Protestantism. Although Reid does not speak in terms of a chosen few, it seems clear that he views his Presbyterian forebears in something of this light, which is another interpretation that has continued to exercise a compelling power on the minds and imaginations of many of his successors. The cultural memory of 1641 itself is carried forward into the present in the depictions of the slaughter of Protestants on Orange banners designed to alert later generations to the supposedly enduring murderous intentions of Catholics, should they be given the chance to implement them.

The formulation of the *Solemn League and Covenant* (1644) and, more importantly, of the *Westminster Confession of Faith* (1646) were vital stages in the development of Presbyterianism and the latter remains the foundation document of the modern Presbyterian Church. Reid regards the *Solemn League and Covenant* as marking

the commencement of the SECOND REFORMATION with which this province has been favoured,

while the *Westminster Confession* and Catechisms were rooted in a theology which was directly opposed to the resurgent Catholic influences of the day, rather as the regrouping of Protestantism in the nineteenth century in Ireland would be motivated by the same imperative.[12] The Calvinistic thought in these documents may be seen in various ways which are worth summarising because of their lasting impact.

The *Westminster Confession* upholds the supreme importance and value of scripture as the Word of God which is to be believed and obeyed (1.4), and which is held to contain all necessary knowledge (1.6), subject to the illumination of the Spirit.[13] Like Calvinism, it adopts a world-view, maintaining that all issues must be regulated in the light of scripture and of what is consistent with it.

The controlling power of God over everything that happens is affirmed (3.1), as is his foreknowledge of history (3.2) which includes the predestined outcomes of every individual's life (3.3–3.7). The elect may be certain of their position (3.8) and all who are predestined to life will be called in time by God's Word and Spirit (10.1). However, others, who are not elected, may be called by the Word, yet cannot be saved (10.4). Thus, many of the harshest austerities of Calvinism are upheld and the image of life as a perpetual battleground between implacable forces of good and evil is retained.

This is further emphasised in the insistence on the depravity of human nature and our incapacity to achieve any spiritual good or merit by dint of our own efforts (7.1, 9.3, 16.3 and elsewhere). Good works are God's command (16.1) and repentance is necessary (15.3), but pardon can never be earned and is the gracious gift of the Almighty to the elect to whom he gives faith (11.1), which is alone the 'instrument of justification' (11.2). Peter Brooke has observed that:

> In stressing man's powerlessness in relation to God; in distinguishing between the elect and non-elect and resting the distinction on the quite arbitrary decree of God, [Presbyterianism] offers no sanctions or incentives for good behaviour – and in its rejection of symbolism and ritual it offers few reminders of a higher reality.[14]

It was a form of religion unrelieved by celebrations to mark the major festivals of the Christian year, because these were believed to have deteriorated into excuses for intemperance and self-indulgence. The Lord's Day alone, commemorating the resurrection, was observed. Even participation in the occasional communion services was subject to recommendation by a district elder who first had to be satisfied with the individual's style of life and state of soul.[15] This very austerity may have encouraged the Arminianism which threatened the church's unity in the eighteenth century and finally divided it in the nineteenth. It may also help to account for the appeal of the more charismatic and evangelical influences which began to make an impact in the later eighteenth century and reached a highpoint in the 1859 revival. There is a further way of viewing this, however, because much of the imaginative writing by individuals brought up within Presbyterian, and later evangelical traditions, reveals a deep-seated reaction against the absence of 'reminders of a higher reality', as we will see.

The Calvinist concern with the integrity of individual conscience and with the supreme importance of the individual's relationship with God, unmediated by church or clergy, is transcribed into the *Westminster Confession* in words still widely repeated at the ordination of Presbyterian ministers and elders in Ireland which counter Catholic ideas of implicit faith and absolute obedience:[16]

> God alone is Lord of the conscience, and hath left it free from the doctrines and commandments of men, which are in any thing contrary to the Word; or beside it, if matters of faith or worship. So that, to believe such doctrines, or to obey such commands, out of conscience, is to betray true liberty of conscience: and the requiring of an implicit faith, and an absolute and blind obedience is to destroy liberty of conscience, and reason also. (20.2)

Ironically, this paragraph proclaims the value of liberty of conscience, yet the issue of compulsory subscription to the *Westminster Confession* by all intending ministers was to bedevil Presbyterianism for the better part of a century. As in Calvinism, the inclination to be both authoritarian and libertarian proved paradoxical and the outcome was fragmentation.

The *Confession* continues the Calvinist tradition of regarding it as the citizen's duty to obey lawful government and civil magistrates, who are God's representatives empowered to exercise authority (20.4, 23.1, 23.4), and warns against acting rebelliously through a mistaken notion of Christian liberty. Here again there is an unresolved tension between the place of conscience and that of external law.

Finally, the hostility to Catholicism apparent in Calvin's *Institutes* is perpetuated in the *Westminster Confession*. Thus, the Pope is described as the 'Antichrist' (25.6) and Christians are instructed not to marry 'infidels, papists or other idolaters' (24.3). Similarly, the doctrine of transubstantiation is rejected (29.6) along with the Catholic view of the mass as a sacrifice rather than a commemoration in which believers are spiritually fed (29.2, 29.7). As in Calvinism, the Lord's Supper and baptism are regarded as the only true sacraments of the church.

Since the *Westminster Confession of Faith* and its accompanying catechisms, which aim to show a clear link between the *Confession* and the wider business of daily living, remain the subordinate standards of the modern Presbyterian Church in Ireland, and have never been revised, it is evident that seventeenth-century theological thought continues to exercise influence in a twentieth-century context.[17] This, of course, is not unique, and while subscription to the *Confession* is still required of all ministers and elders, it is generally understood that this refers to the document as a whole rather than to agreement with it line by line. More specifically, a recent motion was adopted by the General Assembly of the Presbyterian Church in Ireland removing the requirement upon subscribers to believe that the Pope is the Antichrist.[18] However, it is precisely such attempts at amelioration which arouse the most virulent criticism from individuals such as Revd James Hunter, who pressed heresy charges against the Presbyterian scholar Revd J.E. Davey in 1926, and Revd Ian Paisley and his followers who see them as evidence of the weakening of Presbyterianism's commitment to the Protestant Reformation and the appeasement of Catholicism.[19] Paisley, of course, speaks from outside the Presbyterian Church in Ireland and as the leader of the self-styled Free Presbyterians who claim to adhere to the authentic standards of faith which they believe have been betrayed elsewhere. The point remains that the *Westminster Confession* provides useful fuel for those who wish to base their anti-Catholicism on historic theological standards and doctrine.

However, even as Presbyterianism was receiving definition in the *Westminster Confession* and catechisms, and was reviving and expanding in Ulster under the tutelage of a new generation of Scottish ministers who arrived in the aftermath of the 1641 rebellion, so too it was facing fresh challenges from the government which aimed to curb the power of the kirk sessions and presbyteries in ecclesiastical matters. The tension between church and state took on a different complexion in 1649 with the seizure and subsequent execution of Charles I, because the Presbyterians denounced this treatment of their former enemy and upheld the royalist claim of his son's right to succeed him.

This is a classic instance of the Presbyterian understanding of loyal and principled behaviour. They viewed the treatment of the king as worse than anything he had done and the conduct of the parliamentarians as a threat to law and liberty. In doing so, they were, of course, consistent to the principles laid down in the *Westminster Confession*, and despite the extraordinary blossoming of Presbyterianism in Ireland between 1653 and 1660, they backed the restoration of the monarchy, hoping for stability and greater liberty than had been afforded them under the Cromwellian regime.[20]

In practice, the period from 1660 to 1690 was to assume unique importance in Protestant, and more specifically Presbyterian, history and culture as a defining interval of resistance to increasing persecution and threat from Catholicism. Under Charles II, Presbyterians were expelled from their churches, and their ministers were forbidden to preach or baptise unless they were prepared to accept the rule of bishops. J.S. Reid's treatment of the sixty-one Presbyterian ministers in Ulster who withstood this pressure elevates them to heroic status. They are recalled by name in a roll of honour and the significance of their stand is boldly spelt out:

> Neither the privations nor the temptations by which they were beset could induce them to violate the sacred principles of conscience and duty. They cheerfully 'suffered the loss of all things', rather than submit to an unscriptural form of government and worship, and profess allegiance to a church which, while it had renounced the headship of Christ and surrendered the key of discipline to the civil magistrate, had assumed the power of decreeing rites and ceremonies, and adopted too many of the idolatrous and superstitious forms of the church of Rome. . . . Had they, tempted by preferment and worldly ease, apostatized from their principles and deserted their people, few traces of presbyterianism, to which the inhabitants of Ulster owe so much of their civil and religious freedom, would have survived the subsequent persecutions of the prelacy and the ruinous wars of the Revolution.[21]

These Presbyterians are thus seen as the very embodiment of the Calvinistic principles of liberty of conscience, commitment to reformed religion and readiness to sacrifice all worldly interests to preserve the integrity of their faith and the organisation of their church. Their action shows precisely how, in D.W. Miller's words:

> By standing firm for Presbyterian ideals, one becomes an instrument of divine purposes, and potentially of dramatic providential intervention in the external world.[22]

Furthermore, viewed against subsequent events, the resistance of the sixty-one ministers appears to prefigure what is arguably the most symbolic incident in the version of history preferred by many Ulster Protestants – the closing of the city gates in Derry by the Apprentice Boys and the endurance of its citizens under siege.[23] Reid presents this, too, as an event of epic proportions:

> On this sudden and apparently unimportant movement [i.e. the closing of the gates], the fate of the three kingdoms ultimately depended. Had Derry been occupied by a popish garrison, the armies of James would have possessed the whole of Ulster, and thence passed without obstruction into Scotland; where, united with the forces of Claverhouse viscount of Dundee, they would have made an easy conquest of that

kingdom, and afterwards invaded England with accumulated strength. But this important post was thus, at a most critical moment, providentially preserved to be the means of defeating the machinations of a despot and a bigot against the religion and liberties of Britain.[24]

It is significant that Reid speaks of Derry as being 'providentially preserved' and notable that elsewhere he quotes approvingly from a contemporary account which sees the siege and its relief as a clear sign of the Almighty's hand at work.[25] Here again one encounters the Calvinist interest and belief in the value of signs that indicate God's purpose.[26] Despite the passage of time and shifts in consciousness, there are still those who interpret the siege of Derry in this emblematic way, although Ian McBride asserts that recent loyalist literature 'now discloses a sense of isolation in a world where deliverance is constantly deferred and sacrifice goes unrewarded.'[27] Similarly, the defeat of the 'arbitrary monarch and bigoted Romanist', James II, and accession of 'the intrepid assertor of civil and religious freedom', William III, is taken by Reid as a further sign of God's will and of his specifically gracious benignity towards the Presbyterian church in Ireland.[28]

II

The Williamite settlement resulted in renewed expansion of the Presbyterian church and its influence in Ulster, which for the first time flourished with unequivocal royal backing. This was symbolised by the doubling of the regium donum, an annual payment to Presbyterian clergymen instituted by Charles II, and the removal of the long-standing irritation caused by the requirement that Presbyterians should take the Oath of Supremacy. However, the bishops resisted the attempt to remove the Sacramental Test and argued with increasing effect against further concessions to the Presbyterians, particularly as the influence of Bishop (later Archbishop) King grew. Following the death of King William in 1702, the position of Presbyterians again became difficult as both they and the Catholics found themselves persecuted by the Established Church, which refused even to accept that other reformed denominations merited the title 'Protestant'.[29] Thus, ironically, as McBride puts it:

> Memories of the Siege of Derry, far from unifying the Protestant population, helped to crystallise a separate Presbyterian culture of grievance.[30]

As in previous times, the Presbyterian church showed its resilience under attack. Thus, while its members were excluded from positions in the armed forces, customs and excise, and courts and magistracy unless they conformed to the Established Church, and Presbyterians were debarred from teaching by a schism bill (1714), the synod upheld discipline over its members and required stricter educational standards and conduct from candidates for the ministry.

Paradoxically, too, during Queen Anne's reign the Belfast Society was formed (1705) with the purpose of promoting scriptural debate and this became the seed-bed in which some of the most divisive arguments in the Presbyterian Church were first nurtured as doctrinal differences began to emerge. Here again the recurrent tension in Calvinism between liberty of conscience and authoritarianism appeared. Reid brings this into sharp focus in his account of how, although the debates of the Belfast Society

> . . . did not directly impugn any of the leading doctrines of the Gospel, as embodied in the Church's confession of faith, . . . they tended to undermine the entire system of a sinner's acceptance as taught therein, by inculcating the innocency of error when not wilful, and by under-valuing all belief in positive doctrines as uncertain, or, at all events, as non-essential. In reference to ecclesiastical discipline, the members of the society taught, among other things, that the Church had no right to require candidates for the ministry to subscribe to a confession of faith, prepared by any man or body of men, and that such a required subscription was a violation of the right of private judgment, and inconsistent with Christian liberty and true Protestantism.[31]

In this very important passage, Reid describes the origins and sum-marises the essence of the problems that were to beset the Presbyterian Church in Ulster henceforth. Perhaps inevitably, a church so dependent upon a codified formulation of beliefs, and descended from Calvin's Genevan church with its even more elaborately defined theology and practice, faced new kinds of challenge and interrogation in an era of enlightened rationalism. Increasingly the question was raised how a church which placed so much value on freeing its members from the legalistic thraldom of popery, and which asserted the preciousness of private conscience and of the individual's relationship with God, could at the same time expect unquestioning subscription to a humanly devised confession of faith.[32]

Thus by the early 1720s, during the period of the so-called First Subscription Controversy, opponents of the ministerial requirement to accept the *Westminster Confession of Faith* denounced this 'as a tyranny equalled only by the Romish inquisition'.[33] Likewise, the aspiration to embrace every aspect of an individual's life and of a society's activities, inherited from Calvinism, came to rest uneasily alongside a more liberal and less austere view of human nature and of the individual's capacity to repent and find forgiveness. Consequently the consistency of parts of the *Westminster Confession* with scripture was challenged.

(The tensions that surfaced in the Belfast Society's debates also prefigure the unorthodoxies of numerous political activists and writers in future years who held onto the libertarian aspects of Presbyterianism while adopting increasingly hostile attitudes towards its legalism and narrow-mindedness. Here, for the moment, however, the impact and effect of those tensions are viewed through events in the Church itself.)

Despite the decision in 1726 to exclude non-subscribing clergy from the synod and its inferior courts, they were not denied Christian fellowship with other Presbyterian ministers, nor were they debarred from continuing in post. While this indicates the anxiety to avoid an open split in the Church, it resolved nothing. In fact, not only did the non-subscribing influence continue and grow within Presbyterianism, leading, in Reid's view, to a further lapse in standards, but in the 1730s, influenced by the example of the Associate Presbytery which had seceded from the Church of Scotland over the right to determine its own affairs, a secession movement began in Ulster with the intention of restoring evangelical orthodoxy to Presbyterianism. The Presbyterian Church thus found itself exposed to controversy from within by so-called 'New Light' ministers who continued to challenge its procedures and to attack from without by the Seceders who accused it of harbouring preachers of unorthodoxy. Its attempt to defend itself by issuing in 1747 'A Serious Warning to the people of our communion, within the bounds of the synod' to be read from all pulpits, denouncing departures from orthodoxy, affirming scripture, the *Westminster Confession of Faith* and the *Larger and Shorter Catechisms* as the standards of doctrine, and advising of the risks of uneducated reading of 'erroneous books', reveals the extent of its dilemma.[34] It also shows how the Presbyterians found themselves forced into adopting an ever more authoritarian stance which further aggravated 'New Light' clergy while winning no praise from the Seceders, who claimed that the very wording of the 'Serious Warning' admitted the presence of unorthodox influences within the church.

J.S. Reid, who is a steady champion of conservative Presbyterianism, discerns 'the hand of an overruling and gracious Providence' at work again in the development of the secession which restored 'the blessings of a pure Gospel' and counteracted 'the blighting influence of moderation'[35]; and in describing the process of secession in Ulster he adopts overtly biblical language:

> It often happened that those who took an active part in establishing seceding congregations left the communion of the Synod of Ulster with a heavy heart, for it was endeared to them by hallowed recollections; but its fold had been entered by false caretakers, and many could no longer find in it the green pastures and the quiet waters to which faithful shepherds had once guided them.[36]

On the other hand, the influence of the 'New Light' adherents was further stimulated following the appointment of the Ulsterman, Francis Hutcheson, to the Chair of Moral Philosophy at the University of Glasgow in 1729. The son of a traditionalist Presbyterian minister, Hutcheson, who had contacts with the Belfast Society, aroused controversy as early as 1719 by emphasising his belief in the benevolence of God and his optimistic view of human nature and of its potential for good, both of which flew in the face of Calvinist orthodoxy. Almost twenty years later he was unsuccessfully prosecuted by the presbytery in Glasgow for

> . . . teaching to his students in contravention to the *Westminster Confession* the following two false and dangerous doctrines, first that the standard of moral goodness was the promotion of the happiness of others; and second that we could have a knowledge of good and evil without, and prior to a knowledge of God.[37]

Hutcheson's dissenting attitudes made him critical of the inflexible and dogmatic approach taken by conservatives towards the Presbyterian system of church government and its confessions, and of the intolerance and animosity resulting from it, which seemed to him to undermine the real substance of religion. Although he was reluctant to be described as 'New Light', lest the term itself have a divisive effect, this is how he was regarded by conservatives in the church. Given that Irish candidates for the Presbyterian ministry had to go to Glasgow to study, many young men were influenced by his brand of thought. In time, these erstwhile students became members of the Synod of Ulster and by the last quarter of the eighteenth century supporters of the *Confession* in it were probably a minority group. In practice, therefore, although the Presbyterian Church did not formally split during this century, matters were moving towards a critical stage.

Yet for all its internal wrangling – or perhaps because of it – parts of the Presbyterian Church in the late eighteenth century demonstrated a radicalism and commitment to egalitarian principles that are still admired and whose subsequent loss or dilution has often been lamented, not least by a range of writers and poets. John M. Barkley notes that the term 'blackmouth', often used disparagingly of Presbyterians, is of Irish origin and has a specifically political connotation:

> It refers to those whose sympathies lay with the ideals of social polity and human rights in the American and French Revolutions. Eventually the epithet came to be applied to the whole Presbyterian community. . . . The aim of the Blackmouths was to establish unity and brotherhood among all the people of Ireland, to achieve 'parliamentary reform by constitutional means', and to include 'Irishmen of every religious persuasion' in the reform so that it may be 'efficacious and just'. In its origins there was no approval of the use of force.[38]

Such people upheld the radical principles of the Reformation informed by eighteenth-century rationalism and republican idealism. They are represented by William Drennan, Henry Joy and Mary Ann McCracken, Jemmy Hope, Samuel Neilson, the Revds William Steel Dickson and Samuel Barber, and other Presbyterian supporters of the United Irishmen. In them, one encounters again that moral and intellectual courage and independence of mind combined with a readiness for action to affirm cherished principles which are characteristic of Calvinism at its most positive. Much of this radicalism centred on Belfast and David Hempton has written of its 'clubbable character, its close family and economic networks and its mercantile, professional and clerical membership'.[39] While its principal proponents were educated, articulate and able individuals, often exasperated by the constraints on their political influence, they were not typical of Presbyterians more generally, particularly in the tolerance they advocated towards Catholics. Rather, theirs

> . . . was precisely the kind of radicalism that could not sink deep roots into the Ulster countryside where Protestant and Catholic peasants were fighting a life and death struggle against smaller holdings, increasing rents and, ultimately, each other.[40]

The 1790s were, after all, not only the time of the Volunteers and the United Irishmen but the Orange Order was founded in Loughgall in 1795, following one particular sectarian confrontation between Protestant Peep O'Day Boys and Catholic Defenders.

Predictably, W.D. Killen, who completed Reid's historical work, construed events negatively, deploring the period as 'this dark night in the history of Presbyterianism', during which standards of preaching and piety declined as people drifted into misguided political activity.[41] He attributed relaxation of strict observance of the Sabbath and the involvement of Presbyterians in the 1798 rebellion to 'New Light' influences. However, later historians have seriously questioned the simple equation of 'New Light' theology and the political principles of the United Irishmen which it was clearly convenient to Killen's purposes to uphold.[42] What is less contentious is the traumatic impact of 1798 upon the Presbyterian community. For Killen it was nothing less than an apocalyptic warning:

> The melancholy scenes of the Rebellion, to some extent, awakened the ministers, as well as the people of Ulster, from their dream of carnal security, and led them to think with increasing seriousness of the interests of eternity. Shortly after this period, the spiritual eye discerns some faint indications of that revival of religion which has so much improved the character of Irish Presbyterianism.[43]

This clearly implies that the supporters of the United Irishmen had allowed the political, the secular and the temporal to distract them from their true business with the religious, the spiritual and the eternal. Killen's version of Presbyterianism remains rooted in the idea of a contractual or covenantal obligation to the monarch as God's representative, and while this may be consistent with the Calvinistic position set out in the *Institutes*, it does not allow for the changed position of the King and a different concept of politics. Presbyterian adherence to the letter of the law which ascribed unique authority to the monarch did not rest easily with 'the post-1688 concept of the sovereignty of the King *in parliament*'.[44] Nevertheless, as Finlay Holmes writes, the Synod of Ulster's affirmation of loyalty to the King, condemnation of its own rebel ministers, and exhortations to its congregations to recognise that the basis of their liberty of conscience and economic advantages lay in constitutional obedience represented the position of the majority of Presbyterians.[45] This view is further endorsed by the uncharacteristic readiness with which the Synod accepted Castlereagh's subsequent modification of the arrangements for the allocation of the regium donum designed to ensure that Presbyterian ministers would in future be a conservative rather than a radical force.[46]

It may be argued, therefore, that in different ways both the supporters and the opponents of the political radicalism in the late eighteenth century were being true to aspects of their Calvinistic background – and indeed that their differences derived from the paradoxes already observed in that system of belief. However, the deeply divided views of 1798 continued the split in the Church that had started with the Belfast Society and anticipated the struggle in the nineteenth century that centred on Henry Montgomery and Henry Cooke. This continuity is perhaps symbolised by the fact that Montgomery, who admitted that members of his family were sympathetic to the United Irishmen, saw his home burned down by the forces of the crown in 1798 whereas Cooke, who came from Maghera, viewed the rebels as violent anarchists. The degree to which their respective boyhood memories and experiences helped to shape the two men's adult attitudes is therefore an intriguing matter for conjecture.[47]

In spite of its internal divisions, the robust organisational strength of the Presbyterian Church, another important part of its legacy from Calvin, not only enabled it to survive but was instrumental in its resilience against varying degrees of persecution throughout much of the eighteenth and even into the nineteenth century. John M. Barkley has argued that their disadvantaged position in law and negative treatment in propaganda of the period

> . . . contributed to the moulding of the Irish Presbyterians into a closely-knit community and were determining factors in the relationship of minister and people, as well as that of Presbyterian and the community.[48]

This self-protective bonding was further facilitated by the power of the session in each church to monitor and discipline its members, and by the authority of the minister, who was appointed by invitation of the people, not by direction from a bishop or external body. These factors helped to give Presbyterians a strong sense of cultural identity and set them apart from both the Catholic and Church of Ireland communions whose organisational structures were much weaker at this time.[49] Ironically, it was later, in the mid-nineteenth century, when under Cooke's leadership the Presbyterian Church sought to ally itself more closely with the Church of Ireland, to resist the increasingly articulate demands of Catholic nationalists and in response to the growing appeal of evangelicalism which was already becoming a significant force in the 1790s due to the influence of the Moravians and Methodists, that this sharply defined sense of Presbyterian identity began to become blurred.[50]

The importance placed by Presbyterians upon having an educated ministry has already been observed and the educational accomplishments of individual clergymen added further to their status and authority, especially in rural communities. However, the popular acquisition of literacy was also highly valued and has been directly linked to the 'long-established Presbyterian tradition that all members should be able to read the Bible for themselves'.[51] This in turn is associated with a more general aspiration for spiritual and intellectual development, and for economic advancement. For example, Ivan Herbison has shown how the passion for education and self-improvement is reflected in the writings of the Rhyming Weavers in Antrim and Down in the late eighteenth and early nineteenth centuries, and more generally in the rapid growth of book clubs and reading societies in Ulster between 1750 and 1850, and in the fact that Antrim and Down recorded the highest literacy rates in the census returns of 1841 and 1851.[52]

However, those features of Presbyterianism which set its adherents apart and gave them a sense of shared solidarity may also have had the negative effect of reinforcing a siege mentality. In his autobiography, *Blackmouth and Dissenter*, John M. Barkley recalls how the Presbyterian Meetinghouse at Malin in Co. Donegal where his father was minister for a time was built on the sand 'round which the Atlantic sweeps in twice a day'. Likewise, the local Catholic chapel stands in the sandhills, and both are 'a living memorial to the days when Presbyterians and Roman Catholics were treated as religious and social outcasts'.[53] This isolated, marginalised position might be taken to symbolise the way in which Presbyterians saw themselves as well as the way in which they were for long regarded by the Established Church. A.T.Q. Stewart has described the Ulster planters as 'frontiersmen', always unsure of the loyalty and reliability of others around them, forever anticipating or meeting with hostility, and this transferred itself to the mentality of the Presbyterians whose recurrent experience was of persecution, resistance and attempts to discredit and dismantle their church.[54] While this may have helped to give the Presbyterians a sense of common cause, it rendered their relationships with other sections of the community problematic and left them largely isolated – a community within the nation rather than part of it.[55] As time passed and the divisions within Presbyterianism itself deepened, this isolated position threatened to become a source of weakness rather than strength, and in turn helps to explain why Cooke was able to lead his church into a closer alliance with the Church of Ireland and Tory politicians.

III

The history of Irish Presbyterianism in the nineteenth century is essentially the story of the consolidation of the influence of conservative, orthodox views, the departure of the critics of subscription and the move towards greater amity with members of the Established Church. These developments were hastened and encouraged by growing Catholic nationalism which threatened the constitutional relationship with England on the one hand, and by the success of evangelical religion which challenged the hegemony of the Presbyterian and Church of Ireland communions on the other. An increase in the regium donum in 1803 served to encourage the Presbyterian clergy to support the Act of Union, as was noted, while the founding of the Belfast Academical Institution in the early years of the century and the election of the Calvinistic Revd Samuel Hanna to the Chair of Divinity and Church History (1817) were important steps in enabling the Irish Church to provide training for its own candidates for the ministry, rather than sending them on the long-established route to Glasgow. The significance of these developments is suggested in the phraseology adopted by Reid who says that thereafter Irish students

> Trained up in Belfast under the eye of relatives or acquaintances who took an interest in their welfare . . . were preserved from many temptations to which they were exposed in a land of strangers.[56]

However, the revival of orthodoxy did not simply signal the cessation of disagreement within Presbyterianism, rather it was the prologue to the so-called Second Subscription Controversy of the 1820s, which became personalised in the opposition between Montgomery and Cooke.

The almost gladiatorial contest between these extraordinarily gifted orators, who were capable of speaking for several hours each at a time, was of decisive importance in shaping the direction of Presbyterianism for the rest of the nineteenth century and beyond.[57]

Cooke's victory led to the departure from the Presbyterian Church of those who had sought to challenge the requirement to subscribe to the *Westminster Confession* and the creeds. It opened up the way for the foundation of the General Assembly of the Presbyterian Church in Ireland (1840) which became, and remains, its supreme governing body, and in which the earlier divisions between the Ulster Synod and the secession churches were submerged. For W.D. Killen, as he completed Reid's history of the Presbyterian Church, there was no doubt about the desirability of this outcome. Writing at the mid-century he declared:

> The new Assembly is free from the incubus of Unitarianism; it presents Presbyterianism in a consolidated and invigorated form.

And he continues:

> At the present moment, Presbyterians constitute the base and sinew of the Irish Protestant population, as they have more general competence, as well as more diffused intelligence, than any other great religious community.[58]

But the organisational changes that followed the success of Cooke and the 'Old Lights' were not the only, nor the most significant changes in Ulster Presbyterianism. In a very real sense, the departure of Montgomery and his supporters marked the point at which the Presbyterian Church stiffened its resistance towards liberalism of thought and insisted that the affirmation of certain beliefs was its distinguishing mark rather than its commitment to liberty of conscience and the right of private judgement.[59] Thus, the old Calvinist tension between freedom and authoritarianism was resolved in favour of the latter.

Furthermore, whereas Montgomery had supported Catholic emancipation, Cooke was much less enthusiastic, and in the 1830s he increasingly criticised educational reforms and suggestions for integrated Protestant and Catholic schools, although he had been sympathetic to such developments in the previous decade. He found common cause with the Established Church's concern at the way in which the national school system appeared to threaten the erosion of the Protestant influence in education, and this was one of the influences which enouraged him to lead the Presbyterians towards a closer relationship with the Church of Ireland. As Finlay Holmes has put it:

The national education system involved concessions to popery; to many Ulster protestants and presbyterians that was condemnation enough.[60]

An increasingly strident anti-Catholicism reveals itself from the 1830s onwards in the language of Cooke and others, in the suspicion shown towards any attempts by the government to deal with Daniel O'Connell, and in the note of warning against the betrayal of Protestantism through concessions to Catholics which was sounded ever more frequently.[61] Nowhere was opposition to the Catholic Association stiffer than in Ulster and when O'Connell visited Belfast in January 1841 to speak on the invitation of the Loyal National Repeal Association, Cooke challenged him to a public debate – an opportunity the Liberator declined – and there was street violence despite the presence of troops brought in to forestall a serious breakdown of public order.

In their study of evangelical Protestantism in Ulster, David Hempton and Myrtle Hill have shown how the unprecedented efforts of evangelical societies, the most powerful of which were funded from London, to convert Catholics in the first third of the century inadvertently helped to sharpen the sectarian divisions already present in the community. Furthermore, the effectiveness of the itinerant preaching and flexible organisation of many evangelical groups posed a real challenge to the other Protestant churches. The consequences of this

> . . . at once destabilized the old conventional boundaries between Catholic and Protestant churches, and promoted class harmony within Ulster Protestantism.[62]

The movement headed by Cooke to purge the Presbyterian Church of non-subscribers and the encouragement he gave to nurturing better relations with the Church of Ireland must therefore also be understood in part as a reaction to restore orthodox Protestant authority in the community. The influence of evangelicalism and its appeal to many people could not be ignored and henceforth the two main Protestant churches had to take account of it. Indeed, it has been suggested that Cooke's main role in the evolution of evangelical Presbyterianism was his success in linking evangelicalism, doctrinal orthodoxy and anti-Catholicism in the minds of members of the Synod of Ulster.[63]

Ironically, however, and perhaps fatally for the independence of Presbyterianism, Cooke also became drawn into political manoeuvring of a kind which associated his church ever more closely with the Tory cause. This alignment of interests whereby Presbyterianism became joined not only with the more general cause of Protestantism but with the political philosophy of unionism gave it the particular complexion and direction which have sustained it since. Thus, Cooke was perhaps not inappropriately dubbed 'the Presbyterian Pope' by a writer in the *Londonderry Journal* on 4 October, 1837.[64]

It seems clear that modern perceptions of Ulster Presbyterianism and Protestantism – and significantly, the two terms become increasingly blurred – stem from the mid-nineteenth century. The assurances offered by evangelicalism increasingly fostered Protestant feelings of superiority and cultural difference from Catholics, who were seen as superstitious, ignorant and priest-ridden.[65] Lack of success in winning Catholic converts was construed as further evidence of their inability to respond to truth while their continuing and increasingly articulate demands for reform, especially after emancipation was granted in 1829, seemingly proved their treacherous intentions and the threat they posed to the economic prosperity of the region. Cooke proclaimed the notion that Protestantism itself was in danger from reform in favour of Catholics, dismissing O'Connell's demand for repeal of the Act of Union as 'just a discreet word for Romish ascendancy and protestant extermination', and asking for the 'banns of marriage' to be called between the Presbyterian and Church of Ireland communions.[66] His readiness to spot Catholic conspiracy and a threat to self-interest anticipate similar outcries in the face of Gladstone's Home Rule Bills, Parnellism, the 1912 Home Rule crisis, the Anglo-Irish Agreement and the Downing Street Declaration. Although Finlay Holmes shows that Cooke's views aroused deep unhappiness and criticism from within the Presbyterian church and emphasises that he was essentially speaking for himself despite the Tories' inclination, backed by Castlereagh, to regard him as a representative voice, no one mounted an effective challenge to his self-assumed authority.[67] Similarly, although he never joined the Orange Order, Cooke's name was toasted in Derry in 1833 at a dinner following the Apprentice Boys' march, thereby again demonstrating the equivocal position he had come to occupy.[68]

In the conclusion to his biography of Henry Cooke, Finlay Holmes declares that he

> . . . may be fairly described as one of the founding fathers of Ulster unionism, though it was, of course, Irish unionism he stood for. The archetypal Ulster protestant political parson, he epitomised the Ulster

unionist outlook he helped to form, with his anti-Catholicism, his romantic veneration for Britain and his conviction that Ulster's economic interests were linked to the British connection.[69]

It is notable that the word 'Presbyterian' does not feature in this summary and that Cooke's contribution is seen in essentially political and sectarian terms. This confirms the impression that he played a crucial part in refocusing Presbyterianism in Ulster and in making it narrower and more aggressively self-defensive. It is difficult, too, not to feel that much of Cooke's career has been repeated as a kind of parody in the second half of this century by Revd Ian Paisley, who might be seen even more justifiably as the 'pope' in his own Free Presbyterian Church.

The character of Ulster Protestantism and of Presbyterianism itself was further affected by the so-called 1859 Revival – the period of intense religious fervour that swept many parts of the province and which has been described recently by one church historian as 'the most important folk event between 1798 and 1913'.[70] W.D. Killen, who lived through it, regarded the Revival as 'the most remarkable religious movement which . . . occurred, in the Irish Presbyterian Church in the nineteenth century', and was surely right to observe that its impact was reflected in the subsequent ministry of many young men whose ardour was first kindled in 1859.[71]

Although the clergy hoped that it would restore the dwindling sense of a covenanted and chosen people, strong in the face of growing Catholic self-confidence, paradoxically, from the point of view of Presbyterianism, perhaps the most significant feature of the Revival was its emphasis on personal conversion and inner experience in the emotionally charged atmosphere of many of the great gatherings, rather than on some form of doctrinal purity. Commenting on this, and placing it in the context of the church which not long before had finally freed itself of the non-subscribers to the *Westminster Confession*, Robert G. Crawford writes:

> Grace and faith had triumphed over rationality, and the ground was prepared for an event which showed the emotional aspect of the Ulster Protestant: the 'Great Revival' of 1859. The Non-Subscribing controversies were a reaction against the severity of Calvinism, and this same Calvinism was opposed by the emotion of the Revival.[72]

This emotion was both fuelled by and exhibited in the physical manifestations – prostration, weeping, shaking and trancelike states – which, as Stewart J. Brown puts it:

seemed to restore Christianity as a living, spontaneous faith in the modern world – not a set of doctrines defined as orthodox by the letter of Scripture or the *Westminster Confession*, but a faith that transcended logic and forced itself on the scientific world, a faith to be expressed in fear and trembling.[73]

Yet even allowing for this idea of a reaction against Calvinist austerity, the high emotionalism of the Revival might seem difficult to square with Presbyterian self-restraint. D.W. Miller sees the growth of evangelical enthusiasm in Presbyterianism not only as a response to the quashing of the energetic doctrinal disputations that had previously characterised the church, but also as a necessary reaction to the growing popularity of Methodists, Baptists and other sects which proclaimed a conversionist theology, and whose influence and popularity had been growing in Ulster during the nineteenth century. He also suggests that religious fervour may have compensated Protestants for the growing identification of Irish nationalism with Catholicism in the same period.[74] However, Norman Vance has questioned the idea that a conversionist strand first appeared in the nineteenth century, and sees it as implicit in the longstanding paradoxes observable in Presbyterian history:

> This mingling of outer and inner, the national-prophetic and the individualist-conversionist components of Presbyterianism, encouraged and reflected an ambivalent sense of identity. This became manifest not only in . . . ecclesiastical schism, but in the apparently incompatible ideological stances of Presbyterian Irishmen, resisting and identifying with the political nation, Dissenters and beneficiaries of royal subsidy, rebels and kingsmen, liberals and conservatives, scholars and writers of imaginative historical vision and philistine fundamentalists. Prophetic and national Presbyterianism looked to the Old Testament God of history; conversionist Presbyterianism looked beyond history and public discontents to eternity, and so was often effectively conservative in social and political terms.[75]

And David Hempton and Myrtle Hill also emphasise that the phenomenon of 1859 had its origins as far back as the Six Mile Water Revival of 1625 and that for thirty or so years before the 'Year of Grace' evangelical influences had been operative in Presbyterianism.[76]

What is clear, however, is the emergence of the emotional conversionist emphasis as never before, and while there were those who regarded the events of 1859 as little more than a dangerous mass hysteria with little or no real religious value, the Revival had an enduring practical and symbolic importance. While to many it seemed that the hand of God was visibly at work among a Protestant people whose own standards had become lax and who were faced with danger from an increasingly assertive Catholic Church under Archbishop (later Cardinal) Cullen, and while the Presbyterian Church benefited from a large increase of new communicants and ministerial candidates, the Revival also eroded its sense of communal identity as the importance of personal conversion experience became the crucial event for individuals. Stewart J. Brown describes the longer term consequences of this for Presbyterianism:

> The revival had served to weaken the Presbyterian tradition of an intellectual and liberal clergy, exercising a moral control over their congregations. The attempts of the Presbyterian clergy to reassert their former authority in the aftermath of the revival had not on the whole proved successful. After 1860, if a minister took an unpopular position, members of the congregation were likely to leave his church for another – as was the case in the churches of many Liberal Presbyterian ministers during the Home Rule Crisis.[77]

The beneficiaries of such movements were commonly the more evangelical denominations, or the numerous gospel hall missions that became, and remain, familiar throughout the north-east of Ireland.

In a perhaps unforeseen way, too, the new found value of conversion experience may actually have reinforced anti-Catholicism. As Miller has pointed out, as long as Catholics were regarded simply as a group, not as individuals, under the Pope's power, it was possible for Presbyterians to allow that some might be among the elect. With the emphasis switched to personal conversion, the reluctance of most Catholics to convert was construed as objective evidence that they were predestined to damnation.[78] Conversely, many of those from Calvinist backgrounds who were affected by the Revival found an assurance of grace and positive joy in Christian living which they had not experienced before.[79]

However, of even greater importance to note here is the way in which the Revival tended to consolidate the movement of Presbyterians towards other Protestant denominations and to further erode their distinctiveness as a self-contained community in Ulster. Increasingly, what was seen to be crucial was the maintenance of a Protestant – as opposed to a specifically Presbyterian – culture and loyalty to that end was elevated beyond a personal moral principle.[80] For this reason it has been claimed that

Evangelical religion intersected with all other frameworks within which Ulster people expressed their cultural aspirations, including politics and national identity.[81]

The outcome of this development has been contrasted with that observed in America where a major revival had swept through cities like New York, Philadelphia and Chicago in 1858. Whereas there

> . . . revivalism was important in revitalizing the life of the individual frontiersman or immigrant who was moving forward to establish a new culture in a land that seemed to have no boundaries, in Ireland there was no frontier to be pushed back, but rather one to be defended, and the legacy of conversion was more apt to be important in a communal than in merely a personal sense.[82]

One consequence was a strengthening of the conservative influences in Presbyterianism following 1859 and increasingly thereafter dissenting voices encountered weighty opposition from within the church, although they have always been present as stimulating and challenging irritants. Thus, J.M. Barkley identifies the sharpest decline of liberalism in the Presbyterian Church with the period from 1885 to the Home Rule crisis and ascribes it especially to the growing influence of Orange-Toryism in the face of threats to the Unionist position and the authoritarianism of the Catholic Church which was reaffirmed by the Ne Temere decree of 1907.[83]

The case of Revd J.B. Armour of Ballymoney illustrates at one and the same time how the Presbyterian Church hardened its position and yet contained within it outspoken individuals who were not afraid to question its political drift to Toryism. However, Armour's support of Gladstonian politics, his backing of Home Rule for Ireland and his later resistance to the partitioning of the country, demonstrate not only his Presbyterian independence and non-conformity, but also his lack of real influence or ability to sway the majority in the General Assembly. He may never have been as influential a liberal as the laudatory biography by his son published soon after his death proposes, but some of his views articulate robust Presbyterian principles.[84] Thus in 1893, Armour argued that 'The principle of Home Rule is a Presbyterian principle', linking it with Presbyterianism's well-established commitment to justice and liberty of conscience.[85] He accused its opponents of forgetting the common history of persecution at the hands of the Established Church which their forebears shared with the Catholics and of allowing themselves to be exploited for political ends by the landowning and privileged classes in Ulster and by ascendancy interests in Dublin, headed by Edward Carson.

When partition came, Armour described it as 'divisive, anti-Unionist, tending to accentuate racial and religious hatreds, and ruinous to the commercial and moral prosperity of Ireland'. Likewise, he was appalled by the abandonment of Protestants and Unionists in other parts of the country and was quick to point out the irony in the readiness of the former opponents of Home Rule for Ireland to embrace Home Rule for Ulster.[86]

J.B. Armour is not the only radical Presbyterian to have seen weakness and betrayal in the Protestant enthusiasm for partition. While J.M. Barkley shows that the General Assembly of the Presbyterian Church made a statement in 1925 which at least encouraged a conciliatory attitude in border areas, he also movingly records how he himself encountered the sense of abandonment felt by Protestants excluded from the Northern State:

> I sometimes visited a Manse in Co. Donegal where on the mantlepiece in the study was a framed copy of the Ulster Covenant. It had been torn in two and written across it were the words 'The broken covenant'. At first sight the writing looked like a dark stain. It had been written in the minister's own blood. He had been a unionist and had been appointed with another to represent the unionists of Donegal at a meeting with Carson at the City Hall in Belfast. Instead of being treated sympathetically, he and his companion were called upon to resign. They refused and were evicted. No longer was it 'Ulster Will Fight and Ulster Will Be Right'. Donegal, Monaghan and Cavan were to be sacrificed. The night he returned home saw the torn and blood-stained covenant placed on the study mantlepiece where it remained until the day he died.[87]

And in more general terms, the records show how by the end of March 1922, Presbyterian numbers, like those of the Church of Ireland, throughout the twenty-six counties had been dramatically reduced. Elsewhere, Terence P. McCaughey has concluded that 'Irish Protestantism quite simply lost its nerve' over the Home Rule crisis. The consequences of this extend beyond the desertion of Protestants in the south, for, he argues:

> Reluctantly, perhaps, one must see this as a betrayal of the Protestant mission and destiny. They were not content to be a mosquito movement, existing not for itself, but for the whole people of God.[88]

In the period since partition, relationships between Presbyterians and Catholics, and even with other Protestant denominations, have fluctuated in their fortunes. The Presbyterian Church historian, Finlay Holmes, has argued that the influence of the evangelical revivalist preacher, Revd W.P. Nicholson, in Ulster in the 1920s affected many individuals who became leading churchmen in the next generation and renewed the puritan and fundamentalist tendencies in Presbyterianism, commonly leading to sectarian attitudes and a

> . . . suspicion of literature, theological scholarship and the arts, thus helping to widen the gulf which was growing between the Ulster Presbyterian world and the worlds both of the modern intelligentsia and of Irish Roman Catholicism.[89]

Ernest Davey's trial for heresy in 1926 is perhaps the most notorious illustration of this trend, while one of those inspired by the example of Nicholson is Ian Paisley who, although never a member of the Presbyterian Church, has repeatedly challenged and confronted it over many years and, in the view of more than one scholar, has almost certainly created difficulties for some of its attempts to improve interdenominational relationships and understanding.[90]

Writing the conclusion to Reid's history of the Irish Presbyterian Church in 1853, W.D. Killen made the following confident assertions:

> Little more than two centuries ago, [Ulster] was the most barbarous and desolate [province] in the land, now it is the most enlightened and prosperous. And if, in the mysterious providence of God, the time should ever come again when Irish Presbyterians must suffer per-secution for their principles, it will, no doubt, be seen that not a few will again submit, for Christ's sake, to the spoiling of their goods, and to the repetition of the tragedies of the martyrs of the covenant.[91]

The followers of Ian Paisley claim that the Presbyterian Church failed to act as Killen predicted in the face of Catholic appeasement and expansionism and that this necessitated the establishment of their own self-styled Free Presbyterian Church. The latter aims to be the guardian of uncompromised adherence to the *Westminster Confession* and the teachings of Knox and Calvin as expounded by its founder and unchallenged leader, Ian Paisley himself. But Paisleyism cannot be seen to uphold the principles of liberty, freedom of conscience and justice that are essential both to Calvinism and Presbyterianism in their radical forms. It has shown itself to be shamelessly and crudely anti-Catholic – Paisley does not even accept that the Catholic Church is Christian – and cynically manipulative of Protestant ignorance and fear. It has been politically opportunist in its relationships with various organisations and parties over the years and hypnotically self-absorbed with the cult of the leader himself. As Tom Paulin has memorably written, Paisley

> ... more than any other Unionist politician appears to belong to a dreamtime of Presbyterian aborigines – great preachers who strode the Antrim Coast long before the birth of Christ.[92]

Like a figure from the past, too, he has skilfully sustained particular perspectives of the fortunes of Protestants in Ulster in the past, constructing his preferred version of history around dates used to reiterate the unending nature of Catholic rebelliousness and treachery and of Protestant fortitude when faced by them (1641, 1690, 1798, 1914). He implicitly links himself with figures from a carefully chosen pantheon of heroes – with Luther, when he burned Revd Professor Ernest Davey's books; with St Paul, when he wrote his commentary on Romans from a prison cell; with Sir Edward Carson and his UVF paramilitaries, by his promotion of a 'third force' and of the 'Carson Trail'; with William Johnston of Ballykilbeg in refusing to accept any restriction on where he could parade as an Orangeman; with fiery rhetoricians of the past like Henry Cooke and 'Roaring' Hugh Hanna in his thunderous proclamations and denunciations.[93] To his followers, Paisley has sometimes seemed to have a prophetic status, or to have been 'a man raised up by God in Ulster's hour of need', the only person who can really see what is happening to both Protestantism and Unionism in Ulster.[94]

Unlike democratic Presbyterianism which encourages debate, promotes education and is grounded in an organisational structure which placed real power in the laity, Paisleyism's characteristic tone is vituperative, intimidating and unconcerned with any exchange of ideas. It is anti-intellectual, drawing more on emotionalism than on rationalism and is resolutely opposed to modern biblical scholarship and theological debate. It is also oppressively authoritarian and so dominated by the personal influence and power of Paisley himself that its future after his eventual departure must remain open to question.[95]

Finally, Paisleyism, unlike Presbyterianism, is rooted wholly in various kinds of negative feeling and fear. At a personal level, there is the individual's fear of damnation if he or she is not 'saved', and Paisley's roots in gospel hall missions gave him an early training in that kind of ministry. More generally, there is the fear that Protestantism in Ulster is under permanent threat from the insidious designs of the neighbouring Catholic Irish Republic and from its sympathisers within the Northern Irish state. The loss of freedom of worship and of civil liberties and the imposition of Catholic standards are viewed as real possibilities if Protestants do not actively defend themselves. Negotiation, accommodation and compromise are taboo subjects – synonyms for defeat. Furthermore, since Paisley has consistently accused the Presbyterian and Church of Ireland communions of compromising Protestant standards, this leaves his Free Presbyterians to stake their claim as the sole defenders of the Reformation. Even the union with Britain itself has ceased to be a reliable protection and Paisley's repeated and sometimes extraordinarily abusive confrontations with various British Prime Ministers and Secretaries of State for Northern Ireland show clearly the sense of betrayal and distrust felt by him and his followers. It is as if they cling to the old seventeenth-century notion of covenantal politics and cannot see its irrelevance in the modern world.[96] Even if one looks beyond the sphere of Anglo-Irish relationships, Paisley has promulgated the theory that the European Union is another creeping Catholic conspiracy extending its influence ever wider and his own presence in the European Parliament is to offer a prophetic witness against this peril.

Perhaps more important than the activities of Paisley and his overt followers has been their influence in a more diffused way upon Protestant opinion in Ulster, upon 'The Coasters' – to use the title of a poem by John Hewitt on the subject – who have found enough apparent truth in what they say to give tacit assent to it, even if they keep themselves aloof from its populist rhetoric and street politics.[97] Insofar as Presbyterians and Presbyterianism have been distracted in this way, Paisleyism has had a negative effect on that church. But insofar as it has confronted Paisleyism and denounced its perversities and obscurantism, Presbyterianism has perhaps been able to redefine its own distinctive and positive values and its links with a more radical past.

That this process of reaffirmation has taken place, at least in part, may be illustrated by reference to the public position taken by the Presbyterian Church on various occasions in recent years. Thus, for example, the Church and Government Committee of the Presbyterian Church made a submission to the Opsahl Commission which urged the indispensability of measures to develop confidence within Northern Ireland, between North and South, and between the Irish Republic and Britain if any political resolution is to be reached. The Committee upheld the constitutional position of Northern Ireland within the United Kingdom so long as a majority supports this relationship, but also argued the imperative need to move away from the 'zero-sum' attitudes that have often dominated attempts to mediate between the communities in the province. It is notable that the views of this important Church committee, which included the then Moderator, Revd Dr John Dunlop, adopted a much more positive and open attitude than that found in the individual submission of a former Moderator, Revd Dr Robert Dickinson, who appeared to reject all possibility of constitutional change, or the idea that Northern Irish Protestants as a whole would wish to be seen as Irish in any sense. Dickinson's submission is a clear reminder of the survival of deeply conservative beliefs within modern Presbyterianism but the Church and Government Committee's position demonstrates a greater openness to other considerations.[98]

The same Committee has also produced a report, *Presbyterian Principles and Political Witness in Northern Ireland*, which reviews the biblical and theological principles guiding the relations between church and state, anchoring each of its key arguments to references from scripture, the *Westminster Confession* and Calvin's teaching. Here one finds modern restatements of essential Calvinist thought, including the idea that the Christian citizen has an obligation towards both government and state, yet making it clear that this is not to be confused with unquestioning allegiance and obedience. Furthermore, the Church's responsibility to give a 'prophetic witness' and to protest against injustices and inequities perpetrated or institutionalised by the the state is clearly laid down. In the last analysis, the Christian's overriding obligation is to God rather than to any individual or organisation and there is even the declaration that

> . . . God himself may summon his servants to set the oppressed free –
> hence Calvinists, historically and today, have often been in the fore-
> front of certain revolutionary movements.[99]

Understandably, this claim is surrounded by cautionary words, particularly regarding the advocacy and use of violence. Equally significantly, however, the report elesewhere summons Presbyterians

> ... to create a distinctively Christian counter-culture in which we distance ourselves from the kind of Protestantism which closely identifies the reformed faith with particular political and cultural aspirations;[100]

and there are unambiguous warnings against

> ... allowing politics, political dogmas and convictions and political loyalties to become a 'religion', in any way supplanting the paramount authority of Christ or equating the realm of politics with the Kingdom of Christ which, though impinging on this world, is not of this world;

and against 'anti-Catholic invective' and 'sectarian murders', which are 'The ugliest perversion of "religion" in the cause of a political goal'.[101]

Such uncompromising statements are characteristic of Presbyterianism at its radical best, as is the declaration of commitment to freedom of religion and respect for those who hold a different viewpoint. (The same spirit is evident in the recent publication, 'A Presbyterian Response to the "Agreement"' and its accompanying nine-point plan, 'Assessing Political Accommodation', issued to help church members to make an informed Christian judgement of the arrangements approved by politicians for the future government of Northern Ireland on Good Friday, 1998.) A genuine sense of humility is also visible in the acknowledgement of past toleration of unjust practices in the province and in the admission that the Protestant majority has learnt what it feels like to be discriminated against as a result of the Anglo-Irish Agreement. There is a ready acceptance of the desirability of greater co-operation not only between the communities in Northern Ireland, but between the two parts of the country, as was seen in the submission to the Opsahl Commission and which is eloquently reaffirmed in the 1994 'Peace Vocation'.[102] All this suggests that the contemporary Presbyterian Church in Ireland has not entirely lost touch with the radical principles from which it originates. Despite the powerful influences that led it away from those roots from the mid-nineteenth century onwards and into a narrower and politically committed form of Protestantism, Presbyterianism has always kept its radical individual voices. Despite, too, the enormous pressures of the past twenty-five years which have both nurtured sectarian prejudices and been fuelled by them and which have made it even more difficult for Presbyterianism to uphold and practice its most constructive principles, the evidence suggests that these have neither been forgotten nor lost. Furthermore, if it is able to reassert its democratic values, its generous view of the individual's liberty of conscience, and its belief in fairness, justice and respect for all, Presbyterianism retains the potential to become a powerful enabling force during a period of transition in Irish affairs. As John Dunlop has written with painstaking honesty:

> We need to evolve an ideological construct or mental attitude which is rooted in reformed convictions about individual liberty and is capable of accommodating diversity. It may be like the Presbyterian thinking which helped to shape notions of liberty and diversity in the early years of American independence . . . This will require a change of mind and a fundamental revision of the prevailing ideological construct of siege, isolation and defensive thinking. Instead of desiring to live in homogeneous cultural and religious communities, we need to welcome inclusive societies which embrace diversity and, in turn, lead to enrichment as we seek peace, justice, security and honour for everyone.[103]

It is significant, too, that these words find their complement in a challenging book by a Church of Ireland clergyman, Timothy Kinahan, who calls for a similarly radical reappraisal of thinking and attitudes among Christians generally and Protestants specifically in Northern Ireland. He demonstrates that Old Testament scripture does not support those who wish to live in an uncritical or unthinking relationship with any form of political system, and argues that

> Northern Irish Christianity, particularly in its Protestant and Anglican forms, has fallen woefully short of, if it has not totally ignored, the challenge of the gospel. It has avoided the prophetic call to justice, and Christ's amplification of that message, to concentrate instead on pietistic individualism, with a socio-political bolt-hole in Romans 13.[104]

Kinahan ascribes this failure to the domination of religion by Unionist politics ('The gospel has become the slave of our political aspirations') and sees it as leading to a betrayal of New Testament Christianity with its emphasis on peace, equity and social relationships – what he calls 'orthopraxy', or right action – not simply on personal 'orthodoxy', often confused with 'good living', or a self-interested notion of salvation.

To achieve the goals called for by Dunlop and Kinahan, Ulster Protestants as a group must dissociate themselves from the negative attitudes which they often seem to espouse – deep distrust, or worse, of Catholics; fear of betrayal by all external parties, and even by some within their own membership; self-righteousness, linked with the idea that other groups are morally, socially, theologically or politically inferior and distrustfulness towards unorthodox, imaginative new responses and ideas. Many of these attitudes are heightened forms of the authoritarian defensiveness which is one tendency within Calvinism. Furthermore, in the Northern Irish context, they have often been more apparent than the liberating, democratic tendency which encourages debate and aspires to a world-view rather than sectarian tunnel-vision. This is why writers and poets coming from such a background have commonly found it necessary to take issue with the Protestant influences which they encountered in their upbringing and have made art out of their arguments with and their reactions against them.

CHAPTER THREE

'This We Will Maintain':
A Commemorative Culture

*Commemoration is a means whereby communities renew
their own religio: literally, what ties them together, the
rope around the individual sticks. But commemoration,
communal religio, does not merely remember. It reinvents
and reconstitutes according to present needs.*

Edna Longley, 'The Rising, The Somme
and Irish Memory' in *The Living Stream*.

*... the northern protestant's historical imagination ... is
one that has in modern times (at least since 1886) had
recourse to a vision of the protestant community's history
which is starkly simple in outline and depressingly lacking
in emotional range and complexity. ... A people who have
known resistance as well as dissent, rebellion, dispute,
religious enthusiasm in the midst of rural and urban
deprivation, have an interesting story to tell themselves –
one of essential homelessness, dependency, anxiety, obdurate
fantasising, sacrifices in the name of liberty, villainous
political opportunism, moments of idealistic aspiration.*

Terence Brown, *The Whole Protestant Community:
The making of a historical myth.*

THE PROVINCE OF ULSTER, and more particularly the state of
Northern Ireland, have long been regarded as fundamentally
different from the rest of the country. The act by which Ireland was
partitioned in 1920 may have institutionalised the separation of six
of the nine counties of Ulster from the island as a whole, but the
sense of Northern Ireland being, as Dervla Murphy's title has it, *A
Place Apart*, extends back much further.[1] The reasons for this
perception are various. Historically, Ulster was particularly resistant
to colonisation and held out until late Elizabethan times against
attempts to subjugate it. Thereafter, it was more densely planted with

settlers of Scottish background than other parts of Ireland and the continuing relationship between Scotland and the north-east of Ulster was enormously influential, as was shown in the previous chapter, not least in determining the unique concentration of Protestants and the particular strength of Presbyterianism in the region. Later again, the industrial development of Belfast differentiated the experience of Ulster people from those in the rest of Ireland and contributed to the idea of the 'Black North'. Politically, Ulster has often seemed out of step with most of the rest of Ireland at crucial points. Although amongst the most radical regions of the country in the 1790s, it was suspicious of Catholic emancipation in the 1830s and by the 1890s deeply opposed to Home Rule. It was ready to fight against the British government should it impose a Home Rule Act in the early twentieth century, yet appalled by the 'treachery' of the 1916 rebels who took arms against the same government. In cultural terms, too, the North has commonly been viewed as different and its people dominated by Protestant values and attitudes. These are stereotyped as anti-literary, materialistic, austere and philistine, wary of the subversive potential not only of art but even of simple enjoyment and pleasure for its own sake and distrustful of 'Catholic' loquacity, easy sociability and casualness about time-keeping. Such perceptions are not limited to those who come from outside the north of Ireland. They are readily and happily accepted by many who live there and who relish their own sense of difference from Catholics whom they find it hard to think of as their near neighbours and fellow countrymen and women.[2]

Crucial to this sense of difference, whether viewed from without or felt from within, has been the religious history of the local Protestant population. The influence upon it of Calvinistic Presbyterianism and of evangelicalism have remained powerful determinants in Northern Irish society. These have commonly been linked with the supposed cultural barrenness of the region, at least in comparison with the flowering of southern literary achievement in the past century. The extreme view is that the very notion of Northern Irish Protestant culture is unworthy of consideration as it amounts to little more than the parades and associated rituals of the Orange Order, sectarian songs, and religiously or politically motivated wall paintings.[3]

Similarly, these influences are adjudged to have shaped negatively the northern Protestant understanding of Irish history as a prolonged struggle against Catholicism, in which a chosen people have been providentially upheld by the grace of God, but must expect that contest to continue, albeit the enemy now appears under different guises such as nationalism, republicanism, socialism, or even Europeanism. It is a perspective which uses selected events in Irish history – like the siege of Derry, the Battle of the Boyne, the signing of the Ulster Covenant and even the sinking of the *Titanic* – almost as extensions of scripture.[4] Thus, as the Jews extrapolate a sign of God's favour from the account of the crossing of the Red Sea, so Ulster Protestants make a comparable use of the successful resistance offered to the forces of James II in 1689–1690. Protestants are therefore seen to be locked into a nostalgic way of regarding history – one which encourages them to strive to keep faith with the past. This contrasts significantly with the use of history made by nationalists who recall earlier defeats and failures to rekindle and reinforce their determination to bring about change now or in the future. While nationalists declare that their day will come, Protestants often seem exercised with finding means of ensuring that they do not surrender the past to the present or the future. And as Terence Brown has written:

> . . . the politics of the lesser evil, in which dependency on Britain must unhesitatingly be preferred to the proven dangers of attempting fraternity with Irish nationalists is an uninspiring creed, hard to celebrate with any dignity. And as such it is conducive to that political lack of generosity which so marks Northern Unionism.[5]

This predisposition of many Ulster Protestants to regard themselves as the guardians of the past, to the memory of which they must remain faithful and unquestioning, may be attributed to their historical experience as the descendents of planters and immigrants. After all, history, as Steve Bruce writes:

> . . . is not just an account of what has gone before. It is also the vital material for contemporary self-images. Popular history often tells us more about those promoting it than it does about the past. People identify the virtues of their ancestors as a way of asserting that they now possess those virtues. They delineate the vices of the fore-runners of their enemies to assert that their descendents too have all those vices and then some. They describe in detail how their ancestors were nearly destroyed by their enemies but were able to triumph and in so doing assure themselves that they too will triumph. Past successes justify a sense of superiority or comfort those to whom recent times have not been so kind. Past failures fuel resentment.[6]

Unwanted and unwelcome from the outset, many northern Protestants subscribe to a version of history which records their ancestors' triumphs over adversity, prejudice, resistance and legal obstructions. Their economic successes, first on the land and later in industries such as shipbuilding, linen and rope-making, are seen to have been achieved in spite of opposition rather than because of any favours shown to them. Bonded and strengthened by a sense of loyalty to church and crown, they have withstood and outlasted the fickle, short-term aims of politicians and rival clerics who have sought, as they see it, to erode or overthrow their position. Lacking a history that extends back to early, or even mythological times, they have tended to rely upon events from the last three and a half centuries which have been invested with canonical status – a process that was clearly seen at work in Reid's history of the Presbyterian Church. What requires closer examination is how and when particular events emerged as focal points in Ulster Protestant history, the needs those events have served at specific moments, and why Ulster Protestants have shown such commitment to a commemorative view of history. These factors all bear upon the broader cultural characteristics of the Protestant community in Northern Ireland.

In his article '"We're Trying to Find Our Identity": Uses of History Among Ulster Protestants', Anthony Buckley cautions against the notion that there is any single version of history upheld by the Protestant community. He goes on to point out that in some contexts history may be used 'as a political rhetoric' to 'uphold the claims of one's own "side" to power, prestige and influence in the present while stigmatizing one's opponents', or to provide 'a set of archetypal situations' as 'rules or guidelines for acting in the present', or again commemoratively, through 'processions and rituals [which] can provide a focus for ethnic allegiance'.[7] In each case, history is applied for a purpose, whether positively by valorising the legitimacy and rights of Protestants or by facilitating commemorations or re-enactments of past events which serve to remind people today of their inheritance from and obligation to their forebears who resisted persecution and upheld specific 'rights', or negatively by channelling hostility and contempt towards the 'other side'. In the latter case, this is usually the Catholic community, although sometimes the animosity may be directed against members of their own community whose activities are regarded as compromising or endangering the integrity of the past.[8] Furthermore, such uses of history have not evolved fortuitously, but in response to the changing needs of particular times. This is a phenomenon which Gearóid Ó Crualaoich has observed elsewhere in Irish affairs. In his discussion of the interaction of cultural process and mythology with the history of the 1916 rising in Dublin, he writes:

> Rather than being fixed, tradition is always a *process* of selective remembering (and not remembering) that is subject to and responsive to both the creative dynamic of the individual memory and the shaping of memorization at individual and communal levels by current circumstances and interests.[9]

In the light of this view, it is notable that historians have shown how some of the most commonly commemorated Protestant anniversaries have not always been ascribed the same significance that they carry today. Brian Walker, for example, questions whether the Protestant belief in the continuity of history with recurrent episodes of betrayal, siege and threat has always been deeply influential in shaping consciousness. He points out that while the centenary of the siege of Derry was marked in the city, the ceremonies included Catholics as well as Protestants, and in July 1790 the *Belfast Newsletter* carried no reports of the Boyne anniversary.[10] As the previous chapter showed, it was during the second half of the nineteenth century in the face of growing Catholic self-confidence and the nationalist demand for Home Rule that Ulster Protestant politicians and churchmen began to rekindle the memory of Catholic treachery in 1641 and the heroics of the defenders of Protestantism in 1689 and 1690. This emphasis also distracted attention from the long history of antagonism between the Presbyterians and the Church of Ireland which was to the strategic advantage of those who, like Henry Cooke, saw it as their priority to form a Protestant alliance against the advance of Catholicism and nationalism.

In a similar vein, Dominic Bryan has shown that the celebrations in the period immediately after William's victory in Ireland did not carry the associations of twentieth-century processions dominated by the presence and influence of the Orange Order; while in the 1770s and 1780s the anniversaries of the Boyne and of William's birthday were also used by the Volunteers to mark the success of the American Revolution and to call for parliamentary reform at home.[11] However, the cultural historian, Belinda Loftus, looking at the uses to which the figure of William III has been put in more recent times by Ulster loyalists, observes that the Revd Martin Smyth (Presbyterian minister, Grand Master of the Orange Order and politician) and Revd Ian Paisley have identified the king on his white horse with Christ at the Second Coming as represented in the book of Revelation.[12] This

projection of William significantly redefines his emblematic value.
Loftus continues:

> Threatened with absorption by republicanism and 'Romanism'
> [loyalists] have turned to the clear distinction and setting apart implied
> in the white horse; under military attack and limited in retaliation to
> strikes and sectarian assaults, they can turn to the figure of a glorious
> and unrestrained conqueror; abandoned by their leadership, they have
> been able, as in the past, to reinvent a a relationship with it in the
> figure of William on his lordly steed; their legitimacy questioned in
> every area of their operations, they can turn to the very personification
> of the Constitution they uphold, seated on a mount which is always
> correctly painted white; and uncertain about their origins, their present
> role and their future, they can turn to a hero figure who established
> them in their land, and foreshadows the rider on the white horse who
> will lead them into the kingdom which is to come.[13]

All this suggests not only how the issue of what properly constitutes
tradition is problematic, but also indicates the degree to which
history is redeployed and remade to match the political interests and
perceived exigencies of specific periods.[14]

Yet however potent the image of William III crossing the Boyne
may be as a sign of Protestant victory, the memory of the siege of Derry
is perhaps an even more compelling symbol, especially in recent times.
Whereas William's victory may be viewed unequivocally, the siege
stirs altogether more complex feelings and recalls dangers both from
within and without an encircled and beleaguered community.[15] This
clearly corresponds with contemporary experience as it is perceived
by many Protestants. Thus, the siege of 1689 *becomes* the Anglo-Irish
Agreement of 1985 or perhaps even the *Frameworks for the Future*
document of 1995. Given the Calvinist view of history as a linear
process leading to the ultimate outworking of God's plan in time, it
is ironic that the Protestant experience in Ulster should be characterised by such repetition and circularity. Presbyterian history as
offered by J.S. Reid and W.D. Killen exuded mid-nineteenth-century
confidence that would appear to have been disappointed by subsequent events which have returned the Protestant community to a
position of insecurity and greatly reduced self-assurance.

Ulster Protestant confidence in the progressive nature of history
has also been undermined in a particular way by the decline of
Britain's role as an imperial power and the disintegration of the
empire. Whereas the position of Northern Ireland, and indeed its very

existence, now appear to some as one of the final vestiges of Britain's former empire, this is at odds with the perceptions of many of its citizens who find it difficult to regard themselves as unfashionable colonial subjects. It is especially awkward since, historically, the Northern Irish community – and particularly its Protestant members – contributed in many ways to the maintenance of British colonial power in its heyday, not only through its industrial output, but by providing numerous recruits to the Civil Service and the army. D.W. Miller has noted how even before Partition Unionists sometimes referred to Ulster as the 'Imperial Province' of Ireland, implying its special position and relationship, not as a subject colony, but as the representative or ambassador for the values of civilisation and development attributed to Britain itself.[16]

This also helps to explain why the involvement of the Ulster Division in the First World War, and the horrendous losses it suffered, form another complex node of memory for Ulster Protestants. Those who joined up did so out of loyalty to defend the empire with which they proudly identified themselves. But there was a further, specifically Irish, political reason which motivated at least some of the men who enlisted, both Protestant and Catholic, and which was certainly prominent in the calculations of those two leaders with rival agendas, John Redmond and Sir Edward Carson. They were relying on the belief that, as George Boyce puts it:

> . . . the sacrifice of life would make it hard for Britain on the one hand to renege on the implementation of the third Home Rule Act or on the other, to force it upon a reluctant Unionist Ulster.[17]

Particularly, although not uniquely, from the point of view of Ulster Protestants the Easter Rising in 1916 was an outrageous act of treachery, yet again affirming Catholic disloyalty and opportunism and reviving the abiding fears and memories of danger within the community, and the need to band together against it. Additionally, the coincidence that the 36th 'Ulster' Division's own great sacrifice at the Somme later that same year began on the anniversary of the Battle of the Boyne (allowing for the difference in the old and new style calendars) inevitably encouraged the linking together of the two events. As the Boyne had been a crucial demonstration of loyalty and faith underwritten by personal sacrifice, so too the Somme could be seen as a latter day reaffirmation of the same principles and determination to uphold them whatever the cost. Furthermore, the unusual composition of the Division negotiated by Carson with the War Office, whereby many men who had formerly been together in the UVF were now bound by a special political oath, made it a potent symbol of the character of Ulster Protestantism. As the historian of the Division, Philip Orr, has observed:

> Their aggressiveness and the fearful reputation they were to acquire as bayonet-fighters were the outcome of the pent-up belligerence of those tense months of drilling, marching and gathering in large public groups. Their efficiency and esprit de corps were marks of the ethnic solidarity and separateness which they felt was being ignored by the British government's Home Rule legislation. Most of the men had signed the Ulster Covenant. They were a covenanting army, oath-bound and committed as much to the collective survival of Protestant Ulster as to the survival of the Britain they fought for and were part of.[18]

Inevitably, too, when they engaged in battle, the dead and wounded were not strangers, but relatives, friends, neighbours and others with whom they felt strong bonds of association. The poet, Thomas Carnduff, indicates the complex loyalties felt by the Ulster soldiers in some lines from 'Messines, 17th June, 1917 – a memory':

> We thought of home – the hills of Down
> Seemed far away, and yet we saw
> With dreamy eyes Slieve Donard's crown
> Erect above the clouds of war.
> Beyond Messines our vision swept
> O'er white-foamed sea and golden strand,
> And silently each spirit kept
> A tryst beneath the crimson hand.[19]

Viewed in this way, the suggestion that the First World War gave to Ulster Unionism the blood sacrifice it needed 'to create a sense of community amongst the disparate and in many ways divided Ulster Protestants' seems justified.[20] This is a point which has received memorable dramatic endorsement in the closing stages of Frank McGuinness's play, *Observe the Sons of Ulster Marching Towards the Somme*, as the group of soldiers representing every part of the province wind themselves up to the moment of attack in which all but one will perish. Here it is given to Pyper, whose cynicism, atheism and homosexuality have previously made him the least bonded to the other recruits, to articulate the words which draw them together in their hour of crisis, to infuse them with both religious and military fervour and to graft their knowledge of their community's past history onto their perception of the immediate situation:

> God in heaven, if you hear the words of man, I speak to you this day. I do it not to ask we be spared. I do it to ask for strength. Strength for these men around me, strength for myself. If you are a just and merciful God, show your mercy this day. Save us. Save our country. Destroy our enemies at home and on this field of battle. Let this day at the Somme be as glorious in the memory of Ulster as that day at the Boyne, when you scattered our enemies. Lead us back from this exile. To Derry, to the Foyle. To Belfast and the Lagan. To Armagh. To Tyrone. To the Bann and its banks. To Erne and its islands. Protect them. Protect us. Protect me. Let us fight bravely. Let us win gloriously. Lord, look down on us. Spare us.[21]

The biblical resonances of this combined invocation and exhortation capture precisely the sense of the greater cause behind the particular battle, marking it as yet another time of testing for God's chosen people and extending the association back far beyond 1690 to Old Testament times and the plight of the Children of Israel.

But McGuinness's play does not stop here. Written seventy years after the Somme, it shows through the figure of Pyper, who alone survived the débâcle, the feeling of loss, confusion and abandonment which characterise contemporary Protestant Unionism despite the sacrificial bloodshed of its earlier heroes. To use part of the title of Sarah Nelson's study of Ulster Protestants, Pyper's descendants in real life have become 'Uncertain Defenders', no longer able to sustain and embolden themselves with the belief that Britain regards them as valued allies. Qualities which were previously praised and described in positive terms – courage, loyalty, determination, piety and principles – are no longer esteemed, but are dismissed in exasperation as stubbornness, irresponsibility, unreasonableness, bigotry and prejudice.[22]

The self-confidence of Protestants in themselves and in their position has received repeated blows since 1969 and amongst other things has given rise to a sense of their own inarticulacy and lack of political skills compared with those of Catholics in the same period, which is not without justification. Arthur Aughey has noted that the repeated failure of Unionist politicians to present their policies adequately has made it 'quite easy for opponents to fix upon unionism the label of an ideology of sectarian supremacism or to dismiss it as nothing but the flotsam and jetsam of Britain's imperial past'.[23] To many, it seems as if the Protestant virtue of straight-talking has commanded less respect and been less influential than what is perceived as Catholic casuistry and weasel-words. This problem is vividly illustrated in the Opsahl Commission's report on Northern Ireland which quotes from the evidence given by several senior Protestant clergymen. All reiterate the tension that is felt between 'Catholic indirectness versus Protestant directness' and which gives rise to 'the Protestant propensity always to think in terms of the hidden agenda'.[24] Moreover, it now seems to those who, like John Wilson Foster, seek to argue a reasoned defence of the Union, that the British and Irish governments are actively involved in disingenuous, or even devious, formulations in their published statements. Foster writes:

> The Irish Ambassador described the [Downing Street] Declaration as a 'very, very carefully balanced document.' But what he alleges to see as balance others might see as a moderately skilful, ultimately transparent attempt to cast prejudgement in terms of open-endedness. *It is not balance that is achieved, so much as a surface ambivalence about the Union overlying a discontinuance of belief in the Union.* The statements of equity are couched in the dialect of inequity. The protestations on behalf of majority consent are subverted by the barely concealed wish to change – and commitment to change – what it is to which the majority consents. *The Joint Decalaration is a stylistic disaster because much of it is deeply insincere, and in language truth will out.*[25]

This spells out the loss of confidence resulting from the apparently cavalier way in which the historically grounded Protestant preoccupation with the conjunction between words and their meanings that is understood as a guarantee of goodwill and integrity has been brushed aside.

Foster argues the urgent need to espouse a new broad-based and generously spirited Unionism which will be capable of 'accommodat[ing] nationalism, whereas Irish republicanism, by definition, cancels unionism'.[26] However it is also essential to take account of the degree to which the restricted code of Ulster Unionism has long reflected poverty of thought, lack of imaginative resourcefulness and a forlorn dependence on continuity with the past. Gearóid Ó Crualaoich has written that acts of historical commemoration perpetrate and perpetuate

> . . . knowledge, attitudes, values and feelings on the part of adherents to the tradition that are formed from an amalgam of memory,

imagination and desire which has only a tenuous relationship to history in the strict sense.[27]

While it would be wholly inaccurate to suggest that the construction and manipulation of history and tradition are peculiar to the Irish or to Protestants, it is necessary to see how such processes have actually occurred among the Ulster Protestant community before looking further at the characteristics of the particular versions of history they have preferred, at the reasons which motivate those formations and at their impact upon the thought and imaginative responses of Protestants.

The defensive situation in which the Presbyterians especially have always felt themselves to be placed, but which has coloured the perceptions of many Ulster Protestants of all denominations since the second half of the nineteenth century, underlies the versions of history and the particular stories which they have promoted. Constant reaffirmation of Protestant feats of survival, triumph, loyalty and defiance are visibly present in the incidents depicted on the banners of the Orange lodges, in battle honours and memorials to the dead of two world wars and at street level in the painted kerbstones, murals, arches, bonfire ceremonies, sham battles, marching bands and songs.[28] As Terence McCaughey has put it:

> Significant history is the events, tragic and triumphant, which happened on Irish soil. . . . It is an extended saga of conquest and endurance.[29]

But, paradoxically, this 'significant history' has not made its tellers more secure in their identity. McCaughey has compared the northern Protestants to the Afrikaners in that both groups have no other home to turn to, yet in a profound way they are ill at ease where they are. This leads to the dilemma repeatedly articulated in recent years, especially since the point at which the prospect of fundamental changes to the structure and government of Northern Ireland became more likely: some Protestants, who are quite unable to contemplate describing themselves as Irish, and who regard the Republic as a foreign country, also feel increasingly unsure about claiming a British identity since in a very practical sense they consider that the British government and many of their fellow citizens in the rest of the United Kingdom are treating them as foreigners.[30] As Arthur Aughey has observed, *'the greatest of all Unionist fears must remain the ultimate humiliation of their own loyalty to the Union being used as a means to undo their position'*.[31]

The very way in which the six counties were partitioned from the rest of Ireland, the Stormont parliament was established and the Unionists ruled without hindrance from successive Westminster governments for half a century, inevitably strengthened the belief of Protestants in their right to hold power indefinitely and made the subsequent criticism and rejection of their conduct by English politicians seem all the more hurtful and unwarranted. The most extreme view is that the British government has acted with treachery and has broken its part in the contractual bond of loyalty to maintain the position of the Protestant church and monarchy which has been faithfully upheld in Northern Ireland. The pain and betrayal engendered by such perceptions are quite clear in various contexts, and nowhere more movingly, perhaps, than in Harold McCusker's contribution to the debate in the House of Commons on 27 November 1985 following the signing of the Anglo-Irish Agreement ten days earlier:

> I felt desolate because as I stood in the cold outside Hillsborough Castle everything that I held dear turned to ashes in my mouth. Even in my most pessimistic moments, reading in precise detail in the Irish press on the Wednesday before, I never believed that the agreement would deliver me, in the context that it has, into the hands of those who for 15 years have murdered personal friends, political associates and hundreds of my constituents. I hope that no one else in the House ever has to stand outside the gates of anywhere and see his most cherished privileges and ideals turn to dust and ashes in his mouth. This is what it felt like to be me.[32]

The sense of bewilderment, loss and deep injury here, and throughout the speech, with its resonances of biblical language and the familiar image of siege, are unmistakable and complete. What is more, the words and sentiments echo closely the same sense of injury and deception voiced by McCusker's political forebear, Lord Carson, when in his attack on the Anglo-Irish Treaty of 1921, he described himself as

> . . . one of the suffering few . . . who, relying on British honour and British justice, have in giving their best to the service of the state seen them now deserted and cast aside without one single line of recollection or recognition in the whole of what you call peace terms in Ireland.[33]

Once again, it appears, any hope of a linear history has turned out to be repetitive, circular and self-defeating.

These feelings of betrayal and injury are complemented by the contempt with which many Ulster Protestants consider that they, and everything associated with them, are viewed by Catholics and Republicans. John Fulton has observed that hardline Republicans perceive Protestant loyalists

> ... either as a pariah group – the mere instrument of British impe-
> rialism – or simply not there. Their culture has no rights, no claim to
> an alternative identity. Intellectually, the problem is the British presence
> in Ireland. But emotionally, the non-people are hated or at least
> detested.[34]

Ironically, the pain of being dismissed now felt by Protestants corresponds precisely with the ways in which Unionist advocates and
propagandists ignored the sensibilities of the Catholic minority in
their midst during the Stormont years.[35] Now, trapped between the
British government's disdain and increasingly obvious desire to
distance itself from Protestant Unionism, and Republican antipathy,
it is scarcely a surprise to find Steve Bruce suggesting that there is
growing evidence of Ulster loyalism displacing the sense of Ulster
Britishness which preceded the conflict of the past thirty years.[36]

Elsewhere, the Unionist leader, David Trimble – who prefers to
describe himself as 'Ulster-British' – has protested at the way in
which, as he sees them, revisionist treatments of Irish history have
played down the importance of Ulster, demeaned Ulster leaders and
neglected the very events which Orangemen, Unionists and Ulster
Protestants regard as crucial. He concluded an address to the Cultural
Traditions Group with a cautionary note which is couched in highly
significant terms:

> My final comment to the Cultural Traditions Group is that you must
> take care as to the way in which the work you are trying to do is
> perceived in the wider community. One of the enduring folk-memories
> of the Ulster-British people is the fear of massacre – the fear that the
> people may cease to be, at least culturally. If the work of this Group is
> seen as having an agenda that refers to Irishness and the creation of a
> modern inclusive Irish nationalism, then this Group will find itself
> talking largely to itself and perhaps only to one tradition and not to
> the wider community that it must also address.[37]

The allusion in this context to the fear of massacre – rather like
McCusker's reference to standing outside the gate – is very revealing.
It is a clear signal of the deep-seated insecurity of many Protestants

and of the suspicion which surrounds any attempt to review preferred versions of history.

That insecurity is made all the more acute because of the way in which, in the past, Ulster Protestants have shown scant concern for a sense of national identity. Their essential self-definition has been anchored in Protestantism itself, with the British monarch as its supreme political representative, and, secondly, the Westminster parliament as its agent. Stripped of confidence in the reliability of the British connection, this creates a real problem which Ulster Protestants have yet to resolve. Gerald Dawe has aptly observed that

> . . . that painful process of finding out 'What we are' characterises the present state of northern Protestants. Yet many are frightened of accepting that question and hide behind the loudest preacher; others are unprepared to face the uncertainty of the time, or else leave it all behind them and emigrate.[38]

But the situation does not seem wholly negative. There is evidence of Protestants wishing to explore Irish history as never before and the issue of the place of the Irish language for Protestants in Northern Ireland has been debated. Because of history, there is fear and suspicion among Protestants that anything to do with Irish culture and language will inevitably be politicised for nationalist or republican ends and will therefore stigmatise them accordingly. However, the way in which Ulster Protestants of earlier generations participated in Irish culture and used the Irish language is also being rediscovered.[39]

A book such as *Styles of Belonging: The Cultural Identities of Ulster* brings together contributions made by a variety of people with differing cultural, religious and political views during a series of talks held at the Conway Education Centre in Belfast. In a less sophisticated but equally important way the pamphlet, *Beyond the Fife and Drum*, reports on a conference held in the Shankill Road area in 1994 to discuss ideas of Protestant identity in Northern Ireland. Here, a woman speaking from the floor revealed her readiness to question her identity from another perspective, claiming that Protestantism 'did not take account of her experience as a woman living in a Protestant area of Northern Ireland today'. She continued:

> I have a *cultural* tradition, but the *religious* Protestantism which was given to me has excluded my experience and my worth as a woman. I feel this is very common, not only in Protestantism but in Catholicism. My whole being and aspirations as a woman have been denied, and I

feel that there is much more to life as a Protestant than simply as a 'religious' Protestant – it has to do with how you relate to society and how you relate to your culture.[40]

Incomplete as this critique is, it nonetheless opens up questions not only about the relationship between Protestantism and culture as it has developed in Northern Ireland, and in some ways returns to Calvin's insistence that religion has to do with the whole of life, but also ventures to see the issue as one for Catholics as much as for Protestants. Even more significantly, perhaps, it raises the matter of women's position within and relationship to both Protestantism and Catholicism which has so often been conspicuous by the absence of attention given to it. Paradoxically, whereas the conservatism of the major churches in Ireland traditionally marginalised women and may have inhibited the progress of feminism at an earlier stage, the speaker's words suggest that it may now be helping to stimulate new demands.

In the light of this concern with identity, the popularity of the work of Ian Adamson also seems particularly instructive. Beginning with his most influential book, *The Cruthin*, Adamson has produced a series of publications in which he has set about offering a version of history that provides Ulster Protestants with an ancient Irish ancestry normally denied them in more familiar accounts. According to this interpretation, the Cruthin were the original settlers in Ireland, preceding even such groups as the Fir Bolg. The Gaels, traditionally regarded by nationalists as their ancestors, arrived much later and the dominance which they achieved was at the expense of the older Cruthin. Thus, writes Adamson:

> That the Irish Gaels suffered under later English domination is but one side of a coin which carries on the obverse the long cruel extermination of the Ancient Kindred of the Ulster People. The claim of the Gael to Ireland is by the sword only, and by the sword was it reclaimed in later days by the descendents of those Ancient Peoples – namely the Belgic Daltriata and the Cruthin. Of these two Ulster Peoples the paramount claim belongs to the Cruthin, the last of the Picts.[41]

Irrespective of the historical reliability of this, its utility and value to a Protestant community increasingly troubled by uncertainty about its own identity are obvious. Whereas previously Ulster Protestants were caricatured as being more British than the English, this is now converted into a claim to be more Irish than the Catholic nationalist descendants of the Gaels. At the same time, this claim is also linked with an assertion that the forebears of the British royal family belonged to the Cruthin, thereby making Ulster the cradle of the monarchy.

Nor does Adamson's argument rest here. He presents the Cruthin as among the first beneficiaries of early Irish Christianity in the fifth century, who were ministered to directly by St Patrick and were subsequently responsible for establishing the centres of learning and religion at Nendrum, Movilla (Newtownards) and Bangor – all in modern day Co. Down.[42] Two centuries later, the Cruthin were expelled to Scotland by the Gaels but returned to Ireland in the early seventeenth century now as the Protestant planters from Galloway. The impact then of their Protestantism in Ulster encouraged a new unity among Catholics and laid the basis for the sectarian divisions between the descendants of the Cruthin which continues to the present day.

The thrust of Adamson's work, therefore, is to give Ulster Protestants an historical – even a legendary – past which they previously lacked. Yet in doing so, it reiterates key features that characterise more conventional versions of that history: oppression, long-suffering, survival, and success. The early opposition to the Cruthin came from those peoples whose descendants are Catholic nationalists and who still offer resistance. The Cruthin are associated, first, with the establishment of Christianity in Ireland and with early cultural achievement, then later, they are at the forefront in bringing reformed religion to the country. Their particular loyalty to the British monarchy is validated by the Cruthinic connection with it, and by implication, the right of the monarchy to rule over Ulster at least, if not over the whole of Ireland, is affirmed. But while all this may go some way towards satisfying the desire for a missing past, it does nothing to provide a vision of the future, and this absence is, in Terence McCaughey's words, 'one of the saddest characteristics today of a people who regard themselves as a provident, hard-headed no-nonsense crowd . . .'.[43]

Allusion has already been made to the Orange Order and although it was not formed until 1795, it has been enormously influential in shaping popular Protestant views of history. Its commitment to upholding the Williamite principles secured by the 'Glorious Revolution', to resisting Catholicism and to the maintenance of the political union between Great Britain and (nowadays) Northern Ireland, are obviously crucial and are reflected in images and texts displayed on many of the banners carried in Orange processions. In his research into the arcane insignia of the Royal Black Institution, which is one of the three 'Orange' organisations in Ulster, Anthony Buckley has identified key texts, banner pictures and emblems and has commented on what the biblical references share in common. He observes that, in fourteen important specimen texts:

> . . . the most prevailing theme is of an individual or people who, though blessed with God's favour, is confronted with other peoples who are in some way alien.[44]

Furthermore, far from encapsulating an overview of scripture as a whole, the texts create a carefully selected impression with particular emphasis falling upon sinners who must be put down and defeated by exemplary heroes such as Noah, Abraham, Jacob, Joseph, Gideon and Elijah. Old Testament scripture is much more prominently represented than New Testament accounts. Emphasis on Christ himself and on his Second Coming or on New Testament teaching on love and forgiveness is limited or wholly absent. Faithfulness is upheld and is rewarded by God's favour either in terms of prosperity or through victory over oppressors. Buckley concludes that

> When these stories are placed in the context of an insitition whose prime declared purpose is to reinforce both the Protestant religion (as against Catholicism) and a social and political situation in which Protestants can predominate, their relevance is unambiguous. It would indeed be difficult for a Protestant unionist who encountered these stories in detail and in depth in the context of the Black Institution not to recognise the similarity between the situation of the Ulster Protestant and that of the heroes of the various stories. Like the people of Israel in Canaan, Ulster Protestants have been given, and now occupy, an alien land. The foreigners whose land they occupy are, like the Canaanites, the Midianites, the Philistines, and all others, adherents of an alien religion. Like Jacob, they steadfastly avoid marrying the daughters of their enemies. Like the heroes of the stories, they lay great stress on loyalty, whether to their religion or to the crown.[45]

This loyalty, reinforced by the premium placed upon obedience, militaristic discipline and commitment first to the lodge and then to the wider organisation, often submerged potentially divisive class interests in favour of the defence of Protestantism and has sometimes disguised complex and even contradictory politics within Orangeism.[46] And crucially, just as Adamson's history aspires to give Ulster Protestants links to an ancient past through the Cruthin, so the Orange societies encourage an identification with the Children of Israel, God's chosen

– and often cruelly oppressed – people, and imply the divinely approved dominance of their religion.[47]

The use of biblical texts in this instructive way, and in order to generate analogies between situations in scripture and more recent events, may well have been influenced by the Calvinist emphasis on the primacy of the Word and of significant signs and on the perceived connections between the chosen people of Israel and the members of the reformed church. However, the rites of initiation associated with the Orange Order, Royal Arch Purple Chapter and Royal Black Institution, and the fascination with symbols, badges, banners and mysteries may also be regarded as a direct reaction against the austerity and simplicity of low church Ulster Protestantism. Here are outlets for symbolism, ornateness and ritual which are largely excluded from Protestant worship as smacking of Roman idolatry.

Yet, as Belinda Loftus has shown, even the emblems and traditions of Orangeism must be understood in the context of a particular view of history. Territorial rights are aggressively asserted by painted kerbstones, by entry into an area through an arch, by flags and symbolic bonfires and perhaps above all by the 'right' to 'march' along certain routes, however obviously provocative to local Catholics this may be.[48] Similarly, old territorial disputes are commemorated in song and on certain bannners which, in Edna Longley's words, 'carry, like lares and penates, the ancestral details of every local lodge'.[49] Militancy and piety are conjoined in a way that adds legitimacy to the former and virility to the latter – and it should be remembered that the Orange Order is an exclusively male organisation and that political Unionism with which it has been closely associated has always been dominated by men.[50] (These facts in themselves provide an eloquent gloss on the words of the disaffected Protestant woman at the Shankill Road conference quoted above.) The formality of men in suits, bowler hats, white gloves and sashes with numerous emblems parading in ranks coexists with the impassioned performances of many of the marching bands (especially those known as 'kick the Pope' bands) and the holiday spirit which characterises the mood and behaviour of the participants when they reach 'the field', where, simultaneously, they are being exhorted by sympathetic politicians and clergymen to maintain their loyalties to church and crown.[51] This paradox also emerges in the fact that many processions which are ostensibly well-organised and disciplined have led directly to outbreaks of civil disorder and violence. From the point of view of the marchers, of course, such incidents are always the fault of members of the 'other side' and provide self-fulfilling evidence of their disloyalty and readiness to deny the liberty of Protestants. An Orange demonstration which is followed by trouble, therefore, not only justifies itself on the usual grounds of defending the right to 'walk', but also 'proves' that Catholics really do behave in the way that certain Protestants maintain, thereby reaffirming the importance of continuing to march.[52] It is in this sense that parades are what Edna Longley has dubbed 'an inner-directed mnemonic' as much or even more than an anti-Catholic gesture.[53] However tortuous this logic may be, it commands considerable authority at street level.

Nor is the influence of Orange images and emblems with their emphasis on legitimacy and formality confined to the Orange Order and its related organisations. As has been argued by Belinda Loftus, visual artists such as Colin Middleton, Dermot Seymour and Colin McCookin have incorporated within their work lines, motifs and references which derive from their background in the Protestant Unionist community. She is led to the conclusion that

> . . . there are two ways of seeing in Northern Ireland, involving not just two sets of emblems, but two different styles of vision. Timeless, abstract, crafted, divided, unarty, hierarchical, legitimate and public images are favoured in the mode of vision which comes most naturally to the unionist community, and historical, figurative, arty, all-encompassing, romantic, rebellious and private images in that which finds favour with the nationalists.[54]

But the religio-political factors which shape the 'styles of vision' of visual artists also operate upon writers, albeit in different ways. This is a view supported by Ivan Herbison, who has observed that

> Presbyterianism is of central importance to Ulster-Scots cultural identity, and has provided a theological framework for the sense of separateness which manifests itself in literary, linguistic and political modes;[55]

and many other commentators including Tom Paulin, Gerald Dawe, Norman Vance, John Wilson Foster, Terence Brown, Anthony Bradley and Edna Longley have variously taken up this theme of the formative influence of Protestantism and the politics that derive from it on the cultural life of Ulster. How then does this show itself in the work of creative writers from the north of Ireland whose backgrounds are in the Protestant community?

We have already seen how, politically, Ulster Protestants have lived in a tension between their sense of superiority and right to rule in perpetual ascendancy over their Catholic neighbours, and an awareness of their increasing vulnerability, compounded, perhaps, by guilt for the readiness with which they shrugged off responsibility for their co-religionists in the Free State when the country was partitioned. This tension complements the even deeper paradox of the Calvinist's world-view which straddles on the one side an inspirational belief in the existence of those who are predestined by God himself to election into salvation and on the other a conviction of human sinfulness and unworthiness that can be disabling in its certainty.

Given in addition to this the crucial importance placed on the individual's relationship with God – one's personal salvation history – it is not surprising that writers as different as W.R. Rodgers, Louis MacNeice, John Hewitt and Derek Mahon engage in repeated and often anguished self-interrogation in their verse, or that still more have turned to autobiography. The fact that Rodgers forsook his religious vocation and that the poetry of the others reveals varying degrees of scepticism or unbelief may be less interesting than the influence on them of the thought patterns of Ulster Protestantism and how they reacted to these.

In his study of the literature of English Dissenters, Donald Davie argues that the influence of the 'chapel' plays 'a crucial and momentous part in the literary history of England', although this has seldom been observed, because it is

> . . . 'the enemy', . . . precisely that which, in each generation, English artists must do battle with and circumvent as best they can.[56]

The similarity between this situation and that of many writers of Northern Irish Protestant stock in their relationship to their religious background is highly suggestive. If the Dissenters initiated the process of breaking images and challenging established pieties in the name of truth and liberty of thought, then the artists who in turn commit their own acts of iconoclasm are, as it were, the new radicals, demanding still greater freedom and scope for individual expression than the austerities of Calvinistic or evangelical Protestantism allow.

Similarly, the process of self-interrogation characteristic of Protestant catechisms readily transmutes itself into a more general disposition to articulate and question which has always been a feature of radical Presbyterianism, but which in its conservative form becomes an attitude of confrontational resistance to whatever is perceived as threatening. Tom Paulin, therefore, seems right to describe the Protestant imagination as 'dialogic' or 'polemical' in character, seeing itself 'dramatically as pitched against certain powerful ideas that threaten its existence and values'.[57] The theatrical quality and coloration of language common in Calvinist and evangelical rhetoric reveals itself across the spectrum of Protestant writing and testimony, whether in the sermons and speeches of clerics like Henry Cooke or Ian Paisley, the political utterances of Edward Carson or Harold McCusker, the interior dramas of poets, or in representations of the Protestant mind and character in fiction and plays.[58] Equally it is indisputable that even in an age of declining church attendance and religious faith, the vocabulary and rhythms of both politics and literature often remain remarkably rooted in the forms of the King James Bible, especially the Psalms and prophetic books, the hymnody of the nineteenth century, and the resonances of earlier styles of preaching, prayer and testimony. It is as if the consequences of the belief that the whole world is the proper sphere of activity for religion linger on, although the substance of that belief has ceased to be credible to many of those who continue to draw upon its rhetoric, even for the purpose of challenging or rejecting its very premises.

Typically, Calvinists are uneasy with relative judgements, preferring clear categories of right and wrong, good and bad, salvation and damnation, and the effects of this are evident in Ulster Protestant thought and opinion. The problems this raises were clearly defined last century in the dispute between Henry Montgomery and Henry Cooke. In his speech to the Synod of Ulster held at Cookstown in 1828, Montgomery deplored what he saw as the betrayal of the Reformation by the Protestant Church's authoritarianism and else-where he denounced creeds and confessions as 'the great bulwarks of error and superstition in all ages', and 'the chief instruments of all sectarian and political persecutions'.[59] For Montgomery, 'Variety, indeed, is the immutable law of nature', and he feared that the move headed by Cooke to impose a test of doctrinal orthodoxy could only lead to 'a dead sea of Presbyterianism'.[60] But for his opponent, Cooke, such liberalism seemed tantamount to the abandonment of integrity: that which appeared to the one man to shackle God-given individual freedom was presented as the necessary guarantee of its preservation by the other. It is no coincidence that the 'element of sensuous responsiveness' in Montgomery's thought and language is in marked contrast to Cooke's apocalyptic references and appeals to the memory of the militant Protestantism of the defenders of Derry and in the battle at Enniskillen.[61]

The same dilemma reappears in the words of an unnamed speaker at a conference a century and a half after the confrontations between Montgomery and Cooke, who said:

> Protestantism deals with 'absolute truths' – the absolute truth of the Bible, of the New Testament. But Protestantism also cherishes civil and religious liberty and the right to question. And the absolute truth of the New Testament was put together by four men – four alternative descriptions of the life of one person. If we were to take without questioning the attitudes revealed by Paul in his letters to the churches, we would still have women sitting in churches with their hats on, or possibly going back home to be beaten by their husbands. That's the paradox: . . . you have that absolute truth, but at the same time the tradition of questioning.[62]

These examples pinpoint the practical outcomes of one of the central tensions which has been shown in the reformed church from its very origins. In its Irish context, it has contributed to the Protestant perception of history as an endlessly renewed contest between forces of good and evil and between Protestant freedom and Catholic repression. In politics, it has sustained belief in the assumed right of Protestants to rule perpetually in Northern Ireland while in matters of civil liberty, out of deference to the absolute strictures taken from scripture, it has led to the retention of prohibitive laws which have been reformed elsewhere. In broader cultural terms, it has often resulted in hostility to or rejection of work which exercises liberty of thought and expression in ways that are oppositional to or sceptical of the accepted norms. This is also why, in Marianne Elliott's words:

> The strange combination of radicalism and reaction at the heart of Presbyterianism can produce quite divergent responses depending on the level of insecurity at a given moment.[63]

And since the situation in Ulster from the late nineteenth century has been consistently exacerbated by Protestant fears and insecurities, Protestant responses throughout the period have equally consistently inclined to the reactionary end of the spectrum.

Whereas fear can, as Thomas Kilroy has argued, generate positive developments, stimulating the recognition that changes must be made or calcification will set in, all too often its outcome among Northern

Protestants has been to induce a sense of helplessness and hope-lessness. In such circumstances, Kilroy claims:

> The very failure to move, to change, to risk, creates, firstly, a highly exaggerated sense of the value of what we are and what we hold. This is a spurious consolation for being unable to become something else or to acquire a different set of possessions. This, in turn, passes to a secondary negative phase in which the fear-ridden mind tries to project its dilemma, its failure, on to another or others since the first condition, that of false self-importance, quickly becomes intolerable under stress. It is at this point that fear generates violence, a destructiveness of the self, of another or others that can be both psychic and physical.[64]

The significance of this atmosphere of fear and narrowness of vision for creative writers has often been to leave them marginalised or to deny their achievements the recognition and honour that they would have rightly been accorded in a more sympathetic cultural environment. One thinks of the obscurity of Forrest Reid's existence, of John Hewitt's humiliating rejection by the appointing body in the Ulster Museum, of the row over the first production of Sam Thompson's play, *Over the Bridge*, or of Michael Longley's difficulties with the Arts Council. Protestant distrust of writers and their work in the North may be further aggravated, as Edna Longley has suggested, precisely because literature has so obviously played a prominent part in the articulation of Irish Nationalist aspirations and feelings.[65] To the suspicious and judgemental Protestant mind, this may serve to link literature with errant beliefs and Catholic casuistry. Conversely, however, these circumstances give added point to Joe McMinn's enquiry whether imaginative literature may not in fact 'have a special significance in a society where perception seems to be the real battleground'.[66]

Where religion is presented as a way of viewing and interpreting the whole of life, as has been the case with Northern Irish Protestantism, there is a real sense in which questions of history and politics inevitably *are* religious questions. Likewise, many of the cultural practices of Protestants are shot through with some form of religious significance or are restricted by a powerfully inbred religious resistance. This contributes to the insecurity felt by Protestant writers about where they belong in such a society if they can neither subscribe to the religion nor the commemorative culture of their background, nor yet feel free to ignore its weighty presence. Gerald Dawe has summed this dilemma up well:

Coming from such a background implicates the writer in a spider's web: the more one tries to draw away, the more entangled one becomes.[67]

This, he argues elsewhere, compels the Protestant writer to think in a literally 'self-conscious' way about his or her cultural position.[68] And while Dawe, like others, has expressed his scepticism of the notion that there is such a thing as a 'Protestant' literary tradition, he upholds the claim first made in the Introduction to *Across a Roaring Hill* that writers who have come from Irish Protestant backgrounds have 'an ineradicable consciousness of *difference*, of being defined in and against another culture . . . '.[69] How this is so, and what it has meant in practical terms – how the spider's web has entangled specific writers – is the subject of the chapters that follow.

CHAPTER FOUR

Journeys into the Protestant Mind: Essays and Autobiographies

*Writers from a Protestant background . . . are faced with
the fact that their culture, historically defined by the
emphasis on Calvinism, has been invoked as a rationale
for Protestant economic and political supremacy, and has a
history of indifference or antagonism to art.*

Anthony Bradley, 'Literature and Culture
in the North of Ireland', in M. Kenneally (ed),
*Cultural Contexts and Literary Idioms in
Contemporary Irish Literature.*

*The classic assumption in Ireland that Protestant equals
Ascendancy, reactionary, imperialist, is vastly at variance
with the history of Protestantism in the North.*

C.L. Dallat, ' Single Flame' in Eve Patten (ed),
*Returning to Ourselves: Second Volume of Papers from
the John Hewitt International Summer School.*

DESPITE ANY NOTIONS of Ulster Protestants' taciturnity and
inhibitions, a remarkable number of writers from this background have turned to autobiography, often on more than one
occasion. In doing so they have inspected and reconsidered not only
their own development, values and beliefs, but also ways in which
these were conditioned by the world around them. In many instances,
as the previous chapter showed, that world was significantly shaped
either by Protestant theology itself, or by its powerful cultural
influence encountered variously in political Unionism, Orangeism,
education, popular celebrations, or more generally in the kinds of
attitudes and assumptions of family members and peers and within
the community as a whole. Gerald Dawe's comments on the Belfast

in which the musician and songwriter, Van Morrison, grew up in the 1940s and 50s evoke this environment succinctly:

> Protestantism was everywhere. From the Union Jack flying above the Orange halls, to billboards proclaiming Proverbial wisdom from the Bible, assemblies and religious instruction at school, it was impossible *not* to absorb the teaching and cultural values of the protestant church.[1]

However, just as Ulster Protestantism itself is not monolithic, neither are the reactions and responses of the writers monochrome. Indeed, they are testimonies to individuality and independence of thought and action, and, in numerous places display typically Protestant readiness to cast off inherited beliefs and practice in search of personal truth and integrity. English autobiography, it has been argued, 'derives from a Protestant tradition of introspection, one that is insistently hermeneutic', that is, which 'has placed in the foreground the act of self-interpretation – the autobiographer's interpretation of himself and his experience'. This idea is complemented by Declan Kiberd's observation that 'The relationship between Protestantism and autobiography . . . is based on the fact that the Protestant confession is made to the self.'[2] In this sense, autobiography upholds a fundamental principle in Protestant understanding of each individual's relationship with the deity. Furthermore, among stricter Protestants, autobiographical writing has long been accorded a seal of approval often withheld from overtly fictional works, particularly if it is devoted to an examination of the religious awakening and spiritual development of the subject. Such writing is taken to reflect at a personal level the providential pattern of history that features elsewhere in Protestant thought, and conveniently satisfies a reader's curiosity about other people's lives and frailties while affording uplifting instances of individual reform, deliverance from evil and dedication to doing good and serving God. In this instance, St Augustine's *Confessions* (c. 400), demonstrating and praising the saving grace of God at work in the author's life, proved the seminal example for many later writers. Similar earnestness of purpose is evident in celebrated post-Reformation autobiographical works such as John Bunyan's *Grace Abounding to the Chief of Sinners*, Richard Baxter's *Reliquiae Baxterianae*, or Jonathan Edwards's *Personal Narrative*. The focus of other autobiographies varies, however, and may make less of the drama of religious awakening and more of the life of faith. Thus, Thomas Witherow's *Autobiography* and W.D. Killen's *Reminiscences of a Long Life* are primarily personal accounts of their ministry and services to the nineteenth-century Irish Presbyterian Church, although both men also examine aspects of their vocation and beliefs.

Alternatively, some autobiographers, influenced more, perhaps, by *The Confessions* (1781) of a famous native of Geneva, Jean-Jacques Rousseau, deal either with loss of faith and the drift away from religion, or with personal development which is understood in quite different terms to those promoted by more conventionally religious writers. Secularised as such writing may be, its motivation and absorption with the author's own fate and implicit self-belief in the importance of the personal account are hallmarks of Protestant influences, however subdued or subverted these may have become in the author's life. In the particular case of Irish writers, varieties of self-interpretation and expiation are evident not only in the auto-biographies of a series of Ulstermen, including Forrest Reid, George Buchanan, Paul Henry, George Birmingham, Louis MacNeice and Robert Harbinson, but also in journalistic and political essays of writers like Robert Lynd and Denis Ireland, who both extrapolate significantly from personal recollection and autobiographical experience. One might add, too, that Buchanan, MacNeice, Henry and Lynd were the sons of clergymen, Birmingham (whose real name was James Hannay) was himself a Church of Ireland minister and Robert Harbinson attended Bible College and was for a time engaged in evangelical missionary work. Yet, while the influence of diverse forms of Ulster Protestantism may have been particularly immediate in the lives of these individuals, its presence and influence are readily acknowledged by others less obviously immersed in its theology, such as Shan Bullock, Lyn Doyle, Thomas Carnduff, John Boyd and Robert Greacen.

As elsewhere, one of the strongest impressions conveyed by many of these writers is that Protestantism imbues those raised under its influence with a sense of their otherness and difference, whether from fellow Irish citizens or from the natives of the British mainland. Thus Robert Lynd declared that

> The Ulsterman may be a Protestant and a Presbyterian, but at least he is an Irish Protestant and Presbyterian, not a Scotch or an English one;[3]

But while Lynd accepts the distinctness of the Ulster Protestant within Ireland, he dismisses the thought that he is 'only a sort of foreigner', locating difference in 'a division of ancient religious ideals, and of a political, intellectual and economic atmosphere created for the most part by those ideals.'[4] His proposed connection between religious, political and economic interests may be a commonplace, but other writers have found it worth recording too. Robert Greacen recalls that

> There was no clash between devotion to the Crown and the half-crown. God, it was widely understood, favoured those who helped themselves. He favoured Presbyterians in particular.[5]

This suggests the degree to which Lynd's 'ancient religious ideals' had been superseded by more materialistic motives, a perception developed in George Birmingham's analysis of Ulster Unionism in 1919, as an improbable alliance between aristocrats, landowners and military men whose real concern was defending the integrity of the Empire, business men driven by the belief that finance and trade would collapse under an Irish government and Belfast working-men's fear of Catholicism. Typically, he claimed, a member of the last group

> . . . dreads the dissolution of the Union because he believes that the Pope would govern a Home-ruled Ireland. The root of his Unionism is religion, not so much attachment to one faith as fear of the domination of another.[6]

Birmingham's perception of Protestantism as having less to do with articles of belief than with the readiness of specific social groups to defend their own economic interests and privileges, through nurturing and exploiting the fears of working people, is usefully complemented by comments made by Thomas Carnduff, sometime shipyard worker, poet, dramatist and autobiographer. Recalling the abject poverty, insecurity of employment, child labour and lack of civil reform in early twentieth-century Belfast, Carnduff refutes the idea that he and others like him shared any sense of privileged relationship with Great Britain. Yet in his account of his own family, he remembers how for his brothers:

> Protestantism and the Orange Society meant more . . . than their daily bread and butter. Conscience, mode of life, their opinions on public affairs, even their family life was mixed up with the importance of keeping Popery at a comfortable distance.[7]

Thus, even those eking out a penurious existence were convinced that in some unclearly defined way their predicament would be still worse in an Ireland governed by Catholic leaders and that Protestantism safeguarded their position and gave them their identity.

If this seems irrational and contrary, it is akin to George Birmingham's simultaneous feelings of antipathy and admiration towards Ulster Protestants when he deplored the partition of Ireland, yet expressed a certain pride in the determination which had forced the imperial parliament to modify its plans for Home Rule. Likewise, he writes:

> I was never an Orangeman and for a great part of my life have been in opposition to the political opinions held so firmly by my fellow Protestants of Northern Ireland, but the spirit of defiance and detestation of authority which inspired them has remained with me.[8]

This mixture of attraction and rejection – perhaps an eccentric product of the injunction to love the sinner but not the sin – reappears in various contexts in the work of other writers influenced by Ulster Protestantism and may indeed be one of its distinctive characteristics.

It is strangely apparent in the representation of Belfast itself where many of the forces associated with Northern Ireland, both positive and negative, are thrown into sharpest relief. The rapid growth and productiveness of this 'city of restless energy' . . . 'pervaded by a spirit of intense and serious earnestness' made it at once an industrial success and an urban nightmare, or 'jungle', as Denis Ireland called it in the title of one of his books.[9] Both outcomes are attributed to the dynamic force of Protestantism 'which is founded on the self-assertion of the individual and always holds individual effort a supreme virtue', and 'is likely to develop that kind of relentless energy which is characteristic of Belfast.'[10] Although that energy often seemed directed merely to soulless and mercenary ends, Denis Ireland identified a striking convergence of the religious and the secular in his account of launches at the shipyards in the Edwardian days of his youth. Perhaps no event symbolised more obviously the worldly success of the city, but Ireland reveals the whole occasion as a type of religious ritual – formal, ceremonial and inescapably Protestant:

> In Presbyterian Belfast a kind of marriage with the sea *may* have taken place down there at the 'Island', on the artificial peninsula at the head of Belfast Lough, but our Belfast version of the Protestant ethic took no account of such fantastic imagery. Down at the shipyards, in that sea of cloth-caps and bowlers, a more accurate analogy would have been a harvest festival in a Presbyterian church – a thanksgiving at which slight variations from the psalms were permitted, a sort of

Protestant inversion of the Mass at which the pagan rite of breaking a bottle of champagne was regarded as a harmless concession, like rolling eggs at Easter.[11]

However miraculous the feat of shipbuilding in a country with virtually none of the natural resources to provide the raw materials, the celebration is void of excesses or superstitions that would have been thought of as 'Catholic'. Instead, Ireland notes ironically the hubristic self-satisfaction of dignitaries who soon after would watch the launch of the greatest of all Belfast's ships, the allegedly unsinkable *Titanic*, and their implicit sense of superiority over their less industrious Catholic fellow countrymen. Here again one of the central paradoxes of Protestantism is evident: the belief in the importance of the self and in the need for the individual to live with heroic discipline and total commitment to right action, which is predicated upon awareness of human unworthiness, may manifest itself in practice as raw triumphalism and crude worldly ambition. Robert Lynd, who was the son of a distinguished minister and one-time Moderator of the Presbyterian Church, offered a shrewd analysis of the temper of his native city when he wrote that

> What gives Belfast its distinction among cities . . . is the strain of almost savage idealism that runs in the veins of the people. I call the idealism savage, because it has never been given a soul by the churches, or an intellect by the schools and colleges. Belfast has grown up like a child whose parents died in its infancy, and the jerry-builders and the catchword orators have taken merciless advantage of it.[12]

The analogies and choice of language here point to the way in which the freedoms of mind and spirit originally conferred by Protestantism may be reduced to alternative forms of servitude and domination when the institutions whose purpose is to nurture and develop them become narrow and fearridden and betray their own origins. The consequences of this failure are, in Lynd's view, destabilising and potentially dangerous because of their very unpredictability: 'The Ulsterman's religion has been at once his making and his undoing. It has sent him about the world with a flame in his head, and this is a virtue or an evil just as accidents may determine'.[13]

Lynd's emphasis on the ambiguous effects of religion and on the shortcomings of the churches receives endorsement in the accounts of the experiences of individual writers. Thus George Birmingham maintained that

In Ireland religion has been a creed – several creeds – with a call for loyal faith. It has been a rule of life demanding obedience and self-sacrifice. It has not, for many centuries, been a region for spiritual adventure, an unknown ocean across which the soul has gone voyaging.[14]

Although he does not distinguish between the Catholic and Protestant Churches here, regarding them as equally authoritarian in their demands and timid in their practice, he also specifically characterised his own Church as 'that rigid, somewhat arid branch of the Anglican communion.'[15] The sense that the Churches have betrayed their mission and become preoccupied merely with negative teaching against other denominations is repeatedly asserted. 'The anti-Catholic passion is almost the first passion that an Ulster non-Catholic child knows', wrote Robert Lynd in 1909, although he followed this up by affirming his belief that this was changing.[16] He ascribed particular blame for anti-Catholicism to the kind of teaching common in the churches:

Protestants are more likely to be warned in their churches against errors of Catholic doctrine than against errors of Protestant conduct towards Catholics in a misbehaving world.[17]

Within the Protestant communion itself, Birmingham recalled how, in the days of his own boyhood, Presbyterians were marginalised by the Church of Ireland which alone claimed the right to describe itself as Protestant, thereby maintaining a long-standing grievance in practice if not in law.[18] And by way of contrast, the Presbyterian, Denis Ireland, was acutely sensitive to the social differences between the worshippers in a whitewashed meeting-house on the Ards penin-sula and those who gathered in the nearby Church of Ireland which he occasionally visited, and where 'The sight of the brass lectern in the form of an eagle with outstretched wings, the (to our ears) popish sound of the responses, gave us a feeling of dangerous liberation, like a trip to Paris'.[19]

Ireland himself, however, also revealed his belief that Ulster Presbyterianism had strayed from its origins when he contrasted the stark simplicity of the meeting-house with its view of the Mull of Galloway on a clear day with the ornate, 'distinctly un-Presbyterian' architecture and decorations of the 'opulent' Belfast city church – testimony to the worldly success of 'the illuminati of the Malone Road' – which he normally attended with his family, and where

Under that Venetian spire opposite the Botanic Gardens, nobody, including my Aunt Lizzie, could be described as stealing away to Jesus – there were too many legal matters, too many scenes in solicitors' offices to be got through first.[20]

The inference is obvious: the Presbyterian church has become entangled in and compromised by the worldly business interests of its members which are now exalted in its architecture and are the primary matters of concern on the lips of the congregation, despite the second and fourth commandments. Ireland's scorn is encapsulated in his record of how a liberal Scottish preacher caused deep offence in the period just before the signing of the Ulster Covenant in 1912 by challenging the political prejudices of his listeners:

> What they wanted, justified by bloodthirsty texts from the Old Testament and trumpet voluntaries from Rudyard Kipling, was a panegyric on imperialist expansion; and the slightest suggestion that imperialist expansion might, like the redecoration of the manse, some day have to be paid for was, to say the least of it, unpopular; the main lesson for the day being the *Investors' Chronicle*.[21]

The repercussions over Sunday lunch in his own home Ireland likens to 'a sort of Presbyterian rough house, a north-eastern version of the dinner table discussion of Parnell in Joyce's *A Portrait of the Artist as a Young Man*', and for the controversial minister it was the start of 'a process of isolation to a sort of Presbyterian Siberia'.[22] While the characteristic disputatiousness of Presbyterianism is again evident in this case, so too is its growing conservatism and preoccupation with economic self-interest.

Despite the Venetian pretensions of Denis Ireland's church, the austerity and plainness of Ulster Protestant places of worship and religious practice imposed themselves lastingly on the memories of many individuals. More importantly, perhaps, this austerity was closely linked with the heavy emphasis on sin and suspicion of anything that might overstimulate the senses or encourage idolatrous tendencies. George Birmingham noted that 'We see sin as it appeared to men like Bunyan. We do not attach any meaning to the saying that to understand all is to forgive all'.[23] In more specific terms, Robert Harbinson described how

> . . . when we were children, Belfast's Gospel Halls scared us into attendance with such phrases *as eternal damnation, vengeance of*

eternal fire, punished with everlasting destruction, the lake of fire, to be cast into hellfire, in fact a regular thesaurus of arson.[24]

Similarly, the painter Paul Henry told of how, having exchanged a friendly look and a few words with a strange girl who attended his father's church one night, his mother confronted him with the question – 'Paul, do you want to ruin your young life for the pleasure of a moment?'. Having failed to get a satisfactory answer from him, she poured out 'the torrent of her righteous wrath, of her love for me and her care for my future, of her hatred for what she would have termed my "looseness"', followed by carefully chosen warning passages from scripture.[25] Henry's father, like his grandfather, was a Presbyterian minister, but left the church in the aftermath of the 1859 revival on an issue of conscience over baptism. He subsequently became the minister of an impoverished Baptist congregation in Great Victoria Street, Belfast, only to break from it over a further matter of conscience. After this he founded his own mission in the neighbour-hood of Sandy Row where he pursued his vocation with courage and passion, motivated, as his son wrote, by 'his very strong sense of religion and his desire to behave as he thought the early Christians would have behaved'.[26] Although in his *Further Reminiscences* Paul Henry's recollection of his father shows a certain admiration for his single-mindedness, desire for integrity and readiness to work amongst the poorest people, he could never overlook the authoritarian, guilt-inducing and freedom-denying character of the theology he preached. Visits to the circus or military displays were forbidden, outings to listen to General Booth or to Moody and Sankey revivalist meetings were compulsory. Smoking, drinking and thinking were 'three unpardonable sins', while sex was unmentionable. So narrow did Henry feel his strict upbringing to be that he became convinced that 'until I had my liberty, complete liberty to do as I liked and think as I liked, my life would be barren and useless'.[27]

Forrest Reid, a relative of the historian of Irish Presbyterianism, James Seaton Reid, would have recognised Paul Henry's frustration and he offered a memorable account of his own reaction to his family's religion in his autobiography which he significantly titled *Apostate*. Here he records his sense of Sunday as 'a veritable nightmare', every aspect of which aroused deep hostility in him.[28] He found the theological emphasis on human sin 'always proved a stumbling-block, because I had never been able to feel sinful' and the doctrine of the Atonement 'offensive and humiliating'.[29] Bible pictures of Christ struck him as 'mawkish and effeminate' and he felt no appeal for the Gospels. Above all, perhaps, the Church's insistence on the cultivation of goodness oppressed and alienated him.[30] Curiously, however, probably the most decisive relationship Reid ever had was with his nursemaid, Emma Holmes, who was a strict English Wesleyan Methodist – in fact, the very sort of person one might assume that he would remember negatively. Yet it was not so. 'Doubtless her creed was narrow, and probably it was gloomy', he wrote, yet she was '. . . the only deeply religious person I have met with whom I have been able to feel quite happy and at my ease'.[31] The explanation he offered for this is that Emma 'herself was so emphatically *not* narrow and *not* gloomy that it mattered very little what she supposed herself to believe' – a way of interpreting the situation which very conveniently enabled Reid to circumvent his antipathy to her faith by simply discounting any connection between Emma's beliefs and her values and dismissively implying that she could have not have known what she believed.[32] For Reid this was proved by Emma's commitment to happiness and justice even more than to the pursuit of goodness, which seemed to him incompatible with any form of Protestantism. No doubt his feeling for his nursemaid was heightened by a number of other factors, including his own youth, the suddenness and finality of Emma's departure (presumably as a result of the family's declining fortunes) and his sense of betrayal and loss provoked by it. It also coloured his early formed conviction that goodness, beauty and happiness are fleeting and fragile. This contributed to his consciousness of isolation and difference from other people which remained with him throughout his life.

Yet, although Emma's religion itself held no appeal whatever for Reid – he recalls that on the one occasion she took him with her to church he howled and protested so loudly that she had to take him home – he was delighted by the stories she told him, and especially, by a serial tale which she read him from a religious magazine. The adult autobiographer wryly concludes that the story failed in its 'purpose of awakening pious longings' in him. However, its account of a distant, idyllic landscape, no doubt intended to evoke the beauty of heaven, stimulated his first imaginative foray back into a timeless and changeless world of youth and thereby subsequently became associated with the repeated quest to achieve such a state which is at the core of all Reid's fiction:

'My world! My world!' I could have shouted; and though Emma might have answered, 'Not there, not there, my child,' I should have known better. It was the only heaven I wanted, or ever was to want. Fleeting glimpses I have had of it, and lost them: and from the flame of that vision I have awakened desolate and sick with longing. For the life I came back to seemed pale and feeble as a candle in the blazing sun; and the knowledge that the other was there – there in all its splendour and beauty and completeness – if only I could reach it, turned all ordinary ambitions and interests to a kind of langour.[33]

Reid's aspiration and longing may therefore be viewed as a personal subversion or adaptation of the conventional Christian pilgrimage to the heavenly country. It became in his case, a striving to recover beauty and innocence which his Protestant upbringing neglected or denied, and which the author knew most fully in the delights of the Northern Irish landscape, the affectionate loyalty of animals and the company of young boys. The austerities of Protestant practice – whether evangelical pressure put upon him after a period of illness by a young curate or the Sabbath ban on reading anything other than religious books and on playing croquet or going out – antagonised him because they were perverse denials of his instinctive wish to live for the present rather than to defer joy to an uncertain hereafter. As he wrote:

If only I had been asked to worship and to love the earth I could have done it so easily! If only the earth had been God. The tender green on the trees, the mossy lawns, the yellow daffodils – all these were lovely, and Sunday made no difference to them. Everything seemed to have a natural life on Sundays except people. . . . It was only people who made difficulties, and thought this was wrong and that was wrong, and did what they didn't enjoy doing. For they *didn't* enjoy it. I had noticed that on Sundays there was an increased irritability even among the most saintly.[34]

This reaction was immediately recognisable to the young John Boyd and Robert Greacen, both of whom mention its impact upon them in their own autobiographies. Despite the differences between Reid's middle-class upbringing and the working-class origins of both Boyd and Greacen, the former even declared: 'I felt as if the book had been written especially for me'.[35]

Like Paul Henry, Forrest Reid's childhood was surrounded by the religious demands of his family, but Boyd and Greacen's experience was less intense, although they too were constantly reminded of their

Protestant background and often puzzled by aspects of it. From an early age Boyd was perplexed by his grandfather's enthusiasm for parading with the Orangemen in July and listening to the pronouncements of clergymen and politicians in 'the field' when he normally had no interest in either. Greacen was equally bemused by apparent self-contradictions in his family's Presbyterianism: the fact that living uprightly seemed more important than being 'saved'; the problem of what constituted 'necessary' work on Sundays; the tension between anxiety over money and the professed belief that God will provide; the dilemma between his mother's endemic anti-Catholicism and her admission that some Catholics were good and some Protestants bad. As boys, Boyd and Greacen were sent to Protestant Sunday schools where both enjoyed the company but were largely unmoved by the religious instruction, Boyd even admitting that it 'accelerated my unbelief'.[36] Their parents' attitude towards church-going was relaxed. Boyd's father went to Albert Bridge Congregational Church in Belfast, but Greacen's parents were not church attenders and he acknowledges that he was sent to Sunday school partly to get him out of the adults' way for a time.[37] In the end, Boyd's move to atheistic socialism was accomplished without lasting bitterness or rancour towards the Protestantism of his upbringing, while Greacen, the one-time 'self-righteous young Presbyterian and would-be sensualist', defined his passage from childhood influences to his own adult perspective in the poem 'Church and Covenant':

> I think of pitch pine pews
> A northern childhood knew.
> I wrestled with John Knox
> Who ghostly in the aisles
> Whispered 'Thou Shalt Not'.
> I think of ancestors who lived
> For Kirk and Covenant.
> They feared the anti-Christ,
> The Roman Man of Sin,
> Scorned English mitres too,
> Aware of thumbscrew, rack,
> They chose a martyr's stance.
> I lack their bigot pride,
> Their certainty of Truth.
> I chose a slacker way,
> An anxious tolerance.[38]

Despite this religious acquiescence, however, Greacen displays an uncompromisingly Protestant belief in the supreme value of individual conscience and announces it in language reminiscent of a pulpit exhortation:

> One voice above all is worth listening to – the inner voice that demands action thus or thus (or at a certain time, inaction, lying low), that undeniable urge which leads as if magnetically to a given point. Deny that voice and illness, mental or physical, will result. Listen for it. Be guided by the red or green or orange flash of the inner light.[39]

Nor is he any less forceful in declaring his commitment to expressing his opinions openly, irrespective of the reaction these may provoke, or in his refusal to submit to 'mediocrities in authority'. These priorities have in turn shaped his concern as a writer not with courting easy popularity, but with addressing 'that permanent interested minority of "common readers" whose continued interest in literature carries it forward from generation to generation'.[40]

An entirely different reaction to a Protestant working-class background emerges from Robert Harbinson's series of four autobiographies which cover the period from his early boyhood up to 1949, when he was twenty-one.[41] Harbinson came from a very poor Belfast family and was raised by his mother following his father's premature death from injuries suffered in an accident while he was working as a window cleaner. His formal education was minimal and was interrupted by a period of wartime evacuation to Co. Fermanagh, which made a profound impression on him, but throughout the period covered by the books he delineates his total immersion in aspects of Protestant culture and religion. Officially a member of the Church of Ireland, Harbinson soon discovered the numerous competing Protestant churches and sects in the streets around his home and realised the opportunity for entertainment and material advantage which they offered. Although he regarded the parish churches as 'dull and forbidding, . . . bare of all iconography', the rhetoric, choruses and lurid emotionalism of the various mission hall meetings gripped his imagination, provided genuine excitement and eventually filled him for a time with the ambition to become a missionary.[42]

Unlike the other writers discussed here, Harbinson found in low-church Protestantism an endless source of fascination and drama. Unmoved by theological considerations or beliefs, he became a religious consumer, selecting venues according to their sensationalism or the likelihood of cadging food, sweets or money:

> Like connoisseurs we picked and chose carefully from the extensive menu of choice religious dishes. A firm favourite were the meetings of sects believing in baptism by immersion. Here we could have our fill of comedy and thrills, spiced with the possibility of an accident. Steam rising from the big tank that represented the Jordan, filled us with passions like those of ancient Romans in the Colosseum, the baptismal waters were our arena.[43]

This kind of opportunism characterises much of Harbinson's writing about his experiences of religion, although the issue is complicated by the adult perspective through which his account is filtered. The author's style is not only informed by a vividness and immediacy of language and image, which may well owe a debt to his time as an evangelical lay preacher, but also by ironies which reflect his changed views at the time of writing. So, for example, although the divisions and rivalries between and within religious sects presented no problem to the child, the adult at once observes his own former behaviour and makes a critique of the circumstances in which it took place:

> All Ireland was divided, the border cut the north from the south, and Mickeys from Protestants, and at the Last Day, the goats would be divided from the sheep. And so even with the mission halls, they took their stand either behind belief in the Second Blessing on the one hand, or disbelief in it on the other. Theological nuances subtler than this passed over their heads. Personally, I was out for any sort of blessing, no matter what the source, so long as it kept me from an early bed.[44]

As the account proceeds and the subject's involvement with evangelical sects becomes more complex and bound up with witnessing and ministry, so his consciousness of factionalism and of the consequences of division become more problematic. Throughout, however, Harbinson presents a view of Protestant religion and practice as having less to do with faith and a coherent set of beliefs than with superstition and the exercise of power. Whether it is his 'unsaved' mother's reluctance to remove any of the framed religious texts from the wall of the house or to throw out damaged and unused hymn books and bibles for fear of bad luck, the humorous account of his own attempt to make up the deficit of prayers left unsaid before he realised he was saved at the age of three, or his later belief in the desirability of trying to act upon a text from Proverbs which he does not understand, the books repeatedly illustrate the effects of living in the midst of a community obsessed with religious forms, but often lacking any deeper engagement with faith or comprehension of it.

More ominous, perhaps, are the numerous ways in which Protestantism run to extremes becomes a vehicle for the assertion of individual authority and the gratification of personal ambition, greed and even perversion. Harbinson not only records this in his representation of other people's conduct, but shows it in his own youthful behaviour with the sects. Back in Belfast after his wartime evacuation, he became drawn into a breakaway Baptist sect where he enjoyed the drama of being at the centre of the group's prayers to save him from spiritualism and lead him to be born again, but was simultaneously motivated by his precocious sexual designs upon one of the female members of the church. Again one senses the gap between the author's amused and humorous account of how he moved towards public acceptance of Christ as his Saviour and his absorption with his own apparently willing self-surrender at the time:

> Wearing sinners down by sheer weight of words, the preacher wound the meeting up like a clockwork mouse. At any minute now, the spring would be released, and the wheels fly round. Who takes the Lord Jesus into his or her heart as their personal Saviour? When we got to that point, I felt quite convinced of the need for this personal witness. In my own fashion I had always been fundamentally religious for as long as I could remember, certainly believing the man Jesus Christ to be my own, in addition to being the Saviour of the world.
>   My hand went up. I did not make it. It just went up of its own accord, as if seized by an ataxic spasm. I could not have pulled it down at that moment if I had wanted to.[45]

The subsequent history of Harbinson's dealings with various evangelical and salvationist groups shows the ruthlessness with which many of the leaders used their positions to cow their followers into blind obedience and the tendency of the sects to fracture and subdivide over bitter internal arguments. It also records the power enjoyed by the teenaged Harbinson when he had established a reputation for himself as an eloquent preacher and giver of testimony, pompously holding forth to his old friends in Fermanagh, posting tracts around the countryside or hiding them in the coat pockets of dancers at the Orange Hall and throwing away the young men's bottles of drink. He repeatedly indicates the shallowness and self-interest of much of his own conduct, ostensibly carried out for religious reasons, and how he was increasingly capable of exploiting other people's credulity or simplicity for his own gratification. The instability of his convictions, both in spite and because of his exposure to intense proselytising, is reflected in the way he succumbs to a succession of religious influences. It reaches its apotheosis in the increasingly bizarre account of his time at the Barry Bible College in South Wales and Tyndale Training College in London. It is also reflected in his entanglement with religious eccentrics, practitioners of the black arts, sexual deviants and members of the British aristocracy – who often turn out to be the same people.

While Harbinson's relationship with the Protestant faith is difficult to define precisely because it is so volatile and frequently opportunistic, the culture of Protestantism is the crucial shaping influence on the story of his life as he tells it. It imposed itself not only in the churches and mission halls, but at school, through the Orange Order, in popular festivals and anniversaries, and in rumours about and general ignorance of Catholics and Catholicism which the writer only gradually began to rectify for himself. In a particularly important way, therefore, the Protestant culture of Robert Harbinson's boyhood and his negotiations with it are the very lifeblood of his autobiographies, while his turbulent relationships with individual Protestants and with various evangelical sects are inseparable from his own growth to maturity. Yet for all the colour and verve with which he tells his story, that culture is shown to be essentially reductive and introverted in its values, distrustful of the unfamiliar, and indifferent to its own self-contradictions and divisions.

It is, perhaps, a commonplace that Northern Irish Protestantism has often defined itself by its rejection and abhorrence of all things Catholic, by what it is not rather than by what it is. At the same time much of the autobiographical writing from the region confirms that lack of knowledge both of individual Catholics and of their beliefs was the norm among many Protestants. Some of the implications of this are apparent when, at the close of *No Surrender*, the first of his autobiographical volumes, Robert Harbinson recalls his fear and distress on discovering that Eoin, an older boy with whom he had established an admiring friendship, is a Catholic, and his later shock when Eoin's sister, Bridget, whom he also liked, left to enter a convent. The boy who was convinced that 'Mickeys existed only in parts of Belfast and nowhere else except the Free State and Rome itself' faced a further dilemma when Bridget sent him a holy medal:

> . . . I could not take the piece of popery into our good Orange household in case it made the roof fall in or brought the sleeping sickness upon us all. But I could not part with the medal either, and so

kept it in my safe, buried pirate-style among the sally-bushes of the railway.[46]

His compromise – to wear the medal when he was with Eoin – is more than youthful tact, because the engraving of the Madonna and child given in such a friendly and unthreatening way prompts him to contrast this image of maternal gentleness and consolation with the unyielding militancy of Protestant icons:

> Fine though Billy King on his charger might be, or however handsome the periwigs and lace portrayed on the Orange banners, the savage element in them was but cold comfort. But Mary, so near to our kind of life, I could well imagine bending over the tinker's fire, warming a sup of milk for 'wee Jaysus'.[47]

This experience, followed by the lessons in neighbourly living which he learned in Co. Fermanagh (and to which he returned in the long celebratory poem, *Song out of Oriel* in 1974), affected Harbinson who, for all his later evangelical excesses, never succumbs to mere bigotry or fear of domination by Catholicism which George Birmingham and Robert Lynd both identified as the underpinning of Ulster Protestant Unionism.[48]

Lynd, indeed, was deeply critical of the failure of the Presbyterian clergy to 'fight against the bigotry so common among their people' and to love Ireland as much as they hated Rome, which, he claims, resulted in intellectual inertia, lack of idealism and the triumph of 'hard dogma'.[49] This accusation must be linked with the accounts of history which were the standard inheritance of generations of Protestant children. Lynd himself castigated training colleges for not providing future teachers with 'the knowledge and spirit of Ireland . . . to capture the imaginations and spirits of Irish children'.[50] Referring to his own school experience, he writes:

> I myself, who was brought up in a district rich in history and in heroic tales, was never allowed to know at school a single human fact suggesting that this country around me and I had any relation to each other – or even, indeed, that this country existed, except in the geographical sense. . . . History, again, meant for me, just as literature did, something about anywhere except Ireland.[51]

As an adult, he regarded the recovery and dissemination of Irish history and literature as indispensable stages on the way to over-coming politically inspired and maintained sectarianism and fear and to the achievement of an integrated Irish nation. He pursued this idea in a deeply subversive essay written during the First World War, 'If the Germans Conquered England'. Here Lynd invited the English to contemplate the consequences of defeat, one of which would be that their children would be taught a different version of their nation's history, reinterpreting the 'glories' of the past as instances of unruliness, ignorance and treachery which German occupation was enabling them to overcome:

> One can guess how the blackening process would go on. It would be done for the most part by reasonable-looking insinuation. The object of every schoolbook would be to make the English child grow up with the feeling that the history was a thing to forget, and that the one bright spot in it was that it had been conquered by cultured Germany.[52]

Naturally, Lynd argued, the English would be deeply hostile to any such imposition and would do everything possible to resist it. However, the unspoken, though inescapable, implication is that this very kind of historical distortion and misrepresentation have been English policy in Ireland and that it behoves the Irish to reject them and reclaim their own national story.

Denis Ireland made the same point in 1930 in *An Ulster Protestant Looks at his World* where he commented on the situation of his co-religionists suffering from a loss of their history in a partitioned country:

> Unconscious of his history, he [i.e. the Ulster Protestant] finds himself without bearings in a swiftly changing world, and his difficulty in orienting himself in the new century is correspondingly increased.[53]

The lost history referred to is that of radical Protestantism, and again like Lynd, Ireland sees the manipulative purposes behind the official occluded version of events upon which children are reared:

> The object, of course, is perfectly clear. Ulstermen must be persuaded that they are in reality West Britons condemned by the sins of their forefathers to live in a rude island beyond the seas. For this reason a little doctored Irish history is better than no Irish history at all – because no Irish history might lead to curiosity.[54]

The apparently simple certainties of Denis Ireland's 'doctored' history were imparted with the authority more commonly associated with religious teaching, because, of course, they were systematically conflated with it. The consequences of this process were examined earlier, but Robert Greacen's record of his own experience illustrates how its implications extended well beyond official instruction in the classroom:

> I did not learn the Protestant version of history from books, but by word of mouth passed on from generation to generation. The 'quality', who had education and leisure, knew the details and the dates, but ordinary folks like ourselves carried the facts – or alleged facts – of history in our very bones and in our hearts. We were the people who had never surrendered and would never surrender. As each Twelfth of July came round, Protestant fervour would rise again and be reaffirmed.[55]

He complements this with a story he was told of a bemused Englishman watching a Twelfth procession who turned to an Ulster bystander and asked what was happening only to be advised to go home and read the Bible.

Harbinson, too, recounts how the schools 'dinned into us over and over again the Protestant story' and how this was closely linked with required learning of a book titled *How We Differ from Rome*. He also claims that he himself believed for a time that Edward Carson was one of the twenty-four elders mentioned in the book of Revelation sent to defend Ulster Protestants against the designs of the Pope.[56] The overlap between these versions of history and religion and popular Protestant street culture not only furnished writers from earlier generations this century, like Carnduff, Greacen and Harbinson, with vivid childhood images, but reappears more recently in Glenn Patterson's novel, *Burning Your Own*, and in separate comments the author has made about his own boyhood on a Protestant working class estate in Belfast, where he admits

> . . . I was a little bigot then. The Eleventh and Twelfth as I experienced them were unmistakably sectarian. I could offer up excuses for my behaviour – it was the mid-'70s, the troubles were at their height – but in the end none of this is excuse enough. I did what I did for the worst possible reason, because I believed in it.[57]

His words affirm the staying power of this provocative mixture of influences.

Furthermore, the importance of these ritual celebrations emphasises the limited opportunities for cultural expression elsewhere in the Protestant community. 'Protestants did not celebrate anything except the Twelfth of July', writes Greacen. 'Many of them were teetotallers and non-smokers and frowned on entertainment of any kind. They would no more play football on a Sunday than a Jew would eat pork'.[58] Gathered round the Eleventh night bonfire, however:

> The crackle and the flames inflamed excitement, and gave some of us Prods a deep sense of belonging. God's Chosen People – not the Jews, but ourselves – would leap and skip and caper round the blaze and, when the great fire had been reduced to a few smoking embers, we would creep sadly away to snatch a few hours' sleep before the start of the truly serious business of the following day.[59]

This telling description draws attention to the complex node of feeling and thought surrounding an event which is both a defiant affirmation and also a fleeting compensation for deeper insecurities. If it suggests a primitive wish to lose oneself briefly in the fireside jollity and party-making, and a form of licence that has no place in strict Protestantism, then it is counterbalanced by the discipline, formal dress and focus on remembering that are the essence of the processions on the next day. Thomas Carnduff's recollections of the Boyne celebrations in the early years of the century capture these aspects precisely, as well as offering a significant – and selective – interpretation of them:

> The hundreds of bands and five miles long procession of marching Orangemen with flaunting banners and varied coloured sashes, seems far removed from any semblance of political or religious rancour.
> Watching these sons of Ulster marching in military formation, sturdy and strong in their belief that they alone are the rightful champions of civil and religious liberty in their native land, one cannot but admire their dignity and orderliness, irrespective whether their cause be just or unjust. Even if ritual and ceremony is [sic] exploited to an extreme degree by Orangemen, they are no worse defaulters from realism or sane argument than most orthodox Christian churches.[60]

Here Carnduff is willing to set aside any questions concerning the motives or values of the Orangemen merely on the grounds of their impressive numbers and dignified and self-confident appearance. The implication is that such a procession is its own justification, whether or not the participants represent truth and justice or bigotry and injustice – the appearance is everything. Paradoxically, the final sentence, which assumes an unquestioning equation between Orangeism and Christian witness, might seem to dismiss all Christian witness as irrational with the Orangemen benefitting only from the discipline of their particular version of it. The shallowness of Carnduff's apprehension of the religious and moral question he begs again bears out the critical comments of writers like Birmingham, Lynd and Ireland on the diminished spirituality and narrow religious teaching in many Protestant churches of the period.

This issue is revealed very precisely in George Buchanan's self-searching memories of how his father, a Church of Ireland clergyman, reacted sympathetically towards the UVF during the Home Rule crisis. Buchanan ponders how it is that as self-disciplined and non-violent a man as his father could feel drawn to support potential rebels:

> Is my father, who studies so much to be submissive, attracted by the insubmission of the Orangemen? He who deprives himself of initiative and audacity, who says, 'Not my will but Thine' – would he be inclined to regard a little rebellion as a relief? Some shadow of truth may lie in these speculations. More accurately, perhaps, rebellion isn't in it; his support of the Ulster volunteers may be rather a further act of submission – this time not to God but to his milieu.[61]

The emphasis on the affective power of the 'milieu' is again notable. Not only Protestant theology itself but, if Buchanan is right, even the attempt to live a life shaped by its discipline, can be overridden by political priorities which have appropriated religion and history and become indistinguishable from them. Thus, it seemed to Buchanan that in his father's case his devout religious life was unwittingly subverted by the Protestant politics of Home Rule and became an expression of this fact rather than of the principled piety which he strove to observe.

For the much more secular Thomas Carnduff, Protestantism meant membership of 'all the normal organisations of my kind' – the Orange Order, the Young Citizen Volunteers and UVF, the Special Constabulary, as well as the Presbyterian Church – and it was the secular bodies which gave him his strongest sense of identity.[62] However, unlike those Protestants whose religion made it difficult for them to consider themselves Irish, Carnduff had no doubts on this matter and is adamant that he has every right to be considered as such and to have his place in the country. Like John Hewitt, he claims ancestors buried beneath a round tower in the grounds of a Protestant church, and like him, he acknowledges that his forebears wrested land from the native Irish. He also shares Hewitt's sense of affinity with the Irish soil and atmosphere, but unlike him, he has no residual guilts or troubled thoughts about the past in which his family was implicated, or about his own position.[63]

Carnduff, like Lynd and Ireland, believed the real problems in the country derived neither from race nor from religion, but from the manipulation and incitement of working-class sectarianism for political ends. In his essay, 'Belfast is an Irish City', he declared:

> Strangely enough, my impatience with sectarian strife in Belfast is not that it delays national unity. That will come one day, but I would rather be as I am meanwhile. My moan is that it delays the mental and spiritual growth of the city. The mind is intimidated and confused by it and, worse than all, it spreads a feeling that the people are powerless before it and cannot dominate their circumstances. This develops a kind of tribal mind in people and, when misfortune hits, all they can do is riot.[64]

Carnduff's frustration and his sense of the distracting and disabling consequences of sectarianism are akin to Robert Lynd and Denis Ireland's disappointment with what they saw as Ulster Protestantism's lost or betrayed radicalism which had been diverted into much shallower channels.

Despite their family origins at the very heart of the Protestant community, and in the case of Ireland a period of service as a British army officer, both he and Lynd became convinced of the case for national unity and were resolute in their opposition to partition. Writing in 1919, Lynd declared that

> . . . Ulster, which had been so eager and integral a part of Ireland at the end of the eighteenth century, became more and more indoctrinated with a seventeenth-century terror of the Pope and threw off the last remnants of her once proud Nationalism. She was Nationalist Ulster at the end of the eighteenth century; she was Unionist Ulster by the end of the nineteenth. That is one of the tragedies of Irish history.[65]

He recognises Protestants' fear of loss of self-government and of the 'reign of a new sort of ascendancy' – Catholic in religion – which might ruin them either by vindictiveness or incompetence and also the difficulty of overcoming such apprehensions by reason. At the same time, he argues that the Ulster Protestant voice would be both louder and more influential in an Irish parliament than it could ever be in Westminster and maintains that the history of reforms gained by the Nationalists in the previous half-century shows them to have been equally beneficial to Protestant interests:

> . . . the demand of Unionist Ulster is not a demand for freedom; it is
> a demand for the right to keep Ireland in subjection – or at least for
> the continuance of a state of affairs which involves the subjection of
> Ireland. It is a demand begotten of sectarian fears, of ignorance of Irish
> history and ignorance of the world's history. Unionist Ulster has never
> affirmed a single positive ideal. She has simply repeated 'No!' a
> thousand times in a hundred thousand voices.[66]

Thus Edward Carson, the hero of Ulster Unionsim, becomes Lynd's
arch-villain and wrecker, worthy of comparison with the Kaiser and
guilty of 'collusion with British statesmen' who have repeatedly
temporised in their handling of Protestant resistance to Irish Home
Rule because it has provided them 'with a plausible palliation for
their guilt in denying freedom to a race of white men'.[67]

Writing ahead of partition, Lynd was convinced that whereas
Ulster had a vital part to play in the development of Ireland as a
whole, its potential would never be realised as a separate entity. He
announced prophetically: 'Outside Ireland she would merely be a
backward and outlying province of Great Britain, with all her best
sons emigrating to some better soil'.[68] The anti-Home Rule movement,
orchestrated and manipulated by English politicians, he believed, was
deluding Ulster Protestants into abandoning their radical integrity
and sense of justice for a mistaken notion of self-interest based on
fear and the capitulation of reason and obscured by rhetorical pronouncements of freedom, defence of their faith and loyalty to the
monarch. Lynd contrasts this lamentable corruption of memory with
what he calls 'the statement of a deeper Ulster mood' which he
illustrates through the words of an elderly Presbyterian minister.
Speaking the day after an Orange rally in Kilkeel at which a young
clergyman had made an inflammatory anti-Catholic and anti-Home
Rule declaration, the older man took up the political issue of the
moment, voicing his own belief that Home Rule might indeed mean
Rome rule and encouraging prayer to avert this calamity:

> 'And if', he concluded . . . 'God sees good to answer our prayer, He
> will drive these clouds away, and if in His providence He should allow
> the changes we dread to come to pass, then we may be sure that it is
> His purpose to make them the means of some great blessing to His
> people of which we do not know.'[69]

This courage rooted in faith exemplified for Lynd what is truest and
most admirable in the Ulster Protestant character and values and is

what he wanted to see recovered. The episode itself shows precisely how Lynd 'had great love for the Ulster unionists whom he knew through and through, but felt great sadness at their rejection of nationhood . . . '.[70]

George Birmingham also faced the same dilemma. Writing shortly before partition he was equally persuaded of the illogicality of any division which would inevitably result in the abandonment of a nationalist minority in the north and of a Protestant minority in the south. However Birmingham sensed a streak of ruthlessness in the Belfast Protestants that was not matched by southern nationalists and which he correctly saw would lead to Unionists elsewhere in Ireland being left to their fate – 'a fate so evil, according to her [i.e. Belfast Protestant] belief, as to be intolerable'.[71] Like Lynd, Birmingham deplored the process whereby, as he saw it, narrow self-interest and lack of faith had been transmuted into claims of courage, fidelity and moral rectitude.

Thomas Carnduff, too, felt that Protestant radicalism failed to seize an opportunity in the early years of the century. As a young man he was recruited into the Independent Orange Order founded by Lindsay Crawford and Tom Sloan. Following the latter's victory as an independent against a Unionist candidate in the South Belfast by-election of 1902, Sloan had been suspended from the Orange Order, but the new organisation set up after this, with a strong working-class membership and a sympathetic attitude towards the labour movement, soon had twenty-five lodges. Carnduff describes his fellow members in the Sandy Row True Blues, Independent Loyal Orange Lodge No 5, as mostly artisans, 'intelligent and reasonable in discussion but fiercely partisan in the Protestant cause'. However, he also claims that 'A national spirit was creeping into Ulster politics at this time and . . . many of the Orangemen [were] intensely Irish in their outlook'.[72] This development found its fullest expression in the Magheramore Manifesto, launched by the Independent Orange Order on 13 July 1905 and dedicated 'to all Irishmen whose country stands first in their affections'. Carnduff is justified in pointing out the radical nature of this document which condemned 'castle government', called for a full democracy, dismissed Unionism as 'a discredited creed' and decried exploitation of the Irish question by both English political parties. Furthermore, the Manifesto lamented the alienated relationship between Irish Protestants and Catholics, called for unity 'on a true basis of Nationality', and declared that 'The man who cannot rise above the trammels of party and of sect on a national issue is a foe to Nationality and human freedom'.[73]

The document blamed Irishmen themselves for failing 'to think nationally' and for invoking 'with disastrous results, the intervention of external influences' since the Act of Union. It predicted a future

> . . . when thoughtful men on both sides will come to realise that the Irish question is not made up of Union or Repeal; that not in acts of parliament nor in their repeal lies the hope and salvation of the country, so much as in the mutual inclination of Irish hearts and minds along the common plane of Nationality – a Nationality that binds the people together in the school, in the workshop, and in the Senate in the promotion of what has long since been neglected, the material interests of our native land, and the increased wealth and happiness of her people.[74]

Ironically, as Carnduff shows, the very radicalism of the Manifesto led to an old Protestant problem. It split the Independent Orange Order, led some members to resign and attracted much public criticism so that by 1910 it was a spent political force. Looking back at these events, Carnduff likened the Independents to the Irish Volunteers of 1782 and regarded their demise as a regrettable setback to the process of broadening 'the national and religious conscience of Ireland.' He attributed their failure to the subservience of what he called 'the cultural classes' to 'the political caucus who ruled Ulster', and who manipulated prejudice and division to preserve their own power and interests – an analysis which corresponds closely with Lynd's view of events during the Home Rule dispute.[75]

Betrayed radicalism also reappears as one of Denis Ireland's most heartfelt claims and he denotes as 'the hall-mark of Ulster Unionism and Liberalism . . . the attempt to think in English terms on Irish soil' – a project doomed to failure in the long run and obstructive to the process of Irish evolution as a whole.[76] Unlike Carnduff, Ireland is contemptuous of the Orange Order – 'excellent as historical pageantry, but religiously inept – in fact, the negation of true Protestantism' – and of the insecure, distrustful mentality it represents.[77] Likewise:

> . . . the erection of a Protestant (or rather of a Presbyterian) Pale in Northern Ireland may be recognised at once for what it was – an unwise, if not a fatal, move for Irish Protestantism.[78]

This is because it involved 'an abandonment of that true Protestantism of the mind and heart which cannot be confined by fences and is incapable of defence by drums and banners'.[79] The consequences of such introversion are not only religious and political, but also cultural, and Ireland claims to see no literature flourishing within the Unionist tradition. For 'the cultured Protestant Ulsterman with a literary bent' the alternatives are to go to London and seek assimilation there, or to stay at home and adopt a nationalist perspective.[80]

The capitulation of Protestant radicalism seemed to him so complete that Ireland was forced to question whether the eighteenth-century tradition of dissent is any more than a myth and he urged the rising generation to explore and recover it. Continuing in this vein elsewhere, he wrote:

> . . . it is the Ulster Presbyterian who is the real juggler with meta-physical subtleties, the dreamer, and the *potential* liberator of Irish art and literature – potentially, that is, when he has abandoned, as some day he must abandon, his present attitude of life-wasting negation.[81]

However, Denis Ireland lived long enough to see the renewed violence in the late 60s and early 70s, and in *From the Jungle of Belfast* he meditated on the failure of Protestant families like his own to rise above the selfish interests of short-term prosperity and, in effect, to adopt his own post-colonial priorities. Here he juxtaposes thoughts of his newly married parents riding to a ball at Edenderry House on the outskirts of Belfast in Victorian times and contemporary news of the discovery of a hooded man's bullet-ridden body in the lane down which they must have passed in their carriage. He contrasts the confidence of the industrialists of his father's generation, building their mills and warehouses, identifying themselves with the manufacturers of Bradford, Leeds and Manchester and never considering the connection between their lives and 'the buried civilization left after Kinsale', with modern Belfast's bomb-damaged buildings which incude his father's old business premises. He finds in this suggestive landscape 'a memento mori' for their way of life and wryly concludes that 'One factor the Belfast Victorians had omitted from their double-entry book-keeping was the title-deeds of the field in which they were so confidently building'.[82]

Whereas in his earlier writing Ireland's anger and dismay at partition and his disappointment at the lack of courage and generosity of his co-religionists are offset by his conviction that another generation might still recover the lost Protestant radicalism, this late work reveals no such optimism. Returning again to a Presbyterian church overlooking Strangford Lough, which is normally kept locked against 'them', he concludes that

Now from the recesses of the once brilliant Ulster Protestant mind nothing emerges but an empty clanging of gates against ghosts that no longer exist. The Ulster Protestant power to floodlight a political scene by clarity of thought – the power that helped to found those United States of America – has now been paralysed by sheer negation, by a refusal to face the founding of the united states of Ireland.[83]

This predicament is attributed directly to the failure to make the change from seventeenth to twentieth-century terms of thought, to set aside arguments that are no longer relevant and to rediscover means of protest against erosions of individual liberty in forms that relate to modern, secularised life.

As we have seen, Ireland specifically equates the contraction of dissenting Protestantism into Protestant Unionism with the replacement of a radical, challenging cast of mind by timidity and self-defensiveness. The obverse of sturdy individualism and belief in private judgement turns out to be narrowminded self-righteousness and censoriousness and the outcome of this for creative thought and endeavour can be debilitating. His recognition of the significance of this shift for literary artists has been shared by some of the writers whose autobiographical work has already been discussed. Forrest Reid is perhaps the most striking example. His fiction is resolutely dissenting in the author's rejection of what he regarded as the ugly commercialism, materialism and austere religiosity of Protestant Ulster, as well as in his idealisation of homosexual or paedophiliac relationships over heterosexuality and in the value he places upon individual thought and sensibility. Ironically, however, this does not liberate him, because Reid's novels endlessly pursue a regressive, nostalgic state of permanent boyhood in pastoral surroundings. He fantasises on the possibilities of an idyllic male friendship of the kind which eluded him in his relationships with adults and boys where, paradoxically, he appears to have craved the unflinching loyalty of his companions despite his personal hostility to the authoritarian aspects of his own upbringing.[84]

In his essay, 'On Writing Autobiography', Wallace Fowlie remarks that 'the use of memory, indispensable to autobiography, is a recycling of memories, both conscious and subconscious aspects of living, by means of which a life story may be transformed into a personal myth.'[85] In Reid's case, this description is applicable not only to his autobiographies, and especially to *Apostate*, but also to his novels which are ultimately disconcerting in their protracted erotic self-indulgence and 'disquieting unawareness of external reality'.[86] In fact, the ahistoricism of Reid's fiction is futher evidence that his dissent led him into escapism rather than freeing him to confront and critique the upheavals and divisions which occurred in Ireland during his lifetime. Eamonn Hughes has shrewdly linked this absence of any historical sense in Reid's work with his desire to avoid the instabilities and betrayals of Irish politics in much the same way as he aspires to wish away the insecurities of personal relationships.[87] In the end, therefore, he is a writer of limited resource. While ostensibly reacting against the values and attitudes of his society, he wilfully ignored its history and remained obsessively fixated with an enclosed vision of his own which is bounded by the onset of adolescence.

John Boyd is another example of a writer who felt estranged both from the Protestantism of his background and its materialistic values and also from the politics of Unionism and Nationalism. Unlike Reid, however, Boyd did not turn his back on politics and history. (Indeed, he provides an amusing account of his own vain attempt in later years to arouse Reid's interest in the political process.[88]) He opted for socialism, regarding it as the only credible way of overcoming barriers of religion, prejudice and fear and of enabling society to develop. While sharing Ireland's opinion that many artists and writers have found it necessary to flee the 'dangerous and explosive city' of Belfast, Boyd maintains that he himself 'found it no hardship to stay'.[89] Perhaps because he has never had any strong personal investment in Protestantism or the organisations and politics associated with it, Boyd has shown even-handed detachment from the contesting factions in his plays, although works such as *The Farm, Facing North* and *The Guests* pay particular attention to the dilemmas of Protestants in a changing and insecure political and social situation. Like Thomas Carnduff, Boyd admits to a strong sense of belonging in Belfast despite his distance from the beliefs of many of his fellow citizens, and again like him, is untroubled by doubts about his right to be there. Rather than agonising over the historical grounds of division in the community, Boyd preferred to write a play (*The Street*) based upon a period in 1932 when working-class Protestants and Catholics set aside their differences and united to resist common poverty and unemployment. In looking to the potential of a moment of this kind, and realising the tragedy of its brevity, Boyd may again be likened to Carnduff who, for all his Orange sympathies, also understood the non-denominational interests of working people against those in control of economic and political power.

Suspicion of the motives of those in authority is again apparent in the work of George Birmingham who, like the essayists Robert Lynd and Denis Ireland, was an advocate of Irish Home Rule. His autobiographies make it plain that he had few illusions about the way economic self-interest was likely to sway contemporary Ulster Protestants, while his novel of 1912, *The Red Hand of Ulster*, not only anticipated events such as the Larne gun-running, but also foresaw England's underestimation of Protestant militancy and unwillingness to confront it. The story concludes with the creation of an independent Ulster – what Lord Kilmore, the narrator, describes as 'Home Rule of the most extreme kind' – while the reader is left to contemplate the paradox whereby professed loyalty to the crown is affirmed by rebellion against it.[90] It is, as Tom Paulin has noted, 'an ironic and sympathetically intelligent account of Ulster politics which is still relevant today'. This is precisely because it grasps the dynamics of a situation in which the economic opportunism of a minority, disguised as principled conduct and sealed with pieties about the defence of Protestantism, proves capable of mobilising formidable numbers who are swayed by a rhetoric of fear and abandon individual judgement.[91] Furthermore, the book shows Birmingham's understanding of the Ulster Protestant notion of contractual loyalty and also the practical impossibility of declaring faith in the monarch while simultaneously acting violently against that same king's government.

Earlier, Birmingham had written a novel, *The Northern Iron* (1907), set in the period around 1798, where he had shown the character of radical, rebellious Protestantism before its later capitulation to economic expediency and sectarianism. In it, the Presbyterian minister, Micah Ward, whose first name immediately conjures up one of the sternest Old Testament critics of religious and social corruption, is first seen studying the book of Amos, 'the ruggedest, the fiercest, and the most democratic of the Hebrew prophets'.[92] As an organiser of the United Irishmen, he endorses the idea of an Irish nation in which people of differing religious persuasions work for the country's common good. He deplores the injustices done to both Presbyterians and Catholics and the powers and privileges arrogated by aristocratic landlords like Lord Dunseveric and he cites the defiant text from Jeremiah which gives the novel its title.[93] Significantly, too, Micah's brother, Donald, lately returned from participation in the American War of Independence, proudly boasts the exemplary role of Irishmen – and especially of Ulster Presbyterians – in that liberation struggle.

Perhaps most telling of all, Birmingham introduces the '98 leader, James Hope, as the clearest voice of idealism in the novel and also the prophet of the fate that awaits Ireland if it fails to secure its rightful independence. Hope decries the thought that 'the pursuit of riches' and 'the clink of gold and silver' may have distracted Irishmen from the desire to win liberty and justice. He denounces the betrayal of the people by self-interested landlords, merchants and manufacturers, predicting their inevitable ruin:

> They forget that there is a power greater than theirs – that England is certainly on the watch to win back again her sovereignty over Ireland. Our upper class and our middle class are too jealous of their privileges to share them with us. They will give England the opportunity she wants. Then Ireland will be brought into the old subjection, and her advance towards prosperity will be checked again as it was checked before. She will become a country of haughty squireens – the most contemptible class of all, men of blackened honour and broken faith, men proud, but with nothing to be proud of – and of ruined traders; a land of ill-cultivated fields and ruined mills; a nation crushed by her conqueror.[94]

Hope justifies rebellion as a necessity – the only way of redressing a state he describes as the enslavement of nine-tenths of the people by one tenth of them – and as an obligation substantiated by biblical injunction. The rebel force in Antrim is seen as a momentary embodiment of Tone's ideal of Irishmen of all sorts united in a common cause, but the romantic adventures and escapes of the hero, Neal Ward, cannot disguise the defeat of Hope's men and the failure of his dream. That failure is also reflected in the very different circumstances and motives behind the rebellion envisaged in *The Red Hand of Ulster*, and in Birmingham's thoughts on Irish Protestantism and on the course of events in Ulster recorded in his autobiographies.

Whereas Forrest Reid and John Boyd felt alienated both from the doctrines of Protestantism and the cultural values and codes of conduct it encouraged in Ulster, Birmingham's view as a clergyman was inevitably different. Yet despite their diverse attitudes and beliefs, the work of each of these writers testifies to the compelling power of Protestant influences upon them. According to Paul John Eakin, 'We are willy-nilly the creatures of our culture, marked by its paradigms even in the unfolding of our self-consciousness'.[95] The truth of this is borne out in the autobiographies and autobiographically based work not only of Birmingham, Reid and Boyd, but of all the writers considered here. A key issue for each one was his experience of a form of religion which is deeply embedded in the community, which has often made a point of defining itself by its difference from and incompatibility with the other major churches in the country and of voicing distrust of its priests and members, and which has actively discouraged relationships of any sort between the denominations. This Church claimed on the one hand to be the guarantor of liberty of conscience and respect for the individual, yet in practice often seemed to be the active agent of oppressive judgementalism and narrow respectability. The close equation between Protestant materialism and economic power on the one hand and the politics of partition on the other further complicated the matter and was a particular focus for the dismay of writers like Lynd, Ireland, Carnduff and Birmingham who felt most strongly the loss of radicalism associated with earlier dissenters and its replacement by short-term, sectarian self-interest. Protestant materialism also attracted the notice of those with less overt political views like Reid, Greacen and Harbinson, often leading them to polemicise it or question its moral credibility. Whatever the reactions of individual writers to this background, they share a common awareness of it as an unavoidable influence and crucial determinant not only of religious, but of social, economic and political priorities and judgements and, inevitably, of the products of the creative imagination.

CHAPTER FIVE

W.R. Rodgers and the Gift of Tongues

Is there a fundamental conflict between the 'Protestant'
(Calvinist) moral and spiritual code and the poet's ordering
of reality into a form of art? Is it possible for a rejected
religious background to intervene so persistently in the very
make-up of a writer's vision as to inherently determine it?
What chance has the imagination?

Gerald Dawe, 'Law and Grace:
The Poetry of Iain Crichton Smith' in
False Faces: Poetry, Politics and Place.

My friend, who followed coursing on this ground,
and sought its lore and logic everywhere,
suggested once, the Hare must need the Hound
as surely as the Hound must need the Hare.

John Hewitt, from 'The Iron Circle' in
Collected Poems.

THE LIFE AND WORK OF W.R. Rodgers exemplify in a very particular way the dilemma produced by the convergence of Calvinistic and evangelical influences and a creative imagination. He was born into a lower middle-class Belfast family where life was shaped by austere Presbyterianism and an overriding concern to maintain respectability. Rodgers had little access to the world of literature beyond the Bible and less encouragement to waste his time in idleness or the pursuit of worldly pleasures which would distract him from the serious matter of acknowledging his own frailty and seeking salvation. 'Belfast mothers knew what was good for you, and they gave you the compulsory choice of heaven', he later wrote.[1] As an adult looking back on his boyhood, he evokes his early sense of the tensions and contradictions in the daily life of his native city and their origins in religion:

Life in Belfast was an affair of extremes: we were citizens of no mean city . . . Religion was everywhere. Even the houses in Belfast had it . . . 'Christian Bungalow for Sale'. . . . Strange puritan city of pubs and tabernacles. God-fearing, and devil-may-caring.[2]

And in his radio play, *The Return Room*, the writer juxtaposes sounds and memories associated with his Edwardian youth in ways that dramatise their contrasts and evoke the dominant characteristics of his background. These include his father's voice reading the Bible and the skipping songs of the children; the moralising sanctimoniousness and respectability of his mother and her neighbour, Mrs Bittercup, and the voices of barefooted children from the back streets; gospel songs about the saving power of the Blood of the Lamb and the sight of a pig butcher drinking the blood of a newly slaughtered animal; the beauty of summer in the country interrupted by a summons to attend a mission; the oppressive religiosity of Sundays and the devotion to work and money-making on the other days of the week; and the difference between Catholics and Protestants. Finally, always and everywhere, there was a sense of the reality of sin and of the imminence of death and judgement which broke in on every situation. At each stage in the play, life is poised between opposites: between the demands of a forbidding religion and instinctual joy and sensual delight; between the narrowness of 'good living', and spontaneous behaviour; between the inhibitions of custom and conditioning and the exhibitionist flamboyance of words and imagination. The play's narrator sums up his feelings thus:

> . . . I, Thomas John Todd,
> Made in the image of God
>
> . . .
>
> Was tied to the tail of the blue and orange cart
> Of history, articled to etiquette;
> One part of me, the innumerable boy,
> Tethered to a Christian name and hope,
> While all the lucky ones went dancing off
> Scott-free behind the bushes.[3]

The paradox of an 'innumerable boy' who is simultaneously 'tethered' points to the tension within the poet's own life which finds repeated expression in his exploration of oppositions, and which is the focus of this discussion of his writing.

The elements of self-conflict were, perhaps, already present in two early decisions which Rodgers made. First, his choice of an undergraduate course in English, which might seem somewhat surprising given the unsympathetic attitude to the arts in his home, reveals an interest in the life of the imagination. However, his subsequent entry into the Presbyterian Theological College and ordination as a minister, which again contains an element of the unexpected in that Rodgers had not shown evidence of a vocation beforehand, appear to confirm his commitment to a life of principled obedience and service within a Church that was known for its illiberalism of thought and distrust of the freedoms taken by the imagination.[4] Whether Rodgers initially realised a tension between the 'romantic' and 'Calvinistic' aspects of his character, or if he did, whether he believed it could be resolved in some way, it is difficult to know. What is clear, is that during his ministry at Cloveneden Church, Loughgall he found his position increasingly difficult to occupy.[5] Again, the degree to which the disintegration of his marriage on the one hand and the discovery of his alternative vocation – as a poet – on the other were symptoms or causes in heightening the tensions in Rodgers's life, and in his recognition of them, is problematic. However, a sense of turbulence and urgency plainly lies behind the composition of even his early poems in which Terence Brown detects 'a sensibility under pressure, existing in aesthetic isolation'.[6]

Rodgers's isolation may have been aesthetic, but that is not the whole story. His position as a young minister in a rural community was in itself both burdensome and isolating, conferring upon him the respect and expectations that belonged to his office in the eyes of his parishioners, many of whom were much older than him, but also setting him apart from them. In effect, the minister does not seem to have found any particular support from his congregation as he wrestled with his own vocational and domestic difficulties.[7] The preacher at his ordination service in 1935, Revd R.G. Fry of Ahorey, surely spoke better than he knew when he told the congregation:

> You may take it that your minister, like every other minister, will be 'a man of sorrows and acquainted with grief'. He can only teach you what he has learned himself, and if on any Sabbath Day . . . he seems to speak with unusual power, be sure that he paid a great price for that freedom.[8]

It is instructive to set alongside these words an observation made by John Boyd years later, after Rodgers had left his ministry. Recounting a visit they made to the Presbyterian church in Randalstown, where

Rodgers mounted the pulpit and began to address his 'congregation' of one, Boyd comments:

> Bertie looked to me what at heart he was, a clergyman whose vocation gave him an enormous sense of purpose;

but despite his apparent peacefulness at that moment, Boyd describes him as 'a tortured and guilt-ridden man for most of his adult life.'[9]

There are residual signs of Rodgers's desire to preach in poems where he employs allegorical figures or types such as 'Contempt the caretaker', 'Humbug', or 'the lion, Lust', but more interesting and complex are the ways in which he responds to the power not of the Word, but of language itself.[10] In 'Words', the poem 'arrives' after a kind of pentecostal irruption, storming the poet like a force of nature over which he exercises no control. The words are invasive, irresistible and of no known origin:

> Rebutted and rebounding, on they post
> Past my remembrance, falling all unplanned

– and the poet perceives his own role as a cross between a mediator who somehow harnesses them into form and a bewildered medium possessed by a power that is using him:

> But some day out of darkness they'll come forth,
> Arrowed and narrowed into my tongue's tip,
> And speak for me – their most astonished host.[11]

This view of poetry equates it more closely with the glossolalia associated with certain forms of evangelicalism than with the formality of most Presbyterian preaching. The same point might be made about the endless punning, coining of words, playing with irregular sounds and combining of terms which characterise much of Rodgers's writing, at times to the exasperation of his readers.[12]

In a broadcast later published as an essay, Rodgers attempted to explain the process of composition as he knew it, and although he carefully sidesteps the term 'divine inspiration' suggested by a member of the audience he was addressing, he is willing to speak of 'divination' and 'divining', likening the art of the poet to that of the water dowser who locates hidden springs. He also carefully holds on to the notion that the poet is not entirely in charge of events, declaring that

It's almost as if the poem that is going to be written is already in existence, full-blown, somewhere in the back-end of the world. As if it were some sort of Sleeping Beauty that has only to be reached and set free.

And he moves close to the idea of poetry as inspired religious utterance when he adds:

The shadow, the unwanted word that makes its way in, uninvited, on the tail of another word – why, every poem is full of these uninvited guests. And thank God, too, because they are the divine visitors, and in entertaining them we entertain angels unawares.[13]

No doubt Rodgers owes a debt to romanticism in these formulations – one thinks of Byron's 'lava of the emotions' and of Coleridge's aeolian harp across which the wind blows to release sounds – but there is also the Calvinistic notion of the chosen or elected individual, the recipient of special, unmerited favour.[14]

At intervals throughout his writing, Rodgers returns to the power, potential and character of words themselves. So, in 'The Lovers':

One word, flung in centre like single stone,
Starred and cracked the ice of her resentment
To its edge.

The result of this is to release emotion – here 'eager and extravagant anger'.[15] But in a second poem with the title 'Words', the poet regrets the loss of the former emotional power and spontaneity of language which he equates with its integrity, seeming to prefer non-intellectual, even non-rational formations to the manipulated and calculated idioms of such professional users of words as the Demagogue, Orator or Preacher. His longing is for:

. . . a world where words would always be
The windows of feeling (and not mere blinds),
Revealing and relieving living needs.[16]

Not only has 'the Word' given way to 'words', but the poet laments the corruption that has befallen them, turning them into agents of deception rather than vehicles of truth and discovery. The sense of opposition between words and meanings which Rodgers identifies here is one of a number of divisions and oppositions operative in his poetry.

But if the 'Words' poem cited above is unable to go further than wishing for a world of verbal integrity, in 'Europa and the Bull', there is greater faith in the reconciling power of language when, as the action of the poem moves to its climax, we read:

> O what wonders can happen in woods
> Or in words, what two may touch, what gloom
> Can ignite, halves hyphenate; what dead ends
> And ands join answering hands.[17]

Belief in the power of words to transform a life, or bring a person to a turning point, as well as in the authority of the Word itself, validates the very notion of a preaching ministry. Here Rodgers seizes on the capacity of words not to bring an individual to salvation, but to resolve contradictions, bridge divisions, convert states into their opposites.

The creative power of language is at issue again in 'A Last Word', a late poem written in memory of Rodgers's friend, Louis MacNeice, which, unlike the hyperbolic, pagan 'Europa and the Bull', is quiet, succinct and resonant with Christian religious associations. From the opening reference to 'a green hill' which might recall the first line of a well-known hymn by Mrs Alexander, the wife of a Church of Ireland bishop, Rodgers proceeds to engage with the opposition between life and death and the means by which extinction may be transcended. He juxtaposes life and death in an unexpected way through the use of a cliché which in this context is reinvigorated by wit that helps to blur the distinctions between them:

> It is all,
> You might say, so dead true
>
> To life . . .

Likewise, the fundamental connection between man and clay is presented teasingly through allusive modifications to scripture. Christ's teachings on forgiveness and on how the meek shall inherit the earth are applied to the 'meek clay' which 'turns the other cheek' to receive 'the earth of the man/ Whom it has made', and these last phrases echo both the account of the creation of man in Genesis and words from the Christian burial service.

But the final stanza involves an even more crucial twist of meaning which opens up the poem as a whole:

But he made it
That made him,
He put the word on it that gave
Life and limb.
Now to speak of an end
Is to begin.[18]

Despite man's origins in clay and inevitable return to it, the artist, like Adam himself, has the power to name – to 'put the word on it' – which gives him an authority and control over life and experience, and even over death itself, so that what might seem like an ending becomes, paradoxically, a beginning. Thus, the poem is not only 'A Last Word' in honour of the dead MacNeice, but argues that he himself had *the* last word. Here one sees how for Rodgers the poet possesses the power not merely to mediate experience, but to outlast time and mortality by his use of the word which thereby acquires the kind of abiding value traditionally associated with the Word of scripture. While this is no orthodox Christian poem, it is essentially Protestant in the role it ascribes to the poet and in its acknowledgement of the potency of the word itself.

Yet, however affirmative the view of 'A Last Word', elsewhere Rodgers questions the relationship between Protestants and their language, particularly as a vehicle for conveying emotion. In his 'Epilogue' to the ill-fated book that he and MacNeice never did edit, *The Character of Ireland*, he chooses to focus on Ulster speech with its 'spiky consonants', aggressive tone, and distrust of

. . . the round gift of the gab in Southern mouths.
Mine were not born with silver spoon in gob,
Nor would they thank you for the gift of tongues;
The dry riposte, the bitter repartee's
The Northman's bite and portion, his deep sup
Is silence; though, still within his shell,
He holds the old sea-roar and surge
Of rhetoric and Holy Writ.[19]

Here, the blunt, extensively monosyllabic and forceful vocabulary not only reinforces the sense, but in some measure reproduces characteristic qualities and sounds of the speech it evokes. In this way, the lines complement an unsigned article which Rodgers wrote for *The Bell* in 1942 in which he again set out to describe the distinctive temperament of Ulster Protestants. There he compares the supposed facility of the Catholic to express himself feelingly and responsively to his hearer with the restricted code of his Protestant counterpart, which he diagnoses thus:

> The Protestant Ulsterman has halts and suppressions of feeling in his speech, is slow to communicate, reserved, self-conscious, inarticulate, and therefore makes his connections with other people through logic rather than emotion . . . For the Northern Protestant's feelings are deep because they are not extensive and have not been dissipated in words. He would *like* to have eloquence. But he suspects and hates eloquence that has no bone of logic in it. It seems to him glib, spineless and insincere. It freezes him into silence.[20]

Peter McDonald has rightly commented on both the degree to which Rodgers's analysis of Ulster speech, whether in his verse or his prose, indulges in stereotyping and also how his own effusiveness is at odds with the picture of Protestant linguistic embarassment which he has drawn.[21] Yet there is another point to be made. Both the poem and the prose passage hint at repression of emotional and rhetorical tendencies in Ulster Protestants, rather than denying their existence, and in his article Rodgers goes on to declare that the Protestant has 'a self-consciousness' that is not found among Catholics and an '*inner opposition*' or private conflict which 'forces self-awareness on him'.[22] The general merits of this opinion may be debatable, but it suggests something about the particular situation of a poet who had to learn how to negotiate experiences which his background and training did not easily equip him to articulate, and some of which were complicated by feelings of guilt, fear and uncertainty. That Rodgers found himself caught in a private conflict, and that this was in part a conflict between repressive influences and deeply felt emotional needs, there can be no doubt, as a substantial number of his poems make very clear.

The dynamics of this conflict are metaphorically expressed in 'Beagles', where the image of the hunt and of the necessary relationship between the dogs that chase and the hare that is pursued are convincingly evoked. However, it is in the conclusion of the poem, where the poet implicates himself with the hunted animal, that the full significance of the image unfolds:

> From the far flat scene each shout
> Like jig-saw piece came tumbling out,
> I took and put them all together,
> And then they turned into a tether.

A tether that held me to the hare
Here, there, and everywhere.[23]

D'Arcy O'Brien records that Rodgers, commenting on his fascination with the hunt, said:

> My heart was with the hare, quick and elusive, and yet the loud spectacle of the running hounds wakened some old complicity of the blood.[24]

Here again is an indication of the poet's own conflict and his sense of the oppositions and tensions in life from which there is no final escape, but which must be outrun and eluded for as long as possible by the exercise of energy and cunning. John Hewitt recognised the particular relevance of this image to Rodgers, using it not only in 'The Iron Circle' (quoted at the head of this chapter), but also in his memorial poem, 'W.R. Rodgers (1909–1969)':

> Within that kind, exasperating man,
> devious and gentle, there were grappled fast
> the same tense opposites. He was my friend,
> and through his talk, for thirty years, there ran
> a theme – the Hare – which seemed to have no end:
> now that wild creature is run down at last.[25]

Yet, however inevitable the outcome of the chase, 'Beagles' does not succumb to negative feelings. The emphasis is on the continuing action and on the poet's engagement in it, rather than on destruction or despair.

The same cannot be said for 'The Interned Refugee' which conveys an unrelieved sense of entrapment and victimisation, or of being surrounded and observed without being able to see in a kind of Calvinist nightmare. In another early poem, 'Escape', the prospect of immersion in the chaotic activity of war ('. . . the thoughtless centre of slaughter . . .') is seen as affording greater freedom than 'Standing chained to the telephone-end while the world cracks'.[26] Unresolved personal conflicts also lie behind the ironically titled 'Paired Lives' and 'Life's Circumnavigators', which is essentially a death-wish poem, longing only for an end to the tensions which energised 'Beagles'.[27] Even in poems which ostensibly focus on subjects removed from personal conflicts, experience quickly loses any harmony or equilibrium it may temporarily possess. Thus, the happy flamboyance of 'Stormy Day' gives way to bleak reminders of war and the momentary relaxation in the scenic delights of 'An Irish Lake' yield to a sense of surrounding menace and the poet's 'so-frightened thoughts'.[28] This whole dilemma is summed up in some lines from 'Summer Holidays' which reject the Calvinistic notion of predestination for a view of life which is much less rigid and more prone to chaos:

> . . . not by gradual stealthy steps do we
> Move onwards to a plotted destiny,
> But between antinomies we are stretched
> And pent, and catapulted to new ends
> And angry issues.[29]

The extent to which Rodgers's inner conflict was shaped by doubts about his Presbyterian theology and his position as a minister may be hinted at in 'Summer Holidays', but is much more explicit in 'To the Preacher', which challenges the simplistic dualism that sees the world in terms of readily identifiable and separable 'Good and Ill', and suggests instead that this is an unsustainable self-deception which God himself destabilises by sending 'Bother'.[30] Even more telling, however, is a series of remarkable poems which are at the heart of Rodgers's second collection, *Europa and the Bull*, in which, having left the church, he sets about reinterpreting and subverting major elements in the Christian story. Furthermore, in doing so, he appears bent upon looking for ways of coming to terms with or reconciling the 'antinomies' he had encountered in his own faith.

This new complexity is evident in 'The Fall' which shows a great advance from the earlier 'To the Preacher'.[31] The title invites reference to the Genesis story of Adam and Eve, but the poem also embraces the New Testament account of temptation resisted by Christ who did not fall. Whereas the conventional Christian prayer is for deliverance from temptation and sin, this poem, which opens like a prayer by invoking the 'angel of the ledges of our dread', asks for the courage to fall. Falling becomes the act of faith that is refused by the fears of those who will not let go of 'that safe tree/Of love' in order to fall into deeper knowledge. Paradoxically, just as falling through the air is the prologue to a bird's flight, so falling in faith launches the individual into freedom and discovery. As the poem puts it in its most crucial sentences:

> . . . Only
> By daring do we learn our manyness.
> Safety stints us, turns us to stone, to one.

Such faith exists 'always-gibbering between fear and hope', but it also

> Doubles our life, and is the bloody pulse
> Of every vein.

Stones are thus associated with the petrifaction produced by timidity and a reluctance to take risks. However, the final invocation of the poem recalls not only Christ's refusal to turn stones into bread, but also his observation that no man would give his son a stone if he had asked for bread, which indicates how much greater again is the compassion of God, as well as, of course, closely echoing a phrase from the Lord's Prayer:

> . . . O angel of our dread,
> Delicately cater for us rough feeders
> Who ask a stone; and duly give us bread.

This becomes a prayer for deliverance from immobilising fear which feeds on itself and for the grace of the life-giving bread of trust which will nerve us to fall in faith.

Perhaps an even more surprising subversion is found in 'The Trinity' where the Christian concepts of Father, Son and Holy Spirit are replaced by pain/guilt, thought/consciousness, and the poet himself who is crucified between them as Christ was between the two thieves.[32] The poem is an interior drama reminiscent of some of Donne's writing (indeed, the pun on the words 'the Sun, the Sun' recall Donne's play upon his own name in 'A Hymne to God the Father'). Cat and mouse replace hound and hare in an enactment of the poet's sense of competing antinomies behind which lurk the repressed guilts or anxieties represented by the 'thousand sleepers' that awaken. Having articulated the crucifixion he is undergoing, the poem again turns into a personal prayer to God for grace, which, in this case, will mean a reconciliation of the opposing forces:

> Make these two malefactors one
> Within this I
> That soon must die,
> And then will rise the Sun, the Sun,
> The trinity, the three-in-one.

Wholeness, it seems, will be achieved through the assimilation of thought and guilt, not by trying to exclude them, and will lead to a new beginning which punningly conjoins the promise and warmth of a new day and – by virtue of the sound, the use of the capital 'S' and the context – the resurrection of Christ. The Protestant origins of this highly unorthodox poem are most obviously apparent in the directness with which the poet addresses God and equates his own predicament with that of the crucified Christ. It also reveals a preoccupation which is given fuller attention in other poems – Rodgers's deep sense of Christ's humanity. Thus, not only was it

> God who did send this I to cry
> Between two selves on Calvary,

but God himself has been 'torn' there by 'two thieving moods' – the faith and despair between which Christ hangs for a time equivocally poised. This justifies what otherwise might seem a presumptuous identification by laying particular emphasis on the human solidarity between Christ and humankind.

The idea that Christ is, as it were, within the individual is evident in a poem which boldly takes the same title as a better known work by T.S. Eliot, 'The Journey of the Magi'. Eliot's poem opens with a quotation from one of Lancelot Andrewes' Christmas Day sermons reflecting on the hardships faced by the travellers from afar, but develops thereafter to serve its own purposes. Likewise, while Rodgers's poem recalls Eliot's in that it involves a lengthy journey made by men who are uncertain about what they are doing, but who want a birth (and also, perhaps, alludes more loosely to Andrewes' sermon by referring at the outset to harsh weather conditions), in most other ways it is significantly different. It concerns an 'annual journey', 'a risk', which depends upon an inclusive approach to experience, a readiness to find truth anywhere and a rejection of narrow-mindedness:

> – Things never happen how and when they should . . .
> . . .
>   The guide-book's Star
> Has small relation to things as they are.
> . . .
> God can be sought for in a golden rain
> Of levity and fireworks; piety's not pain.
> . . .
> In passing, one may duly note
> That reverence need not choke the throat
> Or dull the cheek.[33]

Such lines reaffirm the position taken in 'The Fall', and challenge the adequacy of puritanical respectability. These kings are not saintly figures in any conventional sense. They drink, whore and double-deal on the journey which is increasingly obviously a metaphor for their lives. All this is associated with their growth of self-knowledge:

> Strange that, in lands, and countries quite unknown,
> We find, not others' strangeness, but our own;
> That is one use of journeys; if one delves,
> Differently, one's sure to find one's selves.[34]

Once again the poem is concerned with setting free the 'manyness' of the individual which can only happen when the securities of the fixed position and the known are rejected; when, in the image of the poem, one refuses to insure against 'second sight' and 'belief'. Evangelicalism promotes the need to cast off the old self and to be born again in order to reorientate life and enable it to be lived according to different priorities and another way of seeing. This idea lies behind 'The Journey of the Magi', although Rodgers does not use specifically religious language. Furthermore, his references to cars, radios, insurance agents and so on, alongside biblical allusions, insist on the timelessness of this journey – its modernity as well as its traditional nature.

Not surprisingly, the poem dispenses with St Luke's account of the visit to the stable and produces its own conclusion. At their moment of greatest frustration and despair, the kings

> . . .   saw
> In the last ditch, on the last straw,
> In front of them a heavenly child.
> See! it looked up at them and smiled.
> It was the child within themselves
> For which they'd sought, for which Age delves
> – Now Age and Innocence can meet,
> Now, now the circle is complete,
> The journey's done. Lord, Lord, how sweet![35]

Thus, Christ resides within the individual and may only be recognised and discovered there after life in all its wholeness has been embraced. According to this view, no longer is it our prime duty to resist and bemoan our sinfulness, but rather to grow through acceptance of our fallen state to the profoundest discovery of all – our in-dwelling holiness – which will provide a reconciliation of the 'antinomies' between which we live. Whereas Eliot's poem concludes on a note of uncertainty with the narrator still living in a state of disturbance long years after the transforming experience he relays, Rodgers offers a vision of spiritual fulfilment and harmony achieved through living dangerously in precisely the way that characterises strong religious faith.

Another reinterpretation of the Christian story is found in 'Nativity' which deliberately links the birth of Jesus with his death, and his childhood with his adulthood. He not only has the 'holly hair' and 'berry eyes' of an infant, but also a 'chrysanthemum wound' and the 'biscuit-brittle straw' upon which he is laid hints at the bread or wafer of the Last Supper and communion service.[36] Likewise, the description of him as a 'gay young god' who is closely associated with the natural world seems to link him with pre-Christian forms of religion.

Building on these multiple implications, Rodgers represents the nativity as an all-embracing cosmic drama involving the whole of creation:

> And there's the tapering tree of his descent,
> Hitched to a kingly star,
> Earth is its horizontal, heaven and hell
> Its upright centre-spar.
>
> The very tree of life, so base, so wide,
> And with such longing fraught,
> Up the step-ladder of our looks it spires
> Into a point of thought.[37]

The intersection of earth, heaven and hell not only forms a cross, but combines an image of the structure on which Christ died with a reference to the way his conflict between the powers of heaven and hell was worked out on earth. The poem has already suggested that Christ's death was implicit in his birth, and the paradox is renewed in the notion that the cross is also the 'very' – meaning both 'actual' and 'true' – 'tree of life' which is simultaneously lowly (although perhaps there is an additional hint at the word 'basic' or fundamental) and extensive or accommodating. The imagery in the rest of this stanza again triggers dual associations – of the worshipping figures around the crib in a traditional nativity scene, but also of the grieving mother and friends of Christ kneeling at the foot of the cross. In both cases the eyes of the watchers are 'fraught' with 'longing'. But over and beyond these specific allusions, there is the more general attitude of worshippers before the crib and the cross, both of which provide a 'point of thought' for their aspirations and meditations, and the symbolism of church spires which point towards heaven and direct thought upwards.

Yet Rodgers presents his nativity against the backdrop of a frozen, spiritually demoralised world where treachery, warfare and killing continue as of old and which desperately needs regeneration. Once more he leads the poem to a prayerful conclusion, invoking God to purify and empower 'all the frozen bards' as once Isaiah was prepared for his prophetic role:

> Lay the live coal upon their lips that they
> May leap uproariously
> Out of their huff of words, and let the thorns
> Crackle with prophecy.
>
> Resume, and reimburse the silent wood,
> Elaborate its saps,
> Bid the bare trees blurt into bloom, and fill
> With leaf the hungry gaps,
> And in its head set the heart's singing birds.[38]

Here Rodgers seems close to his ministerial role, affirming his belief in the possibility of a redemptive change and blossoming of life, beseeching the means of grace by which it may be encouraged, and anticipating, rather than actually arriving at, its outcome. Finally, the prophetic activity which he ascribes to poets is another notable demonstration of his belief in the power of words.

The focus of 'Christ Walking on the Water' is the paradox of the Son of God confined within a human body. Here Christ's action is imagined as an all-absorbing and hugely draining feat of concentration, a triumph of faith and will over matter that is mediated through him and which depends upon utter single-mindedness and total absence of doubt:

> . . .   In his forward face
> No cave of afterthought opened; to his ear
> No bottom clamour climbed up; nothing blinked.
> For he was the horizon, he the hub,
> Both bone and flesh, finger and ring of all
> This clangourous sea.[39]

This delineates a moment of perfection in which opposites are reconciled, divisions resolved, and the harmony of equilibrium is revealed. It is an inspired interpretation of the significance of the gospel account.

However, the second half of the poem goes further both specu-latively and imaginatively. Christ's entry into the boat is explicitly likened to the moment of sexual penetration and orgasm. The aftermath is characterised metaphorically as detumescence accompanied by feelings of tristesse, followed by his uncertainty about what he has done and a heightened sense of loneliness. Appropriately enough the poem concludes with Christ 'Curled like a question mark asleep' – human exhaustion and doubt having replaced his divine energy of spirit and assurance.[40] The astonishing moment of wholeness repre-sented by Christ walking on the water is, necessarily, a temporary phenomenon because of his humanity, a fleeting insight into and demonstration of lasting perfection, as must be any alleged mortal glimpses of the divine state. It can no more be sustained in this life than the instant of complete sexual satisfaction to which it is compared, and which, for Rodgers, became the physical analogue for spiritual wholeness.

The poem startles, first because it assumes that sexuality was part of Christ's humanity, a notion seldom mentioned in traditional theology and certainly not in the Presbyterianism within which Rodgers trained and ministered, and second, because of the context in which the sexual metaphor is used. It is questionable whether this works wholly persuasively here or whether it relies over-much on an idiosyncratic romanticising of sex. Certainly Rodgers was much more successful in integrating issues of faith and sexuality in the poem 'Lent'. However, he is remarkably effective in suggesting that far from diminishing the divinity of Christ, his human limitations serve to heighten the sense of its wonder and reality.

The reality of Christ's physical existence, and the way in which it aligns him with other men and women, reappears in 'Resurrection – an Easter Sequence', written to provide links between sections of a programme broadcast from various parts of Europe on Easter Sunday 1949. The fourteen poems each focus on different moments in the experience of Christ and his followers from Palm Sunday through to Easter Day. They form, as it were, a non-conformist alternative to the Catholic Stations of the Cross with each poem but one prefaced by a text from St Matthew's gospel. (The exception, the tenth poem in the sequence, has a text from St John.) What is notable are the particular emphases which Rodgers gives his subject. His keen sense of the paradoxes of faith is evident at various points – in Christ's fore-knowledge of how the joy of Palm Sunday will turn to mockery with a rapidity that is mirrored in the juxtaposing of the words 'deified' and 'defy'; in his understanding of how faith thrives through 'the mystery of losing'; in the notion that 'Judas was part of Jesus' and the process whereby Peter becomes a denier; in the way that our lives, like Christ's in Gethsemane, are endlessly poised between 'faith and doubt,/Like breath'; in the apparent insignificance of this one death for many of the passers-by and for the soldiers, and yet of the unique drama of the moment when 'God was dead' and 'Now was the world's back broken'.[41]

Christ's isolation is repeatedly shown, along with his insight into human need and the particular role he must perform. Wordplay is tellingly employed to explore the riddle of his dilemma, which also returns to one of the besetting problems in Rodgers's own life:

> To meet with all and go with none
> That was his doom who mediates and makes one
> The split that was in man since time began.
> But how to heal the breach? how to reach across?
> Ay, that was the only answer now – the Cross![42]

But in his acceptance of the Cross and of his Father's will (the subject of the Gethsemane poem), and in the strength he draws from this, the power of Christ's faith is affirmed. The sense of isolation increases as the poems move to the crucifixion, where Rodgers insists on the untidy brutality and messiness of the events, on the fact that it is only

> . . . later on, the heart edits them lovingly,
> Abstracts the jeers and jags, imports a plan
> Into the pain, and calls it history.
> We always go back to gloss over some roughness,
> To make the past happen properly as we want it to happen;

and on the dreadful agonies of the dying man whose 'eliminating moment' becomes 'The illuminating one' for the soldiers beside the cross.[43]

The violent eruptions in the natural world as Christ dies, which are recorded in the twelfth poem, not only pick up on the biblical reference to St Matthew, ch. 27, v. 51, but capitalise upon the sympathetic bond between Christ and nature already hinted at in the first and fifth poems in the sequence dealing with Palm Sunday and Gethsemane respectively. The association also reaffirms Rodgers's view of Christ in 'Nativity'.

Perhaps the most striking and innovative emphasis falls upon Christ's relationship with his mother and with Mary Magdalene. The tenth poem, headed with a text from St John, ch. 19, v. 25 – 'Now there stood by the cross of Jesus his mother . . .' –, allows Rodgers to focus on the maternal bond between Christ and Mary, on the ties of memory and love between them, and on her paradoxical sense of him as both her son and not her son. It creates an astonishing picture of the interplay of human ordinariness and divine difference:

> He remembered the happy days in Galilee
> When he was heaven's hub; the heap of smoking grass,
> The bubble-pipe, the light upon the wall,
> The children in the far garden looking for the lost ball,
> And Mary calling him. He was always so distant
> In those lonely days. O if only
> He had mattered less, she wondered, if only
> She had mastered him more, would he then
> Have been like other men, a flat satisfied plain?
> But no. In him mountains of onlyness rose
> Snow-high. Dayspring was in his eyes
> At midnight. And he would not come down
> From his far purpose even for her who was
> The root that raised him to this Cross and crown
> Of thorns.[44]

These lines emphatically justify Tom Clyde's claim that Rodgers's 'god is as real as in a Mystery play'.[45] They refuse to regard the crucifixion as an icon to be revered from afar, and seek to make immediate those parts of the experience that are most human, but which are inseparably bound up with the greater purpose and meaning of Christ's death that cannot be wholly realised in words.

The penultimate poem in the sequence invokes women as 'the watchers/ And keepers of life'. It prepares the way for the final poem's emphasis on Mary Magdalene's meeting with Christ on the third day and on the transforming and reconciling power of the resurrection:

> It was there, then, there at the blinding turn
> Of the bare future that she met her past.[46]

As past and future encounter each other, death becomes life, grief gives way to joy, doubt turns to certainty and self-imprisonment ends in liberation.

Rodgers's introduction of the two Marys at the most critical junctures in the sequence suggests how the bond of love between a man and woman, and perhaps particularly a woman's love for a man, provides both the analogy for and the access point to a sense of God's love. This idea is developed even more boldly in the remarkable poem 'Lent', which again centres on Mary Magdalene, 'that easy woman', the archetypal sinner.[47] Mary's Lenten discipline and penitence involve a renunciation of sexual adventuring, complemented by giving herself to Christ. The paradoxical nature of this process is evoked in language heavy with erotic suggestion:

> . . .   Take me
> As one who owes
> Nothing to what she was. Ah, naked.

Her penitence is equated with the suppression of her sexuality which in itself becomes a kind of striptease, a casting off of her 'waves of scent', 'petticoats of foam', and 'lightest veil/ Of feeling', and their replacement by coldness, hardness, stoniness. Rodgers successfully reverses the idea of Mary having been motivated by lust and shows her as its victim and object when she prays:

> . . .   that salt lust stave off
> That slavered me . . .

The simultaneous suggestions of bestiality and enslavement make this a particularly effective pun.

Throughout the first five stanzas the repeated words and images associated with water are similarly ambiguous. Mary's tears of penitence and the familiar notion of being washed of sin are held in tension with her recollections of how she 'once/ Could leap like water' in sexual ecstasy, and of her former lovers 'Surf-riding' in to her and also with the metaphors of water used in relation to the tokens of her trade.

She seems to dissociate herself completely from her own body and to objectify it when she speaks of no longer peeping 'Over the balconies of these curved breasts'. Yet, this is the point at which the poem proceeds to its most daring idea – that Mary 'makes room' for the crucified Christ in the 'alcove' of her womb, and that by metaphorically taking him as her lover, she herself is resurrected to new life and compassionately restored to the fullness and wholeness of self which she renounced in the opening stanzas:

> A grave and icy mask her heart wore twice,
> But on the third day it thawed,
> And only a stone's-flow away

> Mary saw her God.
> Did you hear me? Mary saw her God!
>
> Dance, Mary Magdalene, dance, dance and sing,
> For unto you is born
> This day a King. 'Lady', said He,
> 'To you who relent
> I bring back the petticoat and the bottle of scent.'[48]

In this context the idea of 'relenting' comes close to that of 'falling' or taking risks which is viewed so positively elsewhere in Rodgers's work. The conclusion does not imply advocacy of Mary's previous life, nor her return to it, but affirms the exhilaration of her new one. Rodgers has, it seems, found his own highly individual way of reformulating the familiar Christian paradox that service of Christ is perfect freedom. Furthermore, he has done so by translating an abstract maxim into a poetic drama which has all the immediacy and power of physical experience. It is, perhaps, the poem in which he is most successful in resolving the tensions that prevail in his religious verse.

Yet, however totally Rodgers appears to have freed himself from feelings of sexual inhibition and guilt in 'Lent', other poems indicate that this was not a permanent liberation. Even 'The Net', which is probably his most famous work and certainly his most erotic celebration of sex, concludes on a note of modesty and a reference to 'naked guilt' that are not foreseen in the rest of the poem. When Terence Brown describes it as 'a completely successful poem grounded in puritan assumptions which are in the process of giving way to romantic erotic celebration', he is certainly right to show that although those 'puritan assumptions' may have been weakened, they are still actively present.[49]

By subverting Christ's claim to his disciples that if they followed him he would make them 'fishers of men', and focusing instead on the act of sex as the life-changing event, the notion of conversion is radically recast:

> Quick, woman, in your net
> Catch the silver I fling!
> O I am deep in your debt,
> Draw tight, skin-tight, the string,
> And rake the silver in.
> No fisher ever yet
> Drew such a cunning ring.[50]

The perspective is undeniably male-centred, the woman serving simultaneously as the object of intense desire and the means of redemptive release into a bliss which, the poet mischievously boasts, can only be viewed with impotent envy by St Michael and 'all the Angels':

> But I, being man, can kiss
> And bed-spread-eagle too;
> All flesh shall come to this,
> Being less than angel is,
> Yet higher far in bliss
> As it entwines with you.[51]

Yet, even as he claims the superiority of sexual to heavenly bliss and recasts the biblical maxim that 'all flesh is grass', the poet seems to lose confidence in his own hedonism and gives way to the note of uneasy guilt with which he concludes. The physical ecstasy of 'The Net' is thus ultimately unsustainable and is at best a temporary, if glorious, moment in time, like that in 'Christ Walking on the Water', although it is to be neither despised nor rejected for all its limitations.

Elsewhere, old fears return to dominate. In 'The Harvest Field' Rodgers offers a conventional view of Death as the grim reaper who will cut down all flesh in Time and the poem seems ready to serve as a prologue to a sermon or homily on mortality and the vanities of human life.[52] And a late poem, 'Scapegoat', where the title alludes to the animal metaphorically burdened with the sins of the Children of Israel which was driven out to die and thus to expiate them, and also to Christ's atoning and sacrificial role, is a psychodrama of guilt in which the poet is confronted by God bearing ' . . . the accusing document; all my fears'.[53] But this God who seems like an aggressive bailiff backed by a team of Protestant thugs – they are 'hard-mouthed, bowler hatted', which would immediately make any Ulster reader see them as Orangemen – also has an 'implacably-forgiving face'. The unexpected conjunction of words here captures precisely one of the unresolved paradoxes in Rodgers's attitude to God. Yet, it is also the combination of implacability and forgiveness which leads the 'I' of the poem to humble admission rather than defiance and which reduces him to genuine uncertainty

> If it were His son or my son
> The doomsmen laid upon the floor then,
> The knife to his throat.

Terence McCaughey has located in this uncertainty

> . . . the measure both of the artistic integrity and the theological soundness of the poem. For such is the human tragedy and such is the fate of the executed Jesus that it is impossible at any given moment to say definitively or exclusively that he is only God's or only one of ours. He is ours certainly, upon whom falls the consequence of sins or, in the imagery of the poem, of 'debts' we were scarcely aware of. But he is also God's, who alone could bear so great a weight, so great an injustice.[54]

Unmerited forgiveness may be harder and more confusing than deserved punishment. The dog which begins as a guard against an unnerving 'lack of noise' ends by fleeing 'like a kind of domestic scapegoat', leaving the master to face the consequences of his fears on his own.[55] 'Scapegoat' demonstrates that the poet never shed his Calvinistic sense of human accountability before a God who may call the individual to answer at any moment, nor of endemic human sinfulness, but the harshness of divine judgement is modified by the balancing notion of God's forgiveness and of the atoning sacrifice of Christ on the cross.

Again and again the poetry of W.R. Rodgers turns upon the unresolved tensions in his own life and faith. Some poems can do no more than state the dilemma, some declare the need to embrace life inclusively rather than limiting it by dictates of orthodoxy and respectability, while others again explore what it might mean to immerse oneself trustingly in experience. Christ, at once human and divine, perfect and yet beset by both the limitations and the delights of physical existence and feelings, becomes paradigmatic because in him Rodgers finds the exemplary figure whose earthly life points to the way in which all oppositions might be permanently reconciled through love outside time. In time, however, such moments of reconciliation are both temporary and costly, and Rodgers chooses to equate them with the transience of sexual ecstasy which is followed by heightened feelings of loneliness or guilt. Other poems offer occasional glimpses of what the state to which he aspires might be like. So, in 'The Swan', he produces an image of the bird's detached aloofness from everything around it:

> Far from shore and free from foresight,
> Coiled in its indifferent mood
> It held the heavens, shores, waters and all their brood.[56]

This perhaps reflects the poise which forever eludes the poet. Another vision of balanced and well-adjusted living appears in the account of French Catholic village life in 'Summer Journey':

. . . This morning the world went into the church.
Now the church comes into the world. So,
In life we oppose and appease each other.[57]

However, this easy interaction between sacred and secular is what
Rodgers typically wrestles to forge in the convoluted vocabulary of
his poems. It is not his inheritance, but something which he recovers
and communicates through what John Wilson Foster has dubbed 'a
transposed evangelical fervour' in which 'The spirit of God that
inspires millenarian prophets . . . is, as it were, replaced in [his] verse
by the muse . . .'.[58]

Yet, for all the millenarianism and charged emotionalism of his
verse and despite his verbal profligacy, Rodgers only published two
collections and he wrote only a handful of new poems between 1952,
when *Europa and the Bull* appeared, and his death in 1969. Even
allowing for his important BBC work, including *The Return Room*
which Douglas Carson has called 'the finest radio feature produced
in Northern Ireland after the War', this is a modest output which
became increasingly infrequent as time went on.[59] It is almost as if his
prophetic energies not only shared some of the charismatic qualities
of religious revivalism, but also the tendency of revivalism to run out
of steam and lose the compelling intensity of its heyday. What is
interesting is that, to the end, Rodgers continued to pursue his goal
of reconciliation of opposites and harmony. This is movingly
suggested in 'Field Day', where a small triangle of grass at a road
junction is described as 'A still centre', an image of untouched
perfection, and even more so in 'Neither Here Nor There', one of the
last poems in *Europa and the Bull*.[60]

As this last title implies, the poem evokes an ideal place where '. . . all
is, and nothing's ought'. It is outside social, legal and proprietorial
constraints and barriers and purged of negative feelings. Described as
'lackadaisical', it is not governed by the good Protestant virtues of
planning, purpose and organisation, but by spontaneous living and an
absence, as Keats put it, of any 'irritable reaching after fact and reason':

. . . it is a timeless land, it lies
Between the act and the attrition . . .

This is at once neutrality made perfect, and a sacred space; a kind of
fifth province situated in the middleground of Celtic mythology where
actions do not generate negative consequences.[61] Paradoxically,
although this landscape is evoked largely by noting all that is
excluded from it, it is a place of affirmation and promise:

> There are no homecomings, of course, no good-byes
> In that land, neither yearning nor scorning,
> Though at night there is the smell of morning.

It is indeed a promised land, a metaphor for mental and emotional equilibrium, free of the tensions and psychological extremes which the poet has known and from which he desires release. Fittingly, too, the language is quieter, more restrained than in many of the earlier poems and the imagery no longer needs to startle – let alone embarrass – to secure its effects.

Michael O'Neill has commented on how Rodgers's writing and unorthodox life were interpreted by evangelicals as a sign that 'he was sliding into godlessness', while more liberal thinkers saw him as 'escaping from repressive dogma to a more palatable agnosticism'.[62] Yet, it is clear that however far he may have drifted from the norms of Presbyterian thought and conduct, he never broke free from their influence, and while he was deeply distrustful of narrow-mindedness, judgementalism and the conflation of piety with respectability, the same cannot be said of his attitude to Christianity. Rodgers was a true dissenter in that his poetry is an affirmation of the individual's right to work out his own relationship with God, and a non-subscriber in that finally he would not submit to any man-made code. In some senses he might be seen as the victim of a religious and cultural background and training that crippled him for life, but paradoxically, they also equipped him to be the poet he was. It was in his very struggle to break with the mentally and emotionally intimidating restrictions of Calvinism and the simple certainties of evangelicalism that Rodgers found the poetic voice to express his understanding of Christ and his belief that truth could only be reached by welcoming fearlessly whatever the world had to offer. As the text for his final sermon in Cloveneden Church, Loughgall, Rodgers chose Hebrews, ch. 11, v. 8 – 'By faith Abraham, when he was called to go out into a place which he should after receive as an inheritance, obeyed; and he went out, knowing not whither he went'.[63] There can be no doubt that he had his own situation in mind, but the full appropriateness of the text must be judged against those poems in which Rodgers strives to relate theology and experience in language that at best shares the characteristics of prophecy and revelation customarily associated with the Word itself.

CHAPTER SIX

John Hewitt: 'The Ultimate Protestant'?

Ulster developed a strong Protestant ethos. It became Calvinistic because of John Knox. I'm not a Calvinist, it became too rigid . . . I belong to the Dissenting tradition. But our dissent goes further than Presbyterian dissent.

'A Tree of Identities, A Tradition of Dissent: John Hewitt at 78', interviewed by Ketzel Levine, *Fortnight*, No 213.

. . . if we look closely, we find the poetry demonstrates that non-conformism, even when disavowed or ignored as a religion, can be a powerfully cultural, even aesthetic, and therefore pervasive affair that has its roots in the doctrines ignored or disavowed.

John Wilson Foster, '"The Dissidence of Dissent": John Hewitt and W.R. Rodgers', in *Colonial Consequences*,

IF W.R. RODGERS devoted most of his creative energy to a rebellion against the emotional austerities of his background and the guilts and fears inspired by the narrowness and judgmentalism of the Protestant theology in which he was trained, John Hewitt's dissent took a different form. Where Rodgers seems possessed by an almost evangelical fervour directed to unconventional ends, Hewitt approaches his subjects with restraint, a scrupulous eye for detail, and a forensic style of reasoned debate and enquiry. Indeed, both in temperament and in method, Hewitt seems to be much closer to the sobriety, plainness of language and dispassionately cautious attitudes stereotypically associated with Northern Irish Protestants than the volatile, extravagant and sometimes verbose Rodgers. Yet, it was Hewitt who was much more forthright in rejecting the Church from the outset, but who paradoxically described himself as 'the ultimate Protestant'.[1] Furthermore, throughout his life Hewitt found his own relationship to the Protestant community from which he came, and between that community and his Catholic fellow citizens in Ulster, abiding sources of perplexity, whereas Rodgers does not appear to have been unduly exercised by these questions. For Rodgers, as we have seen, sexual love is the key to personal fulfilment, self-discovery and realisation of identity and he treats it with quasi-religious significance so that it becomes, as it were, the equivalent to a pentecostal rebirth experience. Hewitt, however, looks for and finds himself through the kind of genealogical listing and interrogation of ancestors more readily associated with Old Testament scripture, and this provides a relevant point of access to his work.[2]

One of the most striking features of John Hewitt's writing is his preoccupation with his family history. Early and late, in verse and in prose, he returns to his own memories of relatives and to the stories which he was told about other family members from previous generations.[3] He is constantly at pains to tease out the qualities which, he feels, bond him to his ancestors, yet is equally concerned to locate the ways in which he differs from them too. This continuous and apparently compulsive process of telling and retelling is more than a personal dilemma; it seems also to reflect that specific impulse felt among some Northern Irish Protestants to explain and even justify their presence and right to a continuing place in the region. And just as popular Protestant history defines itself in the commemoration of particular anniversaries, so there are a number of seminal incidents in his familial past to which he ascribes formative and symbolic importance.

Hewitt is, famously, the descendant of a planter family which came from the English midlands in the seventeenth century and settled in the vicinity of Kilmore in Co. Armagh. In this fact lies the origin of the poet's debate with himself, as becomes clear in his 'Essay in Discursive Autobiography' where he tells how the discovery – that 'the old Planter's Gothic tower of Kilmore Church still encloses the stump of a round tower and . . . was built on the site of a Culdee holy place' – provided him with

> . . . the best symbol I have yet found for the strange textures of my response to this island of which I am a native. I may appear Planter's Gothic, but there is a round tower somewhere inside, and needled through every sentence I utter.[4]

The term Planter's Gothic refers to a style of church architecture consisting usually of a nave and chancel with a western tower and designed to facilitate congregational worship. It has been described as 'probably the only Protestant development of the Gothic style in the world' and has few counterparts in the British Isles outside Ulster.[5] The fact that Hewitt used the same term as the title for the published fragments from his autobiography is richly suggestive of the way he perceived himself as simultaneously belonging in Ireland and yet not being wholly native to it. It also acknowledges his relationship to the Protestant settlers who took over the land that was not theirs by inheritance and imposed their religious and cultural values on it. This is a theme which Hewitt addresses with greater complexity in poems such as 'The Colony', 'Once Alien Here', 'Conacre', and the verse play, 'The Bloody Brae', but for the moment it is important to realise how these distant ancestors, unknowable in any detail, provide the poet with an origin in Ulster and a genealogical starting point. As he put it in 'Orchard Country':

> When my grandfather came to live with us
> my past expanded, for he proffered me,
> his lively mind so thronged and populous,
> an open door to our own history.
> That Armagh orchard country.
> . . .   How in those Planter lands
> our name is hearth-rolled. Generation, place,
> he gave you foothold in the human race.[6]

In 'The Lonely Heart' section of 'Freehold' an even more telling image is used to explore this relationship between grandfather and grandson. By sharing his accounts of past generations, the old man 'made them mine' the poet declares, 'by laying-on of hands, by word and sign'.[7] The language here is immediately suggestive of religious ritual. John Hewitt is, as it were, ordained into a type of apostolic succession by becoming the latest inheritor and keeper of his family's history. There is no doubting the status and influence here attributed to that history which has the power associated with myth to give him his identity, his place in the world and his relationship to the past.

Elsewhere Hewitt argues his belief in the importance of a writer possessing a sense of belonging 'to a recognisable focus in place and time', and of having ancestors 'Not just of the blood, but of the emotions, of the quality and slant of mind'.[8] Foremost amongst the figures he invokes in this respect is his own father, Robert Telford Hewitt, 'the greatest man of all the men I love', whose presence recurs throughout his writing life.[9]

Robert Hewitt was a schoolmaster with advanced educational ideas for his day, an admirer of Keir Hardie, enthused with a socialist desire for justice and the moral principles of his Methodist faith, a book lover, story-teller and conversationalist. His life as commemorated by his son was an intriguing fusion of regularity, conformity and frugality with an interest in liberal ideas, politics and the arts. He had high standards of integrity and was never afraid to risk causing displeasure when a cherished principle was at stake. Thus, in his professional life he faced criticism from the school inspectors who were unsympathetic to his attempts to broaden the curriculum according to the views of A.S. Neill, while in the domestic sphere he upset his wife-to-be's family in defence of his belief in abstinence when he returned a wedding present given by a friend who dealt in the liquor trade.[10] Likewise, although Robert Hewitt was a practising Methodist, he chose not to have his son baptised because of his disapproval of the incumbent minister whom he allegedly described as '"looking like a barman or a priest"'.[11] The episode is suggestive of Hewitt senior's characteristically Protestant independence of mind in religious matters as well as hinting at his particular prejudices. It is also an incident upon which John Hewitt placed great symbolic importance, ascribing to his non-baptism 'a sense of liberation' so that 'spiritually I have felt myself to be my own man, the ultimate Protestant'. He adds to this the fact that since he was never vaccinated as a child, ' . . . I have often felt myself doubly free from the twin disciplines of organised religion and science'; and thus escaping implication in them claims to have had the freedom to 'set up my own mythology and magic in opposition to either . . .'.[12] Hewitt's myth, despite his father's central place in it, sturdily rejects any affiliation to the Christian church. Although he acknowledges his respect for George Fox, St Francis of Assisi and those more eccentric non-conformists in religion, John Toland and William Blake, he declares his lack of sympathy with John Wesley, Calvin, St Paul, John Knox, Luther, Aquinas and St Augustine. Nevertheless, despite these rejections, the 'fundamental democratic nonconformity' of Methodism which he encountered in his family life was both appealing and deeply influential in shaping Hewitt's secular Protestantism.[13]

His desire to cast himself as a man free from the constraints of belonging to society's institutions is further illustrated in a sonnet from the *Kites in Spring* sequence where once again Robert Hewitt is celebrated for preserving his son's integrity – this time by discouraging him from joining the Free Masons:

> He said No.
> So, from then on, my path in life was clear;
> unsworn, unbound for ever, I should go
> a free man, freely, to the infinite.[14]

But if John Hewitt was partly shaped by the exclusions insisted on by his father, he was also instilled with a deep sense of moral and social responsibility which can be linked to the questioning and didactic impulses that are repeated features of his poetry and which owe much to the religious environment of his childhood. Thus, although he never shared the piety that underpinned Robert Hewitt's life, John Hewitt absorbed many of the values and attitudes associated with it, even coming to regard his father's influence upon him in semi-religious terms and forever standing in affectionate awe of him and of his memory. This is emblematically represented when Hewitt likens a troubled dream in which he wrestled with his father to the biblical account in Genesis ch. 32, vv. 24–31 of Jacob's decisive struggle with God's angel which results in his change of name to Israel – 'because you strove with God and with man, and prevailed' – but also leaves him permanently lamed:

> I wrestled with my father in my dream,
> holding my ground though he strove powerfully,
> then suddenly remembered who we were,
> and why we need not struggle, he and I;
> thereat desisted. Now the meaning's clear;
> I will not pause to struggle with my past,
> locked in an angry posture with a ghost,
> but, striding forward, trust the shrunken thigh.[15]

But if there is ambiguity about his relationship with his father here – the struggle is both enabling and disabling – in 'Freehold' Hewitt wrote:

> This was my father. I have understood
> just how the meek, the merciful, the good,
> possess the kingdom. And that fact is safe
> from need of proof or danger of disproof;

and the association he makes between his father and some of the qualities extolled in the Beatitudes acknowledges him as an exemplary figure. This is soon followed by the poet's admission that he has failed to match these standards in his own life.[16]

In poems such as 'My Father's Death in Hospital' and 'The Lonely Heart' section of 'Freehold' Hewitt also suggests his father's self-containment and isolation both in life and in death despite his family, faith and involvement in many activities and causes. However, it is difficult to dissociate this from the recurrent expressions of his own loneliness and estrangement, or to know the degree to which Hewitt is projecting personal feelings of solitariness onto his father while lacking the latter's consolations of religion. For Alan Warner, Hewitt's detachment and loneliness are the clearest notes in his poetry, another consequence of his interrogative and doubting cast of mind and refusal merely to perpetuate the norms and attitudes of any creed, party or section of the community.[17] These feelings also lie behind Hewitt's dedication to art, regionalism and socialism as strategies for overcoming separation and division, and for encouraging inclusiveness of vision, understanding and relationships. Seamus Heaney observed in a tribute to Hewitt after his death that as a 'mentor to the imaginative life of the community' he gave

> . . . the Northern Irish planters an image of their predicament based upon perspectives and attitudes more generous and historically aware than their political leaders would risk or admit to.[18]

But it is also true that the loneliness which so often resonates in his writing articulates a feeling that lies at the very heart of much of the Northern Irish Protestant experience.

In addition to his father, Hewitt turned to other members of his family as formative presences or forebears of his own particular talents. 'Year of Grace and My Great-Grandfather' deals with the impact of the 1859 religious revival upon his mother's family whose members 'fell prostrate . . . and rose/redeemed by mercy', with the exception of the poet's great-grandfather who resisted the fervid efforts to bring him to salvation, finding

> . . . the songs they prayed for lilt into
> the hearthside ballads in his heart he knew.[19]

The stubborn dissent of Hewitt's great-grandfather in matters of religion and his instinctive preference for folk ballads to hymns prefigure the poet's own attitudes and his enthusiasm for the verses of the rhyming weavers.

Towards his maternal grandmother, who was a young girl in 1859, Hewitt's feelings are more complex. While on the one hand her strict Methodism and stern propriety intimidated her young grandson and were unattractive to him, he found in her too a sturdy independence and indifference to social nicety which he admires, and a more unexpected affinity through her love of poetry.[20] The latter discovery emerges in 'My Grandmother's Garter', where Hewitt weighs up his feelings and indebtedness to this formidable matriarch who caused her family and servants much heartache:

> Yet she always had a pouch in her garter,
> stuffed with snippets of clipped verse;
> Tennyson, Whittier, Longfellow, George MacDonald,
> the guineas in her purse.
>
> And when at last she died there was scant mourning;
> her eldest son already dead,
> the family had poured its load of sorrow
> over that noble head.
>
> Yet, though I did not like her, nor she me, swearing
> I'd come to a bad end,
> remembering that satin pouch of poems,
> I clasp her bony hand.[21]

This sympathy towards poetry combined with his father's modest gifts at writing, including the alleged attempt to write a novel which ended when the manuscript was stolen, enable Hewitt to mythologise his own predisposition to literature.

Another relative who impressed himself on Hewitt's memory was his paternal Uncle Sam whose home was like a magic island of possibility – indeed the poet describes him as 'truly Prospero'. Creative, versatile, sceptical – he was discharged from his post as a Sunday School teacher because of his belief in Darwinian theory – and eventually estranged from the rest of his family after a marriage of which they disapproved, the poet again likens aspects of his own personality to those he highlights in Sam Hewitt:

> . . . from that teeming mind there must remain
> much which has made and kept me infidel.
> . . .
> So, though I lost him early, I have held
> close to that sceptic and enquiring look
> at the old riddle of the universe.[22]

Given the grip of his family's past upon him, it is not surprising therefore, that their history recurs in poems throughout Hewitt's long writing life, nor that as he approached his seventy-first birthday – a year beyond his biblically allotted span – and the third anniversary of his wife's death, and following six months during which he had produced nothing new, he felt impelled to embark upon the fullest retelling of it.[23] The memorial aspect of this enterprise is noted by Edna Longley, who describes *Kites in Spring* as 'a kind of museum and gallery', while Norman Vance equally relevantly emphasises its intentional instructiveness by speaking of it as 'something of a lay sermon'.[24] Furthermore, although 'Freehold' was written many years earlier, Hewitt chose to publish it as the title piece in the 1986 collection, which was also to be his last. In it he sums up the paradoxes and tensions within that family history, many of which are representative concerns shared by other Northern Irish Protestants. Thus, writing of the mixed strains in his background, he describes his ancestors as

> a stubborn Irishry that would recall
> the famine's curse, the farm that was too small,
> yet with a faith protestant that denied
> the hope of mercy to the papist side,
> tongue-loose with stories of the Ninety-Eight,
> yet proud the British Empire is so great,
> despising royal pomp and rites of Rome,
> but loving sashes, banners, fife and drum,
> so tethered to antinomies it rocks
> in seesaw straddle of a paradox.[25]

The claim that his family is Irish ('stubborn Irishry' may recall Yeats's 'indomitable Irishry', although he can scarcely have been thinking of exactly the same people) and the way he links them with the famine, are justified by an incident commemorated more explicitly in 'The Scar' and 'Orchard Country', which record the death of Hewitt's great-grandmother from famine fever caught from a beggar to whom she had given food.[26] Likewise, although the 'Ninety-Eight' was a Republican rebellion, it enjoyed Protestant support in Ulster (see chapter 2). However, Hewitt also indicates that his family's Irishness or identification with the native Irish is neither harmonious nor straightforward. The allusions to anti-Catholicism, to pride in the British Empire, which consolidated its power in Ireland in the nineteenth century after the suppression of the 1798 rebellion and the Act of Union, and to Protestants' paradoxical contempt for the ceremonies and ritual of the Catholic church despite their fascination with Orange triumphalism and regalia, all point to a complex inheritance in which race and religion are crucial factors.

It becomes apparent that Hewitt found that the historical awareness which his grandfather conferred upon him was not only enabling, as has already been suggested, but also a burden and a responsibility. The final three sonnets in *Kites in Spring* recount the old man's death and funeral in 1923 and announce the symbolic and literal changes which they caused in the poet's own life. Promoted to the bedroom left empty by his grandfather's passing, Hewitt, the young non-believer, completes a rite of passage whereby he first replaced the dead man's material possessions with his own, and then metaphorically fills the space vacated by his departed presence:

> I woke at dawn soon after, sensed he lay
> beside me in the bed. I dared not stir,
> but mused shut-eyed, how long I cannot say,
> remembering he loved me in his way
> as I loved him. No reason now for fear.
> I reached my right hand out; no one was there.[27]

After this, the preservation, repetition and interpretation of the family history become the obligation of the man who was at the threshold of his career as a poet, and who, very appropriately, carried his grandfather's name into another generation. Furthermore, this undertaking is inextricably linked to Hewitt's preoccupation with his place in Ulster society.

It is perhaps unusual for a poet to write extensively and sensitively about the country in which he was born and lived most of his life and in which generations of his family before him also lived, and yet to find his situation and relationship to the land so perplexing. However, this is indubitably the case with John Hewitt. As Gerald Dawe has observed:

> . . . his poetry is all about the attempts to find practicable resolutions to what history has given him by way of a home, a family's past and the 'natural' cultural world into which he was born.[28]

Although Hewitt did not support that view of history which projects Ulster Protestants as the lost tribe of God's chosen people, nonetheless he is a proponent of another kind of special pleading. The purpose of this is to reconcile the invasive behaviour of the original planters with the right of their descendants to be considered wholly Irish. In Hewitt's own case, the justification has nothing to do with religion, but with the passage of time since his ancestors first arrived, the way in which they 'claimed, drained, and gave the land the shapes of use', and the fact that the planters, 'Once Alien Here', now have no other place to call home and feel estranged if they return to the British mainland – as the writer records in the ambiguously titled poem, 'An Irishman in Coventry'.[29] But despite these claims, and although as self-appointed spokesman for his family and kind, Hewitt '. . . would seek a native mode to tell/our stubborn wisdom individual', he is also deeply conscious of the linguistic, cultural and religious differences which divide him from the Catholic Irish. In 'Once Alien Here' he admits imperfect linguistic identity with either the 'graver English' or 'lyric Irish tongue', while in 'O Country People' he concedes that:

> I've tried to learn the smaller parts of speech
> in your slow language, but my thoughts need more
> flexible shapes to move in, if I am to reach
> into the hearth's red heart across the half-door.
> . . .
>
> I recognise the limits I can stretch;
> even a lifetime among you should leave me strange,
> for I could not change enough, and you will not change;
> there'd still be levels neither'd ever reach.[30]

This sense of incomplete belonging appears also in 'Conacre', where the poet admits the gentle rebuffs to his attempts to direct the conversation with a countryman in a bar on market day. It is further complicated when he goes on to describe how as a city-bred man he is always something of a stranger in the country, while at the same time the urban environment fails to nurture 'the quiet depths', engaging him only at a superficial level.[31] Hewitt's conclusion – that he cannot return to the '. . . forgotten coasts/our fathers steered from' – leads him to acceptance of an imperfect situation:

> This is my home and country. Later on
> perhaps I'll find this nation is my own;
> but here and now it is enough to love
> this faulted ledge, this map of cloud above,
> and the great sea that beats against the west
> to swamp the sun.[32]

The strategically placed 'perhaps' emphasises the wholly provisional nature of the poet's hope, and it is notable both here and elsewhere that such sense of belonging as he possesses relies more upon a rather vague feeling of affinity with the weather or climate than on human bonds.

Hewitt had initiated his exploration of many of these issues as far back as 1936 when he finished writing 'The Bloody Brae: A Dramatic Poem', although he did not publish it until 1957. In it, he turned to the historical situation of the planters in Ulster, presenting a confrontation between an old Cromwellian settler and the ghost of a woman he had killed as a means of exploring Protestant guilt for the past. The protagonist, John Hill (who shares the poet's initials), acknowledges the consequences of murdering Bridget Magee and her child:

> I murdered pity when I murdered you,
> and reason and mercy and hope for this vexed land

– but the ghost of his erstwhile fellow soldier, Malcolm Scott, articulates unrepentant Protestant bigotry and contempt for Hill's remorse and desire for forgiveness.[33]

Clearly the response of the victim's ghost is crucial here, but Bridget does not simply offer access to the forgiveness Hill seeks; she also asserts that she can only come to him now because he genuinely needs and wants to receive that forgiveness: 'I came at last when every twig was naked'.[34] This emphasises that Hill, and by implication others like him, must accept responsibility for the past before they can expect to be relieved of its burden. Nor is that all. While Bridget's offer of forgiveness may seem conveniently redeeming for Hill, it carries with it a new and further responsibility. She tells him:

> You have narrowed your mercy round you
> like a close blanket that you should have spread
> over the shivering earth,

and insists that he must give up his hermit-like withdrawal from society, and go abroad as an apostle of mercy, forgiveness and reconciliation.[35] Hill's resistance to this demand, his attempts to excuse himself from it, his claim that

> . . . the strange things you said [are] beyond my wit,
> and so outside my responsibility,

and his failure to say anything about his experience to the characters who have observed the confrontation unbeknown to him, all suggest that he is unlikely to move beyond accepting personal mercy from Bridget to become its agent in the community.[36] Thus, although Frank Ormsby's description of 'The Bloody Brae' as 'a morality on the nature of responsibility and the necessity to escape from the destructive cycles of atrocity and revenge' is accurate, and although the poem intimates what is required to achieve this, the likelihood of it happening remains problematic.[37]

Britta Olinder has suggested that 'The Bloody Brae' was the first occasion on which Hewitt introduced the idea that the planters, too, have rights to the land both in spite of and because of history. However, this question assumes a central position in one of his most sustained explorations of the position of the Protestant community, 'The Colony', which the poet himself later described as 'the definitive statement of my realisation that I am an Ulsterman'.[38]

Using the analogy of Roman conquest, the poem makes an explicit acknowledgement of the role of the original planters as colonists following in the wake of 'the legions', land-grabbing, profiteering and subduing the 'barbarian tribesmen' on behalf of an imperial power. Numerous verbs assert the comprehensive and single-minded nature of this enterprise: 'We planted . . .'; '. . . we felled the trees'; 'We took . . .' – used three times in nine lines; 'We laboured hard'; 'we employed . . .'. The natives are routed, driven off the best land, denied liberty to practise their religion and in some cases used as labourers. Yet the colonists remain timelessly haunted by fear, intensified by memories of a vicious rebellion, that the natives may rise up in vengeance. While this recognises one of the deepest anxieties of the colonists, the poem also rehearses stereotypical Protestant prejudices towards Irish Catholics:

> You may distinguish,
> if you were schooled with us, by pigmentation,
> by cast of features or by turn of phrase,
> or by the clan names on them which are they,
> among the faces moving in the street.
> They worship Heaven strangely, having rites
> we snigger at, are known as superstitious,
> cunning by nature, never to be trusted,
> given to dancing and a kind of song
> seductive to the ear, a whining sorrow.
> Also they breed like flies.[39]

However much he may have stood 'outside the creeds', these lines demonstrate Hewitt's precise knowledge of the rhetoric and attitudes of Protestant bigotry in Northern Ireland. The closing two sections of the poem address the predicament of latter day descendants of the planters, who can no longer assert themselves by brute force, and many of whom lack any strategy either for withdrawing from the country or for ameliorating relationships within the community. In this situation Hewitt again projects himself as the true dissenter, ready to act as a mediator, to '. . . make amends/by fraternising, by small friendly gestures.' Yet, even this apparent generosity is qualified by rejection of 'their code' which is 'farther from the truth' and characterised by 'the spells/and fears their celibates surround them with'.[40] Here, as in other poems, Hewitt not only feels separated from the native Irish because of their Catholicism, but also shows a deep-seated Protestant distrust of the oppressive authoritarianism of that church.

There is a further unresolved tension between the poet's acceptance of the need to 'admit our load of guilt' in relation to the past, and the desire to be wholly accepted as 'co-inhabitants,/as goat and ox may graze in the same field/and each gain something from proximity'.[41] Nothing suggests that restitution can or should be made to the descendants of the dispossessed, whose gratitude for overtures of friendship is assumed; and the analogy of a goat and an ox sharing a field might be taken to distinguish between the two communities in a less than flattering way. Above all, however, the closing lines, which recall the rhetoric of 'Conacre', adopt an insistently defiant note which makes it clear that, whether or not reconciliation is possible, the planters' descendants will not relinquish their place in the land:

> for we have rights drawn from the soil and sky;
>
> . . .
>
> this is our country also, nowhere else;
> and we shall not be outcast on the world.[42]

The nature of these rights is not precisely defined, and they are essentially a rationalisation concluded from a history which, as the poem itself has shown, involved the expropriation of land and denial of other people's rights. This conclusion, which not only comprehends the Protestant dilemma in Northern Ireland, but resorts to a familiar note of truculent self-assertiveness in its defence, bears out Terence Brown's remark that Hewitt's imagination is most deeply stirred 'only by fears of a final homelessness', and discloses his fundamental insecurity.[43]

In 'Ireland', Hewitt is even led to see homelessness as the defining characteristic of all Irish people: 'We are not native here or any-where', he declares, rejecting the vanity of romantic or heroic views of history and dismissing '. . . what we think is love for usual rock/or old affection for our customary ledge' as 'but forgotten longing for the sea'.[44] The conclusion offers a curious inversion of Hewitt's more familiar desire to share fully in the rootedness which he associates with Catholics, but from which he feels himself excluded, and proposes instead a version of unity based on a mutual lack of belonging. The result is an oddly sentimental reconciliation in a poem which at first appears impatient with Irish vanity and self-delusion.

For all his secularism and avowals of dissent from nationalist or unionist politics, Hewitt was dogged on the one hand by feelings of guilt and responsibility for the fractured society in Northern Ireland, and on the other by the desire for personal assurance of unqualified acceptance and belonging in Catholic company, although without ever conceding anything to that faith. He was non-religious, yet troubled by feelings commonly associated with religion. He was a non-believer who wanted a gospel, a layman with an impulse to preach, whose concern with verbal exactitude often seems to have more in common with the Presbyterian niceties of the *Westminster Confession* and catechisms than with the fervid conversionist rhetoric of evangelical Methodism.

It is perhaps excessive to describe Hewitt's project to promote regionalism as his gospel and yet it was intended to answer both personal and social needs, some of which have been addressed more conventionally through religion. In this context the failure of regionalism is less important than the hopes which Hewitt attached to it in the 1940s and 50s, and which in turn are directly linked to the insecurities and exclusions felt by the poet and already observed in his verse.

In his 1947 essay, 'Regionalism: The Last Chance', Hewitt begins the final paragraph by declaring that

> Ulster considered as a region and not as the symbol of any particular creed, can, I believe, command the loyalty of every one of its inhabitants. For regional identity does not preclude, rather it requires, membership of a larger association.[45]

The appeal of regionalism lay partly in its opposition to processes of modernisation which threatened to sweep away local distinctiveness of culture, language and custom, and to submerge the individual in the mass, but also in the possibility of the people of a region such as Ulster acting together like an extended family. (In a later essay, 'No Rootless Colonist', Hewitt wrote of the need for 'some grouping smaller than the nation, larger than the family, with which we could effectively identify, with which we could come to terms of sympathetic comprehension, within which our faculties and human potentialities could find due nurture and proper fulfilment'.)[46] But the deeper motivation was the unsatisfied quest to discover practical and productive ways of grafting the two communities in the province on to one another and of giving Hewitt himself an uncompromised sense of belonging. Taking heart from examples in Wales and Scotland, Hewitt announced in his 'Overture for an Ulster Literature' that the region's 'narrow speech' . . . 'will serve our purpose':

> We can make something of it, something hard
> and clean and honest as the basalt cliffs,

infused with the unique coloration and configurations of sound that are in turn associated with the particular character of the local landscape:

> as nourishing as potatoes out of the mould,
> maybe not more shapely than the potato.[47]

The comparison with the potato suggests not only the modest home-liness of this vision, but affirms faith in its sustaining value, a substitution, perhaps, for the symbolic bread of life eaten by believers. Elsewhere, Hewitt questions whether it is

> . . . the unchristened heart of man
> still hankers for the little friendly clan
> that lives as native as the lark or hare,

and here the poet's unbaptised state is less a matter of pleasing independence than a token of an unsatisfied desire to belong.[48] Nor is this the only occasion on which he subjects his vaunted freedom from the creeds to a more doubting attitude. A passage in 'The Lonely Heart' written as far back as 1939 recalls a visit he made to the Catholic church in Warrenpoint. He tells of observing the building and the few people in it with detachment, of resisting a 'fancy' to light a candle 'against the crowding gloom/which seemed that year descending on our time', and of departing with 'a cynic thought'.[49] However, the poem continues with Hewitt reconsidering his behaviour and revealing much less self-confidence than the previous lines had suggested. For not only did he leave as he had arrived – 'a protestant' – but he was

> . . . all unconscious of my yawning want;
> too much intent on what to criticise
> to give my heart the room to realise
> that which endures the tides of time so long
> cannot be always absolutely wrong;
> . . . The years since then have proved I should have stayed
> And mercy might have touched me till I prayed.
>
> For now I scorn no man's or child's belief
> in any symbol that may succour grief . . .[50]

Thus, although Hewitt himself never subscribed to a religious creed, he seems to have recognised the resources of faith for the believer and here at least implies a sense of loss in his own inability to believe.

Within the four-part structure of 'Freehold', this passage leads on to his exploration of his family's history in Kilmore, Co. Armagh, perhaps the only kind of pilgrimage Hewitt could undertake:

> . . . some notion drew me there,
> illogical, but not to be ignored,
> some need of roots saluted, some sought word
> that might give strength and sense to my slack rein,
> by this directed, not to lose again
> the line and compass so my head and heart
> no longer plunge and tug to drag apart.[51]

Again the language used to describe the irresistible 'notion' and the search for some definitive point of anchorage which will give meaning and direction to life denote the urgency of the poet's needs and the similarity of his quest to a search for religious belief. This is further reinforced when Hewitt likens his journey through Armagh to a passage beyond present place and time, into a rich natural environment charged with memories of his past and barely altered since his ancestors lived there, so that he is able to dream himself out of his loneliness and dislocation and finally announce:

> Now and for ever through the change-rocked years,
> I know my corner in the universe.[52]

The confidence gained from this assertion emboldens him to declare his new-found purpose as both learner and teacher of Ulster regionalism, which forms the subject of the final part of 'Freehold'. For once, Hewitt projects himself as an insider – 'new to sworn service' – and recites the secular creed which defines the terms of his belonging, beginning with a typically Protestant insistence on the fact that it is his 'privilege to choose' what he now affirms.[53] The 'good men/this region bred', its history 'certified and sealed/by blood', its 'images and folkways', and its character-forming weather and remote geographical position all contribute to Ulster's regional identity with which Hewitt aligns himself. This, however, will not be a passive belief, as the poem goes on to make clear with its extensive list of all that remains to be done '. . . before our pride/can move with mercy in its equal stride'.[54] Hewitt outlines a programme of agricultural, urban, educational and cultural development which sounds uncomfortably like a new plantation of Ulster fuelled by Protestant rationalism and belief in the virtue of progress. He also wants the region to be open to libertarian influences from the wider world and directs criticism against both the authoritarianism of the Catholic Church and Protestant 'dullness' which

> . . .   cannot see
> the future gay with possibility,
> and howls dismay at change, though it must come . . .[55]

Finally, in justification of his 'illimitable right' to make such claims, he insists on its basis in his discovery that

> . . . every road I travelled brought me back,
> back to the sunlight on the glittering sod,
> back to my fathers and their silent God.[56]

'Freehold' is a crucial poem in Hewitt's canon because it demonstrates so comprehensively the connection between his personal quest for belonging, his guilt about the past and his desire to find a cause to which he could commit his didactic and socialist impulses as well as his poetic ability. However, despite the confidence with which he makes his claim here to an Ulster identity and to act as spokesman for the region, doubts remain about the credibility of his project. Peter McDonald has rightly pointed out that

As in his poetry, so in his arguments for Regionalism, Hewitt returns again and again to the tropes of stability, rootedness and community; but again, as in the poetry, his argument for these things, and his habitual attraction towards them, serve also to intimate how far they are from successful realisation.[57]

The assurance achieved in 'Freehold' is, in fact, more unusual than the self-doubt followed by rhetorical insistence previously observed in poems like 'The Colony' or 'Once Alien Here', or the sense of unbridgeable separation from Catholic neighbours in 'O Country People', 'The Glens' or 'The Hill Farm'.

Hewitt's aspirations for Regionalism were never fulfilled and the lapse into increasing violence from the late 1960s was incontrovertible proof that old enmities still had greater motivating force than ideals of non-sectarian co-operation, socialism and libertarianism. It is a commonplace that Hewitt himself achieved greater recognition and published more in the 1970s and 1980s than at any previous time, however, as Ormsby's edition of *The Collected Poems* shows, much of the work that appeared in this period had been written earlier or was revised material. Faced with the failure of the Regionalist ideal and the seeming circularity of history, and lacking any other vision for transcending the divisions in Northern Ireland, it becomes even clearer why Hewitt began again to recreate his own lineage as his one reliable claim to belong in Ulster.

His renewed sense of estrangement is evident in 'An Ulsterman' where he insists that the province is his country, but decries the 'creed-crazed zealots and the ignorant crowd' who 'have made our streets a byword of offence'.[58] 'The Dilemma', from the 1971 collection *An Ulster Reckoning*, not only deplores Catholic nationalism and Protestant Unionism, but finishes on a note of personal resentment that 'it long has been my bitter luck to be/caught in the crossfire of their false campaign', while 'The Coasters' satirises the purblind folly of the Protestant middle class which had prospered on the perpetuation of old injustices and failed to make changes while the opportunity existed.[59] Finally, two poems written in 1986, the year before his death, show the extent to which Hewitt's hopes for the region had dwindled. 'The Anglo-Irish Accord' acknowledges the sense of betrayal, confusion and fear felt by many Protestants, and so powerfully voiced at the time in Harold McCusker's speech to the House of Commons, and concludes with a tentative appeal to the standards of humane rationalism which the poet never failed to uphold:

> Slave to and victim of this mirror hate,
> Surely there must be somewhere we could reach
> a solid track across our quagmire state,
> and on a neutral sod renew the old debate
> which all may join without intemperate speech.[60]

The familiar urge to instruct and influence is still present, but the tone is pleading rather than assertive, wishful rather than confident. There is no real conviction that the voice of the reasonable man will be heard above the 'intemperate speech' against which Hewitt instinctively reacts. The same note is sounded in the concluding stanza of 'A Little People', where the title itself indicates his late view of the Protestant community. Here he traces the long lost past when Protestantism stood for '. . . the free spirit and the open mind', through the time when '. . . we saw ourselves a part/of a world-striding endless prime', to the 'embattled' position of contemporary Protestants where high unemployment, the decline of Ulster's established industries and the loss of 'mastery' combine to create confusion and insecurity, which in turn are inflamed into violence by the equally deluded rhetoric of both political factions:

> So now intransigently negative
> our threadbare lexicon provides no scope
> should one of our nay-sayers dare to give
> some gentler phrase of mercy, grace or hope.[61]

Hewitt's understanding of the Protestants' dilemma was as sharp at the end of his life in the midst of renewed civil disorder as it had been in poems written almost half a century earlier, and, as in that work, his response unites sympathy with criticism, understanding of their position with rejection of a creed which, in his view, had lost its courage and independence and declined into the sectarianism and narrow-mindedness that had helped to maintain an unjust state. In the Foreword to *An Ulster Reckoning*, which was dedicated to John Montague, Hewitt recalled how seven years previously Montague had described him as 'the first (and probably the last) deliberately Ulster Protestant poet', and then added: 'That designation carries a heavy obligation these days'.[62] Both comments are significant. Montague points precisely to the unique focus which Hewitt gave to the combined circumstances of being both an Ulsterman and a descendant of the Protestant planters whose presence has had such an effect on the region. It is probably true that no other poet has confronted this as the central dilemma in his work. Hewitt's own remark affirms the absolute seriousness with which he continued to face the issue, and indeed the added importance he felt it was given by the return of intercommunity violence and the blow to his hopes that progress had been made 'towards a more mature and responsible society'.[63]

One poem dating from this period is dedicated to 'the people of my province and the rest of Ireland', and represents well Hewitt's responsible and concerned attitude to current events and also their inhibiting effect upon him. The very title – 'Neither an Elegy Nor a Manifesto' – involves denials, and the whole poem is dominated by the difficult search for words to appeal for compassion and an end to killing without at the same time betraying himself into a narrowly political or partisan statement. Language is now a potential trap, memory 'a cruel web' and awareness largely a matter of knowing what cannot be urged or said:

> The careful words of my injunction
> are unrhetorical, as neutral
> and unaligned as any I know:
> they propose no more than thoughtful response;
> they do not pound with drum-beats
> of patriotism, loyalty, martyrdom.[64]

Such cautiousness and restraint may be both understandable and wise in the context of this poem, but they are recurrent throughout Hewitt's writing, and are also consistent with his view of himself as an artist, and of the priorities he espoused. Furthermore, those views and priorities owe a considerable debt to the Protestant culture of the poet's background. Critics have pointed to the way in which the language and forms of his poetry are characterised by 'clean lines, blunt statement and sturdy realism quickening into intensity, . . . scrupulous orderliness and unemphatic decency' – all qualities perceived as virtuous by Protestants.[65] Norman Vance has carried this type of analysis further, suggesting that

> It is not altogether fanciful to see connections between popular Methodist hymns, carefully shaped to embody and reinforce orthodoxy for a worshipping community, and Hewitt's poems, usually plain and accessible, well crafted to embody more humanisitic pieties for a divided community;[66]

and John Wilson Foster has described Hewitt's style as more akin to the seventeenth-century expository sermon than to the nineteenth-century evangelical rhetoric which is evident in some of W.R. Rodgers' poetry.

Hewitt often evaluated his own abilities, weighing up his limitations and consciously affirming his purpose. Thus, in the early poem, 'Interim', he symbolically renounces '. . . the coloured crags' romantic line/for humbler acre fairly mapped as mine', and indeed he devotes much of what he calls his 'slow skill' to the exploration of low altitude areas of experience where he can safely remain a 'stranger to passion' and 'to those emotions use has not approved'.[67] In his distrust, and perhaps even fear, of emotion, his sense of the modesty of his talent and his diligent application to the task he feels capable of undertaking, Hewitt's temperamental disposition emerges, perhaps also reflecting the more puritanical influences of his background. But he also declares the hope that

> . . . in twenty years I'll find
> wisdom like Marvell's comfortable mind,
> and that my thought and action prove to be
> secure in similar integrity;

and although these lines are withdrawn in a revised and expanded version of the poem written forty years later, there he feels able to declare:

> I've kept on target, and am satisfied
> when I recall behind the placid verse
> a man still stands whose attitude declares
> his loyalty to hope, unquenched belief,
> despite the incidence of age or grief,
> in man's rare-hinted possibility
> of being just, compassionate and free.[68]

Between them, these verses from early and late in his career announce Hewitt's creed, relate it intimately to his choice of language and style and make clear his sympathy with the Protestant preference for straight talk and lack of ambiguity which has been observed elsewhere in Northern Irish culture. This is reaffirmed in 'Style', where he describes his own practice as 'a slow measured art/irrevocably plain', and in 'For Stonecutters' with its delight in the incisive clarity of the mason's skill which avoids abstractions and value judgments so that, quite simply, 'The lettered stone's the metaphor'.[69] It is also implicit in Hewitt's reaction to Wallace Stevens' *Collected Poems* which he finds too clever and contrived, declaring his own preference for

> . . . the crisp neat-witted fellows,
> sharp and laconic, making one word do,
> the clipped couplet, the pointing syllables,
> the clean-beaked sentence, the exact look.[70]

Here Hewitt advocates the very manner of speech which W.R. Rodgers had identified as characteristically Protestant in his essay, 'Conversation Piece: An Ulster Protestant', and shows his instinctive distrust of verbal subtlety and artifice which he equates with dubious integrity.

Whatever the advantages in some contexts of reticence and of wariness of linguistic agility and playfulness, they inevitably impose serious constraints upon a poet, and for the reader Hewitt's verse commonly resembles his own analogical description of it as a familiar, oft-traversed plot of land which has been faithfully drained and cultivated over the years. There is remarkably little innovation or opening up of new territories, whether technically, linguistically or thematically. The honesty with which he confronts a limited range of issues must finally be balanced against his reluctance or inability to grapple with the unfamiliar and uncertain, and the losses which result accordingly. As he put it in 'Substance and Shadow', his verse deals with the

> . . . small republic I have charted out
> as the sure acre where my sense is true,
> while round its boundaries sprawl the screes of doubt;

and in a curiously appropriate way, these lines also suggest an image of the situation of Ulster Protestants clinging tenaciously to what they know, but surrounded by insecurities and unable to move to overcome them.[71]

Hewitt's intellectual and technical cautiousness is matched by his emotional reserve – another trait of which he was aware – so that while his humanity, capacity for friendship and desire for justice and compassion are beyond doubt, he seldom reveals stronger or more intimate bonds of feeling. Perhaps the most notable exception to this is the sequence of five 'Sonnets for Roberta', but even here the fact that these were written in 1954, although not published until 1978 three years after his wife's death, seems further indication of Hewitt's unease with this kind of writing. Furthermore, the sonnets are essentially a form of self-examination in which the writer chides himself for his absorption in his work, his insensitivity towards Roberta and his failure to reciprocate her love and nurture the emotional side of their relationship. The tone is sombre, self-critical, apologetic and solicitous of forgiveness, with the sestet of the final poem amounting to a secular prayer to be allowed to begin again. This is couched as ever in restrained and considered language:

> For I need mercy much, and blessing more,
> if, from the débris of my squandered days
> your hand and mine should these four walls restore,
> beacon and haven in this briery maze,
> and, disciplined by guilt's diminished pain,
> our dialogue of love begin again.[72]

The images of rebuilding and reclaiming overgrown land and the references to discipline and dialogue imply resolution of the difficulties between Hewitt and his wife more by dint of mutual effort than through the power of their love. This has all the marks of Protestant pragmatism which extols the virtue of assiduous commitment to purposeful and productive effort, harbours suspicion of the distracting power of passion and doubts the propriety of freely expressed emotion. Again the general impression is of poetry that is circumscribed by the writer's inhibitions and lack of confidence in articulating a range of emotional experience.

It is clear that Hewitt regarded the business of writing poetry both as a craft and as an honourable form of productive labour. Seamus Heaney noted that he spoke of his study as his 'workroom', and in 'Ars Poetica' Hewitt himself specifically likens his verbal art to the practical skills of a joiner who is celebrated for his patient, systematic method of shaping materials he knows well, for his freedom from dependence on other men and for his reliability which is not subject to chance or whim, 'but like a quarry or a spring-fed well'.[73] Such verse, like the products of the carpenter, will be homely, traditional and serviceable; it will eschew the flashy, the fashionable and the eccentric or original. Hewitt shows that there were times when he doubted the value or purpose of writing verse, which seems powerless to resolve the practical problems of life, but he answers these uncertainties by recourse to another analogy with a traditional form of labour. Just as the farmer does not query where the produce of his land ends up, and resolutely continues in the face of a set-back, or repairs broken equipment:

So be the poet. Let him till his years
follow the laws of language, feeling, thought,
that out of his close labour there be wrought
good sustenance for other hearts than his.
If no one begs it, let him shed no tears,
five or five thousand – none will come amiss.[74]

Stoicism, self-discipline and responsibility are implicitly praised here, and poetry, like the bread of life, is freely offered, although the choice remains with the individual whether or not it is taken.

Such a view might suggest that the poet is little more than a creature of steady habit, pursuing his art with dutiful diligence, but elsewhere Hewitt ascribes to poetry the very mystery and miracle that he fails to find in 'hallowed bread and wine,/the blessed relic or the bell'.[75] In 'The Spectacle of Truth' he movingly examines the need for an art that combines compassion with the unwavering rational vision represented by the lens-polisher's crystals which, paradoxically, distort the view of humanity by their reductiveness and replace the essential flux and movement of life with a frozen abstraction.[76] Thus another exemplary craftsman comes to realise that the gains of a sharper focus are offset by loss of 'charity' – a word which in this context has inevitable biblical resonances. This perception corresponds to the poet's acknowledgement that while part of his task is to be a truth-teller and to enable men to know and understand themselves better, he has an equal responsibility to illuminate his work with compassion for universal human frailty.

The legacy of John Hewitt's Protestant background may therefore be seen in a variety of ways. Although secular-minded and non-religious in a doctrinal sense, the value he placed upon social responsibility and action for justice and equality owes as much to the example of Methodism as it does to socialism. Similarly, the combination of his personal abstemiousness and modest respectability with a readiness to act, speak and write on behalf of principles and causes in which he believed, however unpopular they were elsewhere, are typical features of the kind of dissenting Protestantism he admired. Methodism, like Presbyterianism, is primarily a religion of the word, relying heavily on expository teaching, and the instructive impulse is present in much of Hewitt's poetry, although it is often articulated with Presbyterian plainness. It is, perhaps, not entirely fanciful to see in Hewitt's endless questioning of his place, identity and right to declare himself an Ulsterman, a secular equivalent to the Protestant quest to know oneself among the elect or saved.

This is the point at which the religious and historical aspects of the poet's background intersect. Hewitt is a fully representative voice of the historical dilemma of Protestants in Ulster because the certainty of his claim to belong within the region is forever belied by a guilty awareness of events in the past, a sense of the differences which divide him from his Catholic neighbours and the knowledge that he has no home anywhere else. Hence it is that so many poems become acts of explanation, self-justification and admission. The urge to confess and the certainty that reconciliation is a rational imperative are matched by pride in the industry and practical efficiency of his own people and a deeply engrained sense of Protestant superiority towards priest-ridden Catholics. Ironically, Hewitt commonly ends up reformulating stereotypical views of the two communities, while his own sense of isolation and loneliness is intensified because he cannot wholly subscribe to the religious or political priorities of either. In this way he truly is 'the ultimate Protestant', the individual who asserts the dissenter's right to exercise liberty of conscience and to split away from the orthodoxy of his erstwhile brothers and sisters, yet whose search for greater integrity is always and inevitably coloured and shaped by his inheritance from the past.

CHAPTER SEVEN

Louis MacNeice:
'Questingly Agnostic'

*. . . in a poet belief cannot be disentangled from other things,
from his personal experience and attitude. Again, his personal
experience and attitude do not exist in a vacuum but are
conditioned by time and place, by the general experience
and attitude of the community in which he finds himself.
And if he revolts against that communal experience and
attitude, he is still being none the less conditioned by it.*

Louis MacNeice, *Varieties of Parable.*

*MacNeice is . . . 'religious' in the sense that his poetry shows
a continuing concern to achieve a sense of wholeness or
response to life which, within our culture, has historically
been derived from religious belief and observance . . .*

Alan Peacock, 'Received Religion and Secular Vision:
MacNeice and Kavanagh', in Robert Welch (ed),
Irish Writers and Religion.

RECENT CRITICAL AND biographical studies of Louis MacNeice
have successfully demonstrated his importance as a poet of substance, variety and technical skill whose work continued to evolve up
until his premature death in 1963. No longer is his identity blurred with
that of his contemporaries, Auden, Spender and Day Lewis, but he is
properly recognised for his own particular achievement. An important
aspect of this recovery has been the emphasis upon MacNeice's Irish
background which has captured the attention not only of critics but
of later generations of Irish poets, especially some of those from the
north of Ireland such as Derek Mahon, Michael Longley and Paul
Muldoon. There is now much greater understanding of the degree to
which MacNeice's relationship with Ireland influenced his thought
and practice as a poet, not merely in works which overtly address the
subject, like 'Belfast', 'Carrickfergus', 'Carrick Revisited' or *Autumn*

172

Journal Canto xvi, but more generally. It is clearer, too, that this relationship was complex – both rewarding and disabling in different ways – and that MacNeice himself repeatedly returned to it in his prose and plays as well as in his poetry. His background was specifically defined and coloured by the circumstances of his upbringing as a son of the rectory, which made a powerful and lasting impression upon him. Questions, experiences, emotions, fears, guilts and also happier memories deriving from his childhood permeate his poetry and shaped his adult behaviour and beliefs to a striking degree. Overarching every aspect of these years was his father's role as a clergyman and the forms of theology with which he was surrounded, where there was little concession to the ritual dimensions of worship, and a strong emphasis on the primacy of the Word.

John Frederick MacNeice was a man of integrity, intelligence and personal courage as well as a deeply convinced Christian. When he was a child, his own family were forced to abandon their home on the island of Omey in the west of Ireland after his father, a schoolmaster in the employment of the Irish Church Missions, incurred the violent anger of Catholic neighbours following a row with a local priest. Then, in adulthood, when he was appointed to St Nicholas' Parish Church in Carrickfergus in 1908, he faced strong objections from members of the congregation who had expected their curate to succeed the incumbent for whom he had been deputising during the latter's illness. John MacNeice therefore knew at first hand the bitterness and strength of feeling that matters to do with religion could provoke. However, he also believed that the church and its ministers, guided by Christian beliefs and practising Christian standards, could and should be an influential force for good in the world. So it was that he was an advocate of social justice, a critic of unemployment, and more controversially, a supporter of Home Rule for Ireland who refused to sign Ulster's Solemn League and Covenant in 1912. Later, in 1935, as Bishop of Down, Connor and Dromore, he refused to give permission for the Union Jack to hang in perpetuity over Lord Carson's grave in St Anne's Cathedral, Belfast, arguing that there was no precedent for the flag being given political associations of this kind.[1] The less publicised aspects of MacNeice's ministry were characterised throughout by similar firmness and clarity of purpose linked with tireless work among his parishioners and a disciplined, sober way of life.

However, for the young Louis MacNeice, happy associations with his father, such as when he was entertained by him reciting the names of the railway stations between Carrickfergus and Belfast, were overshadowed by pervading darker memories connected with the religious life and duties from which he felt remote and alienated:

> . . . what my father did by himself was frightening. When I was in bed I could hear his voice below in the study – and I knew he was alone – intoning away, communing with God. And because of his conspiracy with God I was afraid of him.[2]

Later, following his mother's death, MacNeice had to share a bedroom with his father for a time and was distressed nightly by his parent's tossing and groaning in his sleep.[3]

Even the wonderful garden of Carrickfergus rectory with its capacity to stimulate the imaginative fantasies of MacNeice and his sister was juxtaposed with the cemetery from which 'you could hear the voice of the minister tucking people into the ground'.[4] The church itself was a source of other 'terrors' associated in the boy's mind with armour hanging above a monument to the Chichester family and an elderly female parishioner dressed in black who, he convinced himself, was blind.[5] The services, which followed the relatively simple liturgical practices common to much of the Church of Ireland, especially in the North, he later described as a 'stony, joyless anti-time . . . which . . . seemed to preclude music and movement and the growth of anything but stalactites and stalagmites'.[6] When he was too young to follow the sermon, he was encouraged to read Revelation, and in later years he found that 'the rest of the service and the hymns made me feel like crying, in a rather pleasant sugary way, but the parts about sin made me terrified'.[7]

If the religion represented by John MacNeice seemed formidible to his son, this impression was compounded by the influence of Miss MacCready (referred to as Miss Craig in *The Strings Are False*), who was engaged to look after the children during Mrs MacNeice's prolonged ill-health. 'She was small and lean and scrawny, . . . her face was sour and die-hard Puritanical, she had a rasping Northern accent. . . . It was Miss Craig who brought Hell home to me'.[8] Introduced thus in his autobiography, Miss MacCready epitomised everything that the writer found intolerable and distressing in Ulster Protestantism – yet from which he could never finally escape. Her version of religion seemed merciless, loveless and snobbish. Her aim, as MacNeice saw it, was to induce feelings of guilt and sinfulness, fears of imminent death, judgement and condemnation and repression of even the simplest pleasures of life; and she was disturbingly successful in fulfilling it. In 'A Personal Digression' he wrote:

When I went to bed as a child, I was told: 'You don't know where you'll wake up.' When I ran in the garden I was told that running was bad for the heart. Everything had its sinister aspect – milk shrinks the stomach, lemon thins the blood. Against my will I was always given sugar in my tea. The North was tyranny.[9]

This atmosphere, designed to destroy self-confidence and create feelings of failure and worthlessness, made MacNeice believe himself guilty on many different counts. Most importantly, he was haunted by the circumstances surrounding his mother's ill health, departure from the family into medical care and subsequent death in Dublin over a year later when he was only seven. He describes his behaviour during a visit to his mother in hospital when she offered him chocolates:

> Something evil came upon me – I knew it to be evil although it was quite different from the many wrong-doings for which I was going to Hell – and I refused to take the box. I wanted the chocolates very much and also I wanted to be gracious to my mother, but something or other made me spite myself and her and stand there surly and refuse.[10]

This 'something evil' which is similiar to Edgar Allan Poe's 'imp of the perverse', seemed to MacNeice to confirm his irredeemably fallen nature over which he could exercise no control. Later, the guilt returned when he felt unable to cry at the news of his mother's death and when he 'committed a murder' by accidentally upsetting a bird's nest in a hedge beside a path in the garden where his mother and sister used to walk.

The strong and dramatic language in which MacNeice describes these incidents reflects the pervasiveness of this kind of rhetoric in his life and its impact on him. Although his sister records their father's personal disapproval of 'hell-fire' religion, quite apart from Miss MacCready's influence, when Mrs MacNeice was in a depressed state, she too

> . . . developed ideas of having committed unforgivable sins and was inclined to talk even to the children about Death and Judgement, Hell and Heaven and kindred subjects.[11]

Louis MacNeice himself later commented on the Protestant predilection for seeing dramatic signs and significances in symbols and phenomena, and in doing so he coincidentally points out how the Church of Ireland theology he knew, like Presbyterianism, bore the mark of Calvinism. 'Few of the Protestants or Presbyterians can see the Cross merely as a cross', he wrote; and he illustrates how his own thoughts followed this pattern during a childhood incident when he hid in the bushes to avoid having to eat steak for dinner. He listened with a mixture of excitement and fear to the hue and cry as the domestic staff tried to find him. The episode reached its climax when an escaped rooster appeared in the bushes beside him:

> The rooster looked like the Devil with his great scarlet wattles and crest and he was leading his hens straight into my hideout. It was too much for me, I scrambled out onto the lawn and was caught. Miss Craig told me I was bound for Hell and my father told me it was very wrong to make everyone frightened and I ought to think of my mother.[12]

Here the adult shows how the child 'reads' the rooster as an image of the Devil, is overcome by his own guilt and abandons his rebellion, thereby submitting to Miss MacCready's categories of thought. Years later, almost at the end of his life, MacNeice lectured on the nature of parable writing and also developed the use of parable within his poetry. In doing so he brought sophistication and subtlety to the simple, even crude, equations of idea and image which he first encountered through religion in childhood, and produced some of his own most accomplished work. Furthermore, although unable to subscribe to Christian beliefs, MacNeice never lost his conviction that humans have a fundamental need to aspire to meaning and significance beyond mere external forms:

> Man is essentially weak, and he wants power; essentially lonely, he creates familiar daemons, Impossible Shes, and bonds – of race or creed – where no bonds are. He cannot live by bread or Marx alone; he must always be after the Grail.[13]

And questing – for meaning, value, identity, love – is the primary moving force behind MacNeice's poetry at every stage, and the very substance and process of numerous individual poems and many of his plays.

This may also be related to another kind of awareness which began to develop in MacNeice at an early age and which he associated with his first visits to the seaside where the sudden sight of a vast expanse of water – so much bigger than the familiar Belfast Lough – confronted him with size and distance that suggested how much bigger the world was than he had realised. Likewise, he records an epiphanic moment during a family walk which he calls 'a revelation of space':

We were walking along a road between high walls and I could see nothing but the road and the air on the road was quiet and self-contained. On the top of the walls, on the contrary, there were long grasses growing in the stonework and these were blown out, combed, by a wind which I could not see. I wondered what was over those walls and I thought that it must be space. Not fields or roads or houses but an endless stretch of windblown something, something not I nor even my father and mother could ever, however hard we tried, walk to the end of.[14]

Here echoes of the words from St John's gospel – 'The wind bloweth where it listeth, and thou hearest the sound thereof, but canst not tell whence it cometh, and whither it goeth: so is everyone that is born of the Spirit' (ch. 3, v. 8) – combine with a perception of the infinite and invisible which is released through observation of physical phenomena – the grass blowing on top of the wall and the contrast between that and the shelter afforded by the enclosed road. This is the kind of synthesis between tangible reality and sensory experience, and speculative or metaphysical thought which is a marked feature of MacNeice's poetry, but it also shows how, even at an early stage, he had glimpses of a bigger world than that accounted for by Miss MacCready. The point is yet more clearly affirmed in 'Landscape of Childhood and Youth', where MacNeice writes of having 'the sense of infinite possibility, which implied, I think, a sense of eternity' when he looked out to sea from Magilligan Strand, an experience which reappeared years later in the poem 'Round the Corner'.[15]

He also offers a telling commentary on the effects upon him of these sudden, almost overwhelming sightings of the sea:

> This explains perhaps why I have never steered myself much. . . . the things that happen to one often seem better than the things one chooses. Even in writing poetry, which is something I did early choose to do, the few poems or passages which I find wear well have something of accident about them (the poems I did not intend to write) or, to put it more pretentiously, seem 'given'. So Magilligan Strand was like falling in love. For such occasions the word 'falling' is right; one does not step into love any more than one steps asleep – or awake. For awake, like asleep, is what one falls, and to keep falling awake seems to me the salt of life much more than existentialist defiance.[16]

This recommendation of surrendering to life, allowing experience to happen to one rather than seeking to exclude or censor it – unlike Miss MacCready for whom 'you had to be careful who you spoke to' and 'Most of the world was untouchable' – underpins MacNeice's best practice as a poet, but is not easily maintained, as he knew. Paradoxically too, such self-surrender might properly be viewed as evidence of greater spirituality than the eager judgementalism and distrust of life shown by the puritanical 'Mother's Help'.

Unsurprisingly, however, MacNeice's first impulse as he grew up was simply to react against the pressures of his background. The process began when he was sent to Sherborne, where he cultivated eccentricity and discovered 'a new power in myself, the power – and the wish – to criticise'. It continued, albeit in different forms, at Marlborough and Oxford as MacNeice became increasingly distrustful of any philosophy or creed which professed to be all-sufficient, and disturbed by his perception of people whose lives were routine and unquestioning.[17] He summed up his position and his own fear of petrifaction of thought in a characteristically vivid reflection:

> You would think people's minds would get wider, more elastic, but they don't. Quite the contrary. There was that little boy at Sherborne who denied the white foxes, you could put that down to childishness, but when you began to grow up you found out that your own contemporaries, some of whom had been open to ideas before, were all denying white foxes. And you could not thrust white foxes upon them because their whole world hinged on the denial of white foxiness. So you had to choose between the white foxes and them. So you chose the white foxes.[18]

To choose the white foxes was to go against received opinion – or, at least, to place nothing above question – to remain open to all possibilities, physical, intellectual, emotional and spiritual, and as a consequence, often to find oneself alone. The notes of loneliness and homelessness that resonate through MacNeice's poetry derive not only from elements in his family background, but also from his scepticism which partly resulted from his reaction to them, and which in his friend John Hilton's words, made him 'questingly agnostic'.[19] If this gave him an enabling freedom of mind, it also exacted a heavy cost both in terms of escaping from past influences and in living without the consolations of philosophy or belief.

An early poem, 'The Creditor', focuses on the inescapable, and by implication unpayable, debts to God which no placebo or escapism can obliterate and confirms the grip of the past on MacNeice's imagination. However, while it may recall David's sense of the ubiquitousness and omniscience of God in Psalm 139, its tone is troubled rather than celebratory. This Calvinistic deity is endlessly in pursuit of His creditor:

Over and under and all ways
All days and always.[20]

The theology of condemnation and fear which promotes such a view of
God is itself the subject of 'The Preacher'. An intimidating, black expo-
nent of negation, he is no bearer of the Christian gospel of light, but like
a prisoner carrying 'a ball of darkness with him . . . / To find his way by
in streets and rooms'; or like an ironic anti-type of John the Baptist

> He walked in the lost acres crying 'Repent
> For the Kingdom of Death is at hand.'
>
> He took the books of pagan art and read
> Between the lines or worked them out to prove
> Humanism a palimpsest and God's
> Anger a more primal fact than love.[21]

Warnings of impending apocalypse rather than a promise of new life
inform the preacher's message. He views the world as incorrigibly
corrupt and tainted by mortality so that tokens of life and beauty –
roses and gardenias – become emblems of death, and art is rejected
and wilfully construed to produce negative meanings. Perhaps most
striking of all, however, this theology is not only dismissive of joy,
beauty and love, it is ultimately self-centred and self-destructive,
based on a futile attempt to calculate God's grace which conflates
faith and despair (one of the great sins in Christian understanding) in
an unnerving way at the moment of greatest personal need:

> Going upstairs to die in a bare room
> He tried to square the accounts; lying in bed
> He summoned home his deeds, drew back
> Sixty years' expended thread,
>
> Pulled it in through the chink beneath the door,
> Wrapped it around him, all
> His faith and his despair a ball of black
> And he himself at the centre of the ball.[22]

The fact that the preacher rather than God is at the centre of 'the ball'
not only raises questions about the nature of his belief, and perhaps
about the reality of God, it is also a critique of his failure to surrender
to life's experiences and of his egocentric, enclosed existence.

The title of 'Intimations of Mortality' reminds the reader of its
significant difference from Wordsworth's well-known 'Ode', and this

is borne out in its painful autobiographical detail. For this child, God and the Devil are equally frightening creatures of the night, destroying sleep and converting normality into nightmare to which he is abandoned by his parents 'After one perfunctory kiss'. While the preacher announced the nearness of the Kingdom of Death, the closing phrase of this poem – 'The Kingdom comes . . .' – echoes words from the Lord's Prayer, but by changing 'Thy' to 'The' removes the focus from God and creates ambiguity about the nature of 'The Kingdom' and of its ruler. The open ending reinforces this uncertainty and perhaps signals that the nightmare exceeds the resources of language to recount it, rather as Emily Dickinson, another poet with a Puritan background, used dashes at the conclusion of some of her poems to convey a similar sense of the insufficiency of language.

A different kind of crisis produced by the tension between the poet's lost faith and his father's robust belief is recorded in Canto xxii of *Autumn Sequel*. Here the schoolboy MacNeice dreams of outpacing his father as they ascend one of the Wiltshire Downs only to see from the skyline a latter-day version of the crucifixion taking place in an amphitheatre below in front of a 'holiday throng':

> . . . and through the noise I foresaw the world collapse
>
> In my father's mind in a moment, who at my back
> Was still coming up, coming up. This was the worst
> Of my dreams and I had the worst of it, in the lack
>
> Of my own faith and the knowledge of his, the accursed
> Two-ways vision of youth.[23]

Conscious of the central importance of the crucifixion in his father's theology, unable to share that understanding, yet lacking confidence in his own unbelief and troubled with guilt or a sense of having failed his father, the poet feels only his own inadequacy and vulnerability. In *The Strings are False*, MacNeice recalls how, towards the end of his time at Marlborough, he and Anthony Blunt, who was also a clergyman's son, 'both resented the fact that our parents assumed us to be Christian, though neither of us would have dared to stand up in their presence and die for our lack of faith'.[24] As in the poem, this shows the difficulty MacNeice felt in freeing himself from the strong religious convictions with which he had been surrounded, and the pressure they continued to exercise upon him even after he personally did not subscribe to them.

The Christian faith that life is not ultimately bound by human mortality and transience proved particularly difficult for him. Throughout his poetry, MacNeice shows an acute consciousness of the passage of time and of its destructiveness. It is as if the repeated childhood warnings of life's uncertainty and of the possible imminence of his own call to judgement had a far more lasting impact upon him than the resurrection theology preached by his father. In many poems from the mid-1930s MacNeice is obsessed by an ominous sense of the inescapability of time which lurks beneath the surface of life like hidden ice – the metaphorical title of one poem of the period – rendering futile any attempt to ignore it (e.g. 'Spring Voices', 'Museums'), theorise it into insignificance (e.g. 'Turf Stacks', 'Sunday Morning'), or use 'the pretentious word' as a stay against flux and confusion ('Nature Morte'). At its most extreme, this preoccupation leads to a virtual death-wish. Thus, 'Passage Steamer' enacts through its rhymes, repetitions and oppositions the tension between a desire for freedom, change and difference, and an underlying sense of entrapment, negation and inevitability:

> The gulls that bank around the mast
> Insinuate that nothing we pass is past,
>   That all our beginnings were long since begun.[25]

W.T. McKinnon detects 'the mood of Ecclesiastes' in the uncompromising gloom of this poem and its sense of 'the futility of beginning', though this is an attitude of mind that MacNeice strongly rejects elsewhere, for example in 'The Slow Starter'.[26] Similarly, in 'Postscript to Iceland', where MacNeice reviews his famous trip with Auden (to whom the poem is dedicated) as a kind of retreat or equivalent to a biblical withdrawal into the desert in search of self-knowledge and revelation, he is left with a 'death-wish', whereas in his friend the 'lust for life prevails'.[27] Whatever its pleasures, the holiday has not brought MacNeice 'miracles' or 'Visions' – 'No conversions like St Paul,/ No great happenings at all.' Although he declares his resistance to the temptation of a sheltered academic life in a 'forest of dead words', preferring to 'hunt the living birds' of experience despite the risks and solitude involved, and is dismissive of civilised London life ('this desert in disguise'), he finds no comfort or joy in his position:

> For the litany of doubt
> From these walls comes breathing out
> Till the room becomes a pit
> Humming with the fear of it

With the fear of loneliness
And uncommunicableness;
All the wires are cut, my friends
Live beyond the severed ends.

As in the story by another disaffected product of stern Protestantism, Edgar Allan Poe, MacNeice finds himself trapped in isolation between the pit of mortality and the pendulum of time, equipped only with an intercession that is void of faith.

The burden of this position is felt in 'Wolves', where the poet longs to escape from reflection 'and make believe that joined /Hands will keep away the wolves of water /Who howl along our coast'.[28] Other poems, however, accept the transience of experience and the impermanence of life in positive terms and discover the paradoxically lasting value of fleeting moments in the face of change. In 'Train to Dublin', MacNeice contrasts the illusion of continuity and equilibrium suggested by railway travel, with the underlying discontinuities and fragmented experience of the journey of life which break through to consciousness from time to time. He declares that 'during a tiny portion of our lives we are not in trains', and it is in these intervals that we encounter life without illusions or consolations of philosophy. This comes close to what Samuel Beckett described as:

> . . . the perilous zones in the life of the individual, dangerous, precarious, painful, mysterious and fertile, when for a moment the boredom of living is replaced by the suffering of being.[29]

Furthermore, MacNeice finds all of the qualities Beckett attributes to such moments and surrenders to the impossibility of unifying them into any overarching pattern of significance:

> . . . I will not give you any idol or idea, creed or king,
> I give you the incidental things which pass
> Outward through space exactly as each was.[30]

Elsewhere, in 'Snow', he celebrates this as 'The drunkenness of things being various.'[31] Edna Longley finds MacNeice's perspective expressive of his reaction against the single vision and proclaimed certainties of Christianity. Nevertheless, she also points out the total ambiguity of the poem's final line – 'There is more than glass between the snow and the huge roses' – which simultaneously rejects the idea of meaningful relationship between phenomena, and yet keeps open the opposite possibility.[32]

This is a strategy favoured by MacNeice on many occasions and indicates his thorough going agnosticism. It is apparent again in the closing of 'Train to Dublin', where he balances his desire 'to give you more' against his inability to 'hold /This stuff', and his intuition that

> . . . there are further syntheses to which,
> As you have perhaps, people at last attain
> And find that they are rich and breathing gold.[33]

The idea emerges differently in 'Leaving Barra', a poem with both autobiographical and philosophical implications. As the title suggests, it is about departure and the impossibility of return to the same place – a theme which prefigures the quests undertaken by Roland in *The Dark Tower* and Muldoon in *The Mad Islands*, or the homelessness of Odysseus in 'Day of Returning' – and it affirms the poet's fundamental need of 'different values' and his 'hankering after Atlantis':

> Unseen and uncomprehended,
> Dimly divined but keenly
> Felt with a phantom hunger.[34]

Despite the anguish of this 'phantom hunger' he firmly rejects a mindless existence or 'the self-abnegation of Buddha' in favour of life's fleeting phenomena, insisting that

> . . . all the religions are alien
> That allege that life is a fiction,
> And when we agree in denial
> The cock crows in the morning.

The metaphor boldly takes the sign associated with Peter's failure of faith and denial of Christ and redirects it at the theologies of contemptus mundi which the poet regards as betrayals of life. As in 'Train to Dublin', he implies acceptance of the possibility that some greater 'knowledge' or 'solution' to the mystery of life may exist, of which he has 'as yet . . . only an inkling.' Crucially, that 'inkling' derives from perceived and felt experiences of life which he accepts as real and valuable, however passing they may be, and which he found exemplified in the fugue-like movement and vitality of the wife who had abruptly left him for another man. Later, in the 'Dedicatory Poem to *Collected Poems, 1925–1948*', which MacNeice wrote for Hedli, his second wife, he again spoke both of his estrangement from the 'older [gods] /Who had created my fathers in their image', and also of his conviction that in the ground '. . . the Word, like a bulb, is there, is present', apparently another 'inkling' of greater knowledge.[35] Yet, as before, he feels himself groping with:

> . . . half-blind questions that still lack their answers,
> Which lack grows no way less as I grow older.[36]

The process of exploring has its own value and importance even though the end point of belief or philosophical resolution remains elusive – a theme he returned to in his epigraph to the poems of 1950–1951. Here he speaks of

> Dry words dying, dying, dead,
> Burning that the Word may live,

thereby acknowledging the inadequacy and unreliability of language, yet at the same time accepting that only through it may we allude to or try to express that sense of the numinous, the absolute, the ideal which he never wholly abandons as a possibility. This dilemma of the man of words in search of the Word is summed up in the opening stanza of 'Entirely':

> If we could get the hang of it entirely
>   It would take too long;
> All we know is the splash of words in passing
>   And falling twigs of song,
> And when we try to eavesdrop on the great
>   Presences it is rarely
> That by a stroke of luck we can appropriate
>   Even a phrase entirely.[37]

In such circumstances, metaphor, symbol and parable are the most suggestive and stimulating means by which poetry builds, in MacNeice's phrase, a 'bridge to the unknown' – just as does the language of scripture and religion that was so familiar to him.

The relationship between man and his world and the mediating role of language in this is also the subject of 'Plant and Phantom'. Reminiscent of George Herbert's 'Prayer' in its technique of announcing the subject ('Man') at the outset, and then proceeding to explore it through a series of vivid images, the poem insists that man

> . . . cheats the pawky Fates
> By what he does, not is,

By what he makes, imposing
On flux an architectonic –
Cone of marble, calyx of ice,
Spandrel and buttress, iron
Loops across the void,
Stepping stones in the random.[38]

To use words is to act, and only through such action is humanity distinguished from other life forms. Only through such action can we rebel against the realities of time and mortality, 'Smuggling over the frontier /Of fact a sense of value'. Sceptic that he was, MacNeice appears thoroughly Protestant in his commitment to the power of words and in the final stanza of this poem he returns to the notion that behind all language is an age-old, unforgettable, felt 'aura' – 'Dew on the skin' – for which man

Ever since has fumbled, intrigued,
Clambered behind and beyond, and learnt
Words of blessing and cursing, hoping
To find in the end the Word Itself.[39]

As Terence Brown has noted, whereas the first stanzas suggest that man himself creates value, these lines offer a different perspective. Here 'Value is not simply a solipsistic construct but an intuition of something beyond us, something implicit and incarnate in the world of fact'.[40] 'Plant and Phantom' shows how although MacNeice was never able to subscribe to his father's beliefs or accept the authority of Christian teaching and practice, he nonetheless continued to revisit certain elements in them which were not wholly alien to his own view of life.

The treatment of Christmas in a number of poems illustrates this point further. The early 'Eclogue for Christmas' shows MacNeice at his most mordant, commenting on an entropic world of increasingly empty gestures, banal living and spiritual torpor. Far from being the conventional season of goodwill, hope and new beginnings, it is 'an evil time' where 'One place is as bad as another'.[41] Yet the refusal of Speaker B to ascribe any meaning to Christmas in his concluding words –

Goodbye to you, this day remember is Christmas, this morn
They say, interpret it in your own way, Christ is born

– is not only consistent with the uncertainties and scepticism of the whole poem; it also leaves room for multiple understandings of the significance, if any, of Christmas, without judging between them.[42] Denis Ireland once commented that these lines would be a suitable epitaph for MacNeice, 'the unbeliever who believed'.[43]

Later, in Canto xx of *Autumn Journal*, MacNeice again reflected on the approach of Christmas, acknowledging the radical challenge of Christ who came

> . . . armed with more than folly,
> Making the smooth place rough and knocking the heads
>   Of Church and State together.[44]

However, he ironises the modern saturnalian version of Christmas which indulges the flesh, ignores the spirit and leaves Conscience 'crying through the desert /With sackcloth round his loins', and in doing so makes a conventional Christian critique of the refocusing of the festival.

The most sustained meditation on Christmas comes in the final three cantos of *Autumn Sequel* in which MacNeice is literally on his own and on the move – revisiting a display of artefacts from the Ancient East in the British Museum, in Norwich on a BBC Christmas Eve assignment and on a train returning to London on Christmas morning – as well as pursuing his solitary speculations and questions. The museum brings back childhood memories of the awe he felt when confronted by the symbols of an alien religion, prompts adult consideration of whether the 'Wisdom of the East' was 'mere bones and riddles', or whether the Wise Men of the Christmas nativity story may really have come from Egypt, Babylon and India, and leads to the question:

> If so, where were they bound for? Can we sever
> Two thousand years ago from here and now,
> Or Bethlehem from say Birmingham?[45]

The search for meaning and belief expressive of a fundamental need is not limited to a particular time or place, but is repeated throughout human history and superficial changes in the style of people's lives have no bearing on it:

> . . . no chromium gloss
> Could ever disguise a manger, no transmitter,
> Gantry or pylon dare replace the Cross.[46]

In this mood, even the poet

> . . . brought up to scoff rather than bless
> And to say No, unless the facts require

> A neutral verdict, for this once say[s] Yes.[47]

However, Canto xxv resumes a more familiar note of doubt as MacNeice's thoughts turn to past times, deceased friends, the state of the world and his own mortality, all of which seem to deny the significance of birth:

> And yet children are born; once more the light
> Bursts through the shattered rafters and the prism
> Contains all colours yet adds up to white;

> And, in despite of ology and ism,
> Barbicans crumble while the stable stands . . .[48]

While he may not accept the meaning attached by Christians to the birth in the stable, MacNeice still finds it a credible and usable metaphor of the human hope that overrides frailty and disaster. This is borne out by the closing words of the canto which affirm that 'now, /Take it what way you like, is really Christmas morning'. Although recalling the end of 'Eclogue for Christmas', and still withholding any personal commitment, the emphatic use of the word 'really' gives positive energy to the line, which is carried forward into the last canto where MacNeice's 'prayer' for his friends is that 'the wall/Of isolation' may:

> . . . crumble, and the light
> Break in, but also out, the black scales fall

> From all their eyes together in one white
> And final annunciation.[49]

He himself experiences a kind of 'annunciation', symbolised in the breaking light of Christmas morning which brings 'different air', sets 'the pigeons . . . homing, each equipped /With some short message to repulse despair', and floods his imagination with metaphors of vitality, hope and renewed quest.[50] The image of an unknown hero resuming the inevitable search is joined through simile to the exemplary figure from another mythology, Theseus, tracing his way through the labyrinth, just as the poet pursues the question of whether or not life is 'empty' sung out by the wheels of the train that is literally transporting him to London, and metaphorically carrying him forward in his life's journey. Confronted in his mind with people from his own past, some of whom are dead, yet who are mysteriously present to him on the train, he undergoes a form of judgement, feeling guilt and facing their accusations, before he sees other 'more /Inspiriting faces' which subdue 'the horn /Of horror' until:

> . . . I can smell
> A waft of frankincense, maybe this morn
>
> Is really Christmas, maybe (who can tell?)
> The Kings are on this train. All that I know
> Is that good will must mean both will and well
>
> And that, crowded or empty, fast or slow,
> This train is getting somewhere. I return
> To my own seat and wait and, also serving, go
>
> Irrevocably forward.[51]

Again he uses Christmas as a metaphor of hope, despite his many reservations and renewed interrogation of its reality. The reworking of Milton's line – 'They also serve who only stand and wait' – places waiting ahead of serving, thereby reasserting MacNeice's belief in the necessity of surrendering to experience before seeking to impose a form upon it.

The 'prayer' which MacNeice offers for his friends in *Autumn Sequel* is one of several such petitions in his work, the best known being 'Prayer before Birth'. It is unclear to whom this intercession is directed, but it expresses multiple fears of life and anxiety that human potential will be utterly corrupted or destroyed. Like George Herbert's 'Sighs and Grones' on which it is loosely modelled, the poem is a plea for mercy, but whereas Herbert's petition rests on belief in an omnipotent God who is capable of reprieving and relieving him, the voice in MacNeice's poem merely asks to be equipped to play the many roles and meet the harsh demands of life. This difference of emphasis is crucial and while Herbert's poem concludes with the exclamatory 'My God, relieve me!', MacNeice's voice ends by preferring death to being petrified or 'spilt' by those who would destroy him.[52] Thus, in 'Prayer before Birth' death is equated with extinction, but in 'Sighs and Grones' God continues to prevail beyond the grave.

The problem of what to pray for and to whom prayer should be addressed had already surfaced in Canto xviii of *Autumn Journal* where MacNeice shows his dissatisfaction with various approaches to the question of God from Nietzsche's abandonment of Him to pantheism and 'Indian acquiescence', insisting only that

> If everything that happens happens according
>   To the nature and wish of God, then God must go.[53]

Further on in the poem, where he deals with the Spanish Civil War (Canto xxiii), he again strives to formulate a prayer, articulating what he wishes to see blessed and prosper despite his customary qualification when using the word 'God':

> May God, if there is one, send
> As much courage again and greater vision
>   And resolve the antinomies in which we live
> Where man must be either safe because he is negative
>   Or free on the edge of a razor.
> Give those who are gentle strength,
>   Give those who are strong a generous imagination,
> And make their half-truth true and let the crooked
>   Footpath find its parent road at length.[54]

Behind these lines lie allusions to Christ's command to travel lightly, to the Beatitudes and to the prophetic words of Isaiah concerning the Messiah. Thus, once again, although MacNeice's prayer is unconventional, he draws upon biblical teaching as a positive source of reference which is not incompatible with his own ideals. It is also notable that in this same canto, he dismisses the refusal 'to begin /Anything new because we know there is nothing /New' as 'an academic sophistry – /The original sin'.[55] E.R. Dodds has written that

> There were few things he was sure of. He was once challenged to state publicly what he believed. He replied: 'I believe that life is worthwhile, and I believe that I have to do something *for* life. I believe that as a human being it is my duty to make patterns and to contribute to order – good patterns and a good order.'[56]

This is entirely consonant with the responsibly committed approach to life evident in Canto xxiii of *Autumn Journal* (and elsewhere), but is also consistent with the kind of Christian responsibility MacNeice must have observed in his father.

Given the combination of his own difficulties with belief and his abiding interest in religious questions, it is not surprising that MacNeice's imagination was stimulated by instances that highlighted the tensions between faith and uncertainty. An example of this is 'The Springboard', 'the dream picture' of the naked man poised in mid-air over London, motivated by 'the irrational assumption that it is his duty to throw himself down from there as a sort of ritual sacrifice'.[57] The dream situation incorporates elements from Christ's story, but recasts them so that the man is 'crucified' by 'unbelief' rather than set free by faith. He is, in Terence Brown's words, 'a modern Saint Thomas, racked by doubt and scepticism'.[58] Whereas Christ resisted the temptation to throw himself from the top of the temple to prove his divinity and win great wealth, but gave himself up for no material gain as the redemptive sacrificial victim on the cross, the man in the poem accepts the need for sacrifice, but:

> His blood began to haggle over the price
> History would pay if he were to throw himself down.

This poem probes the conflict between the need for an atoning sacrifice and loss of belief in its possibility. The words 'If' and 'But' which begin the first two lines of the third stanza balance against each other the ideal and the likely outcomes of such sacrifice in the modern world, while the projected effect on his friends – so different from that on Christ's followers – is negligible and fails to change them:

> If it would mend the world, that would be worthwhile
> But he, quite rightly, long had ceased to believe
> In any Utopia or in Peace-upon-Earth;
> His friends would find in his death neither ransom nor reprieve
> But only a grain of faith – for what it was worth.

The throw-away conversational phrase, 'for what it was worth', is ambiguous, however, suggesting not only the ease with which his faith may be dismissed as little more than personal eccentricity, but also opening up a more thoughtful reflection upon the possible value of faith.

The leap which the man seems bound to make despite all the reasons against it ('. . . we know he knows what he must do') is wholly destructive – he is likened to a bomber – and of no greater redemptive significance than that of 'ten million others', the victims of war who are also 'dying for the people'. The 'broken steeple' he will plummet past is not simply the casualty of an air raid, but symbolises an age of shattered belief in which 'the leap of faith is impossible, the life of commitment an unreasonable suicide'.[59]

In *Ten Burnt Offerings*, aptly described by Peter McDonald as 'MacNeice's most obviously "religious" book', the problematics of faith again feature prominently.[60] Two poems, 'Areopagus' and 'Didymus', are of particular interest in this context, both of them dealing with biblical figures. The first reflects upon St Paul's mission to Athens, bringing 'A sharp titillation /With a snub, if not threat, in it too'.[61] While the apostle represents 'Iron faith', Athens is 'a city of irony', a place of many deities, but also with an altar to the Unknown God symbolising the felt insufficiency of other gods and ignorance of the one proclaimed as real by Paul:

> Which is why Paul
> Scouring the market found an altar
> Clearly inscribed but between the words
> Was the ghost of a Word who runs may guess,
> Who runs from a fate unclear, unkind.

The doubts of the Athenians are wittily contrasted with Paul's Christian certainties in MacNeice's significant alteration to the line from John Keble's hymn which begins:

> There is a book who runs may read
>   Which heavenly truth imparts,
> And all the lore its scholars need,
>   Pure eyes and Christian hearts.[62]

However, the issue of uncertainty is further complicated by references to 'The Kind Ones' or Eumenides, 'Once avenging, later beneficent', also associated with Athens. Although in Paul's time reduced to 'life-size' by poets and painters, unlike Christ who had not yet been 'scaled down /To ikon or niche', the twentieth-century poet is aware how 'bishop and builder' have 'Gilded the nails, adjourned the verdict, /And boxed the cross in a square' since New Testament times.[63] In one sense, therefore, there is nothing to choose between the Eumenides and Christ: both having been tamed and half-forgotten might seem irrelevant curiosities. Yet MacNeice denies that anything that has happened since 'Could cancel out Christ's death or prove the Furies dead'. Both Christ and the Furies remain linked to the human need to face the Unknown and to make a treaty with it and modern man must still find ways to appease this desire for a saviour:

> Christ, if we could, having Christian fathers;
> But Furies, if we must. For no

> Life is for nothing, all must pay,
> Yet what unknown is dread, we know
> Can yet prove kind; our selves can pay
> Our sons atonement for their fathers.[64]

MacNeice's proposed resolution is through human redemptive effort alone, rather as in 'Prayer in Mid-Passage' he paradoxically asked the deity which is at once monster and guide to enable men to transcend humanity, and climb 'This time-bound ladder out of time' without divine assistance.[65]

Where 'Areopagus' juxtaposes ancient Greek and Christian culture, 'Didymus' contrasts the doubting monotheistic faith of St Thomas and the multiple deities of the Indian subcontinent to which Thomas was, by tradition, the first apostle. As Robyn Marsack has written, 'MacNeice here chose a subject exactly suited to his gifts and his own quandaries: he could verbally imitate the metaphysical tension between the One and the Many'.[66] Unlike Paul, Thomas is hesitant, unsure, 'the saint /Who had left his faith to his hands', 'armed with two plain crossed sticks' to 'flout' the 'banyan riot of dialectic' associated with Hinduism.[67] The second section of the poem focuses on the unlikeliness of Thomas as an apostle, on his apparent unsuitability and imagined feeling of impotence before Shiva and Krishna until he realises that his two hands, forever associated with his doubting faith, are his greatest asset and his means of witness:

> . . . then he thought: I am proud, I have only
> Two hands for all things, including the cross,
> As have the coolies; it is my mission
> To help their lack with mine.[68]

However, the doubts which beset his faith and deny him the supposed consolations of secure belief, make him question the lasting effects of his mission and his right 'to preach or write /In the name of Christ'.[69] Even his personal memory of Christ 'wilts in the heat' so that all he remembers with confidence is hearing his name called. Paradoxically, this motivates his mission to others, because although he doubts Christ's continuing friendship to him, he believes it is a possibility for others and particularly for the Indians whose religion excludes such personal intimacy with God:

> Is he my friend still? No, perhaps. All that I know
>   Is that each rice-farmer, snake-charmer, scavenger, merchant, mahout,

> Each life in this land that is sore has the chance to soar
>   To find and keep that friend. But, for myself, I doubt.[70]

In the final section of the poem, the Indian landscape, overhung by Hindu belief in the insignificance of individual life, is set against 'the gospel of Thomas /Which grants each ant its worth', but which is taught by a man who is himself a proxy:

> ... hawking a faith
> That he knows should be theirs while he dare not assume it is his
> Unless he confirm and remind himself by his hands
> Caressing his walls of rock, batting the flies,
> Or pressing them merely together, those hands that once
> Were tested and proved, yet failed through needing a test.[71]

These lines sum up MacNeice's dilemma precisely. It is only through his lived experience – or in the case of Thomas, through touching the risen Christ's wounds – that he can grope towards a transcendent view of life or belief in lasting value. Yet real faith, as Jesus reminded the doubter, does not rely upon tangible proof. The fourth part of the poem is broken up by two eight-line sections in which a tempter's voice encourages Thomas, and by implication the poet, to abandon doubt and admit unbelief, but it is, paradoxically, in living with his doubts that the apostle – like the poet – proves his faithfulness.

Other exemplary figures or types are the subject of 'The Kingdom', a poem celebrating unconventional individuals who 'vindicate the species', and like Thomas are 'humble /And proud at once, working within their limits /And yet transcending them'.[72] They are like a group of the elect, free spirits in whose lives may be seen independence of mind, integrity and magnanimity. MacNeice's own recently deceased father is included in a tribute which revises some of the more austere and troubling images in his earlier work. Now he is acknowledged as

> One who believed and practised and whose life
> Presumed the Resurrection. What that means
> He may have felt he knew; this much is certain –
> The meaning filled his actions, made him courteous
> And lyrical and strong and kind and truthful,
> A generous puritan.[73]

Whatever the difficulties between father and son had been, the latter discovers the virtues he himself most admired in the very man against whom he had earlier rebelled. As Jon Stallworthy has noted, this is one of a number of poems in which, as the years went by, MacNeice 'would plot the progress of his grieving and reconciliation' with his father.[74]

He was also evolving a more conciliatory attitude towards other aspects of his Irish background. Early poems like 'Belfast' and 'Carrickfergus' gave essentially negative views of it. In 'Valediction' he expressed the desire to 'exorcise' his blood of Ireland, while also reluctantly admitting that he 'cannot deny my past to which my self is wed', and as Ryan in 'Eclogue from Iceland' he announced his sense of exile from 'a nation /Built upon violence and morose vendettas', and from fellow countrymen whose besetting sin was 'Shooting straight in the cause of crooked thinking.'[75] This last condemnation reappears in the celebrated Canto xvi of *Autumn Journal* where MacNeice bitterly attacks the narrowness, inflexibility and sentimentality of so much Irish thought which nurtures self-deception and irresponsibility, and is the premise for sectarianism and brutality. Yet, the intensity of his attacks derives from the acknowledged complexity of his feelings – 'Odi atque amo' – from which he cannot escape.[76] Later again, in 'Carrick Revisited', much of the resentment has died away and the poet accepts that no part of his subsequent experience 'Cancels this interlude' of his northern childhood.[77] His visits to the west of Ireland with its ancestral associations also served to modify his reactions and prompted thoughts of another courageous voyager in pursuit of ultimate truth. According to a ninth-century manuscript, Brendan (or Brandan, as MacNeice calls him in 'Western Landscape') sailed from Ireland in search of the Isles of the Blessed, relying on his faith in God to negotiate the trials and dangers of his journey. Inspired by the 'narcotic' power of the landscape, with its Lethe-like atmosphere which lulls the 'teetotum consciousness' and 'Proves and disproves what it wants', MacNeice imagines how it stimulated Brandan's quest to finally 'undo /Time in quintessential West'.[78] The 'spindrift hermit' is a model for the poet of the perfectly reconciled man:

> One thought of God, one feeling of the ocean,
> Fused in the moving body, the unmoved soul,
> Made him part of a not to be parted whole.
> Whole.
> And the West was all the world, the lonely was the only,
> The chosen – and there was no choice – the Best,
> For the beyond was here . . .[79]

Such a state of reconciliation and equilibrium is impossible for MacNeice for whom the 'beyond' would always be 'still out there'. As a modern man, unsure in his beliefs, merely a visitor to the west, he acknowledges that he can neither be 'free of all roots', like Brandan, 'nor yet a rooted peasant', and while he enjoys the west's seductive lure which is suggestive of transcendence, he simultaneously knows his inability to find lasting peace there.

The compelling power of the same western seaboard reappears in 'The Strand', where MacNeice's father is again an exemplary figure of faith. The poet, metaphorically following in the dead man's footsteps where once they had walked together on the shore, recovers the memory of the 'solitary and wild' element in his father's nature, never completely suppressed by 'all his responsibly compiled /Account books of a devout, precise routine', which was released on visits to the west of Ireland. He is preoccupied by the way in which the wet sand, which now mirrors his own image as once it had reflected his father, appears to vouchsafe permanence but is quickly 'Blotted' by 'the floor-mop of the foam'.[80] As W.T. McKinnon has observed, this raises again the riddle of 'the permanence of what passes' which so greatly exercised MacNeice. He continues:

> The reality that is mirrored is . . . complicated, being inextricably involved in the illusion, for the permanence of what passes may be no illusion. Even if the One, the sea, obliterates the Many, the 'bright reflections', these reflections will recur endlessly, linked in the permanency that is bestowed upon them by the eternal principle whose brightness they reflect. The 'bright reflections' are, like 'the flange of steel in the turning belt of brine', in the category of the jigging or glinting mani- festations of the real.[81]

MacNeice's father, the man of Christian faith, is 'A square black figure whom the horizon understood', a significant description which attributes to him a reconciliation of mind and spirit under the eye of eternity akin to that of Brandan, and again quite different to the poet's own agnostic insecurity. However, his recognition of the belief of individuals like his father and Brandan shows that MacNeice remains open-minded on the question of whether or not there is anything beyond the flux of time and change.

His confidence that there may indeed be more is stronger in 'The Window', a three-part exploration of the power of art to mediate between the ideal, perfected moment and the instability and move- ment of life in which such instants dissolve and pass even as they are recognised. The poem begins by contemplating how a painter of a scene viewed through a window created a 'bridge in timelessness' between the worlds on either side of the glass which, rather like Keats's Grecian urn, belongs to everyone and no-one, and has a self-completeness and finality that allow

> No egress to adventure,
> For life that lives from mind to moment,
> From mouth to mouth, from none to now . . .[82]

MacNeice debates how the kind of 'coherence' achieved through art, and sensed rather than fully understood by the mind, may be related to 'a world of flux and bonfires' where the view through the window of every life is endlessly changing. Although he cannot apprehend any lasting solution to this dilemma, he is convinced of the truth of those epiphanic moments, images photographed for ever onto the consciousness, when

> . . . the hour-glass turns over and lies level,
> The stopwatch clicks, the sand stops trickling, what was remote and raw is blended
> And mended what was torn.[83]

It is appropriate to describe such glimpses as visionary or prophetic, not least because of the religious language and references used in relation to them. Their power inexplicably 'Absolves us from time and tide', temporarily overthrowing the isolation of the individual in a mysterious 'betrothal' between flux and permanence. They may be no more than 'a tentative /Counter attack on the void', but MacNeice invokes one of the archetypal biblical stories of faith and hope to describe them as

> . . . a launching forth from the window
> Of a raven or maybe a dove
> And we do not know what they will find but gambling on their fidelity
> And on other islanded lives we keep open the window and fallibly
> Await the return of love.[84]

The contrast between 'fidelity' and 'fallibly' and the use of the word 'gambling' define the difference between the unhesitating faith of Noah and the poet who can neither wholly believe nor unbelieve, yet who, in the final part of 'The Window', still struggles to find a word adequate to name 'what dare not have occurred /But does occur regardless', which must be taken on trust, and which, paradoxically, means that:

> Even at the heart of lust and conflict
> We can find form, our lives transcended
>   While and because we live.[85]

MacNeice wonders whether the 'Pyrrhic salvoes' of art are 'Pentecost or sacrament', but they seem like answers to his 'Prayer in Mid-Passage' and affirm in practice his belief in the supreme importance and value of creating good patterns.

The later sequence of poems, 'Visitations', the title of which suggests occasions of annunciation or epiphany, revolves around more religio-mystical experiences of momentary intersections between the world of here and now and some state beyond temporality. Here MacNeice possibly approaches closer to an affirmation of belief in God than at any other point in his work, and nowhere more so than in the final poem which is inspired by 1 Kings ch. 19. The chapter records how the prophet Elijah, isolated and desiring death, is directed to make a journey to Mount Horeb where he takes refuge in a cave until the Lord reveals himself to him, not in a whirlwind, earthquake or fire, but in a still, small voice. MacNeice aligns himself with Elijah: he is a solitary observer of the world, in his office at the BBC, in a bar, or above all, 'in the cave of his mind' where the poetic creation that takes place is indistinguishable from the healing and restorative revelation given to Elijah:

> Suddenly Something, or Someone, darkened the entrance
> But shed a new light on the cave and a still small voice in the silence
> In spite of ill winds and ill atoms blossomed in pure affirmation
> Of what lay behind and before it.[86]

In 'Jigsaws V', MacNeice wrote, 'That God exists we cannot show', but as 'Visitations' makes plain, he increasingly implied his belief not simply in the human need for an 'unknown', but also that 'The Unknown is There'.[87]

This is substantiated in a number of poems from his last two collections, several of which show him returning to childhood memories of 'the primal garden of Carrickfergus Rectory' which he invested with associations both of Paradise and of the Fall.[88] Thus, in 'Apple Blossom' he confidently asserts that life is a series of new beginnings, first times and fresh starts, so that the loss of Eden is no final disaster. Only after the shutting of the Garden gates was the endlessly self-renewing capacity of life disclosed, thereby proving that 'the first verdict' was not 'the worst verdict', but, paradoxically, the very means by which the reality of the unknown is affirmed.[89] Likewise, 'Idle Talk' reviews the impossibility of finding words which are completely new and unused to express even our deepest feelings, yet concludes that

> The innocence that our days outmode
> Seems no more innocent than that
>
> Adam achieved when, holding the half-
> bitten, already half-forgotten,
> Fruit in his hand, he looked at Eve
> And, wholly forgetting Eve herself
>
> As he had known her till that moment,
> Looked and felt for the same three words
> Which he had uttered time and again
> But never like this, and said: 'I love you'.[90]

Paradoxically again, loss of innocence liberates new understanding and the profoundest insights are granted to fallen eyes. As another poem 'Vistas' puts it, to emerge into love is to gain 'predestined /Freedom' which reveals the world anew and denies that 'earth and truth are only/Earth, respectively, and words'.[91] Like 'Idle Talk', 'The Wall' and 'Good Dream' 'end in Edenic circumstances', as Edna Longley has noted, 'with a similar sense of barriers – between people, between here and the beyond – dissolving in a garden', and in such 'visionary moments . . . the religious reinforces the secular rather than vice versa'.[92]

The garden is also present in a poem which draws together various strands from MacNeice's earlier life and reopens the question of his relationship to his father. 'The Truisms' is the poet's version of the parable of the prodigal son. He returns to the house where 'His father gave him a box of truisms /Shaped like a coffin', but only by leaving home without them, surrendering to all kinds of experience in life and reaching his own disbeliefs which render the old house unrecognisable at first, is this possible:

> . . . he walked straight in; it was where he had come from
> And something told him the way to behave.
> He raised his hand and blessed his home:

The truisms flew and perched on his shoulders
And a tall tree sprouted from his father's grave.[93]

This image of reconciliation clearly cannot be taken to indicate MacNeice's acceptance of his father's beliefs, but reveals the productive dialectical process which enabled him to open the 'box of truisms' and grasp their significance. In doing so it is recognisable as another enactment of the idea of falling into understanding, insight and compassionate feeling. The sprouting tree inevitably recalls the Tree of Knowledge in Genesis as well as the Tree of Life and atonement into which the cross of death was transformed, but it is only identifiable by a man who has long since 'fallen', as both Adam and the prodigal son did, and who, in Stallworthy's phrase, 'dream(s) of forgiveness and renewal' faced with the fact of his father's death and an increasing sense of his own mortality.[94]

The lifelong course of MacNeice's struggle with religious belief is charted more fully in 'The Blasphemies' which starts with an early memory (first recorded in *The Strings Are False*) of struggling to avoid damning God, thereby committing the theological sin against the Holy Ghost and incurring the dire consequences foretold for such offenders.[95] Fascination with the idea of such a great offence, fear of its penalties and incomprehension of its meaning are interwoven in the child, while later the young man mockingly parodies 'Prayers, hymns, the Apostles' Creed – /Preening himself as a gay blasphemer', although realising the impossibility of joking about God while disbelieving in his existence. By thirty, he reformulates the original doctrine, only to be left with a greater sense of the proliferating questions for which he has no answers. This is reflected in the way the jaunty tone of the poem gives way to broken sentences and an interrogative:

> . . . humanism was the all and the only
> Sin was the sin against the Human –
> But you could not call it Ghost for that
> Was merely emotive; the only – you could not
> Call it sin for that was emotive –
> The only failure was not to face
> The facts. But at thirty what are the facts?

Turning to 'myth', he finds attempts to 'use my childhood symbols/ Divorced from their context, Manger and Cross' unsatisfactory precisely because they can never be detached from personal associations, and the myth without faith does not sustain meaning. In the final stanza, covering his fifth decade, he passes beyond the unresolvable questions of the divinity of Christ and the existence of God, placing reliance on no source of authority beyond himself, yet convinced of the worth of his own quest for meaning and still dogged by the question from childhood:

> He was not Tom or Dick or Harry,
> Let alone God, he was merely fifty,
> No one and nowhere else, a walking
> Question but no more cheap than any
> Question or quest is cheap. The sin
> Against the Holy Ghost – What is it?

Edna Longley is surely right in her observation that 'The Blasphemies' 'narrates a history of negotiations with belief, negotiations at once personal and artistic' and 'makes explicit the structure of question and quest behind many other poems'.[96] By encapsulating stages in MacNeice's quest, it demonstrates the continuity of his engagement with issues of meaning, belief and value, and the degree to which his specific religious background informed and drove that engagement. In the play *Christopher Columbus*, the title character declares:

> I remember all things personally.
> All that has happened to man since the fall of Adam;

and the Prior picks up this comment and continues:

> And you know why Adam fell?
> Because he had eaten the fruit of the Tree of Knowledge –
> The forbidden tree that gives men fancies,
> That makes them cry for the moon.
> You yourself, my Son –
> The taste of that fruit is strong in your mouth.[97]

'The Blasphemies' confirms MacNeice as one who has eaten of the Tree of Knowledge and who also cries for the moon. Aware in this poem not so much of loss as of never having found, he nonetheless remains committed to searching and scrutinising his own experience, refusing to deny or forget the difficult questions, and as other poems have shown, in the process gaining intermittent glimpses of the beyond through the world of time and change which he once described as the 'Mainspring of our striving towards perfection'.[98]

If the rigid austerities of his northern Protestant background were decisive in rendering personal belief in his father's faith impossible, they were inescapable and equally influential in other ways too.

MacNeice always accepted the importance of fundamental religious questions concerning the nature of reality and the source of ultimate value in a temporal world. His deep-seated awareness of the particular emphases of Christian theology and his knowledge of the Bible, prayer book and hymn book show repeatedly in his work, and are seldom treated merely satirically or dismissively. Through biblical figures such as Adam, Elijah, Jacob and Thomas he came to explore how human failure and frailty do not preclude the capacity to perceive value beyond mortality. From his father he learnt how individual faith could be the basis of active courage and compassion in life and in fellow artists he identified a 'cloud of witnesses' whose work is, like his own, a permanent affirmation of life.[99]

MacNeice's longheld and unflinching belief in the unique value of the individual's perception of the world and surrender to experience without seeking to evade it through illusion or mediate it through dogmatism underlies his entire project. His friend, W.R. Rodgers, observed that

> If MacNeice's poetry – or his life – at first sight appears fragmentary or lacking in cohesion, it is not because he failed to edit it or order it; it is simply because he positively refrained from editing or ordering his sensations in advance. He preferred to leave himself open to experience, to the infinitely possible and the suddenly surprising, to the *given*. This, I would suggest, is the very basis of his poetry.[100]

In another person, this might be seen as a description of a life of faith, but at the very least it is consistent with a radically Protestant view of the importance of private judgement. Without a belief in God, in Walter Allen's words, 'He is himself, as it were, his final court of appeal'.[101]

Equally rooted in Protestant values was MacNeice's strong sense of personal accountability and responsibility. In his 'modern morality play', *One for the Grave*, which was first produced after the author's death, Everyman greets the audience with the phrase of the doomed Roman gladiators:

> Moriturus te saluto. I did not choose to be put in this ring to fight, I did not ask to be born, but a babe in arms is in arms in more senses than one and since my birth I've been fighting. Conscript or volunteer – I just don't know which I am – and it may have been a losing battle but at least I've been in it, I've been in it. And now les jeux sont faits and rien ne va plus. To be a human being is a cause for grief – and for pride. Everyman must vindicate himself. In what he does, what he makes, what he is. Oh I know they say one has no choice in the matter, but I don't believe them.[102]

Although this might prompt thoughts of the monologues of Samuel Beckett's characters, it does not plumb the depths of their anguish and or their sense of absurdity. Likewise, in his closing prayer, Everyman offers thanks for having been given the chance of life and asks forgiveness insofar as he failed to use it. Such an attitude is consistent with MacNeice's scepticism of any philosophy, theology or -ism which might compromise the intellectual or moral integrity of an individual, or deflect him away from grasping life in its entirety and accepting his responsibility for doing so.

He possessed something of that older puritan sense of life as a continual drama enacted on a narrow stage between birth and death, light and dark, mortality and eternity (or extinction) and with the frisson of perpetual uncertainty about when it would end. His own attitude to that drama may be illustrated through a comment he made not about theology but, much more typically, about rugby. MacNeice was an enthusiastic follower of this sport which, he said, 'makes two virtues supreme – individual endurance and the open game'.[103] The combination of determination and stamina, lit up by bursts of stylish flair, glorious risk-taking, deft footwork and adventurous running characterises much of what is best in his writing, and is most expressive of the view of life embodied in it. Even in 'Thalassa', possibly his last completed poem, the aged leader challenges his 'broken', 'heartsick' and 'ignoble comrades' to renewed effort and quest:

> The narwhal dares us to be free;
> By a high star our course is set,
> Our end is Life. Put out to sea.[104]

Thus MacNeice continued to the end 'raiding the abyss', restlessly pursuing his responsibilities as an artist, 'Raising a frail scaffold in never-ending flux':

> Conscious of guilt and vast inadequacy and the sick
> Ego and the broken past and the clock that goes too quick,
> Conscious of waste of labour, conscious of spite and hate,
> Of dissension with his neighbour, of beggars at the gate,
> But conscious also of love and the joy of things and the power
> Of going beyond and above the limits of the lagging hour,
> Conscious of sunlight, conscious of death's inveigling touch,
> Not completely conscious but partly – and that is much.[105]

CHAPTER EIGHT

Derek Mahon: 'Singing the darkness into the light'

. . . the religious dimension of Ulster Protestant culture –
devolved into aesthetics and metaphysics – counts for much
in Mahon's poetry and conditions its extremity.

Edna Longley, 'Derek Mahon: Extreme Religion of Art' in
M. Kenneally (ed), *Poetry in Contemporary Irish Literature.*

. . . he was born into an historical community, that of
Northern Irish Protestantism, and his most deeply felt
poems derive from his sympathy for its isolation and its
fading presence rather than from straightforward
repudiation of its stiff rhetorical intransigence.

Seamus Deane, 'Derek Mahon: Freedom from History' in
Celtic Revivals: Essays in Modern Irish Literature.

AFTER GROWING UP in Belfast and attending university in Dublin, Derek Mahon has lived and worked in many different places in England, Ireland, the United States and Canada. This enrichingly varied experience is evident in his poetry, but so too is the sense of rootlessness or homelessness which it might suggest. Mahon's relationship to his native Protestant background has never been easy or relaxed. His precocious ambitions to be a poet were known even as a schoolboy, and his 'amazingly accomplished verses' in the school magazine gave a clear indication that his potential matched a disconcertingly assured sense of vocation that was so markedly different from that of his peers, as his fellow poet, Michael Longley, recalls.[1] Years later, in 'Courtyards in Delft', he characterised himself as having been 'A strange child with a taste for verse' in a culture and environment that showed little sympathy or understanding towards artistic endeavour.[2]

Mahon followed Longley to Trinity College, Dublin, in 1960, and both have described the anarchic living conditions of much of their undergraduate years, in the midst of which writing, reading and arguing about poetry remained their constant obsession. For Longley, Mahon in those days 'embodied the spirit of Pan or Puck'. Both set out to 'undermine Northern Irish middle-class respectability' and to mock 'the more complacent brands of Unionism', but while Longley admired his friend's 'disenchanted vision', he found himself 'less attracted than he to the role of *poete maudit*'.[3] This disenchantment, hostility towards many aspects of his background and personal sense of detachment and alienation from it are as apparent in Mahon's earliest collection as his wit, cosmopolitan artistic and literary interests and technical facility. Yet although the narrow-mindedness of Protestant Unionism provoked his contempt, and the sectarian violence into which the province lurched appalled and dismayed him, Mahon's relationship to that background and its culture was and remains perplexed and influential – a tie that can neither be purged nor abandoned and which has contributed formatively to his artistic preoccupations and poetic sensibility.

The early poem, 'Glengormley' (the name of the area of Belfast in which Mahon grew up), announces his wry view of the respectable suburban domesticity and typically Protestant orderliness that have been raised complacently on top of a more violent and invasive past, now ignored or forgotten, but which despite appearances may not necessarily have disappeared.[4] This is a diminished and demythologised world, impermeable to any 'saint or hero' bringing 'dangerous tokens to the new era'. It is a world in which nature has seemingly been tamed and regulated, and where traditional wisdom is reversed since it is not sticks and stones that can harm 'A generation of such sense and charm', but 'Only words hurt us now'. The apparent security gained by mastering natural forces is ironically undercut by this reference to words, because it is by their use that experiences are ordered and articulated. If words themselves are problematic and disturbing because they are inadequate vehicles to convey the deepest feelings and thoughts, then this exposes the superficiality of 'The terrier-taming, garden-watering days' in which, however, 'By / Necessity, if not choice' the poet himself is implicated, as if by a kind of predestination.

The sense of being implicated without choice in the matter is also apparent in 'In Belfast' (subsequently called 'The Spring Vacation'). Here Mahon speaks of 'Walking among my own . . .', but his relation

to them is ambiguous and at first may seem detached and privileged
– he walks 'In a tide of sunlight between shower and shower' – until
he 'resume(s)' his 'old conspiracy with the wet / Stone and unwieldy
images of the squinting heart'.[5] There is a distinct self-consciousness
suggested here, a deliberateness of purpose summed up in the final
line of the first stanza: 'Once more, as before, I remember not to
forget', and it is ironic that in a culture which places such high value
on remembrance, he has to make an effort to do so. In the next two
stanzas he sets against each other the 'perverse pride in being on the
side / Of the fallen angels and refusing to get up', and subscription to
'the humorous formulae' or 'sullen silence' of social and religious
conformity which is associated with distorted vision (see the earlier
'squinting heart') and gloomy piety, and a refusal to contemplate a
different perspective:

> We could *all* be saved by keeping an eye on the hill
> At the top of every street, for there it is –
> Eternally, if irrelevantly, visible –

Here, as Edna Longley says, the use of the word 'saved' 'suggests that
once more a Protestant writer is turning Protestant orthodoxy,
Protestant conscience, against itself, to outline a very different kind
of salvation to that offered by evangelism'.[6] The hill no longer has the
associations with God ascribed to it by the psalmist, and this non-
denominational 'salvation', which has nothing to do with the the
'elect' of Calvinist theology, would entail freedom from the introversion, calculation and repression of people who, ironically, prefer
to walk in the dark rather than in the light.

The shift from the first person singular to the first person plural
between stanzas one and two signifies that Mahon does not seek to
deny his own participation in the codes and conduct he mocks. The
return to the singular form in the final stanza emphasises that even
though he is intuitively 'on the side / Of the fallen angels', 'One part
of my mind must learn to know its place' – both in terms of knowing
Belfast itself and of knowing his proper relationship to its people and
their culture. The closing lines are the poet's memorandum to himself,
a further invocation of the idea that he must 'remember not to
forget', in which he both acknowledges and chides himself for his
'casual interest' in the realities that another part of his mind shies
away from, 'The things that happen in the kitchen-houses/
And echoing back-streets of this desperate city'. The ambiguity of
the word 'desperate' renews doubt about the spiritual state of the

citizens, while through the repetition of the words 'casual' and 'interest' in the final line, and the financial sense in which the latter is used it seems that 'The streets of Belfast . . . do demand the attention from the narrator, like the continuing cost of servicing a debt'.[7]

Mahon's ambiguous relationship to 'his own' is even more acutely exhibited in 'Ecclesiastes' where his concentrated horror at the oppressive, judgemental narrow-mindedness of Calvinistic Protestantism is balanced against awareness of how easy it would be to conform to it:

> God, you could grow to love it, God-fearing, God-
>   chosen purist little puritan that,
> for all your wiles and smiles, you are . . .[8]

The book of the Bible after which the poem is titled is a meditation on the vanities and futility of life. Mahon equates Protestant theology with life-denying, uncompromisingly joyless attitudes which make virtue out of austerity, the repression of pleasure and pious, unforgiving rhetoric. He envisages local John the Baptists as forerunners of nothing:

> Yes you could
> wear black, drink water, nourish a fierce zeal
>   with locusts and wild honey, and not
> feel called upon to understand and forgive
>   but only to speak with a bleak
> afflatus . . .

This is religion, and a way of life, based upon retreat from knowledge, fear of experience (of the kind of 'Fall' advocated by W.R. Rodgers' poem of the same name), distrust of imagination, and deliberate blindness. Here power is exercised by the one-eyed over 'a credulous people'. Mahon knows and understands the dynamics of the society from the inside, pouring scorn upon its workings and rejecting the possibility of abandoning the role of unconventional and raffish entertainer in exchange for that of street-corner theologian and prophet of doom.

Reductive theology is also the target of the satirical '*Matthew V.29–30*', which uses the text ('And if thy right eye offend thee, pluck it out, and cast it from thee: for it is profitable for thee that one of thy members should perish, and not that thy whole body should be cast into hell. And if thy right hand offend thee, cut it off, and cast it from thee: for it is profitable for thee that one of thy members should perish, and not that thy whole body should be cast into hell') to render absurd Christ's injunction to pursue spirituality over worldliness and physical pleasure. The poem enacts a systematic process of self-mutilation involving not only the dismemberment of the body and destruction of the sensory organs, but also of the mind, and of the manifestations of human creativity and intelligence and their capacity to move or influence others; in short, of

> All evidence whatever
> Of civility and reflection,
> Of laughter and tears.[9]

Nor is that all, because following its own perverse logic to the bitter end, this theology requires the obliteration of the world itself which stimulates mind, imagination and emotions, thereby provoking the 'offence' that must be purged; and so it is in 'silence without bound' that the narrator claims to be 'fit for human society'. Thus '*Matthew V.29–30*' proposes that it is only by 'un-creating' the world which believers claim that God made, and by laying it waste, that they can perfect themselves to live in it. This reductio ad absurdum of a type of theology which the poet regards as irrational in itself is a riposte to his experience of the kind of culture satirised in 'Ecclesiastes' prompted by his distrust and hostility towards it.

What Mahon seizes on is the loss of spirituality he perceives in Northern Protestantism and its replacement either by judgmental legalism or an emptiness which seeks relief in nostalgia and lingering desire for a supposedly lost past. In 'The chair squeaks . . .' (later called 'Nostalgias') he employs images of longing for a return to origins which would give security, comfort and meaning in a stormy world. The final lines:

> In a tiny stone church
> On the desolate headland
> A lost tribe is singing abide with me

reverse the consoling image of the Protestant elect, or chosen people, and suggest instead a vulnerable, uncertain and forlorn few attempting to find succour in Henry Francis Lyte's melancholic hymn which appeals to the 'Help of the helpless' as 'The darkness deepens'.[10] This last phrase actually appears in Mahon's poem, '"Songs of Praise"', where the 'tiny tunes' of the hymn singers are lost against 'Conflicting rhythms of the incurious sea' which 'Take over where our thin ascriptions fail'.[11] Mahon's revised version of this poem (in *Selected Poems*) drops the third and fourth stanzas of the original, thereby leaving it as a bleak comment on all 'songs of praise'. However, the subsequently omitted stanzas go on to question what being 'born again' might mean, picking up on the familiar evangelical exhortation and inverting its usual implication that the sinner must turn away from his previous life – 'Never look back, they said; but they were wrong'. The 'lost lives' of these people – and again it is notable that Mahon includes himself among them, because the poem shifts from the third to the first person plural – may be changed not by a single act of repentance leading to salvation, but by looking back 'constantly'

> On that harsh landscape and its procreant sea,
> Bitter and curative, as tonight we did,
> Listening to our own nearly-voices chime
> In the parochial lives we might have led,
> Praising a stony god who died before our time.

Their lostness is now regarded as the result of their failure to see the world as it is rather than seeking refuge from it in a kind of worship which the poem has already intimated to be irrelevant and inconsequential.

The north Antrim coast, which is the topographical location in 'The chair squeaks . . .' 'Nostalgias' and '"Songs of Praise"', figures prominently in other poems (for example, 'North Wind: Portrush', 'Rathlin' and 'The Sea in Winter'), and Mahon has written of its 'peculiar life-style . . . with its strange combination of derivative hedonism and sabbatarian grimness'. He sees it as *'un beau pays mal habité'* (a phrase he also uses in 'The Sea in Winter') whose people 'probably inhabit some old-fashioned California of the mind, where the Union Jack somehow waves in the breeze over Sunset Boulevard and the natives are deferential'.[12] His feeling for them veers between fascination, even admiration for some of the women who are 'tough as old boots', detachment from their affiliations, values and illusions and interest in 'the Ulster Protestant pathology' characteristically revealed in the 'weird poetry' of a nostalgic wall-slogan which declared: 'We shall never forsake the blue skies of our Ulster for the grey skies of an Irish Republic'.[13] But the very exposure of the coastline and the rough weather which sweeps in on it from the sea have also stimulated the imagination of this poet who so often prefers desolate and remote landscapes.[14] The north wind in the poem of the same name is not like W.R. Rodgers's pentecostal wind of words, but it 'works itself into the mind', and betokens 'the existential, black / Face of the cosmic dark'.[15] Paradoxically, the same location may be temporarily irradiated by sunlight, although the beguiling nature of such trans-formations is emphasised: objects are 'eldritch-bright' and the storm-cleansed freshness which might be mistaken for 'the first day' is merely 'A false sense of reprieve'. Nothing ever changes in this elemental battleground ('Were we not / Raised on such expectations, / Our hearts starred with frost / Through countless generations?') which is void of gentler, more colourful and romantic associations:

> Here only the stricken souls
> No spring can unperturb.

'Stricken souls' are lost and suffering, and the negatives in the fol-lowing line insist on the irredeemable nature of their plight from which no healing magic can relieve them ('Prospero and his people never / Came to these stormy parts'), and in which few would choose to join them:

> Yet, blasting the subtler arts,
> That weird, plaintive voice
> Choirs now and for ever.

For all its remorseless bleakness, and indeed through it, the poet recognises a compelling music in this wind which affirms his own view of man's essentially exposed place in a world unrelieved by metaphysical consolations. This is, as it were, an inversion of the orthodox Calvinistic perspective represented by a writer like the eighteenth-century American puritan, Jonathan Edwards, who 'read' in the evidence of the physical world 'The Images of Divine Things'. He commented that, 'The works of God are but a kind of voice or language of God to instruct intelligent beings in things pertaining to himself'.[16] Mahon, on the other hand, is more inclined to see evidence of the absence of God in his 'readings' of the landscape and elements. Although 'North Wind' is situated very precisely and alludes to the predominantly Protestant community that lives there, it is not simply addressing their predicament, but reaches outwards to become an expression of Mahon's perception of the universal human predicament.

In the early poem, 'Day Trip to Donegal' he arrives at a similar awareness by contrasting the apparent securities and order of shore life, and in this case city life, with the unfettered energy of the sea's 'immeasureable erosions' and the wind, which return in dreams to haunt him and confront him with the reality of his existential fate in terms reminiscent of the castaway in William Cowper's poem of spiritual desolation:

> At dawn I was alone far out at sea
> Without skill or reassurance (nobody
> To show me how, no earnest of rescue),
> Cursing my mindless failure to take due
> Forethought for this, contriving vain
> Overtures to the mindless wind and rain.[17]

Just as Calvinist theology insists upon the futility of the individual's efforts to ameliorate God's judgement or to alter one's predestined personal end, so the poem shows how the limited value of all preparations and plans is exposed by the irresistible power of elemental chaos in which no guiding hand is found. The puns on 'mindless' and 'vain' not only mock the theology, but make an ironic comment on the poet's own failure to understand how illusory the tranquillity is in the 'suburbs / Sunk in a sleep no gale-force wind disturbs', and how easily it may be convulsed. In the light of this view, the smug composure of the residents of Glengormley seems foolish indeed.

The feeling of being unhoused and adrift, exposed to forces which may not ever be susceptible to order, and against which any attempts to raise order seem doomed to limited or provisional success at best, has informed many of Mahon's poems at each stage in his career. It is closely allied to another issue he has repeatedly explored – the task of the artist and the significance of art, in an inexplicable and chaotic world. In 'Rage for Order', Mahon brings together these concerns and, in Terence Brown's words, 'deprecates with self-conscious irony the futility of art in a world of "burnt-out buses" and "scattered glass"'.[18] Here, the poet's is 'a dying art':

> An eddy of semantic scruple
> In an unstructurable sea.

It is 'dying' both in the sense of fading and of dealing with death, but Mahon is bitterly critical of poetic detachment and distance, likening this to the activity of that model of artistic irresponsibility, Nero, who infamously fiddled while Rome was burning. Words, the poet's only tool (and the Protestant's touchstone of truth), and order, the artist's ultimate goal, seem equally unreliable and precarious, and writing an act of 'desperate love' in the face of unmanageable experience.

'History', observes Edna Longley, 'marginalises poetry, not poetry history' and she continues:

> Steven Tuohy provides a superb summary: 'At the heart of [Mahon's] poetry, beneath all the brilliance and sophistication, lies a doomed gesture of appeasement of extraordinary pathos'. This covers all the layers of Mahon's apologia, from Ulster Protestant historic guilt, to human guilt, to the poet's guilt that poetry by definition is not enough.[19]

And yet, as other works make clear, each poem marks a return to the challenge and the problem, a bid to start afresh that involves

> coming
> Into a dark country
> Beyond appraisal or report
> The shape of the human heart.[20]

It also necessitates humility and patience, absence of which

> Betrayed you to a waste
> Of rage, self-pity bordering on self-hate,
> A blind man without comfort at the gate.

No positive outcome or increase in understanding is guaranteed, but 'With practice you might decipher the whole thing / Or enough to suffer the relief and the pity'. As in 'Rage for Order', there is an implied sense of guilt here, but 'A Dark Country' adds a wishful note of atonement, a desire to understand and not simply to dismiss, and shows greater optimism that this may be possible.

Whatever may be understood occurs in the context of lost innocence and the acquisition of experience. From the poem that opens his first collection, 'Girls in their Seasons', which speaks of 'running out of light and love' and 'plunging into the dark forever', Mahon has repeatedly articulated his sense of a world rushing headlong towards terminal collapse or destruction and which resists a more consoling view of the future.[21] When, in 'Homecoming' he writes that

> we cannot start
> at this late date
> with a pure heart,
> or having seen
> the pictures plain
> be ever in-
> nocent again

it is clear that he rejects the possibility of a return to some form of prelapsarian state that precedes knowledge.[22] Homelessness is our natural state now, as inexplicable as predestination and akin to it in its inevitability. Thus, in Mahon's work the kind of quests seen in MacNeice's poetry become more like the dislocated wanderings of some of Samuel Beckett's characters. For example, in 'Going Home', the ghostly figures exist meaninglessly in 'the afterlife / Of the unjudgeable, / Of the desolate and free', crossing the Humber like one of the rivers in Hell 'To the blank Elysium / Predicated on our / Eschewal of metaphysics'.[23]

Mahon measures the growth of his own scepticism in 'Afterlives' where the two parts of the poem are strategically balanced against each other. Dedicated to his fellow poet, James Simmons, in the first part he begins by proclaiming confidence in 'reason' to provide 'long-term solutions' to the brutality and sectarianism of Northern Ireland, and in the enlightenment of 'the dark places' with 'love and poetry' and 'the power of good'.[24] Such easy faith in the transforming power of culture, education and reason is then mockingly upended as the poet rebukes himself and his friend for allowing themselves

> To imagine for one second
> That our privileged ideals
> Are divine wisdom, and the dim
> Forms that kneel at noon
> In the city not ourselves.

Their fault and folly derive from the complacent arrogance with which they have assumed the absolute value and potential of their bourgeois liberalism. The second part of the poem offers the only possible corrective: the poet must return home in humility and learn from experience rather than theorising from afar. However, it becomes progressively clear that such a return is itself no simple act of recovery, but serves to generate new uncertainties. If home remains unaltered in some respects since his last return years ago ('. . . the hills are still the same / Grey-blue above Belfast'), yet in other ways it is so changed as to be scarcely recognisable after 'five years of war'. This prompts Mahon's closing speculation on how his own growth and development might have been different if he had 'stayed behind / And lived it bomb by bomb'. Here, as Elmer Andrews says, 'The rebuke of Part 1 deepens into elegy to lost possibility. But all certainty is gone, for he cannot be sure where the road not taken would have led him'.[25]

The sense of irretrievable remoteness from home and of universal existential homelessness has continued into Mahon's most recent poetry. In part xii of 'The Hudson Letter', titled 'Alien Nation', he reflects on Chicago's dropouts and streetdwellers, and concludes:

> We are all far from home, be our home still
> a Chicago slum, a house under Cave Hill,
> or a caravan parked in a field above Cushendun.[26]

Thus, the homeless in Chicago and the poet now distant from Glengormley or from part of the Antrim coast, which also has specific associations with another 'homeless' poet, Louis MacNeice, have more in common than might be imagined. Similarly, elsewhere in the collection, J.B. Yeats, the father of the poet, is celebrated as another exemplary figure who 'in your own words, lived and died / like all of us, then as now, "an exile and a stranger".'[27]

His discovery that the notions of 'returning' and of 'home' are surrounded with difficulty does not remove his need to keep on exploring what they might mean and to understand them better. Terence Brown has noted that

> Poet after poet in the north has written poems that imagine the journey back to origins, to the primal place . . . such poems enforce a sense that the poet knows there are things in the individual and collective past and present which his art must encompass if it is to be true to Irish reality.[28]

The movement of this journey from comfortingly familiar terrain and self-confidence into places where doubt and insecurity prevail is a recurrent pattern in Mahon's work. Already observed in 'Afterlives' it is characteristically illustrated in 'The Woods'. Here, having first evoked an idyllic, peaceful rural existence in 'A green retreat' (a phrase perhaps recalling Marvell's 'green thought in a green shade'), he suddenly interrogates its very seclusion and sedateness, asking

> . . . how could we
> survive indefinitely
> so far from the city and the sea?[29]

Intuitively, he turns from the 'too creamy' and 'fat profusion' of an arcadian grove to harsher, more bracing locations, declaring that

> we travelled on
> to doubt and speculation,
> our birthright and our proper portion.

There is a puritanical quality in this eschewal of comfort and withdrawal in favour of rigour and engagement, and in the terms in which 'doubt and speculation' – altered to the even starker 'chaos and confusion' in *Selected Poems* – are accepted as a fitting inheritance.

The return to origins in 'Courtyards in Delft', one of Mahon's most admired poems, is mediated through the poet's concentrated study of a seventeenth-century painting by Pieter de Hooch which leads him back to formative aspects of his own childhood and upbringing. The immaculate, unruffled orderliness, functional thriftiness and emotional restraint in the domestic scene captured by the artist are evoked with matching verbal precision. However, Mahon goes further than this, defining the world of the painting not only by what it foregrounds, but also by what it omits – thereby implying what is subdued or absent from the lives of those within this culture:

> No spinet-playing emblematic of
> The harmonies and disharmonies of love;
> No lewd fish, no fruit, no wide-eyed bird
> About to fly its cage while a virgin
> Listens to her seducer, mars the chaste
> Perfection of the thing and the thing made.
> Nothing is random, nothing goes to waste.
> We miss the dirty dog, the fiery gin.[30]

This introduces an ironic dimension which grows in importance as the poem proceeds because, even as it is apparently celebrating a model of disciplined, respectable life, the catalogue of exclusions inevitably points to deficiencies or limitations in it. When it becomes clear that the painting is a 'mnemonic' for Mahon, a picture through which he can re-encounter his own childhood background, this releases insights into both his intimate understanding of such a life –

> I lived there as a boy and know the coal
> Glittering in its shed, late-afternoon
> Lambency informing the deal table,
> The ceiling cradled in a radiant spoon.

– and his alienation from it, because his artistic, imaginative interests had nothing in common with the narrow Protestant values that underpinned life in Belfast. Furthermore, he implies his distaste for the imperialistic tenor he associates with Northern Irish Protestant culture just as Dutch imperial ambitions were nurtured within the society represented by de Hooch:

> I must be lying low in a room there,
> A strange child with a taste for verse,
> While my hard-nosed companions dream of fire
> And sword upon parched veldt and field of wind-swept gorse.[31]

Cleanliness, godliness, repression and a potential for violence, which superficially appears to have nothing to do with the scene evoked by either the painting or the poem, are brought into relationship with each other. Domestic calm and orderliness conceal dangerous impulses which, as history has shown, vent themselves against others with religion as their justification, while the creative thinker – the artist – is marginalised or dismissed. Ironically, a culture raised on Protestant individualism has elevated strict conformity into its prime virtue. Equally ironically, as Maurice Riordan has observed, Mahon has taken the values of this background, 'Frugality, discipline and attention to the ordinary', and has used them 'as the artistic means of the poem' which makes a critique of them.[32]

Contrary to his awareness of the Protestant understanding of history as the outworking of God's design, and of progress as the measure of its march towards fulfilment, Mahon's own view is deeply pessimistic, as 'Courtyards in Delft' suggests. He rejects a positive idea of the modern world as the culmination of human achievement so far, seeing it instead poised uneasily between a lost past and an entropic, reversionary future. Unlike Seamus Heaney, to whom 'Lives' is dedicated in later collections, Mahon is distrustful of the capacity of history or archaeology as a means of uncovering significant connections between past and present:

> . . . if in the distant
>
> Future someone
> Thinks he has once been me
> As I am today,
>
> Let him revise
> His insolent ontology
> Or teach himself to pray.

He issues the warning at the end of a poem which has undermined notions of historical continuity.[33] Likewise, Rathlin Island, where the air was once filled with the victims' screams during an horrific massacre, but which is now 'a sanctuary where amazed / Oneiric species whistle and chatter', is a place where, unlike the mainland, 'they are through with history'.[34] This serves to confuse rather than to clarify the relationship between past, present and future for the poet as he returns to the shore after his visit:

> Spray-blind,
> We leave here the infancy of the race,
> Unsure among the pitching surfaces
> Whether the future lies before us or behind.

He cannot be certain whether the future is contained in the memory of distant violence – and the reference to bombs that 'doze in the housing estates' clearly hints at this possibility – or in the kind of 'dream-time' absence of human activity that he has briefly glimpsed.

While Mahon may not believe that the human race is 'fallen' in the theological sense, Edna Longley's observation that, like W.R. Rodgers, he has 'internalised "all that Adamnation /And hand-me-down of sin"' is very apt.[35] This is seen in the corrupting and debasing effects he attributes to much human activity which, in his view, has produced the barbarism of contemporary urban life that will eventually cause it to fall asunder. Many of his poems refer to the disintegrating detritus of modern civilisation – rusting tins, abandoned cars, scrap metal, deserted buildings, empty cityscapes, cut wires – which serve as 'intimations of collapse, pogrom, apocalypse'.[36] In 'Gipsies Revisited' (later retitled 'Gipsies') the poet who has seen on his television in the comfort and shelter of his house how the police, the guardians of conventional, civilised living, have persecuted these dissenting outsiders camped on the margins of society 'on waste / ground beside motorways', addresses the gipsies directly:

> You might be interested
> to hear, though, that on
> stormy nights our strong
> double glazing groans with
> foreknowledge of death,
> the fridge with a great wound,
> and not surprised to know
> the fate you have so long
> endured is ours also . . . [37]

This might recall the biblical story of Dives and Lazarus, but it is also shot through with a Calvinistic sense of impending retribution which will descend upon everyone.³⁸ In addition, the wind to which the poet is listening in the closing lines seems to be the harbinger of the desolation of the universe prefigured in the images of cars piling up and the growing heap of scrap in his garden.

Elsewhere, a less millenarian note is sounded. 'The Terminal Bar' is a metaphorical ante-room to finality, a Beckettian waiting-place on a planet surrounded only by the 'desolate / silence of the spheres', the 'vast dark' of which offers no hope of transcendence and inevitably defeats all searchers for the grail, or would-be conquerors of space.³⁹ 'Entropy', as the title suggests, imagines the decay as a more gradual process – a running down of energy, the failure of civilisation and retreat to 'the old methods' of survival for which

> We are not quick enough
>
> Having become
> Heavy and slow from
> Long urban idling.⁴⁰

The progress of history is not only denied, but thrown into reverse. Society as we know it gives way, nature resumes its ascendancy and human consciousness recedes to a preconceptual stage.⁴¹

Some poems, such as 'The Snow Party' and 'The Last of the Fire Kings', express the artist's desire to finish altogether with history, to escape its barbarity and to retreat into 'my cold dream / Of a place out of time, / A palace of porcelain'.⁴² However, they do not deny the continuation of atrocity or fail to question the protagonist's own relationship to the events which he would ignore or flee from. Here, as in the poem known successively as 'What Will Remain', 'Thammuz', and 'The Golden Bough', the poet again seeks to understand the links between art and responsibility, aesthetics and politics, not simply in the face of local conflict, but of global collapse. 'The Golden Bough' projects a post-apocalyptic scene – 'after / The twilight of cities, / The flowers of fire' – in which man will have restored to nature all that he had previously seized and devastated in pursuit of progress and civilisation, and will inhabit a landscape that sounds remarkably like paradise regained.⁴³ Although the reversion here reiterates the pattern of 'Entropy', the phrase 'When we give back' suggests a more active human role in facilitating this change and the final stanza proposes a different, conscious relationship between man and nature:

> Once more I shall worship
> The moon, make gods

Of clay, gods of stone,
And celebrate
In a world of waste
Their deaths and their return.

In a world redeemed by its return to elemental forms, and in which
man has atoned for the violations of nature caused by his history and
politics, worship is once more possible, albeit of a most primitive
kind, centred on what another poem calls 'the banished gods' who

. . . sit out the centuries
     In stone, water
   And the hearts of trees,
Lost in a reverie of their own natures –

Of zero-growth economics and seasonal change
   In a world without cars, computers
     Or chemical skies,
     Where thought is a fondling of stones
And wisdom a five-minute silence at moonrise.[44]

The silence and stillness associated with these 'banished gods', and
also with worship of them, are in marked contrast to the assertive
dogmatism, rhetoric and ambition for power that Mahon has mocked
and ironised in his explorations of Protestantism. The greater affinity
of such a view with the contemplative religions of the east than with
the Judaeo-Christian tradition is directly suggested by the title of
another poem, 'The Mayo Tao' (originally 'The Hermit') and its
subject – an artist who has 'been working for years / on a four-line
poem / about the life of a leaf.'[45] Here, as Kathleen Mullaney has
written, we see Mahon's 'respectful, patient and self-effacing effort to
let the natural world speak for itself rather than presuming to speak
for it with human language'.[46] This effort, marked by its intensity
and desire for perfection, pursued with courageous fidelity to
individual perception and subject at times to doubt about its own
worth, has all the characteristics of a religious quest undertaken by a
poet in search of spiritual wholeness through the harmonies of art.

If 'The Mayo Tao' suggests the discipline and method of the
contemplative effort, 'A Garage in County Cork' offers an exegesis of
the insights such an effort yields. Beginning with a luminously exact
observation of the particularities of a former home and business
premises, now deserted and reclaimed by nature, Mahon proceeds to
draw from the scene an expanding series of thoughts that transcend

time, place, culture and specific forms of belief, yet which never loses sight of the starting point in the abandoned garage. The scene itself is unfolded like a text: the empty dwelling prompts reflections on the necessarily unknowable lives of the family who lived there, and on where, like so many Irish people over generations, they may have emigrated to – 'South Boston? Cricklewood?'.[47] 'Somebody, somewhere thinks of this as home', opines the poet, reintroducing this familiar concern and releasing an imaginative construction of the memories the emigrants may carry, and of the scene as it may have looked when it was inhabited. One proposed detail – 'Tyres in the branches such as Noah knew' – suggests not only the place's recent past, but, simultaneously, its timelessness. As the perspective shifts back again from thoughts of when the garage was occupied to the circumstantial facts of its current desertion, the process of decay itself becomes revelatory:

> The intact antiquities of the recent past,
> Dropped from the retail catalogues, return
> To the materials that gave rise to them
> And shine with a late sacramental gleam.

Distinctions between ancient and modern, past and present, one place and another, blur as materials metamorphose and revert to basic forms, so that it becomes an easy transition of thought to read this contemporary landscape, with its abandoned petrol pumps and nearby Catholic shrine, in terms that link it with classical mythology (the story of Bauchis and Philemon). 'We might be anywhere', declares the poet, 'in the Dordogne, / Iquitos, Bethlehem', at any time, within any culture or framework of belief or faith:

> But we are in one place and one place only,
> One of the milestones of earth-residence
> Unique in each particular, the thinly
> Peopled hinterland serenely tense –
> Not in the hope of a resplendent future
> But with a sure sense of its intrinsic nature.

Having uncovered the universal contained within the particular, Mahon brings the poem back to the specific place from which it started, insisting on the truth of the paradox that it is simultaneously unique and representative, 'a poem not about place, but our place in the world', as Hugh Haughton puts it, and that its singularity is a cause for celebration.[48] (This idea is also strongly present in 'A Lighthouse in Maine', which first appeared in the same collection.) Despite the 'sacramental gleam' from the decaying objects, the half-humorous suggestion that the site is 'Nirvana' and the specific reference to the birthplace of Christ, the poem expresses no faith in conventional ideas of transcendence ('a resplendent future') in a 'universe / Decelerating while the fates devise / What outcome for the dawdling galaxies?' The best that may be had – and it is not proposed ironically or cynically – is what Tom Paulin has called 'that condition of supremely unillusioned quietism – the wisest of all passivities', which is 'religious in its negativity.'[49] This remarkable poem articulates the vision of a writer whose 'mild theoptic eye' is both near-sighted and far-seeing – responsive to the trees and also to the wood, we might say – as compassionate as it is perceptive in unfolding the connections between the microcosm and the macrocosm. It is steady in its contemplation of a world unredeemed by the hope of faith, yet whose 'intrinsic nature' is not without beauty and value. It is, in short, what Haughton has described as 'a kind of God's eye global view, though in a world without theology'.[50]

The mediating role of the artist, who is perhaps the most appropriate replacement for theologians when, as another poem puts it, 'There is No-one to blame', is evident and indispensable in 'A Garage in County Cork'.[51] Yet it seems that, as if of necessity, the artist himself must work from a position that leaves him detached from or on the margins of society in order to achieve his 'theoptic' perspective. Brendan Kennelly has observed that

> There is something in [Mahon's] art which is peripheral, watchful, measured, spectatorial, ardently uninvolved, articulately sidelined. This does not diminish his ability to appreciate others. It gives it, in fact, the authority of a certain kind of distance, a certain intellectual chastity that warms and validates his feelings;

and likewise Seamus Heaney finds 'present in all his books, this dominant mood of being on the outside (where one has laboured spiritually to arrive) only to end up looking back nostalgically at what one knows are well-nigh intolerable conditions on the inside'.[52] This has already been seen in his ambiguous attitude to history – the desire for disengagement checked by reluctantly acknowledged involvement – and in his repeated situating of poems on the margins of sea and land, in locations exposed to the elements, or where collapse and decay are in progress. However, it is also evident in poems addressed to or about individuals whom Mahon finds exemplary for their own courageous defiance of conventions and in other works which test the possibilities and limitations of art itself.

From his earliest collection, he has been drawn to figures who are dissenters and outsiders – non-conformists, indifferent to the demands of respectability, even in some cases disgraced. These have included colourful relatives ('Grandfather', 'My Wicked Uncle'), distinguished by their difference from other family members, the film star, Marilyn Monroe, who 'learnt how to shrivel and let live', and Bruce Ismay, chairman of the White Star shipping line who survived the fate of its most famous ship, the 'Titanic', that emblem of Protestant hubris, only to live on in a hell of guilt and shame for having escaped, haunted by recurring memories of victims drowning.[53] There are also fellow artists to whom Mahon looks with admiration and sympathy. Right at the outset, one such is Louis MacNeice, whose humaneness and resilient appreciation of life's fleeting beauty in the face of mortality and uncertainty are affectionately commemorated in a poem which echoes the wit and sophistication of its subject's own style.[54] MacNeice's achievement also exhibited the possibility of art to a young poet who shared certain aspects of the older writer's background in the Northern Protestant community, and his dislike of its narrowness and obsessions.

In the colour and intensity of Van Gogh's paintings he sees another triumphant confirmation of the power of art to transcend darkness, gloom, 'the dying light of truth', and the reduction of God to a metaphor.[55] The familiar subjects of the artist's work – 'chairs, faces and old boots', 'sunflowers and fishing boats' – are in fact 'Each one a miner in disguise', gloriously illuminated and transfigured by the individual vision of the painter who has conferred upon them 'A meteor of golden light', unlocking and unleashing 'light and life' that was previously caged up in their subterranean existences. And in a similar spirit, Mahon pays 'Homage to Malcolm Lowry', and in 'Death and the Sun' celebrates Albert Camus who 'personifies for him the individual's dogged, isolated stance in the face of an increasingly homogenous and hostile world'.[56] Here again the keynote is the power of the imagination in the face of chaos, breakdown and insecurity.

This is also reaffirmed in the carefully counterpointed stanzas of 'Tractatus', the first of which appears to endorse Wittgenstein's proposition that '"The world is everything that is the case"', whether humble fly or heroic work of art, while the second rebuffs such literal-mindedness and asserts that

> The world, though, is also so much more –
> Everything that is the case imaginatively.

Tacitus believed mariners could *hear*
The sun sinking into the western sea;
And who would question that titanic roar,
The steam rising wherever the edge may be?[57]

The truth of imagination is no less real and no less credible than the truth of fact and is not bound by it. As Edna Longley writes, Mahon's second stanza 'outflanks philosophy by appealing to the ear', and 'also outflanks more prosaic historians, or perhaps anyone whose definitions limit history as well as philosophy, by conferring validity on Tacitus's poetic error'.[58] Nothing checks the power of the imagination to illuminate the world in terms unaccounted for by mere logic and reason.

Yet Mahon's faith in the imagination is not always matched by his confidence in the reliability or adequacy of words to express it. This is implicit in 'Preface to a Love Poem' which appeared in *Night Crossing*. The words that constitute the poem circle its subject – love – but cannot approach it directly because any attempt to do so would violate the silence which is at its heart. The poem is therefore at best a necessary compromise, a means of hinting at truth beyond itself – 'at one remove – a substitute / For final answers'.[59] A different view of this dilemma is apparent in 'Heraclitus on Rivers', where the fate of art is linked with the general principle of flux and change that denies the possibility of permanence:

You will tell me that you have executed
A monument more lasting than bronze;
But even bronze is perishable.
Your best poem, you know the one I mean,
The very language in which the poem
Was written, and the idea of language,
All these things will pass away in time.[60]

Here the authority of art, and of the word in particular, has no privileged status, no immunity from change, unlike the Word of Protestant scripture. Yet, paradoxically, for as long as language does last, the acts of poetic composition of which this is an example, like sculpting or painting, are affirmative gestures against transience as well as the means of acknowledging its inevitable consequences.

In two of Mahon's long epistolary poems, 'Beyond Howth Head' and 'The Sea in Winter', he mulls over the problems of language and the efficacy of poetry (if any) in the modern world. The former work, which first appeared in *Lives*, pays particular attention to the impact of the logocentric Judaeo-Christian tradition on western culture generally, and in Ireland in particular. The sound of church bells in Monkstown prompts the poet to think of the legend of Kemoc who rang 'the Christian bell' in Ireland 'to crack a fourth-dimensional / world-picture, never known again'.[61] The coming of Christianity is therefore associated with loss of mythological resources (the 'swan-sons of Lir' are forever changed back to men) and diminished imaginative power, but also with man's confident belief in the sufficiency of words to explain the world, and in his own power to use them. The Ten Commandments, originally inscribed on stone tablets and subsequently broken by Moses when he saw the idolatry of the Israelites, are fundamental to Christian teaching and to the idea of what the poem calls a 'Word-God'. However, the questionable adequacy of such a verbally dependent theology is rendered more doubtful by the absurdity of the sign in Co. Clare – '"Stop here and see the sun go down"' – and by the literally fatal results of language that has frozen into dogma in Northern Ireland where, 'for a word's sake, the plast- / ic bombs go off around Belfast':

> . . . everywhere the ground is thick
> with the dead sparrows rhetoric
> demands as fictive sacrifice
> to prove its substance in our eyes.

This deeply sceptical view of the uses to which language has been put and of its tendency to become reductive, destructive and compromised is consistent with the direction in which the poem as a whole moves. Twice Mahon refers metaphorically to 'the writing on the wall', which 'elsewhere was written long ago', wittily implying that just as the original message announced the inadequacy of Belshazzar and the impending destruction of his kingdom (Daniel, ch. 5, vv. 25–28), so the signs he reads in the world around him are of decline and growing darkness. Thus, once again he writes an epitaph for the Glengormley of his youth.

In 'The Sea in Winter', which closed *Poems 1962–1978*, Mahon takes stock of his situation and of his art, likening himself to Ovid in exile as he writes from 'a draughty bungalow in Portstewart' to Desmond O'Grady in the Mediterranean. His feeling of marginalisation – 'the curious sense / Of working on the circumference' – and uncertainties about what he is doing and its value – '. . . all the time I have my doubts / About this verse-making' – are evident:

> . . . One day,
> Perhaps, the words will find their mark
> And leave a brief glow on the dark,
> Effect mutations of dead things
> Into a form that nearly sings . . . [62]

However, he rebukes his own inclination to feel disgust for the local people whose shouts at closing time 'make as much sense / And carry as much significance / As these lines carefully set down', accepting that he himself is no less entrapped than they are, and that their tormented cries and his poetry may be more deeply connected than he first thought. A new stanza added in *Selected Poems* is a further reminder to himself never to

> . . . forget the weird
> haecceity of this strange sea-board,
> . . .
> or ever again contemptuously
> refuse its plight; for history
> ignores those who ignore it, not
> the ignorant whom it begot.[63]

Although more emphatic than the original stanza this replaces, both versions of the poem conclude by qualifying the bleak teaching of Ecclesiastes ('There is nothing new under the sun') with images of reconciliation, revival and healing glimpsed and kept alive through the imaginative power of art to which the poet is committed anew, even though he has to continue living and working within 'the given life'.

Mahon's commitment to the positive possibilities of art, as well as his reservations and doubts about it, are particularly evident in a number of poems which arise from his responses to paintings. Perhaps it is scarcely surprising that this should be so. Painting invites scrupulous and thoughtful observation, a surrender to what is present on the canvas which necessarily precedes any judgement of it. This is precisely the approach to experience advocated and enacted in many of Mahon's poems. Furthermore, as Terence Brown writes at the start of his arresting essay, 'Derek Mahon: The Poet and Painting':

> Light plays a crucial part in the imaginative world of Derek Mahon's poetry. He is in fact a markedly visual poet, one who attends patiently, even contemplatively, to the look of things and especially to the way the light falls on them.[64]

The poet's preoccupation with the effects of light is naturally complemented by the art form which above all others depends upon understanding and mastery of how light and shadow govern perception.

His alertness and sensitivity to light have been present from the
outset. Thus, the early 'Recalling Aran' celebrates:

> A dream of limestone in sea light
> Where gulls have placed their perfect prints.
> Reflection in that final sky
> Shames vision into simple sight –
> Into pure sense, experience.
> Four thousand miles away tonight,
> Conceived beyond such innocence,
> I clutch the memory still, and I
> Have measured everything with it since.[65]

This formative instant which has permanently modified the poet's
perceptions and sensibility derives from a visual experience – a unique,
momentary configuration of light and shade which has inscribed itself
upon his consciousness just as an artist gives permanence to a
particular point in time in a painting. The power attributed to such a
revelatory moment coincides closely with descriptions of occasions of
highlighted religious awareness which in Christian terms are understood as encounters with the reality of the Spirit in the world. John
V. Taylor, for example, records the unforgettable impact a particular
piece of music made upon him as a child: 'a short passage affected me
with a shock of excitement I had never felt before . . . its appeal was
entirely sensual . . . I had not known that such a language existed'.[66]
He experienced something similar when as an adult he first saw
Mount Kilimanjaro, but although these were particularly intense
moments for him personally, he argues that they are representative of
a kind of 'falling in love' that may occur anywhere and at any time.
What all such 'annunciations', as Taylor calls them, have in common
is that

> The fact that something, or someone, is *there* suddenly becomes impor-
> tant. Instead of simply being part of the landscape, part of existence, it
> presents itself, it becomes present, it commands attention.

Although Mahon would almost certainly not attribute the same
source as Taylor to his 'annunciation' in 'Recalling Aran', the poet
and the theologian are evoking what are recognisably comparable

forms of experience in which unforeseen illumination occurs. Likewise, Taylor's 'annunciations' and Mahon's 'Light Music' have much in common.

However, whereas the 'pure sense experience' of 'Recalling Aran' arose spontaneously, without warning or time for preparation, the poems stimulated by paintings are naturally more meditative. Unlike the light over Aran, a painting does not change, and for Mahon this adds to the wonder of its achievement on the one hand and raises the kind of profound questions about the nature of art already hinted at in 'Rage for Order' on the other. This dilemma is evident in 'Edvard Munch' (later called 'The Studio') where the poet reflects on how the powerfully suggested disruptive energies, which apparently threaten to engulf the orderly domestic objects in the picture by dragging them into a vortex of elemental chaos, are held in permanent abeyance because the painting contains the moment in stasis:

> Instead
> There is this quivering silence
> In which, day by day, the play
> Of light and shadow (shadow mostly)
> Repeats itself, though never exactly.[67]

The picture celebrates fixity, defies the disintegrative forces of entropy or Heraclitean flux present within it, and is paradoxically, true to the instant, yet illusory in its capacity to freeze-frame it. As Terence Brown has said:

> . . . in Mahon's sense of things a fine painting through its effects of light, shade and colour is a paradigm of the way in which all art can affect perception of the world, even if the world customarily is refractory and chaotic. As aesthetician Mahon is instinctively sceptical of high-flown claims for the aesthetic itself, yet he is at the same time markedly loath to abandon the possibility that the truths of art are truths indeed.[68]

These comments are also relevant to another poem dating from *Night Crossing*, 'The Forger'. Not only is this imagined artist one of Mahons's disgraced and marginalised figures, but his offence, if such it is, of producing 'fake Vermeers' renews questions about art itself. Is forgery which involves

> The agony, the fanaticism
> Of working beyond criticism
> And better than the best

a crime at all?[69] May it not, in fact, be a supreme act of artistic creation, not plagiarism but vision in its own right revealed by exercising skills as great as those of the consummate Dutch master of light? (Strict Calvinists would, of course, regard all art as 'unoriginal' in the sense that God is the only creator and humans mere interpreters or commentators.) These questions are answered in the fourth stanza of the poem where the narrator pours contempt on the so-called experts who now try to explain why his paintings are not Vermeers, while wholly failing to see what they are:

> Now, nothing but claptrap
> About mere technique and true vision,
> As if there were a distinction –
> Their way of playing it down.
> But my genius will live on,
> For even at one remove
> The thing I meant was love.

Paradoxically, the forger's integrity to his art, the imaginative power he has nurtured within him ('A light to transform the world') are uncompromised by the circumstantial fact that he sold his '*soul* for potage' and broke with conventional decencies by passing his work off as Vermeer's and dealing with Goering. The kind of truth embodied in his art survives his own moral or political shortcomings. Its value resides in itself, not in the person (or personality) of the artist. By this reckoning, art possesses a kind of scriptural authority: as virtue resides in the Word irrespective of the flawed human nature of the messenger, so too with the painting – or the poem.

Finally, Mahon's patient and watchful contemplation of specific paintings is not passively spectatorial. As in 'Courtyards in Delft', poems like 'Girls on the Bridge' and 'The Hunt by Night' proceed from vividly appreciative observation of what is present on the canvases to creative interrogation of what they omit or evade. Thus, Munch's depiction of the untroubled innocence of the girls is reinterpreted as a lost idyll or dream-time for the wanderers 'in the dazzling dark / Amid the drifting snow' in our own 'insane / And monstrous age'.[70] Mahon's poem remakes the picture in the light of his late twentieth-century consciousness, alerting us to the implications it has now accrued. In doing so he not only pays tribute to Munch's work, but illuminates and adds to it by his own verbal art which introduces new images to contrast with those in the original, and thereby offers a source of imaginative truth and insight in its own right.

The poem prompted by Uccello's painting, 'The Hunt by Night', also balances meticulous evocation of detail against a searching enquiry into art which renders the primitive violence of the life or death chase in the 'neolithic bush' in terms that domesticate or aestheticise it and reduce its importance:

> As if our hunt by night
>   So very tense,
>
>   So long pursued,
>   In what dark cave begun
> And not yet done, were not the great
> Adventure we suppose but some elaborate
>   Spectacle put on for fun
>   And not for food.[71]

However, the phrase 'we suppose' leaves open the question whether or not life is a 'great / Adventure', and therefore whether or not Uccello has misrepresented it. The poet's own agnosticism permits no easy resolution of the issue which his contemplative viewing of the painting has stimulated. 'Art and reality vie in the poem for primacy', writes Brown, 'That neither is victor gives to the poem that tone of charged, meditative tension which is one of Mahon's most compelling registers'.[72]

This is entirely apt. Mahon's masterly practice of his own art in creative interplay with examples from a different art form is a triumphant realisation of the power of poetry to confer order and to convey imaginatively conceived truth which is the direct product of the poet's faith in what he is doing. Yet, part of that interplay involves an interrogation of the paintings which casts doubt upon the images they – and by implication all works of art, including his own – project. Mahon therefore achieves the improbable position of being simultaneously a believer and a doubter, a poet with a luminous imagination and consummate verbal and lyric gifts whose creative activity is toughened and emotionally complicated by the element of scepticism integral to his courageous vision. As such, his writing seems tempered by what Paul Tillich called 'the Protestant element' evident in some modern art, where

> No premature solutions should be tried; rather, the human situation in its conflicts should be expressed courageously. If it is expressed, it is already transcended: he who can bear and express guilt shows that he already knows 'acceptance-in-spite-of'. He who can bear and express

meaninglessness shows that he experiences meaning within his desert of meaninglessness.[73]

His position seems more radically doubting than that of Louis MacNeice, one of Mahon's exemplars, yet not as extreme as that of another, Samuel Beckett. While the world may be in terminal decline, the human state is not interminable in Mahon's verse and repeatedly the darkness is illuminated. 'First there is darkness, then somehow light', he wrote in 'Early Morning', likening the dawn to the first day of creation, and the movement of this line, its note of surprised incomprehension at how the change comes about, yet affirmation that it has indeed occurred, is akin to the process at work within many poems.[74] Recently Mahon has paid tribute to a further influence upon him. In 'The Hudson Letter' he writes of W.H. Auden, who 'remind[s] us of what the examined life involves':

> for what you teach is the courage to be ourselves,
> however ridiculous; and if you were often silly
> or too 'prone to hold forth', you prescribe a cure
> for our civilization and its discontents
> based upon *agapé*, Baroque opera, common sense
> and the creative impulse that brought us here,
> sustaining us now as we face a more boring future.[75]

The humaneness, resolute individualism, breadth of interest and belief in the curative power of art which Mahon applauds in Auden are all characteristics of his own work too. They are also implicit in remarks he made in his essay, 'Poetry in Northern Ireland':

> Battles have been lost, but a war remains to be won. The war I mean is not, of course, between Protestant and Catholic but between the fluidity of a possible life (poetry is a great lubricant) and the *rigor mortis* of archaic postures, political and cultural. The poets themselves have taken no part in political events, but they have contributed to that possible life, or the possibility of that possible life; for the act of writing is itself political in the fullest sense. A good poem is a paradigm of good politics – of people talking to each other, with honest subtlety, at a profound level. It is a light to lighten the darkness.[76]

Here he specifically positions poetry on the side of reconciliation and recovery of potential. It is a counterbalance to the disabling forces of prejudice, judgmentalism and fear, a means of seeing afresh or for the first time.

W.J. McCormack has warned that 'It would be a thoroughly and crudely reductive reader of Mahon's poetry who would see it as primarily concerned with, and valuable as, Ulster Protestantism'.[77] However, it would be an inattentive reader who overlooked the part Ulster Protestantism has played in shaping his work. It is present in the apocalyptic note which sounds in many poems, and in his attitude to modern commodity-led materialism, which Mahon treats with contempt like that of an Old Testament prophet, casting his baleful eye on a society that has lapsed into corrupt practices and lost its vision. This extends to the ambivalence of his feelings towards the specific historical community from which he came: sensing the vulnerability and loneliness of its members, he cannot sympathise with their theological beliefs which he regards as another form of blindness, yet he recognises their feelings of homelessness and abandonment in his own, and sees them as reflective of the existential and spiritual state of humankind in the late twentieth century. Lacking the assurance of the elect, he knows intimately the solitariness and pain of the lost. 'In Mahon's world', observes Elmer Andrews, 'all are damned. To be "born again", in Mahon's version of Calvinist theology, is an aesthetic enterprise, and a repeated challenge to creativity. No longer sure of his society, his language or himself, the poet still feels driven, in these reduced circumstances, to discover an "afterlife" in art'.[78] His Protestant attentiveness to words, if not to the Word, and belief in their potential to reveal truth are sorely tested by his post-Christian, post-modern consciousness, yet he remains deeply committed to the order which words can bestow, however temporary or illusory it may be, through the creative process which he himself has called 'Singing the darkness into the light'.[79]

CHAPTER NINE

Tom Paulin's Puritan Imaginings

The puritan imagination is altogether more complex than its opponents suppose – its essential libertarianism can be ironic, playful, dedicated to the primal lushness of a new beginning, as well as paranoid, self-righteous, aggressive and intransigently committed.

Tom Paulin, 'Political Verse' in *Writing to the Moment: Selected Critical Essays 1980–1996.*

He is a dissenter in every way.

Elmer Andrews, 'Tom Paulin: Underground Resistance Fighter' in M. Kenneally (ed), *Poetry in Contemporary Irish Literature.*

BOTH AS POET AND as critic Tom Paulin has consistently challenged the assumptions of his readers by the content, style and motivation of his writing. By turns combative, ironic, sarcastic, humorous, vulgar, tender, spiky and hermetic, his poetry's capacity to disconcert is complemented by the perspicacity and acumen of his revelatory critical reading of such writers as Milton, Dickinson, Bishop, Hughes and Lawrence. Furthermore, his poetry and critical essays bear closely upon each other and are profoundly influenced by his fascination with the tradition of radical dissenting Protestantism. This interest originates in Paulin's childhood and pre-university education in Belfast which coincided with the last two decades of virtually unchallenged Unionist hegemony. His youthful political interests – he belonged to a Trotskyist group – the breakdown of order in the province in the late 1960s and the suspension of the Stormont parliament in 1972, as well as his own widening horizons, highlighted the failure, injustice and bankruptcy of the Protestant state in Northern Ireland, which are recurrent targets in his poetry. His contempt and disdain for the Unionist regime and sense of detachment from it were announced in his first collection with its telling title, *A State of Justice*

(1977). Nevertheless, it has been Paulin's distinctive aspiration to move beyond such initial reactions to a re-examination of Protestant history in a bid to reclaim and celebrate its lost eighteenth-century radicalism in his own practice both as poet and critic. This project becomes increasingly visible in his poetry from *Liberty Tree* (1983) onwards and with the publication of his Field Day pamphlet, *A New Look at the Irish Question*, in the same year. In 1984, his first collection of essays, *Ireland and the English Crisis*, confirmed his preoccupation with Ulster Protestantism, dissenting radicalism, language, history and the relationship between literature and politics. His subsequent pursuit of these interests has been complemented by his selections and introductions to *The Faber Book of Political Verse* (1986), *The Faber Book of Vernacular Verse* (1990), and to a section in *The Field Day Anthology of Irish Writing* (1991), 'Northern Protestant Oratory and Writing 1791–1985', as well as in his more recent poetry and critical essays.

Throughout, Paulin has shown awareness of his connections with the Ulster Protestant part of his background (his father is English and he was born and lived for the first few years of his life in Leeds), and of his ambivalent feelings towards it. However, he has also resisted provincialism by his attention to Protestant history in a European context and his sympathetic examinations of literary dissent in writers as different as Milton and Mandelstam, Dickinson and Lawrence. His anathema for certain tendencies within Protestant dissent – 'its singleminded driven violence and ferocity' – is finely balanced against his strength of feeling for its libertarianism, iconoclasm, relentless insistence on the importance of the present moment and deep sense of social as well as religious responsibility.[1] Given this tension, it seems particularly relevant to look more closely at Paulin's experience of Protestantism and reactions to it which have contributed significantly to the shaping of his work.

At no point has he shown any real interest in Christian theology as such. It is the social, political, intellectual and aesthetic manifestations of Protestantism that have impressed themselves upon him, and in early poems especially, his conclusions about them are primarily negative. The title of 'Under the Eyes', for example, might hint at the presence of an all-seeing, judgmental God, while the poem itself evokes a hideously mechanistic state where justice has been replaced by retribution and a pseudo-biblical legalism which predetermine the dealings of the citizens who dwell in 'murdering miles of terrace-houses':

Every favour, I must repay with interest,
Any slip against myself, the least slip,
Must be balanced out by an exact revenge.[2]

Fear, anger and self-justification are the key motive forces in a society which lacks solid foundations and faces the destruction foretold in the Bible for all such foolish structures, with the difference that its ruin will be precipitated by internal forces that ultimately cannot be contained when 'All the machinery of a state / Is a set of scales that squeezes out blood'. There is no scope for reform or change when, as the poet ironically observes:

Memory is just, too. A complete system
Nothing can surprise.

To live on memory alone is to live wholly in the past, and to allow the past to exercise total control over the present is to foreclose the future. However, this 'complete system' can only be maintained by manipulation and repression and these in turn engender outrages like the shooting of the Judge, which is a symptom of the collapsing order in the supposedly 'secured city'.

Bleak landscapes and locations, allusions to militarism, violence, entrapment and 'murderous authorities', and evocations of loneliness, fear and failed or unsatisfactory relationships feature in many of the poems in *A State of Justice*, conveying Paulin's own disenchantment and alienation. On occasion these are expressed in overtly abstract language, as when he both scorns and is alarmed by 'massed, exact designs . . . / Anonymous and identical' which have 'little . . . to do with love or care', denying individuality, feeling and compassion, and insisting on conformity ('Practical Values').[3] Likewise, in 'Ballywaire', his sense of displacement ('. . . this is where I live: a town / On the wrong side of the border') and awareness of the surrounding '. . . gunfire, night arrests and searches' leads to the self-protective wish to 'keep myself intact' and to have a stone heart.[4] However, 'Settlers', a much less anguished poem, evokes the gunrunning which took place during the Home Rule crisis in more specific terms and insists on the connection between Protestantism and militarism by referring to the concealment of the weapons 'below the floors / Of sundry kirks and tabernacles in that country'.[5] And elsewhere, 'Inishkeel Parish Church' (revised and retitled 'Dawros Parish Church' in *Selected Poems 1972–1990*) enacts in much more personal terms the contest between the poet's own claustrophobic feelings and his desire for freedom and space. Here places and names are precise and the dramatic contrast between the small high-windowed Donegal parish church, crowded with visitors mostly from Northern Ireland, and the panoramic view across Gweebarra Bay from the church door, is both literally exact and metaphorically effective:

> Only one moment counted with the lessons
> And that was when, the pressure just too much,
> You walked slowly out of that packed church
> Into bright cold air.
> Then, before the recognitions and the talk,
> There was an enormous sight of the sea,
> A silent water beyond society.[6]

It is notable that the moment of crisis occurs within a church, during a service from which the poet derives neither consolation nor reasurance, and that the release he experiences is triggered by a prospect from which people, and by extension the constraints and structures of human social living, are absent.[7]

In his 1994 collection, *Walking a Line*, Paulin returns to this location in 'Matins', but where the earlier poem explores the need to escape from the oppression of the service, and particularly from the language associated with it, here he responds to the 'sad but urgent tang' of the church bell:

> off-key but beating out
> its meek unsettled belief
> on a shore of this small republic

and contemplates crossing the fields to 'go into that half-strange porch'.[8] As he scrutinises his possible motives for doing so, he concludes that

> it must be a tribal thing
> this wanting to go back there
> (d'you want to kneel in prayer?)
> this wishing the words were firm
> with a bit of a kick and a skip
> why couldn't they stay the same
> and sing *bing-ding bing-ding* ?

Thus, if the burden of the lesson drove the poet out in 'Inishkeel Parish Church', it seems in 'Matins' that he would gladly recover some of the reliability and fixity of words whose sonorous authority originally crushed him. These now half-tempt him as a refuge from post-modern relativities and instabilities of language and meaning, just as the bell modestly invites those who hear it to seek spiritual consolation from the secular world of unbelief. This, however, is no more than a longing, deep-seated as it may be, and the poet does not delude himself otherwise.

Paulin's reactions to his background and culture in his second collection, *The Strange Museum* (1980), are complicated by an interest in history itself which has subsequently become one of the major preoccupations both in his poetry and in his critical writing. On the one hand he possesses a somewhat Calvinistic sense of the weight and force of history, and its determinist burden on the present. 'It's an autocracy, the past. / Somewhere costive and unchanging', he writes in 'In the Egyptian Gardens', but elsewhere, in works like 'The Book of Juniper' and 'Presbyterian Study', he sees past radicalism as inspirational and potentially enabling.[9] Another view is present in the opening poem of *The Strange Museum* which evokes '. . . the long lulled pause / Before history happens' – a kind of limbo or interlude before the critical mass is reached when internal tensions ('. . . the tyranny of memories / And factual establishments') collapse. They unleash 'history' in the form of profound change and a decisive break from the inhibitions and oppression of the time before, and 'When the spirit hungers for form'.[10] Such 'history', bringing relief to spiritual emptiness and need, does not seem wholly removed from the theological notion of salvation history in which a decisive and transforming irruption will occur.

A similar idea is present in the punningly titled poem, 'A Partial State', which dramatises the relationship between Great Britain and Northern Ireland in terms of a colonial holding-operation:

> White god to desert god, 'The
> lines are open, what you do
> to your helots is up to
>
> you, no concern of ours.'[11]

'The chosen' are empowered to do whatever is necessary to divide 'their enemies' and impose order – 'no / balance of power. / Just safety'. The ironic ambiguity of 'Just' in this context, picking up on a similar effect in the first stanza where the word 'justly' is used equivocally, indicates the focal concern of the poem. 'A Partial State' is not, by definition, a just state, and Paulin foresees its fate in apocalyptic terms. The artificially enforced condition of 'Just safety' is 'Stillness, without history' – very similar to the 'long lulled pause / Before history happens' – which will last only

> until leviathan spouts,
> bursting through manhole covers
>
> in the streets, making phones ring on
> bare desks.

The practical implications of this image of sudden convulsion are intimated in the final part of the poem which refers to familiar details of urban violence and emphasises its sectarianism by mentioning 'special constables'. This in the context of Northern Ireland signifies the exclusively Protestant 'B' Specials whose services were relied upon in times of tension and unrest until their disbandment in 1969. The metaphor of the clocks 'bleeding now on / public buildings' reaffirms the apocalyptic nature of this disruption – the established time is over. Likewise, the mottoes of officialdom now read as 'emblems of failure' which require reinterpretation and assume a meaning that ironically reverses their original sense: whereas the words '*What the wrong gods established / no army can ever save*' that may formerly have been intended to warn others against the futility of rebellion, they now become a judgment on 'The chosen' themselves and on their 'White god', who are 'wrong' both in the sense of being inappropriate and also *in* the wrong. The motto may possibly be an oblique parody of words from the marriage service – 'Those whom God hath joined together let no man put asunder' – thereby making an ironic comment on the colonial partnership alluded to earlier in the poem.

Paulin also refers to 'Leviathan', the biblical monster of the deep and emblem of huge, unseen force lurking below the surface calm of society, in 'In the Lost Province'. In part this is a memory poem, showing the writer's developing thoughtfulness about his own relationship to the Protestant culture and locations of his childhood. As he retrieves his past, 'brick by smoky brick', he has a sense of estrangement, perhaps even of surprise, reminiscent of Derek Mahon's 'Afterlives', but without the latter's unease and guilt. Retrospectively, he can see the superficial peacefulness of the province as ironic, and questions

> Who would dream of necessity, the angers
> Of Leviathan, or the years of judgement?[12]

The sense of impending doom is reinforced here by the specific references to 'necessity', 'angers' and 'judgment', all terms belonging to the rhetoric of fundamentalist Protestantism and suggestive of one of the ways in which the province is 'lost'. Far from being a promised land ruled by a chosen people, it is a place of lost souls upon whom the judgment that was always waiting them has been visited. Furthermore, just as the poet's childhood is a 'Lost Province', so too he understands that the place itself was lost politically and culturally. Thus, the figure of Brookeborough, a mainstay of the Protestant hegemony, with his antiquated weapon and cry of 'No Surrender', does not suggest an image of heroic defiance so much as of purblind anachronism. Despite the ironies in the poem, however, Paulin shows a new interest in acknowledging his own emergence from that background and youthfully uncritical acceptance of it.

His exploration of this past continues differently in 'Still Century', where he reviews the intimate connection between Protestantism, industrialism and power in Northern Ireland. It is 'The hard captains of industry' and their political collaborators ('Ewart and Bryson, Craig and Carson') to whom the adherents of 'a fierce religion' pray and who in turn are flattered by belief in their own 'chosen status':

> They are tied
> To the shade of a bearded god,
>
> Their dream of happiness is his smile
> And his skilful way with the hardest rod.[13]

This is not simply a satirical portrait; it recognises the Calvinistic, self-punishing streak in Northern Irish Protestantism. Paulin's phrase in the second stanza, 'pious tyranny', aptly characterises a form of religion which has often made a virtue of its own capacity to be exacting and oppressive to those who practise it and which encourages them to show similar sternness to others. Service of this god is a form of entrapment, not of liberation, which returns one to the implications of stasis and inertia – yet another 'long lulled pause / Before history happens' – in the poem's title, 'Still Century'.

There is a similar critical thoughtfulness in 'Surveillances', which again introduces images of the state as a concentration camp and refuses any easy dismissal of its 'functions / For a culture of bungalows / And light verse', because

> You know this is one
> Of the places you belong in,
> And that its public uniform
> Has claimed your service.[14]

However, in 'The Strange Museum', Paulin both acknowledges his past and also claims the right to break out of its constraints. The museum in the poem is a house – 'A patriarch's monument' – metaphorically rich with associations of what another poem calls 'The dry shadows of a culture'.[15] No longer occupied, it has connotations of past wealth ('Was this the estate of some dead, linen / millionaire?' the voice in the poem asks); the allusion to the 'Scottish-baronial style' of other buildings implies an Ulster-Scots connection; and the reference to 'a fierce doctrine of justification' and 'a god of curses' hints at Calvinistic Protestant associations. This god is linked with violence both generally:

> His finger was on the trigger. He was insane.
> The vindictive shadow, I thought, he scatters
> bodies everywhere and has broken the city

– and specifically, in that he wished the speaker and his lover dead. Recognition of this and of the way in which he himself has been 'touched' (which may include the colloquial meaning, 'maddened', here) by the 'god of curses', and of his own inability to act defiantly while remaining in 'that strange museum' without being oppressed 'with its fixed anger', leads the speaker to a moment of revelation:

> I knew then, in that chill morning, that this
> was the house I had lived in once, that I was through
> with the polite dust of bibles, the righteous pulpits.

With its echoes of MacNeice's poem, 'The Truisms', this prepares for the sense of release felt in the final stanza where the liberating discovery that

> History could happen elsewhere, I was free now
> in a neat tame place whose gods were milder

is consolidated by references to a new day, a different season, 'the rickety fizz of starlings / trying to sing, and a grey tenderness' but above all by the possibility of love which could not prosper in the 'strange museum'. The poem therefore recognises the burden of history and background, but does not see them as absolute determinants: history is not a closed circle within which the individual is helplessly and irredeemably trapped. Were it otherwise, the world would be the kind of fatalistic nightmare which Paulin mocks in 'What is Fixed to

Happen' even as he also realises how easy it is to yield to such a view, because

> The eye is such a cunning despot
> We believe its wordless travelogues
> And call them *History* or *Let it Happen*.[16]

The concern with history remains central to *Liberty Tree*, which is probably the most controversial of Paulin's collections so far. In particular, the history of the United Irishmen movement in the late eighteenth century and the contribution to it of Protestant dissenters from Ulster are crucial stimuli to the poet's imagination. These provide him with a radically different view of the community from which he comes and with which he has found himself engaged in critical argument from the outset. The activities and aspirations of the 1798 radicals, which are not part of contemporary Protestant Unionist mythology, appeal to Paulin's own values and hopes, unlike the priorities of the modern Northern Irish state. In the Introduction to *Ireland and the English Crisis*, Paulin took up the complaint of an older poet, John Hewitt, and lamented the fate of the dissenting tradition in Ulster, which 'went underground after the Act of Union and has not been given the attention it deserves . . . largely because most Unionists have a highly selective historical memory and cling desperately to a raft constructed from two dates – 1690 and 1912.'[17] A number of the poems in *Liberty Tree* specifically set about recovering and reinstating this submerged Protestant tradition. This is not merely for nostalgic reasons, but as an indispensable part of the writer's efforts to clarify his own identity and to propose a dynamic and visionary way out of what he sees as the petrifaction of contemporary Protestant culture and Unionist politics which are satirised and mocked elsewhere in the book.

Although in 'L'Envie de Commencement' he relishes the thought of

> how simple it is in the beginning
> for the historian to walk at dawn,
> seeing a pure narrative before him

he knows that his own situation is much less clear and beset with complex memories and uncertainties.[18] 'Can you *describe* history I'd like to know?', he asks in 'Martello':

> Isn't it a fiction that pretends to be fact
> like *A Journal of the Plague Year*?

> And the answer that snaps back at me
> is a winter's afternoon in Dungannon,
> the gothic barracks where the policemen
> were signing out their weapons in a stained register,
> a thick turbid light and that brisk smell of fear
> as I described the accident and felt guilty –
> guilty for no reason, or cause, I could think of.[19]

The difficulty – perhaps the impossibility – of discriminating confidently between fact and fiction, the power of fiction which assumes the status of fact, and the manipulation of both fact and fiction for contingent purposes, are exemplified by the reference to a dissenting Protestant maker of fictive histories in a poem written to celebrate the centenary of the birth of the consummate weaver of fact and fiction, James Joyce. It is also dedicated to a leading Irish 'revisionist' historian, Roy Foster, and his wife, Aisling. However, the recollection of groundless guilt felt in the police barracks makes the same point in a more personal way. The irrationality (fiction) of the poet's guilt diminishes neither its reality (fact) nor its power to disturb which derives from his historical awareness of the injustices associated with the police and the ambient sense of menace. This guilt is inherited, rather like a variant form of original sin, and is connected with a history of rule by force applied to maintain an artificially contrived state created to defend the interests of one section of the population which subscribes to a particular fictive view of the past. It is also disabling and dispiriting in its effects – again like belief in original sin.

The struggle to understand and make sense continues elsewhere, too. In the opening poem of the collection, 'Under Creon', Paulin celebrates his discovery of Protestant radicalism ('a free voice sang / dissenting green'), and invokes the names of Henry Joy McCracken and James Hope, two of the pre-eminent leaders of the 1798 rising in Ulster, although he is still unclear about the exact nature of his own relationship to this past:

> Maybe one day I'll get the hang of it
> and find joy, not justice, in a snapped connection,
> that Jacobin oath on the black mountain.[20]

However, as the poem 'Descendency' wryly suggests, there is no clear way back to these 'snapped connection(s)', because:

> All those family histories
> are like sucking a polo mint –

you're pulled right through
a tight wee sphincter
that loses you.[21]

The complexity and extensiveness of many family trees (often referred to as 'the connection') in Northern Ireland, which are a source of popular fascination, virtually ensures that any line of descent will not only be far flung, but will include individuals of widely differing, and even radically opposed, sympathies and allegiances. By implication, therefore, the quest to make links back to the past will be neither straightforward nor unambiguous.

Yet it is the aspiration to pick up the 'snapped connection' that also informs 'The Book of Juniper', the most ambitious poem in *Liberty Tree*. It begins by invoking a kind of pilgrimage, or quest for meaning, to the site of a ruined church on the island of Inishkeel which is approached after an almost biblical parting of the waters. (This is also a literal fact: the island can be reached by foot across a sandbar when there are spring tides.) However, the 'sea wind' offers neither 'yeasty word' nor comfort:

> Only a lichened stone
> is given you,
>
> and juniper,
> green juniper.[22]

To be given stone rather than bread is a biblical symbol of dereliction and treachery, but the tough and resilient juniper is linked with the emblematic Jacobin liberty tree, and therefore also with the moment of revolutionary potential when French troops joined the United Irishmen in 1798. The juniper both testifies to that past and is a symbol of enduring hope for the future:

> Rugged, fecund,
> with resined spines,
> the gymnosperm
> hugs the hillside
> and wills its own survival.[23]

The potential it signifies has implications not only in Ireland but in a wider context because juniper, with its 'springy resistance', flourishes in a variety of climates. Thus, it is associated with one of Paulin's exemplary writers, Mandelstam ('Exiled in Voronezh / the leavening priest of the Word / receives the Host on his tongue – / frost, stars, a dark berry . . .'). For the poet himself it is both a summons to imagine 'a swelling army . . . marching / from Memory Harbour and Killala' and 'the green tide rising / through Mayo and Antrim', and a stimulus to dream 'of that sweet / equal republic' characterised by inclusiveness and reconciliation which are symbolised by the talk between trees representative both of Ireland and of England.[24]

What Elmer Andrews has described as 'the exorbitance of this vision' is also apparent in the language of 'Father of History' which celebrates late eighteenth-century Presbyterianism's radical commitment to the 'rights of man' and 'New Light' theology.[25] Traced by the poet in the Linen Hall, which is now a library but was formerly a centre of Protestant commercial activity, the records of 'Munro, Hope, Porter and McCracken' are 'Folded like bark, like cinnamon things', 'like sweet yams buried deep'. Such exotic similes, like the conclusion of 'The Book of Juniper', evince Paulin's admiring, even romantic, affinity with 'these rebel minds' who 'endure posterity without a monument', and whose 'relished dialect' of dissent he wishes to redeem for the present. The same might be said of 'Presbyterian Study', an affectionate rehearsal of the almost forgotten virtues of 'Those linen saints, lithe radicals', which are conjured into consciousness by this

> . . . room without song
> That believes in flint, salt,
> And new bread rising
> Like a people who share
> A dream of grace and reason.[26]

Here the austerity of the room is not to be confused with the narrowness of thought and timid conformity which Paulin mocks in contemporary Protestant Unionism; rather, its associations are with 'choosing the free way, / Not the formal, / And warming the walls with its knowing'. The study acts as a mnemonic, preserving the ideals of this noble past and prompting the poet's frustration with the ineffectual passivity and procrastination of thought and conduct in the 'jacked corpse' of the modern state.[27]

However, it is the very idealism and aspirational features of these poems which some critics have found most troubling. Edna Longley sees them as deriving from 'the corporate Field Day position'; Elmer Andrews claims that Paulin is 'so absorbed in a Utopian model of redeemed Presbyterianism that he blinds himself to complication', that his myth of the United Irishmen 'has little in common with orthodox Republican politics, and his attempt to associate Republican Socialism with Protestantism has no relation to contemporary reality'.[28] Yet, Paulin's aspirations may be viewed more positively as part of his overall attempt to engage seriously with Protestant culture, to excoriate its contemporary failures of imagination and courage and to recover its lost energy and integrity. As Peter McDonald has shrewdly observed:

> The dissenting radical tradition is in *Liberty Tree* a crucial tool for analysing the shortcomings of the present-day Protestant community. It is important to remember that what Paulin is actually doing is making an *imaginative* appropriation of history, creating symbols from history.[29]

Paulin shows his own puritan sympathies in boldly attacking latter-day losses of original purpose and idealism and their replacement by the politics of injustice and fear, and by spiritual, moral and intellectual torpor.

It is in the light of this aspiration, too, that a second striking and controversial feature of *Liberty Tree* – the extensive use of Ulster dialect and vernacular words – may be understood. Dialect words, wrote Paulin in his Field Day pamphlet, 'A New Look at the Language Question':

> . . . express something very near to a familial relationship because every family has its hoard of relished words which express its members' sense of kinship. These words act as a kind of secret sign and serve to exclude the outside world. They constitute a dialect of endearment within the wider dialect.[30]

Such words essentially belong to the spoken language of a community, hallmarking and distinguishing it by their unique coloration, history and sounds. Paulin has long been fascinated by the rich dialect vocabulary particularly associated with Ulster Protestants of Scottish descent. His extensive recourse to it in *Liberty Tree*, *Fivemiletown*, and to a lesser degree, in *Walking a Line*, reflects this and is motivated by his wish to disrupt orthodox, 'polite' literary rhetoric with the informal and dissenting vigour of dialect.

Elsewhere, especially in some of the essays collected in *Minotaur: Poetry and the Nation State*, his comments on other poets cast further light on his enthusiasm for verse which aspires to the immediacy of speech and defies the canonical fixity of the language of authority. 'Orality – the vernacular imagination – can be a means of resisting the dominance of the nation state', he declares in 'Observing the Fathers: Christina Rossetti', and in a brilliant essay on Emily Dickinson he notes that her 'eruptive, intense vernacular challenges the way in which men use language as a means of achieving and consolidating power'.[31]

He elaborates on this in his admiring emphasis on Dickinson's quest for 'a type of gestural or body language which combines accent, attitude and physical gesture', making it seem 'as if [her] actual, living voice is addressing us as we read'.[32] Such poetry is a calculated act of dissent which aims to defy the very conventions and constraints of print and to retain the freedoms and unpredictability the spoken word possesses over the written. Paulin describes this style as 'one extreme of puritan authenticity', and traces its origins to St Paul's aspiration to an ideal form of 'writing beyond writing'. Alluding to the apostle's affirmation of God's empowerment of His 'ministers of the new testament; not of the letter, but of the spirit: for the letter killeth, but the spirit giveth life' (2 Corinthians, ch. 3, v. 6), he argues that Dickinson is strongly influenced by this 'concept of immortal speech' which is 'infinite and eternal because in not being a series of signs it does not submit to the deadly bondage of the letter'.[33] For such a writer, the aim must be 'to go beyond writing into a kind of speech continuum'.[34] All of this provides an oblique comment on Paulin's own poetic practice and ambition from *Liberty Tree* onwards. It also helps to situate him in a tradition which originates in the convulsive pentecostal experience of the early Christians when the gift of inspired speech was a direct challenge to orthodox teaching based on the codified Mosaic law. However, after the formation and institutionalisation of the Church, it in turn became law-bound and rigid, free speech giving way to liturgy, so that throughout its history the motivation of dissenters has been to recover the immediacy and spontaneity known by the New Testament Christians. Such a process can never end because, by definition, without it the dynamic sense of urgency and of living continually on the edge departs. It is replaced by a form of stasis which is soon graced by the name of tradition, but which may easily become comfortable, unthinking habit endorsed by regulatory controls and prejudices. The imagination of the true dissenter like Dickinson 'exists in a condition of profound ontological insecurity and unfinished knowing, where the Angst of consciousness is often imaged as oppression, threat, terror . . .'.[35] And so too for Tom Paulin himself, whose poetry commonly conveys impressions of an imagination in just such a state, and combines what Bernard

O'Donoghue has called 'a rather puritan notion of perfectability with a sense of the urgent need for greater justice in the body politic'.[36] That 'puritan notion' also fuels a strong satirical element in many poems which registers varying levels of intensity from angry contempt to wry sympathy for its targets.

Thus 'Desertmartin' shows clearly the poet's bitter dismissiveness of what he regards as the shrunken, sado-masochistic mentality of much contemporary Unionism – 'a culture of twigs and bird-shit / Waving a gaudy flag it loves and curses'.[37] Throughout the poem negative associations accumulate around 'This bitter village' which is, punningly, 'in the dead centre of a faith'. The 'Word' sown here has 'withered to a few / Parched certainties', a reductive process which has created an oppressive burden of 'Law' rather than liberating those who have heard it. Here, Paulin implies, the entropic decline from the energising verbal freedom and vigorous exercise of personal conscience associated with radical Protestantism is complete. Furthermore, the perverse politics of the situation mean that the 'Jock squaddy', whose background might be expected to link him with the ancestry of the Protestant natives of Desertmartin, and who is there to 'defend' them, is viewed ambiguously by people who are no longer sure of the reliability of the Union, or of the role of the British army in upholding it.

Edna Longley has attacked 'Desertmartin' as a 'clichéd, external impression of the Protestant community [which] exposes Paulin's own "parched certainty"', but it is also possible to find in it a hurt disillusionment, especially in the third stanza:

> It's a limed nest, this place. I see a plain
> Presbyterian grace sour, then harden,
> As a free strenuous spirit changes
> To a servile defiance that whines and shrieks
> For the bondage of the letter: it shouts
> For the Big Man to lead his wee people
> To a clean white prison, their scorched tomorrow.

The problem is that the sense of what has been lost, of decline and diminution, and of the replacement of the admirable virtues of 'grace' and 'a free strenuous spirit' by self-demeaning, herdlike submissiveness, avoidance of personal responsibility and an empty future, amounts to a comprehensive sneer unrelieved by any imaginative compassion, or even a flicker of humour. It is unclear how a connection is to be restored between the kind of Protestant culture represented in 'Desertmartin' and Paulin's idealised eighteenth-century radical version of it, or how a poem such as this is going to address contemporary Protestant readers without simply alienating them.

Difficulties also arise in some of the poems which make free use of dialect words (for example, 'S/He', 'Exogamy', 'Waftage') and Gerald Dawe's concern that many of the terms are employed in oddly contrived ways seems entirely justified. Who, he asks, uses such phrases as 'lunk July', 'bum hour', 'scroggy town', 'gummy warmth', 'yompy farts' or 'dwammy sick'?[38] Far from capturing the immediacy of the spoken word, these expressions have an essentially literary self-consciousness and a deliberate knowingness that have little to do with a 'relished dialect' or 'writing beyond writing'. The effect of this is heightened by the fact that in both *Liberty Tree* and *Fivemiletown* Ulster dialect words jostle for position with theoretical terminology and jargon. For instance, terms such as 'fictionary universe', 'metonymy', 'autarkic', 'foreground', '*subterfuge text*', '*différence*', which imply the presence of a highly educated and sophisticated reader, have led Clair Wills to question how 'The increasing hermeticism of Paulin's work' is to be related to his 'commitment to poetry's public address, and . . . his interest in dialect and the vernacular'.[39] The issue again arises concerning the poet's own view of the society he is writing about, and whether he regards himself as inside or outside it, using its idioms because they 'belong' to him, or merely exploiting them as one linguistic resource among many in an idiosyncratically mannered way.

His success is more assured in a number of poems which focus on the colonial associations of the link between Britain and Northern Ireland. Satire and humour combine in the creation of a series of 'rum coves' with Protestant loyalist connections who are imagined upholding or representing outposts of British imperialism or white supremacy. These include 'the Reverend Bungo Buller / And his prophet, Joe Gimlet' on their

> . . . coral or guano atoll
> Where a breezy Union Jack
> Flaps above the police station;

the Reverend Spanner McTavish preaching 'a burnt sermon / On the injustice of the Copra Board'; Sol Grout 'On the Barrack Islands far out/ in the South Atlantic / . . . where no maritime elegists sing / of Resolution and Independence'; and Professor 'Deeko' Kerr, 'Chair of Social Justice / At Jan Smuts College in the Orange Free State'.[40] Whether as servants of imperialism, agents of racism, or proponents of the notion of a chosen people, they are eccentric, out of touch and ultimately as absurd as the poem by 'Rupert Brookeborough' (whose name humorously merges that of the iconic British imperial poet and the exemplary champion of Protestant Unionist rule in Northern Ireland) which deals sentimentally with 'fishing and the stout B-men', and by 'use of many metric arts' creates

> . . . a fictionary universe
> which has its own laws and isn't quite
> the same as this place that we call real.[41]

The 'fictionary universes' in these poems are in irreversible decline, their characters perpetuating outmoded views of the past and standing by faded beliefs in the authority conferred by the interrelated power of religion, race and empire.

A further modification and complication of Paulin's attitudes to the position of Protestant Unionists emerges in two poems written in response to the signing of the Anglo-Irish Agreement in 1985. 'An Ulster Unionist Walks the Streets of London' reveals a perhaps unexpected degree of sympathetic understanding for the sense of betrayal and confusion of identity felt as a result of this political settlement. Echoing words of the MP, Harold McCusker, in the House of Commons, it evokes the Unionists' feelings of humiliation and exclusion ('I waited outside the gate-lodge, / waited like a dog / in my own province'), of frustrated bitterness, anger and wounded pride ('Was I meant to beg / and be grateful?'), and above all, of abandonment:

> I called out loud –
> to the three Hebrew children
> for I know at this time
> there is neither prince, prophet, nor leader –
> there is no power
> we can call our own.[42]

The 'three Hebrew children' are Shadrach, Meshach and Abed-nego, the friends of Daniel, loyal believers in God who were compelled to work for Nebuchadnezzar after his occupation of Jerusalem, and who were thrown into a fiery furnace because of their refusal to abandon their faith and worship a golden image at the king's command. Having survived their intended destruction unharmed because of their fidelity, 'Nebuchadnezzar spake, and said, Blessed be the God of Shadrach, Meshach and Abed-nego, who hath sent his angel, and delivered his servants that trusted in him, and have changed the king's word, and yielded their bodies, that they might not serve nor worship any god, except their own God' (Daniel, ch. 3, v. 28). This is an exemplary story of the kind favoured by preachers to illustrate the power of faith. More importantly, however, it is also a proof text of the divine endorsement of individual conscience in matters of faith and principle, even when this involves defiance of a king, and it was alluded to in this way at the time of the Anglo-Irish Agreement. As Paulin explains, this coincidence confronted him with aspects of his own past, and compelled him to a new understanding of it:

> I had been familiar with the story since childhood and had heard excerpts from it read out at primary and Sunday school, where I learnt parts of it off by heart, a process that was more than the apparently personal act of reading and rereading a text in order to memorize certain selected verses – it was the experience of being read into a narrative which is part of the tribal myth of the Protestant community in Ulster. Later on I was to doubt that myth, and then in November 1985 a significant political event took place in the North of Ireland – the British and Irish governments signed the Anglo-Irish Agreement . . . The implicit dilution of British sovereignty [i.e. resulting from the Agreement] profoundly traumatized Ulster's loyalist community, and one of that community's leaders – Ian Paisley – ended a bitter attack on the British government for its 'betrayal' of the loyalists by stating: 'Like the three Hebrew children, we will not budge, we will not bend, we will not burn'.[43]

Paisley's reference to this specific aspect of the story in that context – his ready application of it to the particular circumstances of outraged Protestant loyalists after the signing of the Anglo-Irish Agreement – disclosed to Paulin how 'This story of "peoples, nations and languages" related hermeneutics to state authority, political power and nationhood', giving it both personal and communal significance. However, it also made him aware 'that such an intensely direct interpretation was boxed-in and parochial; it could be of no interest to anyone outside a community that now felt it was a minority within Ireland'.[44] Thus, the familiar Protestant strategy of turning to the Word for consolation or a sign to aid a decision or to direct action is held up to critical scrutiny, for if on the one hand it rallies courage and gives hope to people who feel beleaguered, in other ways it may blind them to larger realities, and thereby be disabling, or render them incomprehensible to anyone else.

Paulin also tells how his 'sense of embattled provincialism' in the way the story was being cited by Paisley grew with his discovery of the additional passage placed between verses 23 and 24 of the third chapter of Daniel in the Catholic *Jerusalem Bible*, in which first Azariah (Abed-nego) and then all three men speak from the midst of the furnace. It is from verse 38 of this version of the story that the lines 'there is neither prince, prophet, nor leader – / there is no power / we can call our own' derive, and Paulin has described them as speaking for 'the deep psychic wound that was reopened by the Anglo-Irish Agreement' – namely the devastating realisation by Protestant Unionists that their security had been removed by the very people on whom they had relied, and that they themselves had become a marginalised group.[45] For this reason the Ulster Unionist finds himself in the same position as the Irish Catholics over whom he and his kind have historically claimed superiority and privilege. In Kentish Town, among the Catholic London Irish, he too feels he is an exile, and suddenly sees their position with a new urgency:

> What does it feel like?
> I wanted to ask them –
> what does it feel like
> to be a child of that nation?

However, he is as alienated from them as he is by the rhetoric of the House of Commons, where he is now a 'stranger' in more senses than one, and the note of loss and displacement on which the poem ends suggests its rich mix of compassionate understanding.[46]

Another poem also alluding to the Anglo-Irish Agreement is 'The Defenestration of Hillsborough' – Hillsborough Castle, formerly the official residence of the Governor of Northern Ireland, was the location for the signing of the Agreement – but it adopts a different attitude. Here the position of the Protestant Unionists 'on a window ledge', stripped of all consoling versions of history ('All our victories / were defeats really'), and cut off from readmission to their former status, may not necessarily signify abject defeat and disgrace. *The Book of Analogies* with which they are left permits an alternative view based upon the energetic seizure of opportunity.[47] Woodrow Wilson and Tomás Masaryk, who became creative statesmen on the world stage despite their family backgrounds in 'the small nations of Europe' (Ireland in the case of Wilson), are therefore exemplary models of possibility:

This means we have a choice:

either to jump or get pushed.

The positive choice in the case of Ulster Protestants would be, in Paulin's view, a return to the dissenting republican ideals of their United Irishmen forebears and the encouragement of what an earlier poem described as '"a form that's classic and secular"'.[48] Just as in 'An Ulster Unionist Walks the Streets of London' he drew upon words uttered by McCusker and Paisley, so too the image of being thrust onto a window ledge has its source in another loyalist leader's 'attempt to find an imaginative image for the sudden shock of being marginalized by two more powerful states'.[49] As Paulin has noted, the image itself recalls the Defenestration of Prague (1618) which initiated the convulsive military and religious turmoil of the Thirty Years War and saw the fragmentation of the Holy Roman Empire. (There is an irony, however, in the fact that it was Protestant extremists who seized the initiative and threw Catholic governors from the windows of Hradčin castle.) This reference suggestively links the provincial crisis affecting a group of people confronted with an Agreement that, in their opinion, turned them from favoured citizens into unwanted outcasts, with a major passage of European history which has conventionally been presented as a conflict between the rising force of Protestantism and Counter Reformation Catholicism.

Paulin's sensitivity to the ways in which Protestant loyalists have turned to the Bible and to the past in the crisis provoked by the Anglo-Irish Agreement results not only from his already established preoccupation with the influence and power of history, but also from his continuing scrutiny of his own relationship to his Protestant background, which is one of the principal features of his *Fivemiletown* collection. Although the title poem begins by renewing the wish for a fresh start, free from the complications and disabilities inherited from the past:

The release of putting off
who and where we've come from,
then meeting in this room
with no clothes on –
to believe in nothing,
to be nothing

– it turns the drama of a furtive lovers' meeting into a metaphor for the risks, dangers and uncertainties involved in a relationship attempted against a background of suspicion and latent violence.[50] The poem's inconclusiveness – does the meeting take place or not? – and other representations of failed, frustrated or loveless relationships in this collection (for example, 'Waftage: An Irregular Ode', 'Breez Marine', and 'Really Naff') reinforce a prevailing sense of distrustfulness and hurt, and of their brutalising consequences. However, as Bernard O'Donoghue has put it:

> That is not to say that [these poems] are propagandist clarion-calls for the Protestant cause; but they are powerful dramatizations of the emotion and dilemma of its interests, by evoking with creative imagination what that desolate, unloved situation is like.[51]

Paulin's examination of his background is particularly evident in 'Why the Good Lord Must Persecute Me', where again the European origins of Protestantism are recalled by the mnemonic pictures of Calvin and Farel (the initial leader of the Reformation movement in Geneva whose recruitment of Calvin in 1536 was decisive). The speaker's reaction to these figures is ambivalent:

> each theologian
> is let into a wall
> like a long thin clock
> – fierce *féroce* feral stiff
> a pair of stone pricks
> or the boots I dig with[52]

But despite his note of contempt for '*tradition*' as defined in *The History of Received Opinions* ('it'll squeak if you touch it / then break up like a baked turd / into tiny wee bits'), he also discovers

> . . . a missing chapter
> that tells what you can't rub out
> however much you might want to

This confirms the problematic paradox of the burden of tradition which is simultaneously no more than the worthless excrement of the past, and yet which cannot be completely erased or abandoned. The intimate and inseparable connections between religion, history and politics that are particularly engrained in the Northen Irish situation admit no easy resolution or escape and become therefore a persecution. Paulin's description of himself as 'the never entirely detribalized me' seems particularly apt in the light of these perplexed and questioning poems.[53]

Fivemiletown also explores the predicament of the artist under pressure. This preoccupation was previously evident in Paulin's celebrations of Mandelstam in 'The Other Voice' and 'The Book of Juniper', of Derek Mahon's 'supremely unillusioned quietism', of Paul Muldoon's poetry and in his admiration for the work of other writers living in 'cold, closed societies' where the practice of art is an inescapably political act.[54] In 'Voronezh' he offers his version of the poem written by Anna Akhmatova in 1936 after her visit to Mandelstam during his exile. It focuses on the endangered position of the artist in an oppressive and punitive society. In the English translation by Stanley Kunitz and Max Haywood, Akhmatova's poem ends:

> But in the room of the banished poet
> Fear and the Muse stand watch by turn,
> and the night falls
> without the hope of dawn.[55]

Paulin's version is significantly different:

> But that tin lamp
> on the poet's table
> was watched last night –
> Judas and the Word
> are stalking each other
> through this scroggy town
> where every line has three stresses,
> and only the one word, *dark*.[56]

Not only does he invite a connection with Northern Ireland by the use of the dialect word 'scroggy' (and others in the poem), but the references to permafrost and darkness used here of Voronezh, have repeatedly featured in Paulin's characterisation of his own country's cultural condition. Most notable of all, however, is the juxtaposition of 'Judas and the Word', where the biblical reference lays particular emphasis on the risky role of the poet. It now falls to the poet to articulate the 'Word' which has the integrity and truth once ascribed only to the Word of God. In Christian belief, Jesus was 'the Word made flesh', and from Paulin's secular point of view Mandelstam is an analogous figure. But just as Christ was betrayed, so the writer labours under pressure and lives in constant danger of treachery in a society which is fundamentally hostile and distrustful towards him and his art.

In the long and difficult final poem in *Fivemiletown*, 'The Caravans on Lüneberg Heath', Paulin strives to bring together his examinations of history with particular significance to Protestants and of the role of the artist in a divided and strife-torn society, with a further consideration of his own position. He again juxtaposes events from different periods – the Thirty Years War, the aftermath of the Second World War and contemporary Northern Ireland – and makes complex use of references to the work of various other writers. Of central importance, as Paulin himself tells us, is a poem by the seventeenth-century German poet from Köningsberg, Simon Dach, 'Klage über den endlichen Untergang und Ruinirung der Musicalischen Kürbs-Hütte und Gärtchens' ('Lamentation over the Final Demise and Ruination of the Musical "Pumpkin Hut" and Little Garden') written towards the end of the Thirty Years War. The 'Pumpkin Hut' or 'Cucumber Lodge' was a meeting place for a literary society started by the composer Heinrich Albert as a focal point for the encouragement of culturally led initiatives to counteract the consequences of prolonged war. It was reprinted in Günter Grass's novella, *The Meeting At Telgte*, which offers a fictional representation of a meeting between Heinrich Albert and Simon Dach. Clair Wills has observed that Grass's work

> . . . is a thinly veiled analogue for the broadly leftist cultural project of the Gruppe 47, set up by Hans Werner Richter in 1947 to foster possibilities for cultural renewal in Germany at a time when the divisions between the Western zones of occupation and the Soviet zone were hardening.[57]

Gruppe 47, therefore, like the Köningsberg literary meeting, was associated with the desire to explore the regenerative potential of art in the context of a shattered society. Given this, as well as Paulin's own commitments at that time, Wills is surely right to infer that 'at one level the poem is also concerned with the cultural project of the Field Day Company to create a "fifth province", a cultural space non-aligned to either the nationalist or Unionist agendas'.[58]

A further issue comes to the fore in the second half of the poem which makes extended reference to Martin Heidegger's conduct under the Nazis and, in particular, to the anti-semitism allegedly evident in his treatment of Edward Husserl. Paulin regards Heidegger as fatally compromised by his beliefs in the separateness of art and politics, against which he himself has repeatedly argued, and in German racial and linguistic superiority which fuelled Nazism:

the West's last thinker, part woodcutter
and part charlatan
is digging trenches on the Rhine
    – lonely uncanny violent
    the artist and the leader
    without expedients
    apolis
    without structure and order
    among all that is –[59]

The fact that Dach's poem was not published until 1936 is both coincidental and felicitous because it invites another suggestive contrast between the creative activities of the 'Cucumber Lodge' artists against the background of the Thirty Years War, and those of Heidegger during the period of the Nazis' increasingly violent seizure of power.

Paulin also alludes to Grimmelshausen's *Der abenteurlichen Simplicissimus Teutsch* (1669), another novel which deals with the Thirty Years War, but from the point of view of a peasant narrator, Simplicius Simplicissimus, who with his fellows suffers endlessly in a conflict that remains incomprehensible and pointless to them. 'Simplex's' view is given in a series of choric comments whose facile rhymes and limited understanding are rebuffed by the much more complex and involved exploration of history which surround them.

In the closing two parts of the poem, Paulin moves from his own imagined presence on Lüneberg Heath at the moment of German surrender at the end of the Second World War, which connects him with Simon Dach at the close of the Thirty Years War, to his position in contemporary Northern Ireland. He declares, 'now I can get born again', because he can revisit his own education (Paulin has recorded how at school he studied the Thirty Years War as part of a syllabus which he now realises 'was designed to reinforce a Protestant identity and to submerge the Catholic population of the province within those dominant values') with a new complexity of understanding, and of the links between local and international events:

lines radiate
in from each pupil
and one tight thread
links Lüneberger *Heide*
to the Clogher Valley
– provincial world history
or the seedbed of soldiers.[60]

Furthermore, although Paulin acknowledges how his background was designed to 'kit' him out 'first / as a blue British citizen' (the 'aluminium school' houses are named after four World War II Generals, all of whom had Ulster backgrounds), it has not precluded his discovery that now

> . . . this flattened trashcan
> has more than enough room
> for Tommy's wee collection
> of aesthetic judgements.[61]

Thus, the individual judgements of the poet exist in defiance of and in spite of the particular historical perspectives inculcated through the formal education system. Once again Paulin demonstrates his desire to refocus the Ulster Protestants' fixation with history and to locate their local predicament in the 1980s within a much larger and more complex framework. He pursues this here in a poem which is aware of and engaged with historical processes, which assumes the artist's social and political, as well as literary, responsibilities, and which goes beyond the treatment of these preoccupations in some of the more simply aspirational works in *Liberty Tree* and elsewhere in *Fivemiletown*.

In his most recent collection, *Walking a Line*, Paulin has once again shown mixed feelings of disaffection, longing and homelessness as he continues to contemplate history, language and the connections between Protestantism and Enlightenment thought. 'Would it – would it ever be / Year One again?', he asks in 'Basta', renewing an old question. If he immediately acknowledges the impossibility of that 'nondate', he nevertheless imagines a 'reverse epic' in which the history of paramilitary violence, injustice and occupation are wound back to leave 'simply / a green field site' of prehistorical and linguistic innocence.[62] Words are, perhaps, more problematic, insecure and provisional than ever, while utterance itself is an act of faith proceeding from inevitable uncertainties and lack of knowledge. As one poem puts it:

> . . . every sentence
> builds itself
> on a kind of clearance
> builds itself on risk
> and an ignorance
> of what's been hacked down
> or packed up[63]

This successfully suggests the effort and challenge involved in the kind of writing he repeatedly applauds, which has the immediacy of speech and the force of action. In '51 Sans Souci Park' he urges himself to '*try writing to the moment*', and the phrase 'writing to the moment' is also the title he gave to a volume of critical essays published in 1996, thereby confirming that the link between his critical preoccupations and his poetry remains as strong as ever.[64]

One of these essays, 'Shakespeare the Catholic', celebrates the qualities of 'bravura performance' and 'puritan theatricality' in Ted Hughes's book on the playwright. Such writing, claims Paulin, 'carries always the preacher's sense of speaking to and through a deeply attentive audience', and reiterating the phrase he had used previously both of St Paul and of Emily Dickinson, he praises Hughes's aim 'to push writing beyond writing, . . . to melt its signs into free expressive performance'.[65] It is a description which seems to match Paulin's own aspirations, particularly in *Walking a Line*, where many of the poems break free from conventional metrical form and punctuation, while others resist closure, ending on a note of ambiguity or a question mark (for example, 'Matins', 'The Firhouse', 'L', 'Unnatural Object', and 'Cadmus and the Dragon').

He returns to a complex free-ranging historical meditation in the longest poem in the collection, 'Cadmus and the Dragon'. Here he employs the figure of the dragon slayer and founder of Thebes metaphorically, as he reflects upon the history of Protestantism from the libertarian rationalism of Lord Shaftesbury and John Locke which contributed to the success of the Glorious Revolution, to the narrow and fearful Protestant nationalism of contemporary paramilitaries.

It is the freedoms and rights ('rights not duties be it said') attributed to the Williamite settlement which Protestants in Northern Ireland have always claimed to be defending through Orange, Masonic and extreme Loyalist organisations in their resistance to Home Rule or any weakening of their power.[66] Thus, the mythical founder of Thebes 'is Sir Edward Carson / raising his bronze fist / against the twisty tail of Home Rule'. Nevertheless, this 'theatrical gesture', permanently captured in the statue that stands in front of the former Northern Ireland parliament building at Stormont, was 'copied from James Larkin / who raised the dragon people / against their bosses' in the Dublin lock-out of 1913, thereby suggesting an unexpected and unacknowledged connection between the arch Unionist and Socialist leaders. Additionally, the poem proposes, there are links between English Tory politicians and government officials who have sometimes supported and sometimes exploited the Protestant Unionists, yet who now seem ready to abandon them.[67] Thus, 'Cadmus was present at a working lunch / in the Stormont Hotel / the winter of 90 or 91', when negotiations on the future of Northern Ireland were taking place, and another modern Cadmus, William Whitelaw, is warned by one of the hooded paramilitaries:

> ye cannae sit in this coul chamber
> wi a bare head
> at a table that's shaped
> like a Wellington boot
> – put you a hood on
> and we'll do business;

and reminded that his ancestry is inseparable from theirs.[68]

The bibical warning – 'as ye sow so shall ye reap' – aptly combines reminders of the story of Cadmus and the dragon's teeth and of the role of the English in shaping the situation in Northern Ireland which can neither be forgotten not disowned with impunity. As the 'hood' humorously tells 'Mr Kidglove Whitelaw':

> we're no Piltdown Planters
> but the real autochthonous thing
> – we're the Cruthin aye
> a remnant of the ancient British people
> who rose again in 98
> in 1912 and . . .
> ack I forget what date it was
> but let Ballylumford
> be our rath and fortress[69]

The 'forgotten date' is 1974 when the Ulster Workers' Council, backed by the UDA and other paramilitary groups, brought the province to a standstill in order to wreck the power-sharing assembly created by the Sunningdale Agreement in December 1973 in which Whitelaw played an instrumental part. Crucial to the effectiveness of the strike which, as Jonathan Bardon has written, 'During fifteen days . . . made an entire region of the United Kingdom ungovernable', was the UWC's control of the power station at Ballylumford.[70]

As has been shown elsewhere, the Cruthinic myth is a loyalist version of history which claims ancient connections between the forebears of the Protestants of Ulster (who lived there long before the Plantation) and the British monarchy that run back to the Children of Israel, and origins in the north of Ireland that predate the arrival of the Celts. From this point of view, if the British turn against the Ulster Protestants, they turn on themselves. The word 'remnant' also recalls the alleged Israelite connection, because, according to Isaiah, the term was used of those Jews allowed by God to survive the exile in Babylon in order to provide the eventual source of renewal for His chosen people, and some Protestants equate their position in Northern Ireland with this biblical situation. Significantly, too, the 'hood' associates his people with the United Irishmen of 1798 as well as with the signatories of the Solemn League and Covenant in 1912 and the UWC and UDA in 1974, all of whom acted rebelliously in defence of the 'rights' they believed in.

Cadmus is further characterised by quintessentially formal, logocentric and masculine modes of thought: he is '. . . all straight lines / he's rule and measure / a rigid prick'.[71] These phrases hint on the one hand at Masonic or Orange iconography, but also imply the imaginative limitations of an angular cast of mind which rejects particularities and is fearful of emotion:

> . . . Cadmus is a grid person
> who must imagine
> not *amor loci*
> not *dinnseanchas*
> but the absolute antithesis of place
> because he fears a parish dragon[72]

But at the same time, as the poem has variously suggested, '*Cadmus is himself the Dragon*', and therefore his fear entails a neurotic repression and denial of another part of himself, the 'Dragon Other', denoted as primeval, female, fertile, exotic and earthy – opposite to Cadmus in every respect and a challenge to his uncompromising masculinity. This tension is not resolved in the poem's conclusion, where the consoling speculation 'that we are all born of the spirit / and not the earth' is followed by the doubt whether '. . . maybe the opposite / just happens to be the case?'.[73] Acceptance of this possibility is the means of escaping from an oppositional mode of thought into imaginative inclusiveness and new potential, whether in the sphere of art or of politics. Implicitly, at least, therefore, the poem might be read as an appeal for what Seamus Heaney has called 'two-mindedness', a reconciliaton of 'two orders of knowledge which we might call the practical and the poetic' – although, typically, it also concludes on a note of uncertainty.[74]

It is clear that Tom Paulin's work so far, both as poet and critic, has drawn heavily upon aspects of his Northern Irish Protestant background. What has been particularly distinctive has been the seriousness with which he has engaged and argued with aspects of a culture that many people find repugnant, offensive or frankly incomprehensible. Paulin is fully aware of the narrow vision, bigotry and emptiness of what he has called 'official Protestant culture' and has expressed his amazement at 'how people can simultaneously wave the Union Jack and yet hate the English, as many Protestants do'.[75] He himself has written of the 'intransigence and destructiveness which are so much a part of the Protestant temperament', and

> For a writer who gives his explicit allegiance to the values of Enlightenment republicanism, . . . is much preoccupied with the hermetic imagery of harsh, dark beliefs, the arcane flip-side of Presbyterianism which is a stylised version of the history of community, grounded in the themes and imagery of the Old Testament.[76]

But it is this very awareness and these interests which have made him so astute an observer of the dynamics of loyalism. In this respect, Bernard O'Donoghue's observation that Ian Paisley has been 'better understood by Paulin than anyone else who has written a serious evaluation, rather than a caricature, of him', is both correct and wholly understandable.[77] And that understanding informs Paulin's argument in 'Northern Protestant Oratory and Writing', where he suggests that Paisley's rhetoric and manner share much in common with those of William Drennan, the United Irishman sympathiser, for all their other differences in outlook. However, Paisley and most contemporary Protestant Unionist culture offer a deformed and debased version of earlier radicalism, in which the potential for intolerance, authoritarianism and repression have become exaggerated at the expense of libertarianism, concern for social justice, and generosity of thought and imagination – the values to which Paulin appeals. Additionally, in contemporary Northern Irish loyalism, dissenting Protestantism's iconoclastic readiness to challenge all conventions, authorities and received wisdom in defence of integrity and fidelity to personal conscience ('The true puritan rejects traditional monarchy and the authority of the Church, and looks instead to the Bible for sanction and inspiration', claims Paulin in 'Political Verse'), risks becoming a parody of itself, motivated by fear and defensiveness and commonly capable only of denials and refusals.[78] These recognitions permeate Paulin's poetry and his critical writing about Northern Protestantism.

More positively, however, a secularised version of Protestant radicalism has shaped both the form and the content of his work. This is evident, first, in the emphasis he places upon the courageous creativity and lack of concern for consensus opinion and acceptability shown by other dissenting writers – for example, he quotes approvingly Whitman's line, 'Not words of routine this song of mine', and cites Milton's constant 'striving to break down inert routines in order to free the imagination from "linen decency", "a gross confirming stupidity, a stark and dead congealment"'.[79] It is also this spirit which Paulin aims to release in his own poetry and which he associates with a style that aspires to the dynamic inventiveness and local coloration of speech. 'Poetry for Paulin', writes Elmer Andrews, 'is a subversive act, a defiance of linguistic and literary order designed for the ideological suppression or pacification of potentially rebellious impulses'.[80] Although no advocate of the Word in the scriptural sense, Paulin is convinced of the energy and power of words themselves – what he quotes Ian Paisley as calling 'the dynamic of heaven' – and particularly of the non-liturgical, spontaneous language of dissenting Protestantism. Thus, in his introduction to the *Field Day Anthology*, Paulin claims that

> In order to establish the distinctive characteristics and values of Ulster loyalist or protestant culture, it is necessary to abandon conventional ideas of the literary and the aesthetic and consider forms of writing that are often dismissed as ephemeral or non-canonical;

and in both his practice of poetry and criticism, his work is marked by unconventional forms, vocabulary and judgements.[81]

Furthermore, he regards a 'constantly challenging or polemical "mind-set"' as 'one result of a belief in the right of private judgement', and in his writing and broadcasts Paulin is well-known for his combative and individual views.[82] His impatience with the Arnoldian idea of 'disinterested' writing is complemented by his insistence on the dangers of ahistoricism. This is the trap into which he sees much Protestant loyalist thought as having fallen, hence his own attempts to widen its horizons and relocate it within the European traditions of the Enlightenment and republicanism. Indeed, Paulin's attitude shares something with the Calvinist whole-world view which rejects the notion of separating the sacred and the secular: 'Theology and politics fuse completely in the Protestant imagination', he has written.[83] Thus, the aesthetic exists within the political, the private and the public intersect, and personal conscience and liberty are inseparable from social responsibility and justice.

Finally, the Protestant complexion of Paulin's thought is apparent in his capacity both to reflect bleakly on the 'fallen' state of man and society and in the idealism with which this pessimism is counter-balanced. Guilt, the threat of violence, fear, loss of vision, absence of or disappointment in love, personal, sexual and social failure of various kinds are recurrent – evidence, as one critic has written, of how 'the Calvinist sense of sin and damnation slips easily into a secular mode'.[84] Yet against all these, there is the imagined possibility of a non-sectarian, libertarian, enlightened republican state, the realised aspiration of the United Irishmen, where the individual and the social good are reconciled – in short, a secular heaven. Inevitably, perhaps, this ideal, however admirable, is less convincing than his sardonic and satirical critiques of the failures and shortcomings of contemporary Protestant culture that has been compromised by political loyalism. The degree to which Paulin is a distinctive, individual dissenting voice, or is likely to have a redeeming influence upon the Northern Protestants, whom he challenges to recover their mislaid radical heritage, remains questionable. However, more than any other contemporary writer, he has recalled neglected aspects of his community's past and the potential within it, and by his own poetic and critical example has demonstrated his personal commit-ment to a modern secular version of the old theologically based tradition of dissent.

CHAPTER TEN

Some Representations of
Protestant Experience: Fiction

If the stereotype is to be believed, Protestants exhibit a
narrower emotional range and a greater, more careful and
on the whole less imaginative stability, a stability that owes
itself to their Protestant religion, the mythless recency of
their Irishness, and their Scottish patrimony.

John Wilson Foster, *Forces and Themes in Ulster Fiction.*

IN THE FIRST CHAPTER of his study of Ulster fiction, which
remains the most comprehensive treatment of the subject, John
Wilson Foster identifies a number of themes or motifs in novels from
the region. These include preoccupations with 'the blighted land' –
a reference to the troubled, impoverished and unpredictable nature of
rural experience, especially in the nineteenth century; 'bad blood', or
the family rivalries and tensions deriving from sectarian grievances
and greed for land which was in short supply; 'lost fields', an allusion
not only to literal expropriation, 'but also to the delayed psychic and
spiritual effects of that loss upon city dwellers', and the desire for an
'eternal return', the recovery of a paradisal state of simple innocence.[1]
These 'forces and themes', he argues, have affected novelists from
both Catholic and Protestant backgrounds to varying degrees, with
the different circumstances and experiences of each community, and
their perceptions of each other and of themselves across the denominational divisions, proving deeply influential. While few, if any, Ulster
novelists have written specifically as proponents of Catholicism or
Protestantism, their fiction commonly foregrounds the community to
which the writers themselves belong, however nominally.

This is evident in the novels discussed here, which are written by
novelists with Protestant backgrounds and focus primarily on
Protestant characters and communities. In three of them – by Sam
Hanna Bell, Janet McNeill and Maurice Leitch – a non-conformist

minister or pastor is a major character and the novelists' representations of them is of particular interest.[2] Compared with the countless
priests who populate Irish novels and short stories, Protestant clerics
make much fewer appearances in fiction, especially this century. This
may in part be a reflection of the differences between the roles of
priest and minister in relation to their people, and of the relative
scope and nature of their authority. The priest has traditionally held
a pivotal position in Catholic communities, exercising considerable
influence over the lives and conduct of his parishioners. In Protestant,
and especially Presbyterian and other non-conformist churches, much
greater power resides with the members who invite and employ their
clergy, rather than receiving appointees sent to them by the ecclesiastical hierarchy. There is a real sense, therefore, in which the laity
feel entitled not only to have certain expectations of their minister in
terms of his theology, learning and way of life, but also to challenge
and question him when they deem it necessary to do so. (One recalls,
for example, John Hewitt's maternal Grandmother Robinson rebuff-
ing her minister for preaching which, in her opinion, failed to arouse
sinners to repentance. See note 20 to chapter 6.) Ultimately, in cases
of extreme disagreement, Protestant churches have subdivided, as
history shows, thereby further emphasising the provisional authority of
the clergy and institutions of the church. The theology of these two
positions originates in the Reformation when the unchecked power
of the priesthood was seen as a key element in the corruption of the
Church. In Ireland however, it has often been presented in simple
sectarian terms as evidence of Protestant, and especially Presbyterian,
respect for liberty of conscience and for the individual's relationship
with God as opposed to the authoritarian invasiveness of Catholicism
embodied in the priest. Yet the demystification of the priesthood and
its replacement in Protestantism by ministers, preachers or pastors
did not wholly remove the special standing of such figures within
their communities. Therefore, the relationship between clergy and
people remained influential and special. The status and authority of
the cleric, his relationship with those to whom he ministers, and the
dilemmas he faces as a result of his position and of the expectations
of his people – all issues which offer particular insights into the
Protestant community – are explored in differing ways in *December
Bride* (1951), *As Strangers Here* (1960), and *Gilchrist* (1994).

The second selection of novels concentrates on young people at
stages in their development when they are beginning for the first time
to question the religious and cultural assumptions of their upbringing

and to discover alternative ways of living and of viewing the world. The protagonists in the books by Anthony C. West, Julie Mitchell and Glenn Patterson all come from strongly defined Protestant communities, although the specific details of their backgrounds vary significantly. The development of the principal character in each book is decisively furthered by friendships with individual Catholics which challenge their ways of thought, bring to consciousness the prejudices they have unthinkingly inherited and lead to reassessments of their relationships with their own families and communities. Since the novels are set against a background of political and religious tension or the upsurge of sectarian violence, this adds to the perplexity of the central characters as they struggle to find their own identities. Thus, it is notable that whereas these fictions represent a commonplace adult Protestant perception of Catholics as unreliable, feckless and oppressed by their Church, the young think they have discovered an enviable freedom in what appears to them a more relaxed, less inhibited and guilt-ridden way of life. While this perspective may be as flawed as that of their elders, and may risk replacing one set of stereotypes with another, the novelists are able to use it as a means of exploring some of the implications of sectarianism for relationships in a divided society from a specifically Protestant point of view.

I

The representation of the various types of ministry performed by Edwin Sorleyson in Bell's *December Bride*, Edward Balleter in McNeill's *As Strangers Here* and Eric Gilchrist in Leitch's book not only explore the predicaments of the individual characters, but also throw into relief other aspects of the Protestantism each purports to uphold and preach. The novels are conceived in markedly different places and times. *December Bride* is located in late-nineteenth and early-twentieth century Co. Down, although there is a felt sense of the growing influence of Belfast and some of the events are set in the city. *As Strangers Here* takes place in Belfast in the 1950s during an upsurge in IRA violence, and *Gilchrist* has near contemporary settings in Ireland, England and Spain, but also makes extensive reference back to the protagonist's rural background in Co. Antrim forty or more years before. Furthermore, while Sorleyson and Balleter are ordained Presbyterian ministers, Gilchrist's credentials are entirely subjective and he has served as pastor to a small, authoritarian evangelical sect which emphasises the need to be washed of sin through baptism by total immersion. Finally, whereas McNeill and Leitch's clerical characters are the central figures in their books, Sorleyson does not occupy a similar position in *December Bride*, although his importance is considerable. Yet, these variations do not preclude instructive points of comparison as well as contrasts. All three writers are engaged by the somewhat paradoxical position of a man who is simultaneously set apart from other people by his vocation and the offices specifically associated with it, but who shares many of the same physical, emotional, spiritual and material needs as those to whom he ministers, though without the channels through which he can satisfy – or even express – them. Central to this dilemma is the ironic absence or disappointment of love in the lives of the three characters which profoundly affects their practice of ministry and even seems exacerbated by the tension between the self-effacing discipline of their vocation and the authoritarian attitudes to which it leads in relation to others. This absence, more than anything else, also precipitates crises of faith, erodes self-belief and heightens each protagonist's sense of acute loneliness – all of which have also been observed in the poetry discussed previously.

In *December Bride* Sorleyson's isolation is revealed in various ways. His relationship with the members of the largely farming community to whom he ministers never seems easy. He himself is not a countryman and his lack of familiarity with rural ways is exposed through his misguided attempt to remonstrate with a farmer who has kept his son off school to help with the harvest. The same incident also indicates the limits to his authority over his congregation, although this is more importantly challenged by his inability to regulate the relationship between Sarah Gomartin and the Echlin brothers, which is the main focus of interest in the novel. Sarah's refusals – to go to church, to accept Sorleyson's theology, to leave the farm at Rathard after Andrew Echlin's death and her mother's return home, to marry either of the brothers although she has slept with both of them and to name which of the men is the father of her child – are direct rebuttals of the Church's teaching and of the individual clergyman's attempt to command her obedience. The fact that it is a woman who shows such defiance adds to its significance, as is highlighted following Andrew Echlin's death by drowning in Strangford Lough after the boat in which Sarah and his sons were travelling with him foundered in a storm. Sorleyson interprets the death as the will of God, prays that the survivors may profit from their affliction and helplessness and reminds them of the futility of human hopes and desires, but Sarah suspects him of bending 'a fortuitous and tragic occurrence to buttress his own beliefs and teachings', and of denying the self-sacrifice she believes Andrew made to save the rest of them.[3]

She is equally resolute when, after her pious mother, whose God is an Old Testament figure of wrath, has exhorted her to remember that Sorleyson is '"the servant o' the Church o' God"' and urged her to attend worship, she retorts:

> Aye! Our folks prospered, didn't they, with their running tae Church on a Sunday! My father died on the roads, and ever since I can mind my life has been nothing else but slaving for other folk. And always . . . its 'be humble, Sarah, God will reward ye.' Well, I'm tired o' it! My ways are my own. I get up in the morn tae my work, and at night I lie down in my bed, and if I fall dead in the midst o' it, there'll be little talk and less weeping![4]

Sarah's daring variant of the words of the Lord in Isaiah ch. 55, v. 8 ('For my thoughts are not your thoughts, neither are your ways my ways') is in striking contrast to her mother Martha's docile compliance in the face of adversity, and she is unmoved by warnings of punishment to follow, responding simply that she will suffer any retribution, but not on her knees.

Sorleyson relies upon the uncritical readiness of the people like Martha in his congregation to observe their religious duties and to accept the authority of his position and when he fails to command obedient conformity from the Echlin household, he is largely powerless. He is particularly perplexed by Sarah's defiance and pointedly neglects to ask her mother to renew the appeal to her daughter to return to church, much to Martha's grief, although pressing her to ask the two men again. His omission is important not simply as a failure of Christian concern, but as a clue to deeper questions about Sorleyson's theology and ministry which are increasingly apparent to the reader, and which are most visible in the character's troubled attempts to subdue Sarah's dissenting spirit.

Bell presents a vain man whose ambitions exceed his ability and whose domestic life and marriage relationship are as hidebound and perfunctory as his vocation is lacking in faith or insight. Unfulfilled both emotionally and spiritually, he has taken refuge in evading anything which threatens to unleash disruptive forces in his life. This is effectively symbolised by the obsessive orderliness and symmetry of his garden and his unease at the less carefully separated beds of his neighbours:

... without being quite able to explain why, Mr Sorleyson felt a strong aversion to this mingling of the orderly with the arbitrary. Perhaps it was because it ran counter to the attitude to which he clung so strenuously. Perhaps it was because it resembled too closely the lives of many of his congregation. He had discovered that these men and women who, from childhood, had been taught to esteem righteousness, could, without any feeling of inconsistency, show a deplorable tolerance to things that were far from righteous or seemly. He had come to the conclusion that Nature, with her continual and invariably indiscreet fertility, was a bad example to simple folk.[5]

Sorleyson's unease about the lives of his flock merely reflects the deeper difficulties in his own life. Paradoxically, though not at all surprisingly, the most irregular relationship in the townland intrigues him as much as it bothers and offends him, especially after Sarah has borne her first child, when her refusal to conform assumes new implications for him and precipitates the crisis between them that he has been trying to avoid.

Although Sorleyson is confounded by Sarah's position and attitude, he finds that he can see nothing evil in the mother and child. He begins to doubt the terms of his language to her and is unable to answer the question which troubles him: 'Of what avail was virtue if lust and irresponsibility were to be crowned with contentment?'[6] Despite his misgivings, on the occasion of his first interview with her after the child's birth, he reverts to the rhetoric of obligation and duty, but Sarah disconcerts him further with her accusation that he is trying to manipulate people and events to justify his own beliefs about the way things should be:

> ... what was it ye said? To marry one of the men. To bend and contrive things so that all would be smooth from the outside, like the way a lazy workman finishes a creel.[7]

This is ironic in view of the superficiality of Sorleyson's own marriage, but it also leaves him envying the relationship Sarah and the Echlins share, which is so different from his own cautious respectability and dependence on external rules. In this tale, it is Sarah, not Sorleyson, who is the real non-conformist, rather as Hester Prynne, not Arthur Dimmesdale, is the true dissenter in Hawthorne's tale. When he returns to see Sarah for the final time, ostensibly to offer to baptise her child, Sorleyson already sees that he is drawn by his own fascination to re-enter this morally freer world in order to gratify 'his natural carnal curiosity in men and women which he had tried to stifle for so long in pious ready-made explanations and half-fulfilments such as his own tepid marriage'.[8] He yields to his repressed curiosity and sexuality when he touches Sarah's breast, but is instantly appalled and frightened by his action, which he interprets as the triumph of evil and the destruction of all to which he had dedicated his life, and the final annihilation of his frail beliefs.

Though Sorleyson is forced to confront himself in this way, he remains incapable of acting honestly upon what he has learnt. His initial intention of telling his wife that he will leave the ministry and become a teacher quickly modifies into the easier, but cowardly, compromise of merely seeking a move to a Belfast church – a change which guarantees that he will remain entrapped by his deference to respectability, rules and public opinion rather than being liberated by experience. Bell adds further ironies when it is revealed that this weak and doubtful minister fathered a son who also becomes a clergyman and succeeds in bringing about the marriage of Sarah Gomartin and Hamilton Echlin years later. Whether, as the young Isaac Sorleyson likes to fancy, this event is the outcome of the Divine Will must be open to question, but it is certain that Sarah's acquiescence in the arrangement is motivated by her customary unerring assessment of what is most advantageous to her family's interests at the time, not by newly discovered religious conviction, deference to the minister, or concern for the opinion of her neighbours.

December Bride, therefore, represents a community in which the outward duties of religion are broadly observed – the Echlins and Sarah being the notable exceptions – but where none of the major characters, including the minister, shows much evidence of the influence of faith in his or her life. The steadily increasing property and wealth of the Echlins, guided by the shrewd business acumen of Sarah, seem to fly in the face of the conventional wisdom of the Church concerning the inevitable downfall of sinners and the hostility of many of their neighbours is inspired as much by jealousy of their success as by moral or religious outrage at their lives. Sorleyson's remoteness and detachment from his people and the insecurities and shallowness of his own beliefs, add to the impression that what goes on at Ravara Meeting-House has increasingly less connection with the fervor and piety of previous generations, traces of which are glimpsed in Martha Gomartin and Andrew Echlin, than with the maintenance of unchallenging social forms and the disciplines of rural religious conformity.

In this way, Bell's book provides a striking contrast with a novel published three years earlier in 1948 by W.F. Marshall. *Planted by a River* is an historical tale set in the time of Queen Anne and centred on characters who had been involved in the siege of Derry. Here the author, who was also a Presbyterian minister, characterises the plantation of Ulster not as a process of expropriation, but as the triumph of piety, industry and discipline over native incompetence. The sturdy Calvinism of the protagonists in this novel is described as '". . . a creed that makes believers with backbone, . . . yet . . . that keeps them modest . . ."', whereas *December Bride* clearly adopts a much less flattering and more unsettling view of the values and conduct of the Presbyterian society it represents, and of clerical authority within it.[9]

Likewise, when one turns to Janet McNeill's novel, it is clear that the troubles of Edward Balleter, the Presbyterian minister, derive in part from his sense of a similar lethargic complacency in the lives of many of his city congregation, although he himself is a man of much firmer convictions than Edwin Sorleyson. McNeill's character must owe a debt to her own background as a daughter of the manse who had observed at first hand the pressures exerted upon a minister. These include the sacrifice of much family privacy and the endless economies necessitated by the low salary paid to clergymen. Although the plot of *As Strangers Here* contains some improbable incidents, McNeill makes a scrupulous and disturbing analysis of the dynamics of the Balleter household and of the way these are the product of Edward Balleter's role as a minister and of his Calvinistic theology.

Like Sorleyson, Balleter is an isolated figure, but whereas the former's separateness seems largely self-imposed to allow him to indulge his day-dreams and avoid awkward questions about his faith and his marriage, Balleter's loneliness derives straight from his vocation. His beliefs are inseparable from a highly disciplined and restrained way of thought and living which makes his relationship with other people difficult. This is most evident within his own family, where his wife Florence's unhappiness and invalidity are in some measure the result of her sense of failure to fulfil other people's expectations of a minister's wife and of Balleter's own unease about the intimacies of marriage. That unease has transferred itself to their children and they force their father to undertake a disturbing interrogation of his marriage. On the one hand, their married son, Colin, who possesses an angrier version of Balleter's puritanism, bitterly interrupts his father's stilted attempts to rejoice in the news of his daughter-in-law's first pregnancy – '"A child completes a marriage. You will find that, Colin. It is very important that a marriage should be complete"' – by questioning the completeness of his parents' relationship, and accusing him of hiding behind '"God's will"' to explain Florence's ill health.[10] (This accusation is very similar to Sarah Gomartin's charge against Sorleyson over the matter of Andrew Echlin's death.) On the other hand, the Balleter's teenage daughter, Joanna, who is embarrassed by her own physical awkwardness and finds the sexual talk of her girlfriend distressing, horrifies her father by revealing her belief that her mother's illness originated when she was pregnant with her, and the guilt she herself feels as a result. Gradually Balleter comes to understand the failure of his marriage, and by implication the other stresses within the family, as the direct consequence of his particular theology and the disciplines he has followed in practising it. His final reflection on his relationship with Florence defines this:

> You were gay and careless and I tried to make you earnest and humble. You wanted my love and I offered you the love of a denominational God. You needed passion and I made humourless and temperate love to you. I always mistrusted ecstasy, and when I found it hugged it to myself. I was sentimental when you wanted sincerity. I only gave you half of myself.[11]

Two points are worth adding. Balleter shows here, and elsewhere, a capacity for honest self-examination and self-criticism which is one of the virtues of his austere creed, but it is equally significant that this remains a personal confession and is not admitted to his wife or anyone else. While everyone may be his or her own confessor to God, this is not necessarily satisfactory or enabling in matters concerning relationships with other people. It is unclear how Florence will be helped by her husband's new recognitions about their marriage when he is unable to share them with her.

The lonely difficulties of Balleter's position are also apparent in his ministry itself and in the pastoral and social obligations that are extensions of it. He is acutely conscious of the expectations people have of him and of his family's exposure to public comment:

> He and his wife were open to observation and to criticism at every step they took, in their way of living, social behaviour, appearance, extent of hospitality, choice of friends, outside interests, upbringing of their children.[12]

Yet, elsewhere, while giving a lift to some female parishioners who begin discussing a birth, he has the sense that 'there was something about his cloth and his function which . . . gave him a kind of invisibility, the neutrality of a eunuch'.[13] When news is received of the death of a policeman in an IRA outrage, he immediately knows that his congregation on Sunday will listen carefully to see if and how he alludes to it. Yet, he also has a troubled awareness of the apparent lack of connection between what he preaches to his people in church and the priorities which govern their lives. Struggling to know what it is his Christian duty to say after the terrorist attack, he is 'ashamed at his hesitation' when he recalls 'the fervour of the Protestant fathers', but his feelings change when he thinks of the Sermon on the Mount and his dilemma deepens: 'He tried to empty his mind of all prejudice – and to balance this to rid himself of a tolerance that paralyses any sense of purpose'.[14]

As a man of fastidious and frugal habits, he is alienated, and sometimes disgusted, by the self-indulgence and materialism of other people. He is uncomfortable even at church social events because he distrusts pleasure for its own sake, regarding it as an unwelcome distraction from 'confronting the sterner realities of life'.[15] This view informs his irritation with people's universal willingness to excuse sin while taking full credit for virtue, and with the complacency he descries in his Sunday morning congregation – 'a well-dressed, well-fed flock whom the Welfare State had robbed of all stimulus to effort and the necessity for fear'.[16] Even the paraphrase (from which the novel's title is taken) chosen to reinforce his text, 'Here we have no continuing city but we seek one to come', seems to Balleter to become parodic rather than pointed in its rendition:

> 'We walk by faith as strangers here,' they sang,
> 'But God shall call us home.'

> The comfortable jog-trot of the metre and the rounded tune only accentuated their content with the way they were walking in and their right to feel at home in it. 'Strangers here?' no, they knew every inch of their territory, and when they sang of 'faith' it wasn't of any personal conviction but a set of inherited beliefs, sitting snug in their pockets.[17]

Balleter wishes that he commanded the rhetoric of Amos or Jeremiah to break into these people's lives with apocalyptic force and yet despite his judgmental attitude and apparent disdain for them, he shows both patience and compassion in his dealings with individuals as well as an awareness of their private griefs. Furthermore, there is another side of his nature which acknowledges both the necessity and the desirability of the ordinary, mundane physical comforts and routines of life, even though so few of them enrich his own.

Balleter's faith is not free of doubt. At a number of key moments, McNeill represents him raising his eyes to the Cave Hill which overlooks Belfast, but unlike the Psalmist, he is not sure that it is the unambiguous source of his aid and reassurance. Thus, following a melodramatic bomb incident in which he escapes unhurt, he sees the hill as 'deepest impenetrable black', and although he looks at it 'in love', it occurs to him that the bomber 'might also . . . have looked to the hill for spiritual ease and in gratitude for work well done, and would resent any instinct of affection that [he] had for it'.[18] His thought here may also imply the kind of uncertainty about his right to be in the country itself, based on his consciousness of Presbyterianism as the religion of the planters, that is recurrent in John Hewitt's poetry. Later, when he turns to it again, 'hoping to find reassurance there, and ease from his irritation, . . . the hill appeared unfamiliar, withdrawn, unwelcoming, as if it denied him, the self-declared stranger'.[19] The implications of this situation are elaborated by Susan Manning in her discussion of the characteristic tension faced by Protestants, and especially Calvinists, whose aim is to live in but not of the world. 'To be a stranger', she observes, 'is not merely not to belong to one's surroundings, to be distanced from their meaning, but to be estranged and set at odds with them. The Calvinist, passing through this world, demands that it yield up its secrets and give him tidings of his Maker; the world looks blankly back'.[20] Balleter is unsettled by precisely this dilemma. However, at the end of the book, his last glance at the Cave Hill is more complex still and includes various possibilities. He now sees

> . . . a place where in the summer evenings climbing boys challenged the daylight, a place where a man could fall and end the argument of life, a place whereby unhappy history chained the future to the past, a place where a man might find, in the sight of it, the evidence of things unseen, which, though they cast confused and conflicting shadows on this beloved borrowed country, were in their true image imperishable and good and full of glory. Each man must make the choice for himself.[21]

This sequence of incidents is extremely important, each one marking a phase in Balleter's spiritual life and in his understanding of his relationship not only with God, but with his family and his country, and of the tensions and divisions that beset them all. The greater richness of his final vision complements the developments in his dealings with other characters and the resolution of some of the problems which he has faced in the course of the novel. While it would be unwarranted to suggest that his way of life has changed, Balleter's experiences have forced him to certain recognitions about himself and to a more compassionate view of the circumstances of others. Ruth Hooley speaks of how Janet McNeill 'dissects the power dynamics of family, examining how people can become mangled in its coils and how social and moral codes can inhibit emotional development', and these remarks are relevant to *As Strangers Here*.[22] However, she has enriched this 'dissection' of the particular complications affecting the family of a Presbyterian minister and of the extraordinary demands upon the clergyman himself. This is achieved by the author's sympathetic, though not uncritical, awareness of what it means to be a minister, his problems in negotiating his relationship with his congregation, of his difficulty in retaining integrity in the face of public pressure to produce stereotyped sectarian responses that contradict the Christian gospel, and of the strain of being a public figure expected to respond supportively to every kind of human crisis without any source of personal replenishment beyond faith in a God whose presence is not always evident to him. It is also this awareness that makes the novel such a perceptive study of Presbyterianism.

Towards the end of *As Strangers Here*, Edward Balleter goes to a gospel hall to interrupt a meeting at which a young man connected with his church is preparing to give his testimony in much the kind of way recorded by Robert Harbinson. Balleter is deeply sceptical of the sort of evangelism practised by such sects 'where salvation could be bought not by the blood of Christ, but by a bit of a thrill and some exhibitionism', and where the pastors were commonly 'local men, rebels from their orthodox Church, enjoying the light of conspicuous piety and the power that went with it'.[23] This kind of religion and pastor are at the centre of Maurice Leitch's novel, *Gilchrist*. If Sorleyson and Balleter are flawed believers, Gilchrist is a preacher who has stumbled out of a fraudulent 'magical' circus act into discovery of a kind of telepathic power which he has adapted to equally theatrical forms of salvationist activity that lead to his own moral corruption and downfall.

The narrative begins late in Gilchrist's story, after he has fled to Spain to escape the consequences of his disappearance with an underage female Catholic convert and the theft of his congregation's finances. It interweaves crucial episodes from his earlier life with an increasingly grotesque series of encounters with Gilchrist's doppel-gänger or alter ego, who establishes power over him and tempts him to further corruption and hypocrisy. Throughout, the novel explores and suggests the interaction between the kind of man Gilchrist is and the religious forms with which he is involved. As a youth, he ran away from his isolated rural family, joining a small troupe of travelling entertainers under the lustful protection of Max, 'The Great Man', who 'christened him Dogsbody', where he immediately succumbed to the mysterious power of performance:

> More than anything he needed to share in whatever it was that held all those people spellbound in the half-dark. He genuinely felt he had found his vocation.[24]

Max instructs him in the chicanery of performance and assures him of the audience's readiness to accept illusion as reality so long as their belief in it is neither challenged nor mocked. Under this tutelage, the youth gains a sense of personal identity for the first time – he becomes one of 'the elect' – and tastes power over people in his role as The Young Bamboozalem with an act which becomes so popular that it arouses the jealousy of his fellow performers.

From the outset Gilchrist conflates his supposed role as visionary medium with that of an inspired recipient of divine favour, thus turning his act into the 'first rung on the ladder of apprenticeship to the higher illusion which will be his life'.[25] Just as he learns to decode information from the words of his fellow-performer in order to impress his audience with his apparent insights, later as a preacher, he interprets scripture for specific ends and to stamp his authority upon his congregations. The obvious dangers of this are heightened when, seduced by his own performances, he begins to believe in his more-than-mortal powers and to take ever greater risks which increasingly alienate him from the company of actors. Ultimately he casts off Max himself in favour of another Great Man – Jesus.

Paradoxically, the power and sense of identity which Gilchrist craved and finds in his role as preacher do not overcome his underlying loneliness or enable him to resolve the sexual insecurity which haunts him. These have their origins in a childhood memory of being left on a rock in the middle of a river by his older brothers while they attempted to have sex with a village girl just out of his sight on the bank. The incident has left him with a lasting association between water and sex – 'Always the two have been connected in some mysterious manner in his life' – and thus the adult baptisms by immersion which he offers those who come to him become expressions both of power and of sublimated sexual gratification.[26] Crucially, this is power without responsibility and sex without involvement, and it is by such strategic detachment that Gilchrist sustains the illusion of his vocation in his own eyes and in those of his followers until Donna Brady presents herself to him for baptism. While he has always taken a vain delight in his particular appeal to women, Donna's obvious vulnerability, childishness and near victim status at the hands of her rough Catholic family overwhelm him. This precipitates the looming crisis in his life. As Gilchrist's involvement with her becomes more complicated and compromising, he is gradually forced to acknowledge his cynical and hypocritical use of religion to mislead the girl, keep his power over her and to justify his own improprieties to himself:

> Never has he felt so inadequate. What a sham he has become. Years of evasion and ready answers, half-truths, platitudes, when what people desperately craved were the certainties. Stones instead of bread was what he fed them.[27]

As the biblical passage to which the last sentence refers forewarns, Gilchrist's actions produce disastrous consequences, because he himself becomes helplessly enthralled by the girl especially when he discovers her familiarity with sex, lost in ever more fabricated versions of his own story and dependent on increasingly incredible self-deceptions:

> . . . he repeats to himself his newest commandment. *Thou shalt not touch.* God have pity on him, he actually did believe it then that if he didn't initiate or reciprocate in any way, somehow he would stay inviolate, uninvolved, more importantly, blameless, a wise monkey playing dead in the dark.[28]

Donna herself ends the illusion, turning his own words back on him when he reminds her that she wanted to be saved, and very properly accusing *him* of merely wanting to save her for himself. Her abandonment of Gilchrist complements his own earlier desertion of Max and fulfils the warning of the Great Man to his upstart protégé about the 'terrible things' that happen to a performer who loses the belief of his audience. It also forces Gilchrist's life into acute spiritual crisis.

His flight to Spain using funds stolen from his former congregation is not only a practical expedient to avoid the law, but is also presented as a metaphorical journey into the wilderness, or a dark night of the soul. The local landscape is likened to a 'biblical desert', and the disgraced Baptist preacher, whose name from the Irish means 'servant of Christ', encounters a grotesque exaggeration of his own worst traits and repressed desires in the equally ironically named Jordan. Dislocated in place, no longer restrained by the oppressive code of respectability required when he was a preacher, unknown to anyone, lacking any public role or position and haunted by the memories of all he has done, Gilchrist surrenders passively to the influence of Jordan and interprets the invasion of his life as punishment for his sins.

Where once Max had encouraged the boy to develop himself as a performer, Jordan denudes him of illusions – 'He had this strange unsettling image of layer after layer of disguises being peeled away to reveal absolutely nothing' – and fills him with self-disgust and the desire for punishment.[29] Initially, Gilchrist senses that a crossover is taking place between Jordan and himself and that he is disappearing 'without trace into the quicksand of the other's personality, body as well as soul'.[30] However, he rebels against a series of temptations to enter into a business partnership to make a fortune out of renewed exploitation of religion and finally comes to recognise Jordan as an embodiment of that very evil from which he himself had previously claimed to offer the way of salvation. At the end of the book, Gilchrist, whose natural element is water, casts off Jordan, who is associated with fire, and strips himself of every vestige of his alien life before plunging into the sea and

> . . . swimming back home, back along those cool, dark, remembered streams of childhood, letting them wash away each stain, every accumulated transgression with each stroke he took.[31]

Gilchrist's death is implied in the conclusion, and thus it is by destroying himself that he is saved and by drowning that he may receive the grace of baptism.

Leitch's novel, declares Robert McLiam Wilson, is 'about the kind of pessimistic Protestant lust that threatens to burst Gilchrist at the seams'.[32] It conveys how a debased form of Protestant individualism without responsibility or coherent theology to contain it can become a vehicle to compensate for personal weakness, timidity and insignificance and may provide a convenient rationale for evading emotional needs and psychological inadequacies. There is no substance to Gilchrist's theology. It derives from his own guilts, fears and desire for recognition and power, and colludes with other people's vulnerability and insecurity to generate unstable emotional gratification without the complications of love or commitment. Gilchrist's austerity, moralising, judgmentalism and bigotry have less to do with reason or principle than with presenting an impression of strong convictions and simultaneously providing a model for people who prefer to live unadventurously and with closed minds. He even acknowledges this to himself after he has connived at smuggling Donna out of the country to escape the supposedly greater tryanny of Catholicism:

> Suddenly he felt sick of his life, these constant admonitions to do this, be that. Yet here he had just sent off another soul to be shackled by those very same commandments.[33]

Such religion, if it merits the name, is entirely disabling rather than liberating or empowering, but the effect of the book is, as John Wilson Foster observed of some of Leitch's earlier fiction, that by its disclosure of the darker face of Ulster Protestantism, it rectifies the inability of some Ulster Protestants to know themselves.[34]

Each of these novels explores aspects of the nature of Protestant ministry, of what that ministry may be and of the pressures it puts upon those involved in it. In particular, they suggest how personal weaknesses and inadequacies become magnified by the minister's consciousness of his public role and the critical expectations of his people. These contribute to the notable loneliness of Sorleyson, Balleter and Gilchrist, none of whom feels upheld by love or is able to express his doubts and insecurities. They are, as it were, not permitted to show weakness and there is little evidence of sympathy or understanding of their needs among their congregations. This isolation is heightened by the solitary nature of their ministry – none of the characters is shown in the company of colleagues – and by the Protestant emphasis on the primacy of the individual's relationship with God.

Doubt, suffering and disillusionment lead to concealment and repression of their vulnerability through fear of losing face and credibility. Likewise, their unease with the worldliness and physical pleasures of many of those to whom they minister is a blend of genuine innocence, frustrated curiosity and desires of their own for a way of life that is less inhibited and less open to the judgmental scrutiny of other people. These feelings also contribute to each character's near inability to have any authentic personal life and to their disappointed or absent sexual relationships which are over-shadowed by the associations of guilt, shame and fear implicit in their theology.

The religion represented by Sorleyson, Balleter and Gilchrist offers salvation and declares the will of God to be active in the lives of people. Nevertheless, it is largely joyless and overbearing and seems to have surprisingly little to do with the daily lives of its adherents which are dominated by moneymaking and worldly gratification, social status and respectability. For many of them it is a code or habitual routine in which they neither seek nor find either the challenge or the blessing of faith. Meanwhile the ministers themselves are entrapped to varying degrees by the forms they uphold and which at times each questions. Sorleyson settles for acquiescence within them, Balleter struggles though uncertainties to a more complex understanding of them and Gilchrist discovers the high price of his hypocritical exploitation of them.

II

If clergymen and preachers are conventionally exemplary figures playing a public role in their communities, exercising a measure of privileged authority over the lives of their congregations and often reinforcing the dominant values in society, children and adolescents normally have no such status. They are among the members of society most open to the influences around them and are often the particular focus of adult efforts to form their thought processes, morality and conduct. Although sometimes unaware of the degree to which they have imbibed the perceptions and values of their elders, young people are also capable of responding to quite different influences and of questioning the received truths on which they have been raised. This readiness to challenge and react against their backgrounds, and the trials of conscience and growth of under-standing which result, are represented in the central characters in novels by Anthony C. West (*The Ferret Fancier* [1963]), Julie Mitchell (*Sunday Afternoons* [1988]) and Glenn Patterson (*Burning Your Own* [1988]). The individual circumstances of the characters, and the degree to which religion itself is a shaping force on them vary con-siderably, but in each case the sectarian differences and the preferred view of history which distort so much Ulster Protestantism are palpably active forces and add to the felt complexity of their situations. This is especially so because in all three novels the major Protestant character becomes involved with a Catholic youth whose differences of background, upbringing and attitude are sources of fascination and attraction, as well as of fear and anxiety, to him or her. The Catholic, therefore, represents the 'other' – that which is opposite to the familiar and acceptable; he or she is forbidden and unknown, religiously and culturally strange, exciting and frightening. In West and Patterson's novels the relationships have to be pursued furtively and concealed from Protestant parents because they would disapprove of them while in Mitchell's the friendship is threatened by sectarian pressures in the community. These friendships play crucial parts in the protagonists' growth of self-awareness and understanding and in enabling them to free themselves from the rigid categories of thought shown by most of their elders and rooted in the community around them. To the degree that they change their perspectives, Simon Green, Noreen Logan and Mal Martin are exceptional rather than representative characters, but through them their creators explore aspects of the society as a whole as well as narrating the stories of these individuals.

The Ferret Fancier is set in staunchly Protestant farming country just inside the newly formed Irish Free State in the period immediately after partition. The principal character, Simon Green, who is entering adolescence, comes from a well-off but frugal farming family. Conor, his father, is a 'respected parishman and an orangeman of long standing', while his mother, Ellen, a semi-invalid, is more strictly puritanical – 'the road of her childhood was paved with stern precepts, parables and proverbs, firsthand contact with and affection for nature the only lightness in it'.[35] At home, at school under the tutelage of a sin-obsessed teacher, Rainey, and in church, Simon is immersed in talk about wickedness, guilt, punishment and human weakness, and is increasingly torn by the conflict between these emphases and his own natural impulses and growing sexual curiosity:

> He was asking to be himself without knowing how to be: Conor stood across one end of his life, Ellen sat at the other and inside these markers were Rainey and the Rector – school and parish, learning and piety attacking both ends of original sin; the cash-and-kind commonalities of day constantly devalued by imagination along with the circus nights of guideless dream.[36]

Simon's consciousness of the disjunction between the theology he is taught and the actual condition and conduct of the lives of the adults he knows also perplexes him. His parents' marriage is acrimonious, the relationship between Rainey and his wife strikes him as grotesque and even the Rector's marital situation is the subject of gossip – yet 'sentimentality and the myth of god-joined marital bliss preserved the paint on the decaying appearances', and the Rector is well-known for pressurising young courting couples to wed.[37] More confusingly still, Rainey and the Rector denounce sex as sin, but Simon cannot understand why, if this is so, God made humans sexual beings and why there is ample evidence of approved sexual activity both in the Bible itself and in the lives of those who speak loudest against it. At the same time as he endlessly fantasises about sex, his fascination is more than matched by fear and even disgust at what it seems to involve. This mixture of feelings is graphically realised in his dealings with Jill, a ferret he is persuaded to buy. Ferreting becomes a metaphor for the sexual experience Simon has not had, but Jill's conscience-free efficiency, whether hunting, killing or copulating and her barely controllable and permanently dangerous nature torment him by emphasising his own timidity, lack of confidence and dread of humiliation and punishment.

The fears which accompany his burgeoning sexual awareness do not exist in isolation. Simon, like his older sister, Agatha, is nervous and insecure in other ways as well, most of which originate in the negative strictures of the religion in which he has been raised. Like Joanna Balleter, he is convinced that his mother's illness was caused or worsened by bearing him and he regards his own existence as evidence of sin. At the same time, he is also terrified that the school-master will wreck his relationship with his mother if he detects Simon's lecherous thoughts and complains of them to her: 'He just had to have someone who believed that he wasn't so bad as he thought he was, whatever the immorality of his daily actions'.[38] He has bad dreams which he later associates with a plague of rats on the farm, seeing them as 'dead end sins' and attributing his hate of them to their symbolic representation of the state of his soul. In each of these instances, Simon's imagination, tainted by doctrines of sin, guilt and punishment, grotesquely dramatises his supposed misdeeds.

As a younger child, terrified by Rainey's Old Testament stories of placatory sacrifices offered to the God of wrath, he secretly tried to appease his teacher by a bungled killing of a rabbit – an action which in itself horrified him. These feelings are renewed after Jill and her cubs kill another rabbit which he has placed in their pen, when the helpless passivity of the victim stirs both Simon's anger and his guilt and makes him connect 'this predetermined end' with

> . . . Rainey's talk about something called the law of predestination with guaranteed salvation for a few and guaranteed deprivation for the many, God Himself dealing off the bottom of the pack and nudging the devil under the table.[39]

The violent brutishness of life and death exemplified by this incident convinces Simon of the falsity of 'the smug life of appearances that friends and neighbours were trying so hard to maintain, praising charity while conniving with distrusts', and leads him him to a nightmarish vision of death as the driving force of life, 'creating and re-creating forms and ghosts of life only to destroy them and then to re-create them for the endless satisfaction of destroying them again'.[40] Faced with such a bleak and unchristian perception, he automatically iterates the petition against temptation and evil in the Lord's Prayer, but derives little comfort from doing so.

Fear also returns to haunt him in the old Quaker burial ground where his renewed thoughts on time and mortality make him contemplate the supposed fecklessness and failures of his own life and contrast his lack of faith with the assumed strength of belief of his predecessors. Ironically, the closest Simon comes to a full sexual experience takes place between the grave mounds and, unlike his fantasies, is forced upon him by the Catholic girl whom he has pursued much more ardently in mind than in deed. Not surprisingly, the combination of her religion and their frustrated sexual activity in this location generates a double sense of sin and shame in Simon's already overactive conscience, leaving him 'more lonely and hopeless than ever'.[41]

Agnes Jameson, the object of his desires, comes from a large, impoverished, chaotic Catholic family which is regarded with disdain by respectable Protestants like the Greens – more especially so since her father converted to his wife's religion. Because of Agnes's background, Simon has a sense of social superiority and also likes to imagine that she will be sexually obliging, but he is paralysed by a combination of guilt about his own motives when he visits the family, fear of betraying his intentions to the girl's mother and lack of confidence to initiate intimacies with her. He is also drawn to the Jamesons' home and family life because it is so much 'softer and more kindly than Simon's speckless own', and particularly to the endlessly fecund, slatternly, but maternal Mrs Jameson, whose carelessness of dress and unashamed attitude to her own body or to exposing her flesh are a startling contrast to his mother's conduct, and arouse a mixture of feelings and desires in him.[42]

Simon is caught between an inclination to romanticise the poverty, instability and squalor of the Jamesons, who seem to him to represent freedom from the Protestant obligation, respectability and judgmentalism that burden his own life and a more realistic awareness of the discomforts and hazards of such a precarious existence. His flirtation with them is a secret defiance of his family's standards, a vicarious sampling of difference. This becomes increasingly uncomfortable as he suspects that Mrs Jameson has seen through him and realises that Agnes's brothers and younger sister are watching him knowingly. Finally, when he sees that Agnes herself is encouraging him, Simon's fears overwhelm him:

> . . . destroying the hitherto protected illusion of hunter and hunted, his body, despite its surging ambition, not strong enough to break through the fastidious fence that ringed round his mind.[43]

Simon's relationship with Agnes recreates many of the conflicts of feeling he had about the ferret. While one part of him wishes to use the girl with the guiltless indifference of an animal following its instincts, another part invokes the moral, religious and social codes of his upbringing, which in this context are disabling and leave him frustrated and confused, rather than with any sense of having acted rightly. In this situation he remembers some words of the independently-minded Paul Noble who criticised 'the moral-human evolution' of both Protestantism and Catholicism for having reached a dead end, and insisted that '"Individual freedom, . . . malice to none, is what we want . . . Without it the world is a wilderness of forelocks and bended knees."'[44] Individual freedom is what Simon longs for, but he has great difficulty in seeing how to achieve it in a society where most adults are like his own father, who 'never even thought, when he called himself a protestant, that the right to protest was buried in the word and was still the first point of liberty'.[45] Simon is, however, described as a member of a new generation 'for whom there was no longer any possibility for easy compromise', and several of the most effective moments in the novel represent his private arguments about the very existence of God which are conducted with the intensity of adolescence combined with some of the boldness of radical Protestantism.

Like his mother, Simon is deeply responsive to the natural world, seeing in its beauty 'the God of brand new Eden, not a worry on Him and not for sure the careworn One whom the Rector mourned in a roast-beef voice of common prayer'.[46] But the onset of puberty, his sexual awakening and his growing awareness that adults denounce aspects of nature as sinful, confuse his intuitive understanding of God and threaten his spontaneous acceptance of the world around him. His sense of reduction and loss as a result of increasing self-consciousness and the activity of conscience is conveyed by a striking simile:

> It was like the flowers: the year before Ellen promised him half-a-crown if he found and named fifty flowers. He found and named a hundred and fifty, pressing them in a book where all the bright colours faded and the green leaves turned black. In finding all these flowers he had lost them, for he couldn't see them for looking for new ones, his search becoming a kind of greed, a whole gay field unseen because he already knew the names of the flowers in it: names, numbers, scentless corpses flattened in a book.[47]

This reverses the biblical notion of the power gained by Adam through naming the creatures in paradise. Simon considers that names are 'sentences of death', diminishing the world and dividing it between rival interpretations – 'The God of wind, sun and weather or Rainey's God, church God, catholic god, or God in a gospel tent. If all the parish gods were under one roof there'd be a holy war – battles of Bibles and riots of prayers'.[48] This contrasts sharply with the innocent simplicity of vision as a child and his readiness to accept the world at face value. Likewise, after he has starved his ferret to death, using the excuse that she bit him to justify his desire to be rid of her, he again discovers too late that actions cannot be undone, nor their significance understood until they have already been committed. Thus he realises the paradoxical state produced by what he has allowed to happen: 'He was free again while dimly divining that he would never again be free'.[49]

When he literally shouts for God, demanding Him to reveal Himself, wanting 'to see Him and live', and 'never once doubting that He would also be beautiful, also kind, and so would give the lie to all the pew-prophets and groaning gospellers', the absence of a response induces a new fear in him of 'a guideless world racing into destruction' – a more unsettling version of Balleter's experience.[50] At another level he is self-critical of his own conduct, questioning whether it is any more than an elaborate game to overcome his boredom. However, at the close of the book Simon experiences a moment of visionary insight halfway between the snow-covered hills of Knockbawn which he has tried in vain to reach and the lowland valley of his home, which from this new perspective appears to him as the world. He renounces the materialistic work ethic of Protestantism, deciding to 'Worship the fullness of God . . . by doing nothing instead of turning pennies into pounds all your life and threatening the images of God with a hatchet if ever they came near the hoard'.[51] Simon accepts that these dissenting thoughts condemn him to loneliness and he also acknowledges the inescapability of time and the necessity of returning to the parish within which he must 'make himself small' and 'keep the law to furnish freedom – to be free was the thing, there were no mind-readers, thank God'.[52] Although the novel ends without Simon having discovered any clear purpose to his life, it shows how he has reached a new stage of self-reliance and self-awareness and has begun to outgrow the arid forms of judgmental Protestantism that surrounded him in childhood and were the source of his disturbing phobias and guilts.

The protagonist of Julie Mitchell's *Sunday Afternoons*, Noreen Logan, is also the product of a strongly religious family, although her father's Methodism and quiet assurance of personal salvation are counterbalanced by Mrs Logan's less fervent and convinced faith. Like Simon Green, Noreen is imbued with a heightened sense of sin. Dancing, smoking, drinking alcohol and sex are all taboo and respectability is again upheld as a protection against temptation and immorality, and an adjunct of piety. This respectability is especially associated with Sunday routines, not only of church-going but also of restrained behaviour, observing quiet and wearing one's best clothes. Noreen, who is an only child, feels increasingly resentful of her parents' values as she goes through adolescence and wants to 'be bad' simply as a rebellion against them, although, again like Simon, she lacks courage and confidence to be so on her own.

It is her chance friendship with a Catholic girl, Eileen McAllister, which initiates important changes in her life. Mitchell's representation of the McAllisters – a large family where money is in short supply, the father drinks, the mother is welcoming and the atmosphere is informal and warm – bears notable similarity to West's depiction of the Jamesons. Likewise, Noreen finds consolation and comfort there that she misses in her own home. Her parents are tolerant of the friendship, however, although her father does not consider the

McAllisters 'respectable', but Eileen is also the temptress whose example leads Noreen into truancy, shoplifting, sneaking out at night to a dance and drinking. This rebellion against her parents and the teaching of her Church is strongly influenced by Noreen's loneliness and wish to belong to another social group. All the same, her naivety results in her estrangement from Eileen's family, after she joins in singing an Orange song at a dance without appreciating its offensiveness to her friend, and in a growing sense of having cut herself off from her parents' world by her own deceitfulness.

Through Noreen's temporary compliance with her father's encouragement to attend an Evangelical Mission Hall, Mitchell explores how the strong emphasis there on sin, guilt, damnation and the need for repentence increase her burden of oppression:

> Being saved, Noreen concluded, was all about stopping doing things. That was how it seemed. You stopped drinking, smoking, dancing – you turned good-living, like Da.[53]

Like Simon Green, she regrets the absence of a means of confession, regarding the occasional penances that Eileen does as an enviable consolation compared with what her Protestant Church offers – 'only the assurance that the wicked would burn in the fires of Hell'.[54] Even more strikingly, she finds the religious ceremony and ritual of the Mass, which she attended once with Eileen, 'with its promise of something hidden, magical, something dark', more credible and appealing than her own austere church experience:

> . . . the Protestant Church was dry, the light too bright in her own religion. You felt that here was something that seared and cut, divided: good or bad, saved or damned, Heaven or Hell. It couldn't be that simple. For Ma was not bad; no, she was lovely and warm and good, yet she was not saved, and so would go to Hell. Noreen couldn't believe that. But they told you it was all to do with grace and faith, rather than goodness; and anyway, God had his own reasons for doing things, which mere humans couldn't hope to understand. They had to just follow blindly, have faith, even if they didn't know what in.[55]

Thus, the forms and practices that are the very essence of strict Protestantism are what make it off-putting and objectionable. The oversimplicity and preference for clear-cut, uncompromising judgments that trouble Noreen here are equated with authoritarianism, intolerance and a sinister menace that are evident in other contexts. These include the set faces of marching Orangemen (and also of

Republican nationalists parading to commemorate the anniversary of a hunger striker's death); the words of the Protestant paramilitary who tells Noreen, '"We must never forget . . . Never. We must avenge our dead, see – for there's no bloody God to do it"'; and also the hard, unforgiving eyes of Paul Megarry, the evangelical preacher who dismisses Eileen's forthcoming marriage as an unholy alliance and refuses to countenance Noreen attending it.[56]

Although she is temporarily drawn into the company first of political and then of religious bigots and seeks to submerge herself unquestioningly in their prejudices, Noreen's experience and intelligence enable her to pass beyond them. When she tries to revive her friendship with Eileen, she herself is subjected to abuse from children on the estate which forces her to recognise the destructiveness of the sectarianism she has mindlessly endorsed. For a time she attempts to lose herself in the sureties of fundamentalist religion, finding that the leader's insistence that thinking and questioning are the Devil's tricks 'fitted her inner landscape exactly' and wanting only to feel loved and united with her fellow evangelicals. She is initially dismissive of her father's warnings against narrow-minded intolerance ('Da's religion was essentially private, just between himself and God. It was extended, at most, to his family, by way of his prayers. He failed to see the greater purpose in evangelizing the world.'), but becomes disturbed by the group's overt anti-Catholicism.[57] This unease deepens when Eileen, whom she meets by chance during a mission to win Protestant converts in the Irish Republic, renews her father's advocacy of religious tolerance:

> . . . it shamed her all of a sudden that their God, the Evangelical God, was too narrow for a generosity which would respect all humanity, as it danced, drank, prayed, loved, fought, died.[58]

However, it is after Mr Logan dies in a terrorist explosion that Noreen begins to understand the complexity of her relationship with and feelings for her father, and realises that she will be 'picking up bits of him for the rest of her life'.[59] Above all, she understands that his moderation, which she had scorned, is precious and creative, whereas fanatical monovision, whether political or religious, destroys lives, as her father's fate demonstrates. This leads to Noreen Logan's most important and enabling discovery – she perceives how the very desire to believe can itself become distorting:

> . . . then it seemed that all sorts of things happened, and you believed all the more that you were right. It was so easy to fit what happened into the framework of your belief; so easy, when you had all those people together, believing in the same thing. You thought you saw everything – but really you saw nothing.[60]

To see nothing in this sense means to lose sight of individuals and to replace love with 'causes and battles and slogans'.[61] This insight gives Noreen the freedom that has eluded her previously. It does not overcome her loneliness – indeed, she is more isolated than ever by her new understanding – and in this she is like Simon Green, but it enables her to see life from a tolerantly agnostic perspective, releases her from the prejudiced modes of thought in which she sought both rebellion and refuge and prepares the ground for her future development, represented in the conclusion of the novel by her preparations to go to university in England.

Mal Martin, the principal character in Glenn Patterson's *Burning Your Own*, is younger than Simon Green and Noreen Logan, and unlike them, lives on a working-class estate on the edge of Belfast. Furthermore, the action of this novel takes place within a few weeks coinciding with the early stages of the 'troubles' in Northern Ireland and culminating with the arrival of British troops on the streets of Derry and Belfast in 1969. Mal also differs from Simon and Noreen in that the religious teaching of the Church has no visible influence on the lives of his family or of the community in the Larkview estate. Indeed, on the single occasion on which Mal's family goes to church, they arrive too early because they are unaware of the service times and appear to be motivated merely by an intuitive wish to show Protestant solidarity in the face of growing sectarianism.

At the outset, Protestantism on the estate is largely a matter of the commemorative rituals of Eleventh Night bonfires and Twelfth of July parades. Larkview itself is an experiment in 'mixed' community living and, among the youngsters at least, boys from both traditions share in games and social activities. There is a more urgent sense of threat from other Protestant gangs, who may seek to sabotage the Larkview bonfire, than from Catholics. While Mal is aware that some families are Catholics he gives this little thought until the reality of sectarianism begins to impose itself as violence elsewhere in the province increases, and the Protestants in Larkview start to force Catholics to leave their homes. His bewilderment at the unexplained departure of the Catholic Campbell family and the evasive answers to his questions about it irritate him at first, but he quickly concludes that

> . . . things *did* change, and if you couldn't accept the changes you simply got left behind. He was coming to see that, in this new order of things, the safest policy was not to pry too much.[62]

Mal's acquiescence here suggests the power of the pressure to conform and is coupled with his pleasure in finding that he himself is more acceptable to his peers after his return to the estate following a temporary family separation. His improved standing owes something to the fact that he now possesses a good football, but even more to the dynamics of events which are driving the Protestants together and focusing their enmity on Catholics. Mal, at last, feels he is on the 'right' side, having previously been marginalised as a newcomer to the estate, mocked for his physical immaturity and exploited because of his obvious wish to belong to the local gang.

One part of Patterson's achievement, which might be regarded as bleak, is to show how deeply engrained Protestant bigotry and fear of an increase in Catholic power are even in such a non-religious, secularised community and how quickly they manifest themselves as circumstances begin to change. Eve Patten is right to emphasise that 'from Mal's perspective' the building of the Eleventh Night bonfire is 'a social occasion on which the local residents who form the corporate identity of the neighbourhood are suddenly and painstakingly illuminated in their individuality', more than a gesture of sectarian triumphalism.[63] However, the brief interval between Eleventh Night and the second conflagration with which the novel concludes produces not only social disintegration and open violence, but is also a forcing house for Mal's physical and mental growth and development. By the end, he has begun to recognise that the environment in which he has been brought up, and its attendant values and attitudes, are neither neutral nor immutable and may be experienced and understood in radically different ways. Patterson himself has very tellingly observed that 'Rushdie's treatment of countries as collective fictions (willed or imposed) and as significant *characters* in their inhabitants' lives accorded perfectly with my own ideas of how to begin reimagining Northern Ireland'.[64] This is the more radical and optimistic dimension to the book, affirming the possibility of revisioning the world and reaching different conclusions. Crucial to Mal's expanding view within the novel is his relationship with Francy Hagan.

Francy is an extraordinary creation. An adolescent with wisdom far beyond his years, he lives outside the control of family, church, school and social convention in an elaborately constructed den and surrounding network of booby-trapped tunnels on wasteground at the edge of the Larkview estate. Protestants have him marked from the outset as 'a mad Taig bastard' after he wields a hatchet against a binman who is trying to kill a rat. Francy himself tells how he first sought sanctuary on the wasteground when he was bullied and chased from school by his Catholic classmates, overcoming his own terror of the hordes of rats on the site and taming them sufficiently to assume a precarious mastery of the territory. (There is some similiarity between this and Simon Green's less confident control of his ferret.) His distance from the aspirations to respectability and conformity of Mal's family is much greater even than that between the Greens and Jamesons in *The Ferret Fancier*, or the Logans and McAllisters in *Sunday Afternoons* and much more important than the anarchic squalor of his life, or his Catholicism, which is as nominal as Mal's Protestantism, is Francy's capacity for independent thought.

The opening words of the novel – '"In the beginning" – said Francy – "was the dump"' – are a bold reformulation of the first verse of St John's gospel, which in itself looks back to the opening of Genesis. Francy therefore, announces a radically different world-view which he elaborates incrementally to his younger follower, binding him first by a parodic oath of fealty – although he immediately cancels the pledge of obedience – and giving him new perspectives on the familiar. In a very literal way, Mal is surprised at how different the estate looks viewed from the wasteground and how its assumed order and inevitability are suddenly deconstructed:

> Beyond the dump, across the grass, a solid mass of redbrick walled in his vision. Roofs emerged in strange teetering formations, half-houses, quarter-houses were grafted onto the sides of others, filling every gap, blinding every alley and driveway. He lived here, but he did not recognise this place, could not reconcile the jumble with the neatly hedged rows he walked through day to day.[65]

This discovery is complemented by Francy's 'history' of the building of the estate. This is presented as a creation story with its origins in the dump, an experiment in postwar social engineering designed to bring together people from all over Northern Ireland and abroad, but which, he implies, has resolved nothing and will eventually return to primal chaos. For Mal, whose sense of the past consists of little more than the Protestant version of King William's victory at the Boyne, this is just one of a whole series of disturbing reinterpretations of the familiar which extend from the grotesquely humorous to the profoundly serious.

One of the first lessons that Francy teaches Mal is that '"their rules" – he jerked a thumb vaguely over his shoulder – "stop at the fence"'.[66] As a result, he claims the right to ascribe his own meanings and significances to the symbols, slogans and proprieties of the rest of society, Catholic or Protestant, and to deny them conventional respect and gravity. Thus, the flower urn taken from a grave and dumped becomes a 'spiturn'; an abandoned toilet is Francy's throne; stones from a ruined chapel form the walls of his sanctuary; a Union Jack egg cup becomes a candlestick and so on. Mal quickly realises that Francy cannot be contained by any stereotypical label. Others dismiss him as 'a Rebel and a Taig', but:

> The words had no history in Mal's mind. They had been coined for Civil Rights marchers and student demonstrators; coined for rioters in Londonderry, Dungannon and Armagh, places Mal had never been; coined for John Hume and Gerry Fitt, Bernadette Devlin and Eamonn McCann, faces on TV. Why, then, for Francy Hagan? Because he sat on a toilet and not a seat, in a filthy dump infested with rats?[67]

As the disorder and sectarianism increase and come closer to Larkview, Mal is temporarily betrayed into linking Francy with the Civil Rights demonstrators, and blames them equally for wrecking things because they feel left out, while at the same time, paradoxically, they refuse to join in. This is, perhaps, the closest Mal comes to rejecting Francy, but because he has already started to see the world differently following his friend's example, he soon feels guilty of an act of treachery despite the attractions of a place in the Protestant gang if he is prepared to collude in their prejudices.

Mal's realisation of new perspectives is confirmed by watching television pictures of the first moon landing which prompt a series of bewildering thoughts about the smallness of the particularities and location of his own existence when placed in the context of a whole country, of the world and of the immensity of space itself. In the same spirit, looking over Belfast from the perspective of the Cave Hill, where it is impossible to distinguish the city's discrete sectarian territories and flashpoints of violence, he comes to understand how easy it is to delude oneself that there are no divisions and that people live naturally together, and how things are much harsher in reality:

But it was no kind of togetherness really. Whatever didn't fit in, got excluded; that's what it boiled down to. The Ardoyne, Unity Flats – Derrybeg, for that matter – all seemed as far away as Armagh, Rossville Flats and Londonderry itself had earlier that year. But just ignoring things didn't make them go away.[68]

This insight determines his decision to return to Francy at the dump and he knows that by doing so he is significantly altering his relationships with his community: 'It was as if, in refusing to be cowed any longer by the dire warnings of his elders, he had broken through some invisible barrier, across which he now faced them'.[69]

Mal's education continues as Francy demythologises his single scrap of local 'history', pointing out that the chapel King William allegedly passed on his way to the Boyne was not built until 1875, when its opening was celebrated by Protestants as well as Catholics, and that it was destroyed by Protestants during Home Rule demonstrations. The process has its apotheosis in Francy's 'sale of a fucking lifetime' where he makes his most public and comprehensive mockery of society's shibboleths before accidentally immolating himself. Each item with which he taunts the crowd has its significance. He jeers at the unreliability of words and the manipulative ways in which they are used when he hurls a dictionary at them, scorns progress by offering a wheelless pram frame and denies respect for the dead when he suggests a series of irreverent uses for the funeral urn. Even more provocative is his offer of an Orange sash for towelling or toiletry purposes and of the Irish tricolour which, he claims, is big enough to give everyone a piece – but which precipitates his own death when it catches alight. This second bonfire with a Catholic boy at its centre rather than a dummy of Gerry Fitt makes explicit the darkness that underlay the Eleventh Night celebrations and shows the cost of Francy's radical rejection of a rigid society whose narrow assumptions lead the characters, in Patterson's own words, to 'blame themselves, becoming self-destructive, or blame other working people, creating social unrest, rather than accept that the assumptions themselves are at fault'.[70]

Therefore, the story of Mal Martin traces his growing self-consciousness of the society in which he lives and of the illusions and unexamined attitudes which perpetuate its tensions and divisions, and which he himself has inevitably assimilated. These are brought into sharp relief by the Civil Rights demonstrators' challenge to the establishment which helps to unleash the underlying sectarianism in the community, but, symbolically, it is a Catholic who teaches Mal to see his family, peers and history afresh. As a result, he grows in understanding of the nature of the fixed attitudes that govern his community and is confronted with the horror of their consequences. However, Francy's vision implies equal interrogation of the assumptions and prejudices of his own part of society, from which he is also conspicuously alienated, and in this way the novel refuses to privilege the politics or religion of either side.

The troubled relationship between an adolescent character and the influence of Catholicism has been fertile territory for numerous Irish novelists from Joyce onwards, but the dilemmas of the youth whose background has been equally decisively shaped by Protestantism and the cultural practices associated with it in the North of Ireland are less familiar. In charting that experience in their various ways, these novels explore particular forms of Protestant angst. Of central importance are the fear and guilt about actions that will be seen as disloyal to the Protestant community itself. In practice, such disloyalty usually means entering into relationships with Catholics who are understood from an early age to be 'different' in an unacceptable way, and who, even if they are tolerated, can never be accepted on equal terms because they represent a permanent threat to the survival of the Protestant community itself. Even Mal Martin, whose upbringing is unambiguously non-religious, becomes conscious of the rigid associations ascribed to the terms Protestant and Catholic, and their significance in maintaining the divisions on the estate. Thus, the characters' dealings with Catholics become underhand or secretive, or are viewed as somewhat disreputable.

On the other hand, these novels show little evidence of guilt over rejecting the Church itself, or of fear of the authority of the institution or its ministers. Ironically, Simon Green and Noreen Logan's real struggles are to secure for themselves the freedom of conscience which Protestantism notionally upholds, but which they find restricted by a burdensome insistence on human sinfulness, formulaic teaching and the connection between outward religious conformity and respectability.

Just as the Protestant clerics were represented as isolated and lonely figures, so too are the young protagonists of West, Mitchell and Patterson. Likewise, the home lives of Simon, Noreen and Mal share some of the tensions, emotional coolness and neurotic concern with orderliness and tidiness that figure in the domestic circumstances and personal habits of Sorleyson, Balleter and Gilchrist. All these characters are at least temporarily attracted by what they see as the greater freedoms and lesser discipline of other people's lives – often a Catholic. At the same time they remain inhibited by psychological and emotional anxieties deriving from a deeply engrained sense of personal responsibility and accountability which has its origins in Protestant theology. These novels suggest, therefore, that while the young Protestant's *non serviam* may be less tortuous and traumatic than that of the Catholic, especially in previous generations, in a community as sensitive to the politics of religious difference as that in Northern Ireland, it is unavoidably painful, costly and alienating.

CHAPTER ELEVEN

Some Representations of Protestant Experience: Drama

*If ever a time and place cried out for the solace and rigour
and passionate rejoinder of great drama, it is here and now.
There is a whole culture to be achieved. The politicians,
visionless almost to a man, are withdrawing into their
stockades. It falls to the artists to construct a working model
of wholeness by means of which the society can begin to
hold up its head in the world.*

Stewart Parker, *John Malone Memorial Lecture.*

A CYNIC MIGHT SAY that the Northern Irish state was invented
for the benefit of dramatists, and certainly the divisions and
confrontations that characterise the region have provided playwrights
with endless and ready-made sources of drama which have been
exploited since the early years of this century. The personal and social
consequences of living in a communtiy which at its most benign and
secular remains permeated by consciousness of religious identities and
differences and in its most bitter and tribal moments fractures along
the sectarian faultline, are notably recurrent issues in the plays of
dramatists from Protestant backgrounds.[1] John Boyd sums up the
situation very clearly in his claim that, as a playwright, he reckons he
has been given two advantages:

> First, my life has been lived in my native city, and Belfast happens to
> be the most 'dramatic' of cities. Things happen here all the time that
> concentrate the mind on the 'dramatic experience', with the city itself
> a stage, exploding daily with tragedy, comedy and farce. Belfast also
> happens to be the most violent, dangerous, bigoted, politically and
> socially stagnant city in Western Europe.
>
> . . .
>
> The second advantage is that between the warring tribes of Protestants
> and Catholics I owe allegiance to neither: a liberating position that
> suits a playwright.[2]

294

His personal disinclination to side with either religious group, his implied detachment from the specific beliefs and mutual fears that motivate their animosity and the resulting wide-angle vision that this gives him, are not unique. In differing ways, each of the dramatists under consideration here – principally St John Ervine, Sam Thompson, Christina Reid and Stewart Parker, as well as Boyd himself – writes with particular knowledge and experience of the life and culture of Belfast Protestant working-class communities. They understand how certain shared loyalties and beliefs motivate and give definition to the lives of the characters in their plays who come from such communities. Each is also a critical observer of the ease with which these same loyalties and beliefs can be manipulated and mobilised into prejudice and action that are both divisive and self-destructive. For the most part, they avoid sentimentalisation of their characters or their lives. They focus instead on the ways in which are circumscribed by insecurities that are never far below the surface, limited by ways of thought that are resistant to change and suspicious of the unfamiliar, and overshadowed by conservative notions of respectability and narrowly defined gender roles. Although religion itself and the substance of religious beliefs do not figure prominently, they are repeatedly alluded to by characters as loose justifications of their attitudes and actions, and are clearly represented as a consciously – if often uncritically – internalised framework of reference. Likewise, history and the past weigh heavily upon the lives of many of them, whether in terms of commemorative celebrations of key Protestant 'triumphs', memories of Catholic 'treachery', a sense of the repetitive nature of history, or concern with threats to continuity with the past precipitated by lack of an heir or social change. In some of the plays the dramatists venture further, imagining the means by which the future might assume different patterns if alternative perspectives and priorities were allowed to emerge, governed by socialist and humanitarian rather than sectarian considerations.

Certain images and thematic preoccupations recur in a number of works by these dramatists, and in what follows the emphasis is on three of these. First, there is the question of troubled inheritances. Ownership of land and property, concern to protect it and pass it on to another generation, and the threat of losing control of it or seeing it divided up raise important issues in plays by St John Ervine and John Boyd. These may be understood in part as a reflection of residual Protestant insecurity of possession, but they are also an offshoot of Protestant materialism based on the belief that God favours those whom he has chosen, and on the originally biblical notion of the importance of protecting inherited territory for the future. Ervine's *John Ferguson* and Boyd's *The Farm* and *Facing North* provide the principal focus of examination for this theme.

The dramatised representation of the consequences of sectarianism are the second area of exploration. In particular Ervine's *Mixed Marriage*, Sam Thompson's *Over the Bridge* and Bill Morrison's *A Love Song for Ulster* (which is also much concerned with inheritance) suggest how playwrights have not only understood and conveyed the dynamics of sectarianism, but also its ruinous effects in both the private and public spheres of life, and its usefulness to unscrupulous politicians and businessmen whose own interests were best served by having a polarised working class.

In the final selection of plays, by Christina Reid and Stewart Parker, a haunted house or a house tenanted by ghosts of the dead as well as by the living, is the common setting for examinations of the interplay and influence of the past upon the present. *Tea in a China Cup* and *Pentecost* are the principal texts which reveal how these dramatists explore the determining influence of personal, religious and cultural history on their characters, and the degree to which their lives are found to be irretrievably entrapped by ghosts of the past, or possess the potential to be liberated from them.

I

John Ferguson, first performed in 1915, is located in the Co. Down countryside in the 1880s – the same period as that represented by Sam Hanna Bell in the early part of *December Bride*. However, where the novel focused on Sarah Gomartin's defiance of her expected religious obligations in pursuit of her own will and material ambitions, Ervine's title character is initially presented as a model of piety, reading his Bible regularly, citing scripture and ascribing everything to the will of God. In the introductory stage directions he is likened to a portrait of Moses, but 'not that Moses who led the Israelites out of Egypt and was a great captain of hosts, but the Moses who surveyed the Promised Land from Mount Nebo in the Plains of Moab' – a hint, perhaps, of his declining status.[3] Even before the details of his current difficulties are known – a mortgaged farm which he is no longer fit to work and which his son, Andrew, is incompetent to manage, and the threat of losing it to the grasping Henry Witherow – his philosophy is revealed in his opening words, a reading from Psalm 30 expressing joy in the comfort of God, confidence that foes will not prevail, and faith that although 'weeping may endure for a night, . . . joy cometh in the morning'. On the face of it, Ferguson seems to exemplify the kind of fundamentalist Protestant faith that Ervine knew well through his grandmother, Margaret Greer, who had played a large part in his upbringing and to whose memory he dedicated the play. However, events soon show a more complicated character, and the playwright probes the tension between a life led wholly in the faith represented in the Psalm and one in which the individual acts in an attempt to exercise influence or take control of a situation.

The strict logic of Ferguson's declared faith demands that he should wait on God to resolve his problems – 'Don't be complaining now', he tells his wife, 'for sure God never deserts His own people. We have His word for that, Sarah. We're tried a while, and then we're given our reward'.[4] Yet almost at once we see that he has not upheld this belief in practice. Although he 'dedicated' his son to the ministry 'the day he was born', he has reneged on this and put him to work on the land, unsuited as he is for the job, because of their financial crisis. Material necessity, but above all the desire to keep the land, have motivated Ferguson's actions: 'Our da was born here too, and his da before him. Andrew couldn't let the farm go out of the family after all them generations'.[5] Commenting on this attitude, Norman Vance has observed that there is

> . . . a specifically Presbyterian dimension to the motif of generational continuity on the land. Continued Scots settlement in Ulster could be seen as an effect of the covenant relationship between God and His people, renewed from generation to generation as it had been with Abraham, Isaac and Jacob.[6]

Ferguson's imperfect reliance on God is further emphasised by the alternative source of help to which he has turned, seemingly to no avail – his brother, Andrew, who has made money in America, presumably after having had to emigrate because there was no land for him to inherit. Yet when his wife (Sarah) and daughter (Hannah) protest against the unfairness of life's misfortunes which affect 'people that never done nothing to deserve it' (like themselves, they imply), Ferguson's rapid defence of God's providence under which 'Everything that happens is made to happen, and everything in the world . . . has a purpose and a meaning' asserts conventional Calvinist wisdom.[7] However, it also serves to rule out any contemplation of the degree to which the Fergusons may have contributed to their own problems.

Such professions of belief are not so much sustaining as a means of evading the need to address uncomfortable realities.

This becomes particularly clear if one compares Ferguson's reactions during two key stages in the action. Threatened by new demands from Witherow, and thrown a lifeline by the pitifully weak and boastful Jimmy Caesar who offers to settle the mortgage payment in exchange for marriage to Hannah Ferguson, the most spirited character in the play, John refuses to put pressure on his daughter (unlike his wife) referring again to God's providence and plan in all things. He blesses her acceptance of Jimmy's offer, yet seems equally ready to abide by her subsequent wholly credible admission that she cannot bear to marry him, and rejects Sarah's suggestion that he should insist on their daughter keeping her word even though her failure to do so means losing the farm. In this instance Ferguson appears to act upon his beliefs, as he also does when Hannah is raped by Witherow ('God's scourged us hard, and it isn't easy to bear. We must just . . . just try and be patient', he tells her by way of comfort), and when he rejects his son's call for vengeance ('You have your own work to do in the world, and you must leave God to do His; it's His work to judge, not ours!'), and sets out to stop Caesar fulfilling his boast that he will kill the offender.[8] However, the issue is further complicated when Ferguson makes an important admission in an exchange with his wife and son. Expressing concern over the continued disappearance of Caesar and fear that he may have attacked Witherow, he continues:

> I feel my own responsibility, son. I'll admit to you I was hoping Hannah'd marry him [i.e. Caesar], and I didn't discourage her from saying 'yes' to him when he asked her, for all I knew she was only doing it for the farm. I knew the girl couldn't bear him, but I pretended to myself it would come all right in the end. I . . . I love this house, Andrew! That's the excuse I have for not being honest with Hannah.
>
> Sarah: Ah, sure, you left it to her own free will.
>
> John: Ay, I tried to salve my conscience that way, but I said it in a way that showed plain what my desire was. If I had been firm, there would have been none of this bother now. You understand me, son, don't you? I feel I won't be happy till I see Jimmy safe and sound from harm, because I put him in danger.[9]

This is not only an explicit recognition that he has tried to sway events, irrespective of his outer conduct and words at the time, but also suggests the self-defeating and futile nature of all such efforts and their tendency to release unforeseen repercussions.

Thus far Ferguson is unaware of the full extent of these consequences, because he does not know that his son, Andrew, rather than Jimmy Caesar, has shot Witherow. Andrew's action results from provocation – one might even say temptation – by 'Clutie' John, a character 'hover[ing] upsettingly somewhere between an active and a choric part', who rouses him to action by questioning Caesar's courage to kill and playing upon the outrage to Hannah's honour.[10] Andrew's eventual confession follows the belated arrival of the long-awaited letter with money from America, which was posted late because of a misunderstanding – a Hardyesque device that again mocks all the efforts of individuals in the play by rendering them as unnecessary as they are irreversible. It results in Ferguson's complete abandonment of trust in God at this point. Significantly, the stage direction describes how, as he retires to his chair in shock, 'his hand touches his Bible. He pushes it away from him'.[11] While the father's sole concern is to help his son to escape punishment for his misdeed, it is Andrew who now demonstrates in practice the scrupulousness of conscience that Ferguson had previously advocated, insisting on the overriding priority of securing the release from prison of the wrongly charged Jimmy Caesar. Equally important, Hannah who, like Andrew, had been impatiently critical of her father's religion, agrees with her brother against the appeals of both their parents that he should save his life by running away. Although Ferguson recovers his poise when faced with his son's declaration of faith – '. . . a man must clean himself . . . It's no good other people doing things for him. He must do them himself' – returns to his Bible and consoles his wife with the thought that 'we must just bear it, for God knows better nor we do what's right to be done', the reading with which the play closes – David's lament for the death of his son Absalom – calls into question one last time the degree to which even now he is able to accept this as truth.[12]

Although *John Ferguson* is generally accepted as Ervine's best play, the main character's attitudes are not entirely typical of those shown by some of his other other protagonists who are equally concerned with problems of inheritance. Ferguson's ineffectuality, which is related to, if not caused by, his professed religious beliefs, is in marked contrast to the pragmatism of shopkeepers like Mrs MacDermott and Mrs Dunwoody in the novels *The Foolish Lovers* and *The Wayward Man* respectively. Here, the repressed opportunism and readiness to make a deal glimpsed in Sarah Ferguson find full expression in the business enterprise of these hard-headed, industrious Presbyterian women. Mrs MacDermott, who regards books and reading as an unprofitable waste of time and ruinous to the mind, does not rest content until she has tied her son into the long-standing family shop in Ballyards, which he has done his best to avoid entering, and convinced him that he has discovered the superiority of the aesthetics of business to those of the literary art he originally intended to master: '. . . he knew that there was Beauty in the labours of men, that bargaining and competition and striving energies and rivalry in skill were elements of loveliness. "These little poets sitting in their stuffy attics scribbling about the moon! – yah-rr-r!" he said, putting his hat on to his head again'.[13]

Mrs Dunwoody's aims are even more grandiose. She imagines herself as a latter-day Abraham surrounded in her twilight years by children and family members each of whom manages a flourishing shop: 'If she were to settle her children in comfortable circumstances, she would never fear to lose them from her side. Dunwoody's would be in every part of Belfast, all of them owing allegiance to her'.[14] In both novels, the mothers regard their sons' wish to leave home as an incomprehensible and unacceptable threat to family unity and the almost mystical value they attach to rootedness in one place. Despite her failure with her wayward son, Robert, Mrs Dunwoody's shrewd assessment of the binding power of economic prosperity typifies the calculation and determination with which she pursues her ambition to secure and advance her inheritance.

Ervine's interest in strong, business-minded women no doubt owes much to the circumstances of his own background, but as a self-made man himself, he was also a champion of individual initiative. In one of his later plays, *Friends and Relations* (1941), which again deals with a question of inheritance, the ambitious Fanny Cairns rejects utterly her son's opinion that people are victims of their environment, insisting on the individual's responsibility to master his or her circumstances and denying sympathy to those who fail to do so. Adam Bothwell, to whom she is talking, agrees 'In theory', and declares himself 'a follower of Pelagius', 'A distinguished Ulsterman who lived in the time of St Augustine' and 'believed that we can lift ourselves up if we want to'.[15] However, Bothwell also points out that Pelagius did not share Fanny's contempt for those who have not raised themselves and regrets that the philosopher did not return to his alleged native shore to spread this part of his teaching more widely. On the whole, nevertheless, Ervine's strongest characters, both in his plays and his fiction, show greater determination than tolerance, embody a work ethic that has little patience with incompetence or idleness and are content to be Protestant without being pious or feeling constrained by religious beliefs, as John Ferguson is. In later years his outlook on the Protestant community became increasingly conservative and more softly focused – as the perennially popular *Boyd's Shop* demonstrates.

Here, comments David Kennedy, Ervine saw 'the Presbyterian middle class . . . through the rose-tinted spectacles of exile. Presbyterian Ulster liked this picture of itself'.[16] It did so because the play upholds the values of the past and rebuffs those who would replace them. John Haslett, the entrepreneurial young grocer with modern marketing ideas, fails to replace Boyd's general store which has been in the family for three generations. His watchword – 'Efficiency first, last an' all the while!' – and training in a College of Modern Commerce prove no match for Boyd's unreformed store management and customer relations – and the young man who possesses the ambition and drive of some of Ervine's earlier tradespeople is obliged to turn to his elder for help with his chaotic business affairs.

The second moderniser in the play is the designing Revd Dunwoody whose successful efforts to force the elderly Revd Patterson into retirement and institute a ministry which emphasises social service rather than theology are the object of mild satire throughout. At the intersection of these lines of plot are two linked questions: the future of Boyd's shop since there is no son to succeed the ageing Andrew, and who his daughter, Agnes, will marry. Ervine's resolution of these issues is revealing, for although Dunwoody initially wins the woman's acceptance, she is unprepared to distance herself from the shop to satisfy his snobbish ambitions and she punishes his apparently irresistible rise in the community by breaking her engagement and choosing Haslett for her husband. Since Haslett has repented of his modernising ways and acknowledged Boyd's wisdom, this is an affirmation of old values over new ones. It also fulfils Boyd's desire to see the future of the shop secured, whereas Agnes's prospective marriage to Dunwoody had threatened this. As Boyd says:

> The Boyds always married intil shops or farms. That's the style we're accustomed to, an' shops an' farms is what I like. What'll happen to this place after I'm gone, if Agnes is a minister's wife? It worries me when I think of that. I sit here of a night, an' think of the generations that have passed though this house an' served in that shop.[17]

Finally, but no less importantly, the family name will remain on the shop – it will be known as 'Boyd and Son' – thereby allaying the owner's fear of disturbing convention had he altered it to 'Boyd and

Daughter'. Once again the decisiveness of a spirited female is critical, but here it serves mainly to consolidate traditional Protestant patriarchy rather than to give Agnes any real independence of her own.

John Boyd, a friend of Ervine and admirer of his early work – he even adapted one of his novels, *Mrs Martin's Man*, for the stage – also makes issues of inheritance and the future of property central in two of his plays, *The Farm* (first performed in 1972) and *Facing North* (first performed in 1979). The former opens with a set description of a cottage which matches that in *John Ferguson* in many details, including a prominently positioned family Bible. However, there is one important difference: 'The room looks deserted and dusty as if not lived in for many months . . . The overwhelming impression is one of gloom'.[18] Its previous occupant, Sam MacCann, a parsimonious, bible-reading reclusive bachelor, has died and the action of the play turns on the future of his property and small farm. Consisting of two small cottages and four overgrown fields, this might be taken as a symbol of Ireland itself and of its condition as the playwright sees it. From this point of view, it is also significant that MacCann insisted on keeping the doors and windows of his own cottage shut out of fear of burglars, thieves and marauders.[19]

As elsewhere in Boyd's drama, the characters are strongly associated with particular points of view, and differences and tensions between these are the source of much of the interest. Of central importance is Sam MacCann's younger brother, known as Mac, who also grew up in the house, but was obliged to seek work in the shipyards when the farm went to the elder son 'by right'. This break with the rural family past has been deepened by his desertion of religion – he cannot understand what good his brother's religion did him, especially since it appears to have encouraged his withdrawal from other people – and by his own pursuit of socialism and refusal to accept preferment or promotion within the capitalist system. Mac combines socialist belief in the dignity of labour with the Protestant work ethic – 'If a man hasn't work to do he might as well be dead', he says, and he immediately sets about retrieving Sam's cottage and the land from years of neglect.[20] Windows are symbolically opened, fresh air is allowed to circulate, and an overgrown well is cleaned out. Despite Mac's long absence from the farm, he, unlike his children, 'seems completely at home' on it. He simply ignores the fact that the property has been left to his son, Ed, who is preparing to sell it to a neighbouring large landowner until he discovers an impromptu dalliance between the latter's son and his wife. This rather crude piece of plotting creates a situation whereby the farm remains in the family and Mac is placed in charge of it while his children pursue their lives in Belfast and Canada.

Boyd uses the family members to advance a series of attitudes not only to the inheritance of the farm, but, by implication, to Ireland itself, and to contrast them with Mac's own views. Although his children eventually rally round the plan to save the farm for Mac's sake, none of them has any real commitment to it. His elder daughter, Babs, and her husband, Mike, have settled in Canada, but whereas she wants to dismiss her Irish origins completely and is disgusted by the prejudice, violence and lack of change she still finds in the country, he has experienced a loss of identity, has taken to studying Irish history and Gaelic and has a nostalgic desire to return, although it is unlikely he will ever do so. The other daughter, Beth, points out to her husband, Jim, a liberal-minded school teacher in the city, how frustrating and narrow he would find life in the country. They resist Babs' suggestion of emigrating to Canada, yet Beth is dismissive of any responsibility for the extremism represented by the sound of Lambeg drums, claiming, 'They've got nothing to do with me! If I had my way I'd lock them up'.[21] Ed, whose career in the Civil Service and marriage to Dolly both seem unsuccessful, simply wishes to realise money from the sale of the farm, having no further interest in it, and is prepared to accept the offer from his sisters and brothers-in-law. The outcome is presented as the means by which 'the family is still together, in a sense; this old place becomes a kinda focal point for us all'.[22] But its rehabilitation depends on Mac himself who stands as much at odds with the opinions of his family as with the sectarian prejudices of Old Ben, the one-armed tenant of the second cottage on the land. Mac locates the problems of the country in religious bigotry which divides the workers and yields their potential power to politicians who perpetuate sectarian division for their own ends. Yet for all Mac's greater liberalism, his tolerance towards the gipsies from the Irish Republic who offend Ben and the energy with which he sets to work on the farm, the ending is muted. He is also elderly and the strain of the tasks ahead may be too great, as he is forced to recognise when he struggles to shift an obstructive tree stump. He is also, as Ben comments several times, increasingly like his brother, and the final visual image of Mac settled in his brother's chair, the oil lamp lit and reading from the Bible, realises the scene implied at the beginning of the play, as well as furnishing another reminder of *John Ferguson*. Significantly, however, the passage he reads, and with which the scene ends, from the Song of Solomon (ch. 4, vv. 12–16) offers images of harmony, unity and fulfilment nurtured by winds from both the North and the South, and is once again suggestive of the inclusiveness and generosity of Mac's vision which distinguishes him from Sam.

This might be compared with the attitudes of Adam Grant in *Facing North*, who is the owner of an ancestral property on a much larger scale than the MacCann farm. His footloose son, Peter, airily sums up the history of the original house as 'Seventeenth century. Plantation barn, built for self-defence, colonists agin natives, Prods agin Papes, expropriators agin expropriated'.[23] Its century-old successor, ominously named Cromwell House, was built 'facing north' with almond trees in the garden by Adam Grant's father, another 'great reader of the Bible', who took his inspiration from verses 11 and 13 in the first chapter of Jeremiah. These form part of the Lord's call to the prophet to speak out against apostasy, the reference to the budding almond being taken to signify God's purpose and imminent activity, while the problematic allusion to 'a seething pot; and the face thereof is toward the north' is interpreted as foretelling the punishment of the people of Israel for worshipping false gods. In the context of the play, the exposed north side of the house leaves it open to attack from the IRA and presents a security problem for the neighbouring British army base.

In spite of what this might suggest about the position and politics of the Grants, the introductory stage directions state that they 'were never a homogeneous family in the past and certainly are not in the present', and the rather improbable and overladen plot is designed to play off Adam's more liberal views against the political Unionism of his brother-in-law, Sir Kenneth McCann. Grant, like Mac in *The Farm*, does not share the prejudices and assumptions of his class. He is described as 'a much more reflexive, introverted person than is usual among "hard-headed" Ulster businessmen', and his minor English public school education, 'instead of making him more English, has had the opposite effect. He feels himself to be almost Irish. But not quite. "Northern Irish Protestant" is his cumbrous term for his identity'.[24] His thoughtfulness and complex sense of identity manifest themselves in his openly sceptical attitude to the British army's role in the province ('The British Army, like any other, is but an instrument of the state. And the state can give it the most devilish work to do.'), and to the 'pretty messy and corrupt job' the English have done in Ireland throughout history.[25] Likewise, his non-discriminatory employment practices and opposition to sectarianism in his factory are further evidence of his open-mindedness. However, the real test of his attitudes comes when the government announces a compulsory purchase order on Cromwell House in order to build a housing estate for Catholics. Whereas this is construed by Adam's wife, older son, Oliver, and brother-in-law not only as a violation of personal rights of property and inheritance, but as 'just another concession to the Catholics' which threatens the position of Protestants, Adam is much more sanguine.[26] He tells his wife:

> A retreat is not necessarily a defeat. . . . I try not to think of people as Protestants or Catholics. That's the poison in all our blood . . . it's our duty to be critical of our own tribe. And it's your duty in the factory, Oliver, not to take sides. It's good ethics, and happens to be good business.[27]

Although he dismisses his brother-in-law's predictable rallying promise to the factory workers that the government will be resisted 'every inch of the way' as 'a voice crying in the wilderness', the increasingly extravagant action in the closing stages suggests that the biblical reference applies more aptly to Adam Grant himself. It is his own liberalism and readiness to question Protestant rights of possession and power, and to think critically about the Anglo-Irish relationship which are unheard as the old forces of sectarianism take up their positions again. Just as the hope of alternative perspectives flourishing is muted at the end of *The Farm*, so too Adam Grant's reforming attitudes to tradition and inheritance are left looking eccentric and isolated.

These works by Ervine and Boyd show how issues of inheritance and of land and property recur in dramas centred on the future of Protestant families. Retention or expansion of ownership and emphasis upon continuity from one generation to the next in a fixed place are powerful motivating factors for Ervine's characters, whereas inheritance becomes more complex in Boyd's plays. His progressive figures like Mac and Adam Grant react against entrenched anti-Catholic suspicions and defensiveness and are less narrowly possessive. Despite his youthful Fabianism and his admiration for Bernard Shaw, Ervine's plays do not question conservative ideas of inheritance and ownership, which he represents as characteristically Protestant. It is Boyd who suggests how in the Northern Irish context that Protestant attitude has also become sectarian, resulting in a conflation of religion with politics which frustrates socialist attempts to challenge the basis of ownership and inheritance.

II

St John Ervine understood very well the dynamics of sectarianism, however, and these are foregrounded in his 1911 play, *Mixed Marriage*, which explores their divisive consequences within both the domestic and the public spheres. Sectarianism not only compromises working-class unity in a strike action, it also tears apart the Rainey family. In the 1914 edition, the stage directions announce that the scene is suggestively situated in a home 'midway between the Falls Road and the Shankill Road, Belfast', while the principal characters are quickly associated with specific points of view. John Rainey's authoritarianism and deeply engrained anti-Catholicism are pitched against his wife's long-suffering submissiveness to him and ineffectual advocacy of tolerance, as well as the stereotypical female virtues of homemaking and looking after men folk who are little more than overgrown children. One of Rainey's sons, Tom, is dismissive of his father's prejudices and uninterested in the politics of the impending strike, whereas the other, Hugh, incurs his growing displeasure, first by consorting with the Sinn Féin supporter, Michael O'Hara, but more importantly by proposing to marry the Catholic Nora Murray.

The opening act quickly focuses on the elements in the situation which will precipitate the later crisis and is arguably the most effective part of the play. Rainey's simplistic attitudes are immediately apparent. He is contemptuous of his wife's concern for the social and economic consequences of a strike and of her conciliatory view of Catholics, partly on the grounds that these are a woman's opinion, and partly because they differ from his own. Where she chooses to emphasise Michael O'Hara's character, Rainey cannot see beyond his Catholicism, and when she suggests that the denominations will mix in the next world, he counters that Catholics cause trouble on the Twelfth of July in this one. His perverse illogicality is neatly demonstrated when he rounds on Tom for his lack of interest in the strike, suddenly linking this with his preferred version of history and his sectarian fears:

> Rainey: The young men o' this day don't think enough. There's not one o' them knows a thing about the battle o' the Boyne. What happened on the first day o' July in the year sixteen hundred and ninety, will ye tell me that, now? (Tom *sits at the table*)
>
> Tom: Aw, fur dear sake, hould your tongue. A left school long ago.
>
> Mrs Rainey: Mebbe some ould men lost their tempers.

Rainey: Aye, ye can make fun, but it was the gran' day fur Englan' and Irelan' that was, when William o' Or'nge driv Popery out o' Irelan'.

Tom: He didden drive it far. Sure, there's plenty o' Papishes in Bilfast, an' there's more o' them in Irelan' nor Prodesans.

Mrs Rainey: A can't help thinkin' it's their country we've got.

Rainey: Their country indeed! What d'ye think 'ud become o' us if this wur their country? There isn't a Prodesan in Irelan' wud be left alive.[28]

The subversive mockery of Mrs Rainey and Tom serves only to fuel Rainey's aggressively defensive attitude. He is as blind to the self-contradiction involved when he announces to his son that 'The working class has got t' hing thegither' as he is to the irony of Michael O'Hara's rather improbable compliment that he is 'a man that's held in great respect be the men, Cathliks and Prodesans', and in his own self-righteous response that he has 'always tried t' live a straight life an' do me duty by my fellow men'.[29] The unacknowledged problem is that it depends which 'fellow men' Rainey has in mind, for although he appears to have a genuine sense of injustice over the industrial issue, it is clear that the 'religious rancour' which O'Hara fears will be used to split the workers is always likely to determine his actions. The justification of O'Hara's concern is emphasised by a reference to the way in which the influential *Belfast Telegraph* is promoting the strike in sectarian terms, describing its leaders as Dublin Nationalists and calling on Protestants to recognise that their interests lie with their employers – although Rainey himself has already insisted that it is an economic dispute. The pact into which Rainey enters with O'Hara and Hugh, whereby he will address the strikers and call for solidarity, is chiefly distinguished by its obvious fragility. He is caught between the competing demands of class and sectarian or tribal loyalty, and whereas O'Hara and Hugh regard religious differences as superficial and Mrs Rainey opines that the crucial thing is to 'act up til yer religion', Rainey himself is unable to surmount his unreasoned conviction that 'There's a differs' between Protestants and Catholics which is fundamental and immutable.

The limits of Rainey's tolerance are exposed when he discovers Hugh's secret engagement to Nora Murray. Although he has denied the imputation of bigotry, pointing out that he allows Catholics into his home and his son to go out with one, and has asserted the value of being a peacemaker – 'y've on'y got til putt out yer han's til wan another, an' grip them, an' it's all over' –, he cannot stomach the prospect of a mixed marriage. It immediately releases his latent paranoia against Catholics, so that the strike itself, O'Hara's encouragement to him to address the men and Nora's friendship with Hugh are reinterpreted as a calculated conspiracy to mislead and betray him. As Hugh angrily tells him:

> Ye've somethin' in yer min' about Cathliks an' Prodesans, an' ye're thinkin' o' that all the time. Ye're not thinkin' o' her an' me, an' ye don't care about us bein' happy.[30]

Unmoved by his son's determination, his prospective daughter-in-law's refusal to give up either her religion or her man and his wife's warning that the relationship will not cease to be a reality even if he denies it, Rainey is prepared to lose his whole family rather than assent to Hugh and Nora's marriage. Unsurprisingly, he is equally deaf to O'Hara's appeals to save the strike. However, it is notable that Ervine shows O'Hara and Rainey to be kindred spirits at this particular juncture, because the former urges Nora to leave Hugh for the sake of Ireland (thereby anticipating the same nationalist appeal which O'Casey satirised over twenty years later in *The Plough and the Stars*), insisting on the prior claim of loyalty to the nation over that to the individual and extolling patriotic self-sacrifice. The mutual recognition of narrow minds is affirmed when O'Hara rounds on Hugh for criticising his father's bigotry with the words: 'Sure it's his faith. He can't go back on his faith'.[31]

It is left to Mrs Rainey, who increasingly seems like a forerunner of Juno Boyle, to argue that the peaceful unity of Ireland O'Hara wants is prefigured in the love between an individual Catholic and Protestant which he is bent on wrecking for an abstract cause:

> Him an' her, Mickie, are bigger than the wurl', if ye on'y knew it. That man o' mine can't see fardher nor churches an' Or'nge Lodges, an' all the time there's men an' weemen stan'in' about waitin' fur somethin' til bring them thegither.[32]

However, the humane logic of this is as impotent against O'Hara's nationalism as it is against her husband's idea of Protestantism, and the action proceeds remorselessly to its violent conclusion which Rainey, with unintended aptness, likens to 'the Day o' Judgment'. The cumulative effects of sectarianism are unfolded. The family is about to be permanently broken up; the Raineys have incurred the hostility of fellow Protestants for consorting with Catholics; the strike is broken over the issue of religion; Protestant and Catholic mobs are on the streets and the military has been called out, and O'Hara's authority over his co-religionists has collapsed. In yet another twist which foreshadows O'Casey, Nora is shot and killed, ironically blaming herself for the chaos and accepting that it is right for her to die while Rainey ends the play still insisting that he 'wus right. A know A wus right'.[33] The impasse, it seems, is total because where sectarianism is able to marginalise liberal-minded attitudes and values, and to undercut other social and economic concerns, then division and confrontation are the inevitable outcomes, as the play demonstrates. The Protestantism to which Rainey repeatedly appeals is void of Christian doctrine. Furthermore, it has surrendered its original commitments to the rights of individual conscience and justice for a series of inflexible and dictatorial attitudes, and has allowed its anti-Catholic tendencies to become irrationally absolute, and the key determinant in all situations which bring the denominations together. If Ervine's play is guilty of being too schematic and over-obviously planned, as D.E.S. Maxwell has claimed, that predictability may also be seen as an accurate representation of the relentless workings of sectarianism.[34]

These workings are also central to the one act play, *The Orangeman*, although the focus here is entirely domestic. Ervine again locates the kind of intransigence found in Rainey in his male protagonist, John McClurg, describing him in the stage directions as 'a man of forceful character, quick in his speech and temper . . . what the Belfast people call "a fine man" – that is to say, . . . a sober, industrious, decent bigot, with a mind like concrete'.[35] Patriarchal, authoritarian, nursing 'dull angers' and 'ancient rages' which are all the more evident because the action occurs on 'Eleventh Night', he 'has many fine qualities, but they are negatived by a narrow nature and a revolting religious belief'.[36] His long-suffering wife is another of Ervine's sympathetic Protestant females, 'full of the sweetness of the women of Ulster', who shares her husband's religious convictions, but in whom they 'become transmuted to something fine and lovely'.[37] Unable to play his Lambeg drum in the Orange procession because of his rheumatism, McClurg expects his son to go in his place, and the scene is set for the inevitable family row when Tom refuses to comply, scorns his father's Orangeism ('Sure, an Orange sash isn't the Protestant religion') and belief that sons should maintain its traditions, and finally destroys the drum after he has been assaulted and told to 'Go and live up the Falls Road with the Fenians . . .'.[38]

This slight play again propounds the destructiveness of sectarianism: 'Sure, all the drums of the world won't make up for a son that's angry with his da', concludes Mrs McClurg, and she proposes a cup of tea to restore calm and humour among her childish menfolk.[39] However, the play touches on two points of wider interest. Set at the height of the Home Rule crisis, it is significant that McClurg regards the Orange parades as a means of warning England about Protestant resistance to constitutional change as much as they are a reminder to the Nationalists not to assert themelves. The history McClurg invokes is not only that of the Boyne, but of demonstrations 'when ould Gladstone brought in his first Bill, and . . . when he brought in his second Bill'.[40] The second point is raised when McClurg's friend, Andy Haveron, declares that 'The drumming's more important nor the speeches' which 'Nobody listens to . . . when they can read them in the *Telegraph* at their ease the next day'.[41] This implicit admission that the emotional tribalism of the Twelfth is its real source of power and attraction, rather than any religious or historical justifications, is further suggestive of why sectarian passions are so inaccessible to reason and restraint.

Two more recent plays which reopen the issue of the destructiveness of sectarianism to relationships are John Boyd's *The Flats* (first performed in 1971) and Bill Morrison's trilogy, *A Love Song for Ulster* (1993). Boyd focuses on a Catholic family, the Donnellans, and their sole remaining Protestant neighbours in a block of flats in Belfast, Monica Moore and her invalid mother. Monica is a Protestant variant of Ervine's Nora Murray – a non-sectarian, caring, morally upright victim (she is fatally wounded by an unknown killer during the sectarian clash with which the play ends). She is carefully kept off-stage for much of the time, which thereby preserves her integrity, keeps her clear of the cross-currents of varying political opinion that characterise the individual members of the Donnellan family and renders more potent the sense of futile waste when she dies. Boyd also draws out the bewilderment of the young, working-class British soldier, Phil, stationed at the flats, who cannot understand why he is in Belfast, what the factions are fighting about and why the girl he has begun to court has been killed. Earlier in the play he is dismissive of the history lesson Joe Donnellan tries to give him – ''Istory is 'istory . . . What can you do abawt what's all ovah? Forget y' 'istroy, Paddy . . . Think of the future' – and Monica's death at the end is a blunt reminder that in Ireland the old arguments go on taking their toll.[42] Phil's ignorance and naivety give him no greater exemption from the consequences of sectarianism than Monica Moore's innocence affords her. Likewise, the socialist rationalism of

Gerard Donnellan, who uses Radio Free Belfast to urge all working-class people to unite against their common capitalist enemy, has as little influence in checking the atavistic motives that set the two communities against each other as his mother's Junoesque desire to be allowed to live in peace.

Bill Morrison's aim is more ambitious. He uses the dramatic metaphors of an arranged mixed marriage, consummated in rape, and a shared house to explore the history of the Northern Irish State and its relationships with the Irish Republic and England from partition to the modern day. The Protestant Orangeman, John, informs the Catholic Nationalist, Kate:

> I'm the son of the son of the son of the son of some poor gam who was washed over from Scotland and stayed. Worked till they dropped. Built where there was nothing. Trusted nobody. Danced to nobody's tune. Believed that each man was his own conscience. Thought perversity was a virtue. A man of the North. Proud of it. And that's what you are now, a woman of the North.[43]

The character's sense of historical destiny and his assumption here that his mastery and the (Catholic) woman's submission are natural and unquestionable take on added significance in the light of recurrent exchanges throughout the plays on how the biblical story of Abraham and Isaac is to be understood. These take place between Willie and Mick, ghosts waiting to be born at the start of the first play, who enter the action as 'characters' later on and become ghosts again before the end. (Mick dies on hunger strike, while Willie, who has cultivated both extremist Protestants and the British army, is murdered by unidentified killers.) They puzzle over the uncertainties of the story: why did Isaac not rebel? was his life ever in danger? do free will and choice exist or are all actions predestined? is the story accurate as it is told in the Bible, or was it edited afterwards to suit events?

Given the predilection of some Northern Irish Protestants to link their story with that of God's chosen people, and to view their possession of the land as an historical destiny, this interrogation of one of the foundation myths of the special relationship between the Lord and the Israelites has particular relevance. It questions by implication the inevitability, or otherwise, of the Protestant hegemony in Northern Ireland, the justification, if any, of the oppression of Catholics, and whether history can be shaped and redirected by human will and agency, or is an imposition from which no escape is possible, a fated re-enactment of the same feuds from generation to generation.

The brutal violation which initiates the mixed marriage sets in train an endless cycle of suspicion, cruelty, insecurity and unhappiness affecting both parties. The Protestant desire for absolute power and for unequivocal certainty of possessing it is impossible to fulfil and is ultimately self-destructive, as Kate prophetically warns her second and even more ruthless husband, Victor:

> . . . you are nurturing a worm that will grow into a snake that will eat you from the inside out until its gleaming eye will be the centre of your eyeball and its tongue will slither out of your mouth and poison your spit so that all the words you speak will shower out hate and you will poison your own seed.[44]

The events of the play, paralleling some of the major stages in the state's history, realise this vision of approaching apocalypse, and it seems that the only way to escape its relentless outworking may be a refusal to accept the terms of the past. However, not only the necessity for this, but also the seeming impossibility of it emerge in exchanges between Boyd, who has been raised in the image of his father (or stepfather – it is uncertain which of the two brothers, John and Victor, is his natural parent) and his mother, Kate:

> Boyd: I was left to be his.
> Kate: What choice did I have?
> Boyd: What choice do I have now? I don't know to this day whose I am. Who am I?
> Kate: Yourself. Be yourself. Not your history. Not living up to a father living up to a father.
> Boyd: It's too late.
> Kate: It can't be.
> Boyd: It's way too late to stop now. I have to go with him. I have to go with Victor. He's my father. The only father I have. I have to go wherever he takes me. I can't turn against him. It would be the death of him.
> Kate: It could be life for everybody else.
> Boyd: Do you want me to kill him? Is that what you wanted all along?
> Kate: I did once.
> Boyd: I know.
> Kate: For what?
> Boyd: For land. Mother, the truth is you sacrificed me. The deed was done long ago. And I have sacrificed in my turn. I can no more escape than a ram caught in a thicket. For love of land.[45]

Boyd can neither commit the Oedipal act of killing his father for love of his mother, nor console himself as the chosen sacrificial offering who was saved, like Isaac. His allusion to the ram only serves to emphasise how completely he himself is an impotent victim of circumstances. In the closing moments of the play more positive images are offered when the ghost of Mick suggests that the whole idea of God speaking to Abraham 'was a dream in Abraham's mind', and likewise the voice that told him not to kill his son was his own – 'he undreamt his own dream'.[46] Having disposed of belief in a God who determines events, man is released into individual responsibility for his actions: 'If you dream one dream to live by you can undream it because it is only yours and not unchangeable'.[47] This thought is complemented by Anne's dream for her baby's future:

> That you will understand your history and the dangerous dreams that made it . . . That you will have no dreams to torment you. That you will see that we all of us have a choice. We can say good morning instead of passing by. We can not lift a gun, we can take back the bitter words, we can perform these small acts of love that are our salvation.[48]

Yet however laudable and desirable these words, they remain a dream, an aspirational statement at the end of a three-part play characterised by graphic visual images of domestic and communal suffering, grief and violent confrontations directly attributable to a history driven and fuelled by sectarian passions and insecurities.

Whereas *The Flats* and *A Love Song for Ulster* pursued in particular the domestic and personal consequences of a sectarian society, Sam Thompson's *Over the Bridge* develops the second strand in Ervine's *Mixed Marriage* – the divisions among workers caused by religion. In his introduction to the published text, Stewart Parker observed that Thompson 'saw right from the start that poverty and sectarian violence were root and branch of the one ugly tree'.[49] Drawing upon his personal experience of working in the Belfast shipyards, which were as notorious for their occasional anti-Catholic pogroms as they were renowned for their world-class vessels, he laid bare the pernicious way in which sectarianism was a route to power for some, but crippled union attempts to achieve parity and win improvements for all. The sharpness of Thompson's vision received an unwanted form of endorsement in the statement issued by the directors of the Group Theatre in Belfast, who panicked about the feelings the play might unleash, and having failed to persuade the author to make changes to his script, cancelled the intended first production when rehearsals were under way. They publicly defended this decision by declaring their determination

> ... not to mount any play which would offend or affront the religious or political beliefs or sensibilities of the man in the street of any denomination or class in the community and which would give rise to sectarian or political controversy of an extreme nature.[50]

The faint-hearted directors missed the point that the sell-out audiences who eventually saw the play in 1960 recognised at once, that Thompson's play is not an incitement to sectarian or political violence but a serious observation of how these are unleashed. It is a warning (which has subsequently proved all too true) that without changes of heart and perspective, events like those represented on stage could recur in workplaces and on the streets.

The alternative to sectarian groupings among the workforce is trade unionism, and Davy Mitchell (who may be hinted at in John Boyd's Mac in *The Farm*) is the character whose firmness, fairness, courage and selfless brotherly love offer an inspirational model of union leadership in action. However, Thompson does not idealise the conduct of the union itself. It abjectly fails to prevent a sectarian riot in which Mitchell is killed by a mob of his own Protestant members for defending a solitary Catholic's right to work, and is repeatedly divided by petty internal arguments. Mitchell's exemplary conduct and pursuit of justice are continually rebuffed and frustrated by the selfishness of those who cheat on their fellow members and by the intrusion of religious and sectarian issues into the workplace. In the end, his innocence and moral uprightness give him neither protection not respect and he dies as a secular martyr.

The conversations and tensions between the characters disclose the elaborate network of sectarian attitudes and consciousness among the men. Warren Baxter is perfectly happy to exploit bigotry to win votes for a union office, regarding this as 'common sense' instead of the folly of Mitchell's 'principles'; Ephraim Kerr loses his position as a teaboy for filling a Catholic's can, and is threatened with violence; Archie Kerr is bitterly hostile to having a Catholic union organiser and contemptuous of the Protestants who nominated him; a sinister, anonymous mob leader appears to warn the Catholic Peter O'Boyle to quit work after an explosion in the shipyard is automatically attributed to the IRA; rumours and gossip have labelled O'Boyle a Republican although nothing in the play confirms this, and within the shipyard, rival Protestant and Catholic Vigilance Groups operate to defeat the goal of union brotherhood.

Religion also intrudes when Billy Morgan tenders his resignation from the 'ungodly' union following a conversion experience. His wish (and need) to continue working conflicts with the union's closed-shop policy and precipitates another confrontation between absolute points of view. Thompson spares neither Morgan's new-found religious exclusivity nor Rabbie White's legalistic application of the union rule book, using the head foreman, Fox, to criticise both men for inconsistencies in their own behaviour and an irresponsible lack of concern for the wider consequences of their actions. It is also Fox who, at the end of the play, pinpoints both the strength and the weakness of the trade unionism it has represented in action when he tells Davy Mitchell's daughter:

> . . . I learnt a great lesson the other day, Miss Mitchell. I saw the wheels of trade unionism deprive a man of his livelihood because he wanted to leave on religious grounds, and I witnessed the very same day the loyalty of your father who stood by a workmate in defending his right to work without intimidation.[51]

This may imply that the union can only ever be as strong and effective as its weakest members and that without a general reformation of attitudes, examples like that of Mitchell will always be marginalised and ignored under pressure. However, the final speech of the play, delivered 'as if in a trance' by a greatly altered Warren Baxter, reaches out to the consciences of the audience as well as to the other characters with the idea that if they do not accept their own share of responsibility for Mitchell's death, but walk away because it is 'none of their business', then selfishness and sectarianism will continue to distort both trade unionism and Christianity.

In each of these plays the writers have not only exploited the obvious dramatic potential of sectarian confrontations, often sharpened by what has been called 'the sardonically abusive speech of Belfast', they have also shown how deeply sectarian attitudes and responses are embedded in Northern Irish society, permeating relationships and determining the judgment and actions of people who do not even think of themselves as bigoted.[52] Sectarianism is intimately bound up with the exercise and maintenance of power, and conversely, with fear of losing it, which may be why it is so strongly – though not exclusively – associated with Protestant characters in these dramas. Ironically, as

Ervine, Boyd and Thompson all imply, sectarianism is also a weapon that has been used by some Protestants to protect their own political and business interests against the threat that a united working class would pose to them. In all these circumstances, the religious rhetoric of sectarianism has little or no visible connection with the practice of faith or with coherent beliefs, but flourishes alarmingly independent of them like a grotesque, unsanctioned by-product with no framework of accountability.

The very success of the dramatists in representing the power of sectarianism militates against the alternative perspectives and possibilities each one brings forward. Within the plays, socialism, trade unionism, moving on from old memories, breaking with 'tradition', seeing past denominational labels and stereotyped attitudes, tolerance and common sense are all advocated and demonstrated. Yet, however compelling and reasonable their exponents may be, and however exemplary their behaviour, the plays primarily serve to affirm the corrosive effects of sectarianism and its enduring resistance to every version of moderation and change.

III

The entrapping cycle of history which reinforces itself by its own repetitions and haunts those condemned to live it has also engaged the attention of Christina Reid and Stewart Parker, who offer radically different dramatic explorations of it, and of their characters' reactions to its processes. In *Tea in a China Cup* (first performed in 1983), Christina Reid presents formative episodes in the lives of three generations of the same Belfast Protestant family. Crucially, this is a female-centred drama. The men in each generation are absences rather than presences. The father and husband of the main character, Beth, never even appear, while her grandfather occupies only a marginal place in the home, which is the women's domain, preferring to slip off to the pub where he is out of the way. Beth's maternal uncle is seen briefly as he prepares to go to war in 1939, following his father's example in 1914, but he is fatally injured, while her brother is glimpsed only as a child and we later learn that he is with the modern British army in Germany and unable to return home for security reasons. Whereas the men are typified by the women as feckless, irresponsible or uncaring in their family relationships and are preoccupied with misplaced fantasies of military glory or wealth, the women combine the practical skills of running a home on insufficient money and of dealing with the realities of birth, childrearing and death, with the perpetuation of superstitions, rituals and ignorance which simultaneously bond them together and disable them.

Reid deliberately blurs any distinction between the present time and scene – Beth's house in 1972, where her mother, Sarah, is dying of cancer – and episodes set in her original family home and elsewhere at intervals from 1939 onwards. Beth herself narrates the past as well as the present, investing events which took place before her own birth with the same immediacy as those in which she participated. The effect of this is to persuade us that the stories of the past have in a real sense become part of Beth's personal family memory and history, even when in a literal sense this is impossible. The importance of preserving these stories and of passing them on to future generations is explicitly declared early on when Sarah instructs her daughter to 'mind all the old family stories, tell them to your children after I'm gone'.[53] Thus, the experience of one generation of women becomes that of the next without moving forward in any very discernible way.

The private stories and memories of Beth's family are additionally reinforced by being interwoven with the wider community's Protestant identity and Orange commemorations through which they also define themselves. The sound of bands rehearsing for the Twelfth of July opens the play and Sarah's last wish is that she will live to see one more parade:

> It's the sound of the flute bands . . . always gets the oul Protestant blood going. I tell you, a daily dose of the True Blue Defenders would do me more good than them hateful transfusions they give me up at the hospital,

she tells Beth.[54] Thoughts of going to 'the Field' (the location to which the Orangemen march during the Twelfth of July commemorations) link up with Beth's 'memory' of the Orangeman in a clerical collar who praised her mother for carrying her to Finaghy when she was four months old ('Women like you are the backbone of Ulster.'), and of the bands playing 'On the green grassy slope of the Boyne' on the day her uncle, who died before she was born, joined up in 1939. Her own birthday coincided with the anniversary of the death of William of Orange, which the Grand Master of the local Orange Lodge predicted would ensure her survival, despite her initial frailty.

However, her mother named her after the heir to the throne rather than after William's wife, because, ironically, Mary is 'a very Catholic sort of name in Northern Ireland' – a revelation which is immediately followed by bands playing to mark the coronation in 1953.[55] Later, at Beth's first encounter with death, when she goes to watch her grandmother and Maisie laying out a corpse, the women abuse the spitefulness of the dead man for passing away on the Twelfth. These Orange celebrations are less significant as anti-Catholic triumphalism than as acts of bonding and affirmation within the Protestant community itself – a point which reflects how the mood of parades may vary considerably depending on the current state of community relations. So too, recalling her own childhood memories of Orange marches, Reid has said, 'this was the highlight of the year, going to see the parade, you know the . . . waving to your uncles. And you knew so many people in the parade'.[56] The sense of belonging conferred by the familiar Orange tunes and cultural practices is implicit in the recurrent strategic use of the band music in *Tea in a China Cup*, and is manifestly part of the means by which these 'people who fear absorption into another group . . . counteract the threat of extinction by telling the story of the past and of themselves to their own community'.[57]

The women's counterparts to the public, male Orange rituals are specifically private female routines, superstitions and protected areas of knowledge. Some of these are also affirmations of Protestant distinctiveness and of their supposed superiority to Catholics. They perpetuate the myth of the cleanliness of Protestant children and homes, whereas Catholics are allegedly 'clarty and poor', and when Beth points to her own family's poverty, her Grandmother enigmatically replies that 'There's poor and poor'.[58] The women move quickly to curb the child's readiness to speak of her mother's economies, 'Because if you do, you bring yourself down to the level of the Catholics, whining and complainin' and puttin' a poor mouth on yourself'.[59] Possession of 'a bit of fine bone china and good table linen' epitomises Protestant decency and respectability, affirmed in the play by the ritual of drinking tea from a china cup. It is a damning indictment of Beth's father, and a family disgrace, that because of his fecklessness, her mother has had to sell her china cabinet to a Catholic to pay the rentman, saving just one cup and saucer to salve her injured pride and to preserve a token of her compromised respectability. At the end of the play when Beth oversees the disposal of the remaining goods in her mother's house, including the cabinet of Belleek china that ironically seemed to Sarah the very symbol of her daughter's 'good' marriage, she re-enacts this gesture, keeping back one cup and saucer even though it greatly lowers the financial value of the set.

This repetition, one of many in the play, is indicative of the degree to which Beth's life lacks scope for individual development and growth. Like the annual marches of the Orangemen the domestic superstitions are repeated. For example, Beth immediately covers the mirrors in 'white starched linen clothes, just as my grandmother had shown me', when her mother dies and she accepts the two wedding rings from Sarah because they are 'charms' – even though her own marriage has failed and the ring her grandmother gave her son to protect him in 1939 served no purpose.

But Beth is also circumscribed by the silence of older women about the onset of menstruation and the physical realities of marriage, so that the ignorance of one generation is inherited by the next. Beth and her Catholic friend, Theresa, who is no better informed, half-excite and half-frighten themselves as teenagers with lurid stories about sex and religion but both fall into disastrous relationships. Beth's marriage is a sham, although she conceals this from Sarah to preserve the illusion that she has done well, while Theresa is an unmarried single parent living in poverty in London whose mother back at home boasts of her daughter's career, flat and numerous offers of marriage. With the death of Sarah, Beth faces a future in which most of the rituals and patterns that shaped and determined her life have altered or broken down completely. The onset of the troubles rends apart the community in which her family have lived for generations – ironically, Sarah is ordered to leave her home by a Protestant youth who wants to burn it to prevent Catholics moving in. Beth herself has become a property owner in middle-class Belfast through her marriage, but, childless, she has no daughter through whom she will perpetuate the interlocking history of her family and her society. She voices her predicament to Theresa:

> All my life people have been telling me what I should do! . . . I'm scared, Theresa . . . my mother's dying and very soon for the first time in my life I am going to be alone . . . and I'm scared . . . my head is full of other people's memories I don't know who I am . . . or what I am . . .[60]

Beth's personal dilemma – her sense of loss and isolation, her uncertain identity and apprehension for the future – represents on a personal level the problem of a whole community which is dependent on perpetuating a particular view of itself through rituals of self-affirmation, and which is thrown into crisis when these securities are threatened or break down. Held in thrall by the history and cultural practices of her Protestant community, and of her individual family and its womenfolk in particular, Beth experiences disability rather than freedom when her mother dies and seems condemned more than ever to live among the ghosts of the past.

The hero of Stewart Parker's *Northern Star*, the Protestant leader of the United Irishmen in Ulster, Henry Joy McCracken, is also represented as the victim of history rather than its liberator, as he aspired to be. Early in the play he declares the 'new idea' of the unity of 'Catholic Protestant Dissenter' in 'one big mongrel family' against the common oppression of power and wealth, but by the end he is forced to admit not only the failure to realise this, but also the unforeseen consequences that have followed:

> . . . all we've done, you see, is to reinforce the locks, cram the cells fuller than ever of mangled bodies crawling round in their own shite and lunacy, and the cycle just goes on, playing out the same demented comedy of terrors from generation to generation, trapped in the same malignant legend, condemned to re-endure it as if the Anti-Christ who dreamed it up was driven astray in the wits by it and the entire pattern of depravity just goes spinning on out of control . . .[61]

The self-conscious theatricality of the structure and style of *Northern Star*, linking McCracken's story to a version of the Seven Ages of Man, each one of which brilliantly parodies an earlier Irish dramatist, and its setting in 'the continuous past' reinforce this powerful sense of entrapment and repetition.[62]

McCracken's own fate is further ironised because despite his advocacy of reason to overthow the ghosts of the past, he himself is embraced by the Phantom Bride of another freethinker whose mysterious death is attributed locally to his attempt to build a house using stones taken from a fairy fort. As Csilla Bertha has observed, the Phantom Bride

> . . . coming from the past, is both life-saving and life-taking. She protects the half-made, crumbling house (itself a metaphor of a united Ireland, or of the abortive attempts to create one) and those who find refuge there, and saves McCracken from an undignified fall into the hands of the soldiers. On the other hand she is dangerous: she urges the hero to choose death instead of life; to seek martyrdom.[63]

In this way, the relationship between the Protestant rationalist and the Phantom Bride is not significantly different to the Catholic nationalist's devotion to Kathleen ní Houlihan. Because of it, McCracken's mistress, and the mother of his child, Mary Bodle, confronts him with his infidelity to life – 'It's living you fear. That's the sore spot on your soul. Living the way I do, most people do. Humdrum, ordinary, soon enough forgotten' – which is probably the most serious accusation against him.[64] This, she tells him, is 'why you're more in love with that rope than you are with me and the child', and the play affirms her judgment, showing McCracken's vain preoccupation with the 'famous last words' he may or may not utter.[65]

His inability to control history and the way he will be used by it after his death, which anticipates the dilemma of Hugh O'Neill in Friel's *Making History* four years after the first performance of *Northern Star* in 1984, is variously introduced. Mary-Anne McCracken, already preparing her brother's story as that of a 'national hero' and exemplary model for the 'coming generations', rejects his horror at this prospect: 'Pious phrasemaking over a butcher's shambles, valiant defeat, maudlin self-pity – "we wuz robbed!" – defeat! What an example', he protests.[66] Mary Bodle warns him that his death will be ugly, not glamorous, but that what will be done in his name afterwards will be even worse, and in the end McCracken himself curses the uses to which history will put him in language that deliberately echoes a Beckettian character's existential nightmare:

> To finish. Unless only to begin anew, there is of course that. Only to glimmer on in the effigy of another time, other times, other effigies, never to know end's mercy, never to be let end, never to know mercy so much for the rope's comfort, I shall soon be quite enshrined in spite of all. A whore's pox then on the future! And I forgive it nothing, for there's nothing it will learn from those of us who swung for it, no peace to be got from it, for those of us who want nothing more now than to finish, a cat's flux on whatever holy picture they may fashion of me![67]

Here the Protestant understanding of history as a progress toward final consummation is looped back on itself to become an apparently closed circle without prospect of advance or completion.

Northern Star is a drama of failure and anguish. As Parker presents it, McCracken's weakness is partly due to traits in his character and partly to his erroneous belief that a non-racial, non-sectarian rational vision of the future could prevail in an archetypal internecine struggle, 'two men fighting over a field'.[68] These flaws combine to ensnare him fatally in the coils of history and leave him to articulate the paradox of his undiminished love for what might have been in a place that is 'Braindamaged and dangerous, continuously violating itself, a place of perpetual breakdown, incompatible voices, screeching obscenely away through the smoky dark wet . . . a ghost town now and always will be, angry and implacable ghosts'.[69] Terence Brown has claimed that this pessimism is alleviated by the 'future ghost' of Jemmy Hope who offers a glimpse of 'the revolutionary possibilities of a socialist analysis of Irish history', but it is at best a frail counterbalance, an aspirational alternative briefly introduced well before the closing speeches of the play with their insistence on history as repetition.[70] It is in the last of his *Three Plays for Ireland* that Parker achieves a more fully realised vision of how the ghosts of history may be assuaged and new possibilities initiated.

Like *Northern Star* and *Tea in a China Cup*, *Pentecost* is set in a haunted house which has its own emblematic history. The home of the late Lily Matthews, whose life spanned the first seventy-four years of the twentieth century to the time in which the action occurs, has been 'the object of a desperate, lifelong struggle for cleanliness, tidiness, orderliness – godliness', the Protestant virtues.[71] 'This house was my life', declares Lily's ghost, with more significance than is at first apparent, and it has survived burning by Catholics in the 1920s and German airraids in World War II to stand vulnerably between the warring communities in contemporary Belfast, 'eloquent with the history of this city'.[72] It also becomes what Anthony Roche calls 'a kind of stay or refuge, an asylum or temporary holding-ground one step removed from the (war) zone of historical circumstance', occupied by four characters – two from Catholic and two from Protestant backgrounds – in need of spiritual and psychological healing for their injurious personal and social past.[73]

The interior drama is firmly located in the context of the current political troubles, both actual and imagined: Harold Wilson's voice is heard infamously denouncing the Northern Irish as spongers and Protestant anger is reflected in the reactions of Ruth and Peter; the progress of the Ulster Workers' strike is closely followed, two of the characters are roughed up in street incidents, and the sounds of explosions, drunken shouting, an Orange band and a military helicopter punctuate the action. These signals of external breakdown and confrontation have their counterparts in the crises in the lives of the characters on stage. Lenny's estrangement from his wife, Marian, follows their loss of love after the death of their infant son, Christopher, five years earlier. He is drifting, evading responsibility, trying to console himself with his trombone playing. She has survived by selling antiques to people whose avaricious vulgarity she despises, but can no longer live with her own contempt and has sold her business. Marian's impulsive desire to buy the house Lenny has inherited and her decision to keep it as a time capsule or heritage home (she proposes to make it over to the National Trust) is at first indicative of her wish to withdraw from the present and immerse herself in the past. The third character, Ruth, seeks refuge in the house from her policeman husband whose repeated violence has already caused her to have three miscarriages and left her with little future hope of childbearing, while the fourth, Peter, the son of a Methodist minister, has returned from England to mock indiscriminately and sneer at Ulster Protestant bigotry and history which he can neither forget nor come to terms with.

Marian's quest to know more about the former occupant of the house begins as a reconstruction of the circumstances of Lily Matthews' death, but leads to a deconstruction of the superficial respectability of her life and a revelation of the hypocrisy at its core which exorcises the guilt of the past, lays the ghost to rest, and enables Marian's own regeneration and potentially that of the other characters too. Lily's initial resentment of Marian probing her past is expressed in sectarian terms. She sees her as 'an idolator', related to the 'pack of Fenian savages' who once wrecked her home, her very presence a violation of the idealised Protestant decency she and her husband built up over the years and which she maintained alone after his death in 1959. Under closer questioning, she increases her opposition by singing 'O God our help in ages past' and denouncing Marian as the Antichrist when she confronts her, an apparently childless woman, with a christening gown which she has found in her home. Marian correctly suggests that, in an inversion of the customary pattern, it is she who is haunting Lily's ghost by pressing on past her explanation of her childlessness as God's will, the Protestant snobbery with which she sneers at the size of Catholic families and her criticism of the state of Marian's marriage, until Lily finally takes over and tells her own story, admitting her affair with her English lodger, secret pregnancy, abandonment of her baby and endless guilt thereafter:

> I sinned against my own flesh in lust and fornication, I had to desert my own baby, nobody ever knew only the Lord our God knew and His eye was on me all right, burning into the very soul of me, He alone was witness to the torment that I've suffered every living hour in this

house where the very walls and doors cry out against me . . . until I was all consumed with my own wickedness, on the inside, nothing left but the shell of me, for appearance's sake . . . still and all. At least I never let myself down – never cracked. Never surrendered. Not one inch. I went to my grave a respectable woman, Mrs Alfred George Matthews, I never betrayed him. That was the way I atoned, you see. I done him proud.[74]

This powerfully moving confession, completed by Marian's gesture of holding Lily's hand to her own heart and asking her forgiveness, becomes the means by which the problem of escaping from the burden of the past is resolved. Lily's ghost does not appear again and the scene prefigures the events at the close of the play. Anthony Roche writes that Lily's 'denial of life and her sense of abandonment are the emotional truths which her Unionist cry of "no surrender" tries to deny and silence'.[75] Conversely, when her life is accepted and spoken for in its entirety, when vulnerability, weakness and personal responsibility are admitted, guilt may be put aside and the unending defensiveness and tensions of hypocrisy removed in an act of liberation which has relevance for both private and political spheres of activity.

The inherent religiousness of this redemptive process is more explicit in the closing moments of the play. In contrast to the triumphal rowdiness of a Protestant mob outside celebrating the success of their strike in reinforcing the old divisions by compelling the government to abandon its plan for power-sharing, the four characters in the house embark upon an orchestrated series of confessional stories which centre on ways of resolving conflict. These start with the comic absurdity of an alleged plan by Peter, Lenny and another student to spike the Silent Valley reservoir with LSD and 'turn on the population, comprehensively, with one simple transcendental gesture'.[76] Peter's invitation to Marian to follow his story by 'dishing the dirt on Orange Lily Matthews' prompts her to reveal her knowledge that Peter and Ruth have earlier made love in the parlour, and to tell how the sofa they used was the one where Lily's child was conceived and on which she had waited in vain during the blitz 'for the chosen bomb to fall on her and cleanse her terrible sinfulness and shame'.[77] Marian's announcement at this point that she no longer wants to preserve the house as a museum piece ('What this house needs most is air and light') shows how her perspective is changing as her understanding grows, but Lenny seizes on the issue of religious guilt and describes an idealised scene of uninhibited and unselfconscious sexual and spiritual freedom which he imagines may have characterised pre-Christian Ireland before the impositions of the Church. When Ruth disowns Lenny's negative view of Christianity – 'You think it's only denial, but that's wrong. It's meant to be love and celebration' – this leads to the revelation that it is Pentecost Sunday, and her recitation with Peter of the relevant passage from The Acts of the Apostles, ch. 2.[78]

From a Christian point of view, the account of Pentecost is crucial, signifying God's continuing covenant with humans, and the unprecedented, liberating empowerment of the disciples. This is also why it is a favourite source for evangelical preachers. However, Ruth and Peter's quotation of scripture is confrontational rather than complementary. Her belief is offset by his increasingly apparent cynicism which finally vents itself in bitter accusations –

> . . . it hasn't entirely held up, Ruthie. I mean they're never done calling on the name of the Lord in this wee province of ours, so it ought to be the most saved place on God's earth, instead of the most absolutely godforsaken, not so?

– and nihilistic mockery of the four of them as a parodic version of the holy family, until it occurs to him that they are missing the 'most important member . . . the Prince of Peace Himself'.[79] He taunts the others with the idea of Jesus entering into the world of Northern Ireland's sectarian violence and hatred, which provokes Lenny to a renewed outburst against all religion and churches until Marian's crucial intervention challenges their 'righteous anger' against other individuals and organisations and insists on the overriding importance of individual responsibility.[80] Marian's confession of the impact of her own child's death upon her, told now for the first time, parallels that of Lily earlier on and as Lily's story released her, so Marian's is equally cathartic. Her passage beyond the belief she shared at first with Lenny that somehow 'this town' and 'these times' had killed Christopher, through the phase of blaming the child himself for her own suffering, has led her to the transforming realisation that

> I denied him. The christ in him. Which he had entrusted to my care, the ghost of him that I do still carry, as I carried his little body. The christ in him absorbed into the christ in me. We have got to love that in ourselves. In ourselves first and then in them. That's the only future there is.[81]

Here, as Csilla Bertha has put it, 'the resurrection of Easter and the understanding of Pentecost happen at the same time since resurrection becomes possible only after arriving at acceptance.'[82] That acceptance opens up the future to creative possibilities and the final part of Marian's testimony is a renewed commitment to life. It does not seem inappropriate to say that she has been 'born again', albeit not with the usual connotations of this phrase, and while the past cannot be forgotten, her relationship to it has been radically altered. Likewise, she understands that the proper obligation to 'our innocent dead' (whether Christopher or any of the victims of the Northern Ireland troubles) and to themselves will be to live 'the fullest life for which they could ever have hoped'.[83] This secularised version of Pentecost may lack the convulsive drama of the mighty rushing wind and tongues of fire in the original story, but Parker has created a complex score of lighting, music, gesture, movement and words – many of them picked up from earlier in the action and invested now with new significance – in which the characters are absorbed and reconciled.[84]

Elsewhere he had warned against cheap and easy exploitation of the sensational elements in the Northern Irish situation before going on to proclaim the potential revelatory power of drama, which

> can confirm the conflicts and contradictions, the cruelty and the killings, the implacable ghosts, the unending rancour, pettiness and meanness of spirit, the poverty of imagination and evasion of truth which unites our two communities in their compact of mutual impotence and sterility – all in a single image. Within that same frame, it can demonstrate and celebrate a language as wholesome and nutritious as a wheaten farl, a stony wit and devious humour, an experiential vivacity and wholeheartedness, a true instinct for hospitality and generosity, which also and equally unite our two communities.[85]

In the crucial confrontation between Lily Matthews and Marian, and again in the interaction between the four characters in the closing moments of the play, Parker employs all his imaginative and theatrical skills to realise this vision of drama that is inspirational rather than instructive, inclusive rather than exclusive, and above all, which 'assert[s] the play-impulse over the deathwish'.[86]

Yet it is an ending which troubles some critics. Robert Johnstone senses 'a straining for significance and resolution in the final act', while Elmer Andrews describes it as 'somewhat clumsily forced and impatient' and regrets that it moves 'toward a final, overwhelming stasis, a consummate declaration – rather than a consummate act – beyond which the audience must not think'.[87] These judgments underestimate the almost operatic way in which Parker uses the voices of his characters in solos and duets, complementing and counterpointing each other, in different combinations and with diverse tones, over a sustained period, until they are united in the profoundly humane final harmonies. Through Lily Matthews, wrote Parker, 'the cycle of retribution is in fact finally laid to rest, in the only way I can foresee as having any possible meaning'.[88] Through Marian that way is given its spokesperson in a drama which encourages the Protestant principle of personal responsibility, invests it with a humane and generous awareness of social obligation, liberates it from the disabilities of sectarianism and lays the malign ghosts of history. It is a final thought-provoking irony that a play, the art form most suspected by the Protestant fathers, should be so deeply committed to the ancient religious function of drama, the vehicle for reimagining a contemporary version of the pentecostal experience with its regenerative and enabling potential, and the means of offering what Parker himself called 'a gesture of charity and solidarity which transforms the whole human journey for us at last with a possibility of hope'.[89]

Notes

1 Declan Kiberd, *Anglo-Irish Attitudes* in T. Paulin, S. Heaney, S. Deane, R. Kearney, D. Kiberd, *Ireland's Field Day*, p 100. Iain Crichton Smith, *Collected Poems*, p 322.
2 Peter McDonald, *Mistaken Identities: Poetry and Northern Ireland*, p 39.
3 *Ibid.*, p 83.
4 R.S. Thomas, *Collected Poems 1945–1990*, p 54.
5 Robert McLiam Wilson, 'Rhythm Method', *Fortnight*, No 331, Sept 1994, p 45.
6 Susan Manning, *The Puritan-Provincial Vision (Scottish and American Literature in the Nineteenth Century)*, p 1.
7 Brendan Kennelly, *Journey into Joy: Selected Prose*, p 127.
8 *Ibid.*, p 128.
9 Crichton Smith, *op. cit.*, pp 20–21.

CHAPTER ONE

1 In the case of Ireland, the encounter between Calvinist influences mediated not only through the seventeenth-century Scottish planters in Ulster with Presbyterian convictions, but also strongly present within the Church of Ireland, and native Roman Catholicism soon created a lastingly volatile situation in which religious and political allegiances became in time ever more intertwined.
2 Henry R. Van Til, *The Calvinistic Concept of Culture*, p 20.
3 John Calvin, *Institutes of the Christian Religion*, Vol 1, Bk1, ch 1, sect 1, p 38 and Vol 1, Bk 1, ch 2, sect 1, pp 40–41.
4 Susan Manning, *The Puritan-Provincial Vision (Scottish and American Literature in the Nineteenth Century)*, p 7. Such division is evident in the theological disputes *within* the church itself which, for example, have contributed to the proliferation of small sects and free churches in the north of Ireland (see the case of Paul Henry's father and Robert Harbinson's experiences discussed in chapter 4 below. Another instance is found in Thomas Witherow's nineteenth-century account of a Mr Bryce who withdrew from the Synod of Ulster on a point of principle concerning the *regium donum*. See *Thomas Witherow 1824–1890*, [Graham Mawhinney and Eull Dunlop, eds], Draperstown: Ballinascreen Historical Society, 1990, pp 23–24). This is quite apart from the arguments pursued by Calvinists with those outside their beliefs.
5 Calvin, *op. cit.*, Vol 1, Bk 1, ch 3, sect 1, p 43 and Vol 1, Bk 1, ch 2, sect 3, p 42.
6 *Ibid.*, Vol 1, Bk 1, ch 5, sect 11, p 59 and Vol 1, Bk 1, ch 5, sect 12, p 60.
7 Van Til, *op. cit.*, p 33. In the light of this, it is interesting that Forrest Reid was to call the first volume of his autobiography, *Apostate* – see chapter 4.
8 Calvin, *op. cit.*, Vol 1, Bk 1, ch 5, sect 12, p 59.
9 Van Til, *op. cit.*, p 49.
10 Calvin, *op. cit.*, Vol 2, Bk 4, ch 17, sect 39, p 596.
11 Van Til, *op. cit.*, p 161.
12 See Calvin, *op. cit.*, Vol 1, Bk 1, ch 6, sect 1, p 64.
13 *Ibid.*, Vol 1, Bk 1, ch 16, sect 9, p 181.
14 *Ibid.*, Vol 1, Bk 1, ch 18, sect 4, p 205.

15   *Ibid.*, Vol 1, Bk 2, ch 2, sect 15, p 236. However, it should be added that such 'truth' in no way 'contradicts' the supreme truth of the Word in scripture.
16   *Ibid.*, Vol 1, Bk 2, ch 5, sect 3, p 275.
17   Tony Tanner, *Scenes of Nature, Signs of Men*, p 11. Calvinist influenced culture in Northern Ireland also makes extensive use of signs and emblems which are interpreted as external tokens of religious and political commitments. See, for instance, Anthony D. Buckley, 'Walls Within Walls: Religion and 'Rough' Behaviour in an Ulster Community', *Sociology*, Vol 18, No 1, Feb 1984, pp 19–32, and the same author's 'The Chosen Few: Biblical Texts in the Regalia of an Ulster Secret Society', *Folk Life*, Vol 24, part 19, 1985–1986, pp 5–24. Also section III of this chapter and chapter 3 below.
18   Calvin, *op. cit.*, Vol 2, Bk 4, ch 14, sect 17, p 503.
19   *Ibid.*, Vol 2, Bk 4, ch 14, sect 18, p 504.
20   One thinks, for instance, of what is signified by the crossing of the Boyne, the closing of the city gates in Derry, withstanding the siege and the breaking of the boom on the River Foyle. These are discussed further, especially in chapters 2 and 3 below.
21   See James Joyce, *Ulysses*, 1922, London: Bodley Head, new ed 1960, 5th imprint, 1966, p 42. Mr Deasy's view contrasts with the Joycean sense of history as nightmare which it is the artist's goal to transcend by aesthetic means.
22   Don Cupitt, *The Long-Legged Fly*, p 163.
23   *Ibid.*, p 163.
24   John Milton, *Paradise Lost*, Book 1, ll. 25–26, in *John Milton: Complete Poetry and Selected Prose*, edited by E.H. Visiak, p 79.
25   Calvin, *op. cit.*, Vol 2, Bk 3, ch 10, sect 1, p 32.
26   *Ibid.*, Vol 2, Bk 3, ch 19, sect 9, p 136.
27   Van Til, *op. cit.*, pp 99–100.
28   Calvin, *op. cit.*, Vol 2, Bk 3, ch 19, sect 14, p 140.
29   *Ibid.*, Vol 2, Bk 3, ch 19, sect 15, p 140.
30   Owen Chadwick quotes John Knox's view of Geneva as 'the most perfect school of Christ that ever was on earth since the days of the Apostles' in *The Reformation*, p 91.
31   Calvin, *op. cit.*, Vol 2, Bk 4, ch 10, sect 5, pp 416–417.
32   *Ibid.*, Vol 2, Bk 4, ch 20, sect 3, p 653.
33   *Ibid.*, Vol 2, Bk 4, ch 20, sect 6, p 655.
34   Van Til, *op. cit.*, p 95.
35   Calvin, *op. cit.*, Vol 2, Bk 4, ch 20, sect 22, p 668.
36   *Ibid.*, Vol 2, Bk 4, ch 20, sect 27, p 672.
37   *Ibid.*, Vol 2, Bk 3, ch 21, sect 5, p 206.
38   See especially *ibid.*, Vol 2, Bk 3, ch 23, sects 6–8, pp 230–233.
39   G.R. Elton, *Reformation Europe 1517–1559*, p 236.
40   G.R. Potter, 'Zwingli and Calvin' in Joel Hurstfield (ed), *The Reformation Crisis*, p 42.
41   Ian McBride, *The Siege of Derry in Ulster Protestant Mythology*, pp 12–13.
42   McBride's book examines the shifting ways in which the siege of Derry has been 'remembered, commemorated, and interpreted over the last three centuries . . .' *ibid.*, p 13. The significance of the siege is considered further in chapters 2 and 3.
43   Elton, *op. cit.*, p 236.
44   Van Til, *op. cit.*, p 42. Harro Höpfl, *The Christian Polity of John Calvin*, p 37.
45   Höpfl, *ibid.*, p 75.
46   *Ibid.*, pp 212–216.
47   Anthony D. Buckley, 'The Chosen Few: Biblical Texts in the Regalia of an Ulster Secret Society', see 17 above.
48   D.W. Miller, *Queen's Rebels: Ulster Loyalism in Historical Perspective*, p 119.
49   Abraham Kuyper, *Calvinism*, p 206.
50   Van Til, *op. cit.*, p 26.
51   Kuyper, *op. cit.*, p 202.
52   *Ibid.*, p 245.
53   Van Til, *op. cit.*, p 34.
54   *Ibid.*, pp 60–61.

55 *Ibid.*, p 61.
56 Sallie McFague, *Metaphorical Language: Models of God in Religious Language*,
    p 13. Interestingly, Kuyper, too, makes the same point, commenting that Calvinism
    is a more highly evolved form of religion than Roman Catholicism because it has
    graduated from the symbolical to the 'clearly-conscious'. He continues: 'The purely
    spiritual breaks through the nebula of the symbolical.' *op. cit.*, pp 196–197.
57 Paul Tillich, *Theology of Culture*, p 68.
58 Kuyper, *op. cit.*, p 198.
59 Van Til, *op. cit.*, p 62.
60 See James Joyce, *A Portrait of the Artist as a Young Man*, p 240. At the time when
    Joyce was writing, it was accepted that the priest was God-like at the moment of the
    consecration of the elements, rather than the mediator through whom transubstantiation
    occurred, which represents a more modern understanding. Thus Joyce has Stephen
    claiming the God-like power of the priest for the artist in what he does with the bread
    and wine of life.
61 The phrase is cited by Van Til, *op. cit.*, p 129. Also see Kuyper, *op. cit.*, pp 26–28
    and p 225.
62 Kuyper, *ibid.*, p 141.
63 Van Til, *op. cit.*, pp 129–130.
64 Kuyper, *op. cit.*, p 216.
65 *Ibid.*, p 209.
66 *Ibid.*, p 31.
67 Desmond Bowen quotes sources which estimate that at least 200,000 Presbyterians
    (out of a total community of 400,000–600,000) left Ulster between 1700 and 1776,
    with up to 6,000 per year entering the American colonies just prior to the War of
    Independence. See Desmond Bowen, *History and Shaping of Irish Protestantism*,
    p 466 and p 636.
68 Donald Davie, *A Gathered Church*, p 3.

CHAPTER TWO

1 David Hempton, *Religion and Political Culture in Britain and Ireland*, p 93.
   Hempton comments that in the seventeenth century, no European country, with the
   possible exception of Bohemia, underwent a comparable shift of population or
   religious composition and points out that while Catholics owned about 80% of the
   land in 1600, by 1700 this had slumped to 14% and was still falling.
2 Desmond Bowen, *History and the Shaping of Irish Protestantism*, p 69.
3 *Ibid.*, p 78.
4 It should also be noted that Calvinism in Ireland has itself been subject to a variety
   of influences that have affected or modified it. Thus while Knox's Scottish Calvinism
   is obviously important, English Calvinism also played its part as has already been
   indicated. At different stages in its subsequent history, the Irish church experienced
   the influence of European religious groups such as the Huguenots, Moravians, and
   Palatines, as well as of North American Protestantism, which was often deeply
   conservative and the conversionist theology of the Methodists and Baptists from the
   eighteenth century onwards. The fissile tendency of Calvinism is fully reflected in the
   internal arguments and divisions within Irish Presbyterianism. This chapter highlights a number of these disputes to illustrate the complex history of Protestantism
   in Ulster and its inseparability from the wider cultural inheritance and attitudes of
   the Protestant community.
5 John Dunlop, *A Precarious Belonging: Presbyterians and the Conflict in Ireland*,
   op. cit., p 17.
6 Bowen, p 66.
7 A contemporary church historian, Finlay Holmes, locates the formal origins of
   modern Irish Presbyterianism in 1642 when the first Presbytery was organised, but
   he readily acknowledges that there were Presbyterians in Ireland before then. See
   Finlay Holmes, *Our Irish Presbyterian Heritage*, p 3.

8   J.S. Reid, *The History of the Presbyterian Church in Ireland*, Vol 1, p 119.

9   Bowen, *op. cit.*, p 87.

10   Reid, *op. cit.*, Vol 1, pp 271–272.

11   Bowen, *op. cit.*, p 91. See also p 101 where, referring to the men who founded the Carrickfergus Presbytery, he quotes from G.B. Henderson, *Religious Life in Seventeenth-Century Scotland* (1937), as follows: 'The Covenanters stood for Reformation (against Rome), Calvinism (against Arminianism), Presbyterianism (against prelacy), Scottish independence (against English interference), and Puritanism in morals, art and everything (against the Devil).'

12   Reid, *op. cit.*, Vol 2, p 44.

13   All references are to the *Westminster Confession of Faith*, 1646, republished Glasgow: Free Presbyterian Publications, 1994. The numbers refer to the chapter and paragraph. The volume also contains *The Larger and Shorter Catechisms*, The National Covenant, The Solemn League and Covenant, and other significant documents.

14   Peter Brooke, *Ulster Presbyterianism: The Historical Perspective 1610–1970*, p 175.

15   See R.F.G. Holmes, pp 72–73 for elaboration of these points. He observes:
       So the great enterprise of Christian preaching, teaching and the enforcement of discipline, the great characteristic of the life of the reformed churches, 'the very sinews of religion' as Calvin described it, went forward in Ireland. (p 73)

16   This point is made by John Thompson in 'The Westminster Confession of Faith', an essay included in *Challenge and Conflict: Essays in Presbyterian History and Doctrine*, p 15.

17   *Ibid.*, p 14.

18   I am grateful to Lindsay Green, an elder in the Irish Presbyterian Church, for clarification of this point. It is worth noting, however, that the notion of the Pope as the AntiChrist remained prominent for a long time within Presbyterianism. Thus, W.D. Killen attacks the Pope and Catholicism in precisely the terms of the *Westminster Confession* in his *Reminiscences of a Long Life*, pp 204–218. Killen was Professor of Church History, Church Government and Pastoral Theology and completed the final volume of Reid's *The History of the Presbyterian Church in Ireland* after the latter's death.

19   For the case of Hunter against Davey, see R.F.G. Holmes, *op. cit.*, pp 153–156. In *Persecuting Zeal: A Portrait of Ian Paisley*, Dennis Cooke cites Paisley's declaration that 'The whole ecclesiastical setup of Protestantism has become corrupted, has become de-Protestantised, has become apostate' (p 69).

20   Reid records that in 1653 there were only about six Presbyterian ministers in Ulster, whereas by 1660 there were over seventy, organised in eighty parishes with a total membership of over 100,000. He observes:
       It was during this period that Presbyterianism struck its roots so deeply and extensively throughout the province, as to enable it to endure in safety the subsequent storms of persecution and to stand erect and flourishing, while all the while the other contemporary scions of dissent were broken down and prostrated in the dust. (*op. cit.*, Vol 2, p 337.)

21   Reid, *ibid.*, Vol 2, pp 349–351.

22   D.W. Miller, *Queen's Rebels: Ulster Loyalism in Historical Perspective*, p 83.

23   Anthony D. Buckley has described the story of the siege of Derry and its relief as 'a cultural landmark, a point of orientation for all who inhabit the society', and he goes on to use the metaphor of the siege to express the complex sense of threat and persecution felt by beleaguered Ulster Protestants. See 'Walls Within Walls: Religion and "Rough" Behaviour in an Ulster Community', *Sociology*, Vol 18, No 1, Feb 1984, pp 19–32.

24   Reid, *op. cit.*, Vol 2, p 440. The historian, A.T.Q. Stewart, puts a rather different gloss on these events, questioning what really happened at Derry, denying that the closing of the gates was a sign of loyalty to William and interpreting it as a simple act of self-preservation – a view he supports by quoting from a contemporary historian of the siege. See A.T.Q. Stewart, *The Narrow Ground*, pp 63–66.

25   Reid, *op. cit.*, Vol 2, p 471.

26   It is notable that Reid's exaltation of the significance of the siege of Derry was complemented by the account in an almost exactly contemporary work – Macaulay's

hugely successful *History of England from the Accession of James II* (1848–1855). In it, it has been claimed, he 'gave Ulster Protestants a central place in the myth of the unfolding British, and the book is still quoted by Unionists to show Ulster's importance in the struggle for civil and religious liberty, for representative institutions and ultimately for democracy itself.' (Ian Mc Bride, *The Siege of Derry in Ulster Protestant Mythology*, p 60).

27 *Ibid.*, p 77.

28 Reid, *op. cit.*, Vol 2, p 427 and p 480.

29 Commenting on King William's demise, Reid observes:
> No heavier blow could have fallen upon the cause of toleration, and the interests of the Presbyterian Church in Ireland, than the death of this truly great man. Reid, *ibid.*, Vol 3, 1853, p 84.

William King was the son of a Presbyterian who fled from Scotland after refusing to subscribe to the *Solemn League and Covenant*, and had himself suffered hardship and imprisonment under James II. Thus, this Church of Ireland cleric had no love for either Presbyterians or Catholics. However, although he had no hesitation in provoking the former by claiming that the Church of Ireland followed more closely the pattern of religious life implicit in scripture, he also wanted solidarity with them against Catholicism. See Bowen, pp 121–136.

30 McBride, *op. cit.*, p 25.

31 Reid, *op. cit.*, Vol 3, pp 236–237.

32 Marianne Elliott has written:
> The association of popery and prelacy with excessive authoritarianism was . . . at the heart of early Presbyterianism and explains the intensely anti-papal language of the *Westminster Confession of Faith* which still causes considerable embarrassment to the Presbyterian General Assembly. But the *Westminster Confession* also embodied that central Calvinistic belief in a direct communion between God and man and it expressed the need to purify protestantism from the kind of absolute obedience, by which it felt Roman Catholicism and Judaism shackled men's minds. Christ had purchased liberty for believers, delivering them from sin, giving them free access to God and destroying 'slavish fear'. Above all he had freed men from doctrines and commandments contrary to his word: 'so that, to believe such doctrines, or to obey such commands, out of conscience, is to betray true liberty of conscience: and the requiring of an implicit faith, and an absolute and blind obedience, is to destroy liberty of conscience, and reason also.'

Watchmen in Sion: The Protestant Ideal of Liberty, p 8. This articulates clearly the dilemma that existed when a document designed to define individual freedom in matters of faith assumed a dogmatic and imposing quality of its own.

33 Reid, *op. cit.*, Vol 3, p 270. In his essay, 'A Theological Interpretation of the First Subscription Controversy (1719–1728)', Revd Dr A.W. Godfrey Brown set out in some detail the issues at stake in the argument, and while these need not detain us here, the overriding point of relevance is that it was essentially a dispute about liberty of conscience and the absolute value of individual conscience. Significantly, too, many of the most capable opponents of subscription were men who had travelled widely and studied under teachers who were influenced by newer modes of thought, increasing secularism, and eighteenth-century optimism about human potential. This essay is included in *Challenge and Conflict: Essays in Irish Presbyterian History and Doctrine.*

34 See Reid, *op. cit.*, Vol 3, pp 376–377.

35 *Ibid.*, Vol 3, p 393.

36 *Ibid.*

37 Cited in R.F. Stalley, 'Admiring the Lovely Action' in Francis Hutcheson, a supplement to *Fortnight*, No 308, July 1992, p 11.

38 John M. Barkley, *Blackmouth and Dissenter*, p 10.

39 David Hempton, *op. cit.*, p 96.

40 *Ibid.*

41 Reid, *op. cit.*, Vol 3, p 486.

42 See R.F.G. Holmes, *op. cit.*, p 86, and D.W. Miller, 'Presbyterianism and "Modernization" in Ulster', *Past and Present*, No 80, 1978, pp 77–84.

43   Reid, *op. cit.*, Vol 3, p 509.
44   Elliott, *op. cit.*, p 9.
45   Holmes, *op. cit.*, p 90.
46   *Ibid.*, p 97
47   This point is raised by R Finlay Holmes in *Henry Cooke*, p 5
48   John M. Barkley, 'Presbyterian Ministers in the Eighteenth Century' in *Challenge and Conflict: Essays in Irish Presbyterian History and Doctrine*, p 48.
49   See Sean Connolly, *Religion and Society in Nineteenth-Century Ireland*, p 15.
50   See Bowen, *op. cit.*, p 476, where the point is made that the Moravians had 30–40 itinerant preachers active in Ulster by the mid-eighteenth century, while John Wesley paid twenty-one visits to the province, where by 1770 almost half the Methodist missions in Ireland were operative.
51   Ivan Herbison, 'Language, Literature and Cultural Identity: An Ulster-Scots Perspective' in Jean Lundy and Aodán Mac Póilin (eds), *Styles of Belonging: The Cultural Identities of Ulster*, p 59.
52   *Ibid.*, pp 58–59. Herbison draws in part on work done by John Hewitt in his *Rhyming Weavers and other country poets of Antrim and Down* (1974). See also J.R.R. Adams, *The Printed Word and the Common Man: Popular Culture in Ulster 1700–1900* (1987).
53   Barkley, *op. cit.*, p 19.
54   Stewart, *op. cit.*, p 47.
55   This point has been argued in some detail by Peter Brooke, *op. cit.*, p 120. Brooke sees this as having had a weakening effect upon the position of Presbyterians in the long run.
56   Reid, *op. cit.*, Vol 3, p 543.
57   The account of the debate between Montgomery and Cooke at the Synod held on 30 June 1829, given in Reid's history, shows clearly how the occasion was viewed by a contemporary who was present:
     . . . the Synod of Ulster witnessed a display of eloquence which would have been pronounced magnificent, had it occurred even in the most illustrious assembly in the empire. Mr Montgomery had evidently summoned all his strength for the occasion; and, as if anticipating his speedy secession, seemed resolved to make his last appearance in the synod memorable, by the infliction of a fatal wound on the reputation of his great ecclesiastical antagonist.
     After speaking for nearly three hours in support of the appointment of Revd Ferné as Professor of Moral Philosophy at the Belfast Academical Institution, the synod broke for half an hour for lunch, after which:
     . . . Mr Cooke entered forthwith on his defence; and though his reply was obviously altogether unpremeditated, never did the representative of a great cause acquit himself on a great occasion, more to the satisfaction of his party.
     Cooke, 'the Goliath of orthodoxy', spoke for two hours. *ibid.*, Vol 3, pp 562–564.
58   *Ibid.*, Vol 3, p 589. Finlay Holmes, too, affirms that the union with the Seceders gave a new evangelical energy to the Presbyterian Church, *Henry Cooke*, pp 102–103.
59   Holmes, *ibid.*, p 52.
60   *Ibid.*, p 100.
61   For example, Desmond Bowen quotes from Revd Thomas Drew, Grand Chaplain of the Orange Order, who told Ulster Protestants in 1852:
     You possess your churches and your meeting-houses, and your churchyards only until popery has gained sufficient power to nail up the one and to rob you of the other.
     Desmond Bowen, *The Protestant Crusade in Ireland 1800–1870*, p 289. Elsewhere W.D. Killen devotes two chapters (xxv and xxvi) of his autobiography to deeply critical and largely hostile comments on the Pope, the Catholic priesthood and Catholic worship, and the general moral and personal standards of the Catholic laity. Killen was ordained in 1829 and ministered for over seventy years. See *Reminiscences of a Long Life*.
62   David Hempton and Myrtle Hill, *Evangelical Protestantism in Ulster Society 1740–1890*, p 61.
63   *Ibid.*, p 73.

64 Holmes, *op. cit.*, p 125.
65 David Hempton writes that evangelicalism 'imbued the Ulster Protestant community with a sense of divine approval in its continued resistance to assimilation into the wider Irish culture, in which the Roman Catholic religion was regarded as the most central and most pernicious element.' See R*eligion and Political Culture in Britain and Ireland*, p 101.
66 Quoted by Holmes, *op. cit.*, p 115.
67 *Ibid.*, pp 116–117. Elsewhere Holmes has shown that Castlereagh, who was an Ulsterman and a baptised Presbyterian, had actively involved himself in discouraging the kind of republican radicalism associated with Presbyterians like William Drennan in the late eighteenth century by modifying the basis on which the regium donum was disbursed and linking it to an oath of loyalty taken by ministers before they received it. He also suggests that this may have influenced Cooke's views on unionism. See Revd Professor R.F.G. Holmes, 'Controversy and Schism in the Synod of Ulster in the 1820s' in *Challenge and Conflict: Essays in Irish Presbyterian History and Doctrine*, pp 124–125.
68 Holmes, *Henry Cooke*, p 120.
69 *Ibid.*, p 208.
70 Bowen, *History and the Shaping of Irish Protestantism*, p 490.
71 W.D. Killen, *op. cit.*, p 64. Not all Presbyterian commentators felt equal enthusiasm for the Revival, however, as the title of Isaac Nelson's *Year of Delusion* (1860), written in response to Gibson's *Year of Grace* makes plain. Other sceptical responses include W. Hamilton, *An Inquiry into the Scriptural Character of the Revival of 1859* (1886), and T. MacNeece, *Words of Caution and Counsel on the Present Religious Revival Addressed to his Parishioners* (1859) – see Hempton and Hill, *op. cit.*, p 153. A more positive view of the Revival is given by Thomas Witherow in his *Autobiography*, p 95 and p 97.
72 Robert G. Crawford, *Loyal to King Billy: A Portrait of the Ulster Protestants*, p 52.
73 Stewart J. Brown, 'Presbyterian Communities, Transatlantic Visions and the Ulster Revival of 1859', in J.P. Mackey (ed), *The Cultures of Europe: The Irish Contribution*, p 99.
74 D.W. Miller, *Queen's Rebels: Ulster Loyalism in Historical Perspective*, pp 84–86.
75 Norman Vance, *Irish Literature: A Social History*, p 35. One might add to this that millenarian prophecies were prominent during the period of the United Irishmen in the 1790s. See Sean Connolly, p 44.
76 Hempton and Hill, *op. cit.*, pp 148–149. They conclude:
    The revival was not a catalyst for change, but a kind of mid-century stepping-stone reflecting the consolidation of earlier evangelical enthusiasm. Its importance lies in the boost it gave to Protestant confidence, and its articulation of values perceived as central to the prosperity and unity of the province. (p 160).
77 Stewart J. Brown, *op. cit.*, pp 103–104. In the period prior to 1859, church attendance had begun to drop, public houses and shops were open on Sundays, and prostitution and the incidence of unmarried couples living together had increased, according to John T. Carson in *God's River in Spate: The Story of the Religious Awakening of Ulster in 1859*. Carson declares that:
    The whole movement brought to Ulster character a strength of conviction and a resoluteness of purpose, as well as a sense of Divine authority and of human responsibility. (p 93)
    The impact of the 1859 revival on Ellen Harrison, John Hewitt's maternal grandmother (and its failure to touch his great-grandfather) are recorded in the sonnet, 'Year of Grace and My Great-Grandmother'. See *The Collected Poems of John Hewitt*, p 259.
78 D.W. Miller, *op. cit.*, p 85. See also Bowen, *op. cit.*, p 490, where he asserts that 'An immediate consequence of the revival was the reinforcement it gave to the popular anti-Catholic preachers of the time like Hugh Hanna, Tommy Toye or Thomas Drew in Belfast.'
79 Holmes, *Our Presbyterian Heritage*, p 123. Holmes also quotes from J.E. Davey's *The Story of a Hundred Years* (1940) to reinforce the same point.

80   See Miller, *op. cit.*, pp 119–121.
81   Hempton and Hill, *op. cit.*, p xii.
82   Bowen, *op. cit.*, p 490.
83   Barkley, *op. cit.*, pp 151–152. Barkley shows how, in 1893, in the General Assembly 304 voted against Home Rule and 11 in favour – but 341 abstained. In 1913, 921 voted against, and 43 in favour of Home Rule.
84   The biography is W.S. Armour, *Armour of Ballymoney* (1934). The heroic status the author accords to his father is questioned in J.R.B. McMinn, *Against the Tide: A Calendar of the Papers of Revd J.B. Armour, Irish Presbyterian Minister and Home Ruler 1869–1914* (1985).
85   Armour, *op. cit.*, p 104. Quoted from Armour's speech to the General Assembly on 15 March 1893.
86   *Ibid.*, p 320 and pp 322–323.
87   Barkley, *op. cit.*, p 152.
88   Terence P. McCaughey, *Memory and Redemption: Church, Politics and Prophetic Theology in Ireland*, p 133.
89   Holmes, *op. cit.*, pp 152–153.
90   Barkley, *op. cit.*, p 147, considers that Paisleyism influenced the decisions of the Presbyterian Church to withdraw from the World Council of Churches, the Tripartite Talks with Methodists and the Church of Ireland, and the Council of Churches in Britain and Ireland. In his 'portrait' of Ian Paisley, *Persecuting Zeal* (p 89), Dennis Cooke inclines to the same conclusion. More positive evidence of attempts at constructive relationships are mentioned in Josiah Horton Beeman and Robert Mahony, 'The Institutional Churches and the Process of Reconciliation in Northern Ireland: Recent Progress in Presbyterian-Roman Catholic Relations'. This essay appears in Dermot Keogh and Michael H. Haltzel (eds), *Northern Ireland and the Politics of Reconciliation*, pp 150–159, and see also John Dunlop, *op. cit.*, Finlay Holmes has also identified the Orange Order's hostility to Presbyterian involvement in the WCC as a significant pressure. He cites Reports of the Grand Lodge of Ireland half-yearly meeting in June 1966 which formulated resolutions against ecumenism and called for 'a return to the principles of the sixteen (sic) century.' See Finlay Holmes, *Presbyterianism and Orangeism 1795–1995*, p 9.
91   Reid, *op. cit.*, Vol 3, p 593.
92   Tom Paulin, 'Paisley's Progress' in *Ireland and the English Crisis*, p 157.
93   See Dennis Cooke, *op. cit.*, pp 80–81 on Paisley's selective use of Henry Cooke's views, which ignores the latter's recognition of Roman Catholic baptism and insistence on the need for cooperation between the various Protestant churches. William Johnston (1829–1902) was an evangelical member of the Church of Ireland, an Orangeman and a Unionist politician. He is remembered (and represented on Orange banners) for his campaign against the Party Processions Act in the 1860s, despite resistance to his efforts by members of the Grand Orange Lodge. Having run a commercially unsuccessful, but controversial, paper, the *Downshire Protestant* (1855–1862), advocating the doctrines of the Reformation and the principles of the 1688 Revolution, Johnston's attention was attracted to the case of eight mill workers charged under the Party Processions and Emblems Act with parading behind pipes and drums on their way home from work in Gilford in July 1863. After various unsuccessful attempts to win high level support from the Orange Order to resist the Act, on 12 July 1867, Johnston led a parade from Newtownards to Bangor and sent a memorial to the Prime Minister calling for a change in the law. He was subsequently prosecuted and gaoled for his actions, refusing all offers of compromise, and as a result achieving his legendary status. Hugh Hanna ministered in Berry Street and St Enoch's, Carlisle Circus, Belfast, and was one of the more virulent anti-Catholic preachers of his day, and one of the few Presbyterian ministers who was a member of the Orange Order. He helped William Johnston draft his address for the 1868 parliamentary election. Some of his most inflammatory preaching occurred during the 1886 riots over Gladstone's proposed Home Rule Act and Hanna acquired a reputation on the British mainland as the epitome of Protestant extremism. For a fuller account of Johnston's career, see Aiken McClelland, *William Johnston of Ballykilbeg* (1990).

94 This phrase is from a supporter of Paisley quoted in Ed Moloney and Andy Pollak, *Paisley*, p 2.
95 Moloney and Pollak argue that Paisleyism provides a mirror image of conservative Catholicism in many of its features – *ibid.*, p 256. The ruthless way in which Paisley has ousted individuals who have threatened his position or departed from his preferred way of doing things is recorded in various places in this book, and also by Dennis Cooke, who, in his last chapter questions the likelihood of a Paisley 'dynasty', pointing out that after Paisley himself no one is likely to command the dual roles of Moderator of the Free Presbyterian Church and leader of the DUP which have contributed greatly to his power and influence. See *op. cit.*, pp 216–224.
96 Ruth Fleischmann has observed that Paisley 'treats the Bible as though it were a recent account of life in Northern Ireland, figuring his colleagues, the prophets, and his Chosen People, the Loyalists', and she goes on to analyse an example of his expository rhetoric in which he merges quotation from and paraphrase of the *Book of Amos* with his own contemporary additions. See '"The Blood Our Fathers Spilt"': Rhetoric and Poetry' in Tjebbe A. Westendorp and Jane Mallinson (eds), *Politics and the Rhetoric of Poetry – Perspectives on Modern Anglo-Irish Poetry*, p 69.
97 John Hewitt, *op. cit.*, p 135.
98 Andy Pollak (ed) *A Citizens' Enquiry: The Opsahl Report on Northern Ireland*, pp 130, 195–196, 100–104. Dunlop's views have since been more fully elaborated in *A Precarious Belonging*.
99 *Presbyterian Principles and Political Witness in Northern Ireland*, p 10.
100 *Ibid.*, p 7.
101 *Ibid.*, p 12 and p 20.
102 Dunlop, *op. cit.*, pp 40–42 cites the full text.
103 *Ibid.*, pp 81–82.
104 Timothy Kinahan, *Where Do We Go From Here? Protestants and the Future of Northern Ireland*, p 50. In Romans ch 13, vv 1–2, Paul writes: 'Let every soul be subject unto the higher powers. For there is no power but of God: the powers that be are ordained of God. Whosoever therefore resisteth the power, resisteth the ordinance of God: and they that resist shall receive to themselves damnation.'

CHAPTER THREE

1 Dervala Murphy, *A Place Apart* (1978).
2 Thus John Dunlop writes:
> This culture has not produced many poets, authors or artists. It is a culture more interested in engineering than in art; more likely to rejoice in the launch of a ship than the production of a painting.
A Precarious Belonging, p 84.
3 Norman Vance begins an article, 'Presbyterian Culture and Revival', by observing:
> For some commentators the very idea of Presbyterian culture or imaginative life, in Ireland or elsewhere, seems almost a contradiction in terms.
The Bulletin of the Presbyterian Historical Society of Ireland, Vol 22, 1993, p 16. It is not a view which Vance himself supports.
4 John Wilson Foster records how in recent times he received an evangelistic tract linking the fate of the *Titanic* with a series of precise biblical texts and warnings, and urging the reader to accept Christ who, unlike the lifeboats on the ship, has room for all. See 'Imaging the *Titanic*' in Eve Patten (ed), *Returning to Ourselves*, p 334.
5 Terence Brown, *The Whole Protestant Community: The Making of a Historical Myth*, p 14.
6 Steve Bruce, 'Cultural Traditions: A Double-edged Sword?' in *Causeway*, Vol 1, No 4, Autumn 1994, pp 21–22.
7 Anthony D Buckley, '"We're Trying to Find Our Identity": Uses of History Among Ulster Protestants', in E. Tonkin, M. McDonald and M. Chapman (eds), *History and Ethnicity*, p 184.

8 Thus, for example, many individuals have been victimised, or worse, for having a relationship with a person from 'the other side'. St John Ervine's play, *Mixed Marriage* (see chapter 11), takes this as its subject.

9 Gearóid Ó Crualaoich, 'Responding to the Rising' in M. Ní Dhonnchadha and T. Dorgan (eds), *Revising the Rising*, p 65.

10 Brian Walker, '1641, 1689, 1690 And All That: The Unionist Sense of History' in *The Irish Review*, No 12, Spring/Summer 1992, pp 56–64. Belinda Loftus has also noted how the ceremony of burning an effigy of Lundy became increasingly bitter and sectarian during the nineteenth century as Catholics gained political and religious freedoms. See *Mirrors: Orange and Green*, p 35. For a fuller discussion of the changing significance of the siege of Derry, see also Ian McBride, *The Siege of Derry in Ulster Protestant Mythology* (1997).

11 Dominic Bryan, 'Interpreting the Twelfth', in *History Ireland*, Summer 1994, pp 37–41.

12 'And I saw heaven opened, and behold a white horse; and he that sat upon him was called Faithful and True, and in righteousness he did judge and make war.' Revelation, ch 19, v 11.

13 Belinda Loftus, *Mirrors: William III and Mother Ireland*, p 38. Although on Orange banners and murals William is always represented crossing the Boyne on a white horse, this itself is a piece of myth-making – in fact, he rode a chestnut mount and is depicted as doing so in the large tapestry that hangs in the former House of Lords (now part of the Bank of Ireland) in College Green, Dublin.

14 This question has not only exercised Irish historians and anthropologists, but has been dealt with by playwrights such as Stewart Parker (*Northern Star*, 1984), Frank McGuinness (*Observe the Sons of Ulster Marching Towards the Somme*, 1986), Brian Friel (*Making History*, 1988), as well as by numerous poets including Brendan Kennelly, Eavan Boland, Paul Durcan, Tom Paulin, and John Hewitt. See also Edna Longley's essay, 'The Rising, the Somme and Irish Memory', included in *The Living Stream* (1994).

15 This is explored in A.D. Buckley's 'Walls Within Walls: Religion and "Rough" Behaviour in an Ulster Community', *Sociology*, Vol 18, No 1, 1984, pp 19–32. See also John Fulton, *The Tragedy of Belief: Division, Politics and Religion in Ireland*, pp 122–125.

16 D.W. Miller, *Queen's Rebels: Ulster Loyalism in Historical Perspective*, p 118.

17 George Boyce, 'Ireland in the First World War' in *History Ireland*, Autumn 1994, p 48.

18 Philip Orr, *The Road to the Somme*, p 45.

19 Thomas Carnduff, *Poverty Street and Other Belfast Poems*, p 42.

20 Boyce, op. cit., p 51.

21 Frank McGuinness, *Observe the Sons of Ulster Marching Towards the Somme*, pp 79–80. It is interesting that the author is an Ulsterman, but from a Donegal Catholic background.

22 James Loughlin, *Ulster Unionism and British National Identity since 1885*, also demonstrates how these altered perceptions reflect the changed attitudes and values in Britain itself, especially in the period since World War II.

23 Arthur Aughey, 'The Idea of the Union' in John Wilson Foster (ed), *The Idea of the Union*, p 8.

24 A Pollak (ed), *A Citizens' Inquiry: The Opsahl Report on Northern Ireland*, p 37. See also John Dunlop, *op. cit.*, p 84 and pp 99–100 where he observes that for Presbyterians:

> . . . the meaning of a document is the sum total of the words used. If they want to understand it, they don't ask what it is getting at, they don't look for spaces, they delve into the meaning of the words.

The author was also one of the Presbyterian representatives to the Opsahl Commission.

25 John Wilson Foster, 'The Declaration and the Union' in Foster (ed), *op. cit.*, pp 102–103.

26 John Wilson Foster, 'The Task of the Unionists', *ibid.*, p 72.

27 Ó Crualaoich, *op. cit.*, p 65.

28 Recalling his boyhood, Robert Johnstone captures the spirit of this motivation vividly:
    Everything about the Twelfth has to be bigger than life – larger than reality
    perhaps; the numbers in the procession, the crowds, the music, the excitement.
    The very movements of the participants might be designed to make him look
    bigger and broader-shouldered than they are. It was as if we have to convince
    ourselves that the Protestants are stronger and more numerous than they feel
    themselves to be.
    See Robert Johnstone and Bill Kirk, *Images of Belfast*, p 21. This issue also arises in
    the discussion of Christina Reid's play, *Tea in a China Cup* in chapter 11.

29 Terence McCaughey, *Memory and Redemption: Church, Politics and Prophetic
    Theology in Ireland*, p 20.

30 Loughlin, *op. cit.*, deals in detail with this issue.

31 Arthur Aughey, 'The Constitutional Challenge' in Foster (ed), *op. cit.*, p 52.

32 Harold McCusker, in his speech to the House of Commons on 27 November 1985,
    cited in *The Field Day Anthology of Irish Writing*, Vol 3, p 372.

33 Lord Carson, in his speech to the House of Lords on 14 December 1921, cited in
    Ibid., Vol 3, p 354.

34 John Fulton, *op. cit.*, pp 104–105. Foster provides another angle on this in describing
    the personal feeling of alienation he has felt in the Irish Republic: 'One of the most
    sacred spots in the South of Ireland is the Easter Rising room in the National
    Museum: I stand in it and feel utterly estranged, as I do if I stand in a Roman
    Catholic church: both are mighty formidable spaces, but they exclude me and
    moreover wish to exclude me.' See 'Why I Am a Unionist' in *op. cit.*, p 61.

35 See, for example, Loughlin, *op. cit.*, p 146, p 152, p 166.

36 Steve Bruce, *The Edge of the Union: The Ulster Loyalist Political Vision*, see p 30.

37 David Trimble, from the text of an untitled speech included in M Crozier (ed),
    Cultural Traditions in Northern Ireland, p 50. The reference to 'fear of massacre'
    is presumably an allusion to folk memories of atrocities associated with the Catholic
    rebellion of 1641 (see chapter 2). The survival of this kind of memory is also evident
    in John Hewitt's play, *The Bloody Brae*, discussed in chapter 6.

38 Gerald Dawe, 'The Sound of the Shuttle' in *A Life Elsewhere*, p 66.

39 See, for instance, Pilib Mistéil (ed), *The Irish Language and the Unionist Tradition*,
    (1994). For fuller accounts, see also Pádraig Ó Snodaigh, *Hidden Ulster: Protestants
    and the Irish Language* (1995) and Roger Blaney, *Presbyterians and the Irish
    Language* (1996).

40 *Beyond the Fife and Drum*, p 10.

41 Ian Adamson, *The Cruthin: The Ancient Kindred*, p 15. His thesis shares ideas also
    propagated by the British Israelites. Adamson followed this volume with *The Identity
    of Ulster* (1982) and *The Ulster People* (1991) in which he pursues his ideas further.
    It is interesting to note that at another crucial juncture for Irish Protestantism, in the
    period prior to the disestablishment of the Church of Ireland, when Cardinal Cullen
    argued that the episcopalian church was not Irish at all but imposed on the people
    and maintained by force, Church of Ireland apologists replied by insisting that *their*
    church, rather than Cullen's, derived from St Patrick, who, they claimed, had no
    commission from Pope Celestine. As in Adamson's case, the objective appears in part
    to have been aimed at outflanking the opposition's case by asserting an even longer
    indigenous history. See Desmond Bowen, *History and the Shaping of Irish
    Protestantism*, pp 307–308.

42 *Ibid.*, pp 41–42.

43 McCaughey, *op. cit.*, p 42,

44 Anthony D. Buckley, 'The Chosen Few: Biblical Texts in the Regalia of an Ulster
    Secret Society', *Folk Life*, Vol 24, pt 19, 1985–1986, p 21.

45 *Ibid.*, p 23. The idea of the association between Ulster Protestants and the Children
    of Israel is also taken up by Very Revd Dr A.A. Fulton, who writes:
    In relation to the 'native' Irish [the Presbyterian planters] saw themselves, or
    many of their descendants did, as being like the Israelites fighting their way into
    Canaan to possess the promised land. They must needs keep a watchful eye for
    the movements of the enemy, whose swamps they drained and whose forests they
    felled. The Ulster-Israelite mythology evolved survives in the Old Testament

scenes depicted on many of the gorgeous Orange banners carried on 12 July each year, and in the minds of those who march under them.
'Church in Tension – in the Twentieth Century – Mainly' in *Challenge and Conflict: Essays in Irish Presbyterian History and Doctrine*, pp 150–151.

46   For a discussion of this, see Dominic Bryan, *op. cit.*, pp 37–41.

47   This point is noted by Terence McCaughey, *op. cit.*, p 23. He, too, offers a discussion of images and texts commonly found on Orange banners which complements Buckley's work, but he also shows how Orange songs and many Protestant sermons exploit the allegorical possibilities of the Old Testament. See especially pp 23–25. Belinda Loftus makes yet another examination of and commentary on Orange regalia, banners and sashes in *Mirrors: Orange and Green*.

48   In the 1990s, the demand of the Portadown Orangemen to walk down the Garvaghy Road, where there is a large Catholic housing estate, on their way back from a service at Drumcree parish church has become a *locus classicus* in this respect.

49   Edna Longley, *op. cit.*, p 75.

50   Women did play an important role in support of Unionism during the Home Rule crisis. Diane Urquhart has shown that the Ulster Women's Unionist Council organised petitions against the Ne Temere Decree and opposing Home Rule in 1912. They were sending up to 10,000 leaflets and newspapers per week to Britain and elsewhere arguing against Home Rule and raised funds and trained nurses, drivers and signallers to back up the UVF. While men only were permitted to sign the Solemn League and Covenant, a greater number of women signed the supporting declaration. However, all these were activities in support of the men, rather than as principals and leaders, and the UWUC was generally unsympathetic to the contemporary campaign for female suffrage. See Diane Urquhart, '"The Female of the Species is more Deadlier than the Male"? The Ulster Women's Unionist Council' in Janice Holmes and Diane Urquhart (eds), *Coming into the Light: The Work, Politics and Religion of Women in Ulster 1840–1940*, pp 99–102.

51   F.S.L. Lyons, commenting on the stark contrasts visible in Orange parades, observed:
       Here, in formidable juxtaposition, were the immobility and dynamism of the Protestant culture, the mingling of resolution and hysteria.
       Culture and Anarchy in Ireland 1890–1939, p 137.

52   One might relate this to a point made by Terence McCaughey in his discussion of the Calvinist doctrine of double predestination and the way in which this became politicised to provide justification both for the elect/Protestant occupation of land formerly held by Catholics, and also for the abandonment of any attempt to convert them. See McCaughey, *op. cit.*, p 28. See also Bill Rolston's article, 'Contemporary Political Wall Murals in the North of Ireland: "Drawing Support"', which examines the motives of both Loyalist and Republican mural painters. He discusses how, after partition, the symbols of Unionism became identified with the state itself, thereby intensifying Nationalist feelings of exclusion, and how the Twelfth of July celebrations became an important mechanism for reinforcing the sense of a divided community in which one faction possessed authority and rights at the expense of the other. *Eire-Ireland*, Vol xxiii, No 3, Fall 1988, pp 3–18.

53   Edna Longley, *op. cit.*, p 76.

54   Belinda Loftus, *op. cit.*, p 109. For her discussion of the influence of Orange emblems on Protestant artists, see especially pp 45–46.

55   Ivan Herbison, 'Language, Literature and Cultural Identity: An Ulster-Scots Perspective' in J. Lundy and A. Mac Póilin (eds), *Styles of Belonging: The Cultural Identities of Ulster*, p 62.

56   Donald Davie, *A Gathered Church: The Literature of the English Dissenting Interest 1700–1930*, p 2.

57   Tom Paulin, 'Northern Protestant Oratory and Writing 1791–1985' in the *Field Day Anthology of Irish Writing*, Vol 3, p 318.

58   Examples of such writers and their work are treated in detail in the later chapters of this study.

59   H. Montgomery, 'Letter to Henry Cooke' (1829), reprinted in *ibid.*, Vol 3, p 340.

60   H. Montgomery, 'The Cookstown Speech' (1828), *ibid.*, Vol 3, p 338 and p 339.

61   The phrase is Tom Paulin's. See *ibid.*, p 317. Cooke's 'Hillsborough Speech' (1834) exemplifies his rhetoric. See *ibid.*, pp 348–349.

62   *Beyond the Fife and Drum*, p 9.
63   Marianne Elliott, *Watchmen of Sion: The Protestant Idea of Liberty*, p 22.
64   Thomas Kilroy, 'Secularised Ireland' in E. Longley (ed), *Culture in Ireland: Division or Diversity*, p 136.
65   Edna Longley, 'Writing, Revisionism and Grass-seed: Literary Mythologies in Ireland' in J. Lundy and A. Mac Póilin (eds) *op. cit.*, p 15.
66   Joe McMinn, 'Language, Literature and Cultural Identity: Irish and Anglo-Irish', in *ibid.*, p 47.
67   Gerald Dawe, 'Telling a Story: on "Region" and "Nation"' in *op. cit.*, p 90.
68   Gerald Dawe, 'The Sound of the Shuttle' in *ibid.*, p 65. See also p 66.
69   Gerald Dawe and Edna Longley (eds), *Across a Roaring Hill*, p iii. John Wilson Foster approaches the same point by asking:
     . . . to what extent is an Ulster Protestant an Ulster Protestant because he is not an Ulster Catholic of whom he is nevertheless incessantly conscious?
     See 'The Critical Condition of Ulster' in *Colonial Consequences*, p 225.

CHAPTER FOUR

1   Gerald Dawe, *The Rest is History*, pp 23–24. On pp 12–21 of this book Dawe conveys more of his own compelling sense of Belfast as a place.
2   Linda H. Peterson, 'Gender and Autobiographical Form: The Case of the Spiritual Autobiography', in James Olney (ed), *Studies in Autobiography*, p 213; and Declan Kiberd, *Inventing Ireland*, p 428.
3   Robert Lynd, *Home Life in Ireland*, p 152.
4   *Ibid.*, p 151.
5   Robert Greacen, *Even Without Irene*, p 38.
6   George A. Birmingham, *An Irishman Looks at his World*, p 38. A similar connection between Protestantism, economics and the Empire is found in Shan Bullock's *After Sixty Years* (1931) where he recalls his father's account of the differences between Protestants and Catholics. The former are described as materialistic, respectable, proud, law-abiding and solemn: 'What you and I strive after, money, power, all the rest, means little to him [i.e. the Catholic], and the majesty and dominion of the British Empire never stirs his head' (see pp 126–127).
7   Thomas Carnduff, *Life and Writings* (John Gray, ed), pp 75–76.
8   George A. Birmingham, *Pleasant Places*, p 4.
9   Birmingham, *An Irishman Looks at his World*, p 260 and p 263.
10 *Ibid.*, p 266.
11 Denis Ireland, *From the Jungle of Belfast*, p 28.
12 Lynd, *op. cit.*, p 186.
13 *Ibid.*, p 152.
14 Birmingham, *op. cit.*, p 92.
15 *Ibid.*, p 97.
16 Lynd, *op. cit.*, p 156.
17 *Ibid.*, p 164.
18 Birmingham, *Pleasant Places*, p 5.
19 Ireland, *op. cit.*, p 25.
20 *Ibid.*, p 23.
21 *Ibid.*, p 38. Kipling's 'Ulster 1912' was a popular inflamatory poem against Irish Home Rule and in support of Ulster Protestant resistance to it.
22 *Ibid.*
23 Birmingham, *An Irishman Looks at his World*, p 86.
24 Robert Harbinson, *The Protégé*, p 51.
25 Paul Henry, *An Irish Portrait*, p 7.
26 Paul Henry, *Further Reminiscences*, pp 30–31.
27 Henry, *An Irish Portrait*, p 6.
28 Forrest Reid, *Apostate*, p 19.

29   *Ibid.*, p 130 and p 131.
30   *Ibid.*, p 130.
31   *Ibid.*, p 18.
32   *Ibid.*
33   *Ibid.*, p 28.
34   *Ibid.*, p 148.
35   John Boyd, *Out of my Class*, p 81; Greacen, *op. cit.*, p 128.
36   Boyd, *ibid.*, p 74.
37   *Ibid.*, p 73 and Greacen, *ibid.*, p 27.
38   Greacen, *ibid.*, p 133 and *Collected Poems 1944–1994*, pp 139–140.
39   Greacen, *Even Without Irene*, (first edn) pp 79–80.
40   *Ibid.*, p 81.
41   Robert Harbinson is the pseudonym of Robin Bryans who is well known as a travel
     writer.
42   Robert Harbinson, *No Surrender: An Ulster Childhood*, p 30.
43   *Ibid.*, p 57. It is interesting to set Harbinson's account alongside Gerald Dawe's
     description of evangelical meetings which also emphasises how religion, drama
     and entertainment are all important ingredients in what the congregations
     experience:
         While the routines of an evangelical meeting might appear to be soulless in
         comparison with, say, the ceremony of catholic Mass or the pomp of High
         Church, the language of 'being healed' or 'saved', the plain witness of one man's
         voice bearing testimony to finding the Lord, has a poignancy and theatricality all
         its own. Largely based upon the Old Testament, adamant in its fundamental
         convictions of right and wrong, sin and forgiveness, speaking out against self-
         deception, and seeking the Lord through being Born Again, the language and
         performance of such preachers provided as much entertainment as it did spiritual
         guidance. *op. cit.*, p 25.
     For other representations of this kind of theology, see the discussion of Janet
     McNeill's *As Strangers Here* and, particularly, of Maurice Leitch's *Gilchrist* in
     chapter 10 below.
44   Harbinson, *ibid.*, p 54. Harbinson's dual role as teller of his own story and ironic
     commentator on it reproduces the 'bifurcation of the puritan personality into actor
     and observer' which Susan Manning identifies as a tenet of Calvinistic doctrine,
     whereby the conscience was conceived of as a 'kind of sentinel' (Calvin's phrase) to
     keep watch on man and bring into the light all his deficiencies and errors. See Susan
     Manning, *The Puritan-Provincial Vision (Scottish and American Literature in the
     Nineteenth Century)*, p 11.
45   Robert Harbinson, *Up Spake the Cabin Boy*, p 134.
46   Harbinson, *No Surrender*, p 132 and p 183.
47   *Ibid.*, p 184.
48   Birmingham, *An Irishman Looks at his World*, p 38 and Robert Lynd, *Ireland a
     Nation*, p 76.
49   Lynd, *Home Life in Ireland*, p 149.
50   *Ibid.*, p 94.
51   *Ibid.*, pp 95–96.
52   Robert Lynd, *If the Germans Conquered England, and other essays*, p 5.
53   Denis Ireland, *An Ulster Protestant Looks at his World*, p 11.
54   *Ibid.*, p 38.
55   Greacen, *Even Without Irene*, (revised edn) p 38.
56   Harbinson, *No Surrender*, pp 121–122.
57   Glenn Patterson, 'Twelfth Nights', *The Tribune Magazine*, 9 July, 1995, p 7.
58   Greacen, *op. cit.*, p 108.
59   *Ibid.*, p 40.
60   Carnduff, *op. cit.*, p 82.
61   George Buchanan, *Green Seacoast*, *op. cit.*, p 37.
62   Carnduff, *op. cit.*, 'Belfast is an Irish City', p 121.
63   *Ibid.*, 'I Have Faith in Ireland', pp 157–158.
64   *Ibid.*, 'Belfast is an Irish City', p 122.

65 Lynd, *Ireland a Nation*, pp 46–47.
66 *Ibid.*, pp 91–92.
67 *Ibid.*, p 240.
68 *Ibid.*, p 80.
69 *Ibid.*, p 147.
70 Séan McMahon, Introduction to *Galway of the Races: Selected Essays by Robert Lynd*, p 24.
71 Birmingham, *op. cit.*, p 272.
72 Carnduff, *op. cit.*, p 78.
73 *Ibid.*, pp 78–79 where Carnduff quotes from the Magheramore Manifesto.
74 *Ibid.*, p 79.
75 *Ibid.*, p 81.
76 Ireland, *op. cit.*, p 10.
77 *Ibid.*, p 33.
78 *Ibid.*, p 33.
79 *Ibid.*, p 33.
80 *Ibid.*, p 38.
81 Denis Ireland, *From the Irish Shore*, p 200.
82 Ireland, *From the Jungle of Belfast*, pp 170–171.
83 *Ibid.*, p 175.
84 See Brian Taylor, *The Green Avenue: The Life and Writings of Forrest Reid, 1875–1947*, pp 98–105.
85 Wallace Fowlie, 'On Writing Autobiography' in Olney (ed), *op. cit.*, p 166.
86 Peter Coveney, *The Image of Childhood*, p 274.
87 Eamonn Hughes, 'Ulsters of the Senses' in *Lost Fields* (a supplement to *Fortnight*, No 306), May 1992, p 11.
88 See John Boyd, *The Middle of My Journey*, pp 62–71.
89 *Ibid.*, p 101 and p 197.
90 George A. Birmingham, *The Red Hand of Ulster*, p 241.
91 Tom Paulin, 'Nineteen Twelve' in *Ireland and the English Crisis*, p 120.
92 George A. Birmingham, *The Northern Iron*, p 3.
93 'Shall iron break the northern iron and the steel?' Jeremiah ch 15, v 12.
94 Birmingham, *op. cit.*, p 116.
95 Paul John Eakin, 'Narrative and Chronology as Structures of Reference and the New Model Autobiographer' in Olney (ed), *op. cit.*, p 36.

CHAPTER FIVE

1 W.R. Rodgers, *The Return Room*, p 17. The readiest source of biographical information on Rodgers is still Darcy O'Brien, *W.R. Rodgers* (1970). Rodgers's radio play referred to above is also semi-autobiographical. It was first broadcast on 23 December, 1955. He returned to the subject of his childhood in *Essex Roundabout* (1963).
2 Rodgers, *Essex Roundabout*, pp 46–7 and p 50.
3 Rodgers, *The Return Room*, pp 3–4.
4 See O'Brien, *op. cit.*, p 23, where he comments:
   Rodgers looked upon joining the ministry as a way of not having to choose a career. He thought of it chiefly as a means of being left alone to be or to become himself. He feared having a job with regular hours and a boss giving him orders.
5 Terence Brown's essay, 'W.R. Rodgers: Romantic Calvinist', is included in *Northern Voices* (1975).
6 *Ibid.*, p 115.
7 Darcy O'Brien, *op. cit.*, pp 30–31, quotes from an unpublished essay in which the poet commented on the challenges and isolation he felt during his ministry.
8 Reported in the *Armagh Standard*, 18 January 1935, and cited by Michael Longley in his introduction to *Poems: W.R. Rodgers*, pp 12–13.
9 John Boyd, *The Middle of My Journey*, p 92.

10   The references are to 'The Party' in *Poems: W.R. Rodgers*, p 31, and 'The Pier', and 'Spring' in W.R. Rodgers, *Collected Poems*, p 4 and p 13.
11   *Poems: W.R. Rodgers*, p 27.
12   'Glossolalia', or 'speaking in tongues', appears to have been a common phenomenon in New Testament times. It is perhaps most famously described in chapter 2 of The Acts of the Apostles when, on the day of Pentecost, the disciples 'were all filled with the Holy Ghost'. 'Speaking in tongues' has often been a characteristic of periods of religious revival where it is commonly construed as a sign of blessing. In the case of Rodgers's poetry, however, some critics have judged matters very differently and one of the harshest indictments of Rodgers's verse in this respect came in a review of *Europa and the Bull* by Kingsley Amis:
     The typical poetic method . . . is twofold. A mythological or religious subject is chosen, and then verse is written round it in which the meaning is frequently guided by the sound, or, sometimes, altogether sacrificed to the sound.
     'Ulster Bull: The Case of W.R. Rodgers' in *Essays in Criticism*, Vol 3, No 4, Oct 1953, p 470.
13   W.R. Rodgers, 'Balloons and Maggots', *Rann*, No 14, p 9 and p 12.
14   For other comments on this idea see Terence Brown, p 119 and Darcy O'Brien, pp 33–34.
15   *Poems: W.R. Rodgers*, p 30.
16   Rodgers, *Collected Poems*, p 49. In her study, *The Puritan-Provincial Vision (Scottish and American Literature in the Nineteenth Century)*, Susan Manning observes a similar uncertainty and sense of breakdown between words and meanings when she notes that 'the Fall, as described by Calvin and explicated for a provincial society by Jonathan Edwards, opened a gulf between words and objects, an ontological distance which accounts for the failure of words to mean and of objects to reveal their "significance". For puritan and provincial this is, threateningly, not so much a failure to signify . . . as a failure of confidence that the signs may be interpreted correctly' (p 107).
17   *Poems: W.R. Rodgers*, p 48.
18   *Ibid.*, p 105.
19   *Ibid.*, pp 106–107.
20   W.R. Rodgers, 'Conversation Piece: An Ulster Protestant', *The Bell*, Vol 4, No 5, Aug 1942, p 309. *The Bell* (1940–1954) was an important periodical founded by Seán O'Faolain which aimed not only to publish poetry and fiction, but also social, political and cultural commentary – much of it deliberately challenging the prevailing orthodoxies in De Valera's Ireland. Equally significantly, at a time of particular coldness betweeen south and north, it had a policy of encouraging and publishing work by writers from Northern Ireland such as John Hewitt, Sam Hanna Bell, Michael McLaverty, and Rodgers himself.
21   Peter McDonald, 'The Fate of "Identity": John Hewitt, W.R. Rodgers and Louis MacNeice', *The Irish Review*, No 12, Spring/Summer 1992, pp 79–80.
22   Rodgers, *op. cit.*, p 310.
23   *Poems: W.R. Rodgers*, p 29.
24   O'Brien, *op. cit.*, p 37.
25   John Hewitt, *The Collected Poems of John Hewitt*, F. Ormsby (ed), p 167.
26   Rodgers, *op. cit.*, p 35.
27   *Ibid.*, p 32 and p 43.
28   *Ibid.*, p 38–9 and p 36.
29   Rodgers, *Collected Poems*, p 25.
30   *Ibid.*, p 45.
31   *Poems: W.R. Rodgers*, p 52.
32   *Ibid.*, p 53.
33   *Ibid.*, p 60.
34   *Ibid.*, pp 60–61.
35   *Ibid.*, pp 63.
36   *Ibid.*, p 54.
37   *Ibid.*, pp 55.
38   *Ibid.*, p 57. The biblical reference is to Isaiah, ch. 6, v. 7.
39   *Ibid.*, p 64.
40   *Ibid.*, p 65.

41   *Ibid.*, p 66; p 67; p 68 and pp 69–70; p 69; p 71 and p 72; p 73; p 74.
42   *Ibid.*, p 67.
43   *Ibid.*, p 72 and p 74.
44   *Ibid.*, pp 72–73.
45   Tom Clyde, 'W.R. Rodgers 1909–1969', *The Honest Ulsterman*, No 92, 1991–1992, p 7.
46   *Poems: W.R. Rodgers*, p 75.
47   *Ibid.*, p 76.
48   *Ibid.*, p 77.
49   Terence Brown, *op. cit.*, p 121.
50   Rodgers, *op. cit.*, p 78.
51   *Ibid.*, p 79.
52   *Ibid.*, 'The Harvest Field', p 81.
53   *Ibid.*, p 100.
54   Terence McCaughey, *Memory and Redemption: Church, Politics and Prophetic Theology in Ireland*, p 68.
55   *Ibid.*
56   Rodgers, *op. cit.*, p 83.
57   *Ibid.*, p 89.
58   John Wilson Foster, '"The Dissidence of Dissent": John Hewitt and W.R. Rodgers', in *Colonial Consequences*, p 127 and p 125.
59   Douglas Carson, 'The Pursuit of the Fancy Man – Sam Hanna Bell and W.R. Rodgers 1952–1955', *The Honest Ulsterman*, No 92, p 18.
60   Rodgers, *op. cit.*, p 104, 'Field Day', and pp 96–97, 'Neither Here Nor There'.
61   I owe this suggestion to one of my former undergraduate students, Rosalia Fudio.
62   Michael O'Neill, 'W.R. Rodgers's Revolutionary Theology', *The Honest Ulsterman*, No 92, p 13.
63   See O'Brien, *op. cit.*, p 57.

CHAPTER SIX

1   Tom Clyde (ed), 'Planter's Gothic' in *Ancestral Voices: The Selected Prose of John Hewitt*, p 28.
2   Geraldine Watts, 'Utility Clashes with Emotion', *Fortnight*, No 275 (John Hewitt Supplement), July/Aug 1989, p v, observes that he shows '. . . a Calvinist respect for the elders of the family and almost biblical emphasis on the continuation of a name.'
3   Hewitt is the author of an unpublished autobiography, *A North Light*, from which a number of extracts were published in *The Bell* in 1953 and reprinted in *Ancestral Voices: The Selected Prose of John Hewitt. Kites in Spring: A Belfast Boyhood* (1980) consists of 107 sonnets all devoted to his family and ancestry, and at intervals throughout his poetry he returns to familial subjects.
4   *Ancestral Voices*, p 9.
5   Denis D. O'Hanna, 'Architecture in Ulster' in S.H. Bell, N.A. Robb and J. Hewitt (eds), *The Arts in Ulster*, p 33.
6   Frank Ormsby (ed), *The Collected Poems of John Hewitt*, p 272.
7   *Ibid.*, p 377.
8   'The Bitter Gourd' in *Ancestral Voices*, p 116.
9   *Collected Poems*, p 375. The line occurs in the second part of the long poem, 'Freehold', which provides a composite tribute to Robert Hewitt.
10 *Ibid.*, 'A Dominie's Log', p 290 and 'The Wedding Present', p 263.
11 *Ibid.*, 'Outside the Creeds', p 276.
12 'Planter's Gothic' in *Ancestral Voices*, p 28.
13 *Ibid.*, p 29. Norman Vance suggests that 'Hewitt can be considered not so much a "post-Christian" as a post-Methodist poet, with hymns and preaching still resounding in his head.' See 'Pictures, Singing and the Temple: Some Contexts for Hewitt's Images' in Eve Patten (ed), *Returning to Ourselves*, p 298.
14 *Collected Poems*, 'Free Mason', p 302.
15 *Ibid.*, 'Jacob and the Angel', p 96.
16 *Ibid.*, 'Freehold', p 375.

17 Alan Warner (ed with introd.), *The Selected John Hewitt*, p 7.
18 Seamus Heaney, *John Hewitt 1907–1987, The Universal Poet*, n.p.
19 *Collected Poems*, 'Year of Grace and My Great-Grandfather' and 'My Great-Grandfather's Refusal', p 259.
20 In 'My Grandmother Robinson', Hewitt wrote:
    Church-going, comely, critical, sedate, / deep down my terror often still endures (*ibid.*, p 260).
    He records his grandmother's independence of mind in 'A Victorian Steps Out', which tells of how she left the rest of her family on their way to church in order to fall in behind a Salvation Army band along with a crowd of less reputable followers, much to her daughters' mortification. Likewise in church itself, she was not above challenging the minister over his sermons (p 107).
21 *Ibid.*, pp 105–106.
22 *Ibid.*, 'Consequences', p 272. Sam Hewitt is also the subject of 'The Magician' and 'The Breach', both p 271, and 'The Wheel', pp 101–102.
23 Hewitt records how the sonnets in *Kites in Spring* were written quite rapidly after he started composing them on 16 October 1978. See notes to *ibid.*, p 617.
24 See Edna Longley '"A Barbarous Nook": The Writer and Belfast' in *The Living Stream*, p 96, and Norman Vance, *Irish Literature: A Social History*, p 238.
25 *Collected Poems*, 'Freehold', p 377.
26 *Ibid.*, 'The Scar', p 177, and 'Orchard Country', p 272.
27 *Ibid.*, 'I Lie Alone', p 309.
28 Gerald Dawe, 'Against Piety: A Reading of John Hewitt's Poetry' in G. Dawe and J.W. Foster (eds), *The Poet's Place: Ulster Literature and Society*, p 216.
29 *Collected Poems*, 'Once Alien Here', pp 20–21 and 'An Irishman in Coventry', pp 97–98.
30 *Ibid.*, 'O Country People', pp 72–73.
31 *Ibid.*, 'Conacre', p 4.
32 *Ibid.*, pp 9–10.
33 *Ibid.*, 'The Bloody Brae', p 411.
34 *Ibid.*, p 413.
35 *Ibid.*, p 414.
36 *Ibid.*, p 415.
37 *Ibid.*, Ormsby's Introduction, p xlviii.
38 Britta Olinder, '"The Heartbreak's Relevant": Dramatic and Poetic Qualities of John Hewitt's Verse Play *The Bloody Brae*' in J. Genet and R.A. Cave (eds), *Perspectives of Irish Drama and Theatre*, pp 78–83. 'The Colony' first appeared in *The Bell*, Vol 18, No 11 (Summer 1953), pp 33–37, but the essay in which Hewitt made his claim, 'No Rootless Colonist', was published in *Aquarius* in 1972 and was reprinted in *Ancestral Voices*, pp 146–157. The quotation is from p 157. It is worth adding that the title of the essay refers to a line in a poem, 'Mesgedra', by another Ulster Protestant, Samuel Ferguson.
39 *Collected Poems*, 'The Colony', p 78.
40 *Ibid.*, p 79. Hewitt's unease in the presence of Catholicism appears in poems throughout his career. Examples include 'Mass', p 99, 'May Altar', p 115, 'The Hill Farm', pp 124–125' 'The Glens', p 310.
41 *Ibid.*
42 *Ibid.*
43 Terence Brown, 'The Poetry of W.R. Rodgers and John Hewitt' in D. Dunn (ed), *Two Decades of Irish Writing*, p 94. See also John Wilson Foster, '"The Dissidence of Dissent": John Hewitt and W.R. Rodgers' in *Colonial Consequences*, p 116, for other comments on this point.
44 *Collected Poems*, 'Ireland', p 58.
45 *Ancestral Voices*, p 125.
46 *Ibid.*, p 153.
47 *Collected Poems*, 'Overture for an Ulster Literature', pp 511–512.
48 *Ibid.*, 'Sunset over Glenaan', p 113.
49 *Ibid.*, 'Freehold', p 378.
50 *Ibid.*
51 *Ibid.*, p 379.

52 *Ibid.*, p 382.
53 *Ibid.*, p 383.
54 *Ibid.*, p 384.
55 *Ibid.*, p 385.
56 *Ibid.*, p 386.
57 Peter McDonald, 'The Fate of "Identity": John Hewitt, W.R. Rodgers and Louis MacNeice', *The Irish Review*, No 12, Spring/Summer 1992, p 75.
58 *Collected Poems*, 'An Ulsterman', p 132.
59 *Ibid.*, 'The Dilemma', p 132 and 'The Coasters' pp 135–137.
60 *Ibid.*, 'The Anglo-Irish Accord', pp 537–538. For reference to McCusker's speech, see chapter 3.
61 *Ibid.*, 'A Little People', pp 539–541.
62 *Ibid.*, p 594. Ormsby has reprinted the Foreword in his notes to the poems.
63 *Ibid.*, p 593.
64 *Ibid.*, 'Neither an Elegy Nor a Manifesto', pp 188–189.
65 Terence Brown, *Northern Voices*, p 91. J.W. Foster makes the same point, *op. cit.*, p 121, and in 'The Landscape of Three Irelands: Hewitt, Murphy and Montague', *Ibid.*, p 158, he compares the neatness and regularity of Hewitt's lines to the orderly fields of planter farms.
66 Vance, *op. cit.*, p 225. See also Foster, *ibid.*, p 125 and p 128.
67 *Collected Poems*, 'Interim', p 44.
68 *Ibid.*, 'Retreaded Rhymes', p 366.
69 *Ibid.*, 'Style', pp 311–312 and 'For Stonecutters', p 312.
70 *Ibid.*, 'On Reading Wallace Stevens' *Collected Poems* After Many Years', p 230.
71 *Ibid.*, 'Substance and Shadow', pp 190–191.
72 *Ibid.*, 'Sonnets for Roberta', pp 251–253. The quotation is from the fifth sonnet, pp 252–253.
73 Heaney, *op. cit.*, n.p.; *Collected Poems*, 'Ars Poetica', p 228.
74 *Ibid.*, p 229.
75 *Ibid.*, 'Dedication', p 431.
76 *Ibid.*, 'The Spectacle of Truth', pp 89–90.

CHAPTER SEVEN

 1 For this and further information about J.F. MacNeice, see Jon Stallworthy, *Louis MacNeice* (1995), passim; Terence Brown, 'MacNeice: Father and Son' in T. Brown and A Reid (eds), *Time Was Away: The World of Louis MacNeice* (1974), pp 21–34; George Rutherford, 'John Frederick MacNeice' in *Carrickfergus and District Historical Journal*, Vol 7, 1993, pp 38–46.
 2 Louis MacNeice, *The Strings are False*, p 38.
 3 *Ibid.*, p 54. Also see 'Autobiography' in *Collected Poems*, p 183.
 4 *Ibid.*, p 37. In an alternative version of this passage also included in *The Strings are False*, MacNeice wrote: 'Our life was bounded by this hedge' between the garden and the churchyard (p 216).
 5 *Ibid.*, p 46.
 6 Louis MacNeice, 'Experiences with Images' in A. Heuser (ed), *Selected Literary Criticism of Louis MacNeice*, p 159.
 7 *The Strings are False*, p 54.
 8 *Ibid.*, p 41 and p 42.
 9 Louis MacNeice, 'A Personal Digression' in A Heuser (ed), *Selected Prose of Louis MacNeice*, p 61.
10 *The Strings are False*, p 43.
11 Elizabeth Nicholson, 'Trees were Green' in *Time Was Away*, pp 16–17.
12 *The Strings are False*, pp 44–45.
13 *Ibid.*, pp 77–78.
14 *Ibid.*, pp 39–40.
15 *Ibid.*, Appendix A, p 220, and *Collected Poems*, p 518.
16 *The Strings are False*, Appendix A, p 220.

17 *Ibid.*, p 73.
18 *Ibid.*, p 96.
19 *Ibid.*, Appendix B, John Hilton, 'Louis MacNeice at Marlborough and Oxford', p 282.
20 *Collected Poems*, p 3.
21 *Ibid.*, pp 175–176.
22 *Ibid.*, p 176.
23 *Ibid.*, p 422.
24 *The Strings are False*, p 101.
25 *Collected Poems*, p 72.
26 William T. McKinnon, *Apollos's Blended Dream: A Study of the Poetry of Louis MacNeice*, p 75. Also *Collected Poems*, p 478.
27 *Collected Poems*, pp 73–75.
28 *Ibid.*, p 29.
29 Samuel Beckett, *Proust and Three Dialogues with Georges Duthuit*, p 19.
30 *Collected Poems*, p 28.
31 *Ibid.*, p 30. The use of the term 'drunkenness' in this celebratory context may also be related to MacNeice's personal experience. As he wrote in *The Strings are False*, 'Coming of a temperance family, drunkenness had always been for me a symbol of freedom.' He goes on to explain that his father's chief objection to drink was that the drunkard lost 'self-respect'. For MacNeice, however, 'self-respect' was associated with the people he most disliked – Miss MacCready, Sir Edward Carson, 'half the world's trouble-makers', 'the sectarians and the militants, the nationalists and imperialists, the captains of industry and the moral reformers' – and therefore, loss of 'self-respect' through drink 'was laming and debilitating one's private Satan, one's Tempter' – a course to be warmly welcomed. See *ibid.*, p 103.
32 Edna Longley, 'Louis MacNeice and his Influence' in *Carrickfergus and District Historical Journal*, Vol 7, 1993, p 15.
33 *Collected Poems*, p 28.
34 *Ibid.*, p 87.
35 *Ibid.*, p xvii.
36 *Ibid.*, p xviii.
37 *Ibid.*, pp 158–159.
38 *Ibid.*, p 159.
39 *Ibid.*, p 160.
40 Terence Brown, *Louis MacNeice: Sceptical Vision*, p 91.
41 *Collected Poems*, p 33.
42 *Ibid.*, p 36.
43 Denis Ireland, *From the Jungle of Belfast*, p 143.
44 *Collected Poems*, p 143.
45 *Ibid.*, p 429.
46 *Ibid.*, p 430.
47 *Ibid.*, p 431.
48 *Ibid.*, p 433.
49 *Ibid.*, p 436.
50 *Ibid.*, p 436.
51 *Ibid.*, pp 438–439.
52 R.S. Thomas (ed), *A Choice of George Herbert's Verse*, pp 41–42, and MacNeice, *Collected Poems*, pp 193–194.
53 *Collected Poems*, p 138.
54 *Ibid.*, p 149.
55 *Ibid.*, p 150.
56 E.R. Dodds, 'Louis MacNeice at Birmingham' in *Time Was Away*, p 88.
57 Louis MacNeice, 'Experiences with Images' in *Selected Literary Criticism of Louis MacNeice*, p 163. For the poem, see *Collected Poems*, p 213.
58 Brown, *op. cit.*, p 57.
59 *Ibid.*, p 58.
60 Peter McDonald, *Louis MacNeice: The Poet in his Contexts*, p 143.
61 *Collected Poems*, p 287.
62 *Ibid.*, p 288, and *Church Hymnal*, No 373.
63 *Collected Poems*, pp 288–289.

64 *Ibid.*, pp 289–290.
65 *Ibid.*, p 212.
66 Robyn Marsack, *The Cave of Making: The Poetry of Louis MacNeice*, p 98–99.
67 *Collected Poems*, pp 296 and p 295.
68 *Ibid.*, p 297.
69 *Ibid.*, p 298.
70 *Ibid.*, p 298. Marsack (p 98) points out how the homophones in the the first and third lines of this stanza – and of each stanza of part 3 – emphasise dubiety by playing with words which sound the same but have different meaning.
71 *Ibid.*, p 299.
72 *Ibid.*, p 248.
73 *Ibid.*, p 253.
74 Stallworthy, *op. cit.*, p 309.
75 *Collected Poems*, 'Belfast', p 17; 'Carrickfergus', pp 69–70; 'Valediction', pp 52–54; 'Eclogue from Iceland', pp 40–47.
76 *Ibid.*, pp 131–134.
77 *Ibid.*, pp 224–225.
78 *Ibid.*, p 255 and p 256.
79 *Ibid.*, p 256.
80 *Ibid.*, p 226.
81 McKinnon, *op. cit.*, pp 156–157.
82 *Collected Poems*, pp 275–276.
83 *Ibid.*, p 277.
84 *Ibid.*, p 278.
85 *Ibid.*, p 279 and p 278.
86 *Ibid.*, p 469.
87 *Ibid.*, p 458.
88 Stallworthy, *op. cit.*, p 453.
89 *Collected Poems*, p 473.
90 *Ibid.*, p 488.
91 *Ibid.*, p 502.
92 Edna Longley, *Louis MacNeice: A Study*, p 140.
93 *Collected Poems*, p 507.
94 Stallworthy, *op. cit.*, p 447.
95 See *Collected Poems*, pp 507–509 and *The Strings are False*, p 59. The biblical reference is to Matthew, 12, vv 31–32.
96 Longley, *op. cit.*, p 142 and p 151.
97 A. Heuser and P. McDonald (eds), *Selected Plays of Louis MacNeice*, p 14.
98 *Collected Poems*, 'Plurality', p 244.
99 *Ibid.*, *Autumn Sequel*, Canto vii, p 357.
100 Cited in McKinnon, *op. cit.*, p 216, and sourced as a broadcast Book Talk on the European Service, 18 November, 1965.
101 Walter Allen, introduction to Louis MacNeice, *Modern Poetry*, p xvi.
102 *Selected Plays of Louis MacNeice*, p 247.
103 *The Strings are False*, p 33.
104 *Collected Poems*, p 546.
105 *Ibid.*, 'Plurality', p 244.

CHAPTER EIGHT

1 Michael Longley, *Tuppenny Stung*, p 33.
2 Derek Mahon, *Courtyards in Delft*, p 21.
3 *Tuppenny Stung*, p 38. Mahon's account of his Trinity Days is in 'A Ghostly Rumble Among the Drums' in *Journalism: Derek Mahon*, pp 220– 223.
4 Derek Mahon, *Night Crossing*, p 5.
5 *Ibid.*, p 6.
6 Edna Longley, '"A Barbarous Nook": The Writer and Belfast' in *The Living Stream: Literature and Revisionism in Ireland*, p 106.
7 Kathleen Shields, 'Derek Mahon's Poetry of Belonging', *Irish University Review, Special Issue: Derek Mahon*, Spring/Summer 1994, p 71.

8 Derek Mahon, *Lives*, p 3.
9 Derek Mahon, *The Snow Party*, pp 13–15.
10 *Ibid.*, p 22. The lines quoted might also remind one of Robert Lynd's description of the little meeting-house on the Ards peninsula.
11 *Courtyards in Delft*, p 17.
12 'The Coleraine Triangle' in *Journalism: Derek Mahon*, p 217 and p 219.
13 *Ibid.*
14 Peter McDonald has observed how for Mahon, as for MacNeice and Paulin, the 'stark contrasts . . . of a living community on the edge of an ungovernable perspective' have been extremely important. See McDonald, 'History and Poetry: Derek Mahon and Tom Paulin' in Elmer Andrews (ed), *Contemporary Irish Poetry: A Collection of Critical Essays*, p 90.
15 *Courtyards in Delft*, 'North Wind', pp 10–11. This poem is retitled 'North Wind: Portrush' in later collections.
16 Jonathan Edwards, *Basic Writings* (selected and edited by Ola Elizabeth Winslow), p 250.
17 *Night Crossing*, pp 22–23. For Cowper, see 'The Castaway', especially the last stanza.
18 Terence Brown, 'The Poet and Painting' in *Irish University Review, Special Issue: Derek Mahon*, p 44. The poem first appears in *Lives*, pp 22–23, and then in revised form in *Poems 1962–1978*, p 44.
19 Edna Longley, 'The Singing Line: Form in Derek Mahon's Poetry' in *Poetry in the Wars*, p 173. Longley's citation from Tuohy comes from a review of *The Hunt by Night, P.N. Review*, 10, No 1, p 73.
20 'A Dark Country', *Lives*, p 18.
21 *Night Crossing*, pp 1–2.
22 *Lives*, p 1.
23 *The Snow Party*, pp 5–7.
24 *Ibid.*, pp 1–2.
25 Elmer Andrews, 'The Poetry of Derek Mahon: "places where a thought might grow"', in E. Andrews (ed), *op. cit.*, pp 247–248.
26 Derek Mahon, *The Hudson Letter*, p 62.
27 *Ibid.*, 'The Hudson Letter', part xvii, 'Imbolc: JBY', p 74.
28 Terence Brown, 'A Northern Renaissance: Poets from the North of Ireland 1965–1980' in *Ireland's Literature: Selected Essays*, p 217.
29 Derek Mahon, *The Hunt by Night*, pp 57–58.
30 *Courtyards in Delft*, p 21.
31 The final lines originally read:
     While my hard-nosed companions dream of war
     On parched veldt and fields of wind-swept gorse.
     These were altered in *Selected Poems*, Harmondsworth: Viking, 1991, pp 120–121, to the version quoted in the text. In *The Hunt by Night*, pp 9–10, Mahon added an extra stanza, which he then dropped in *Selected Poems*. It is reproduced below and introduces a much more direct note of bitterness and anger, and explicitly points out the religiously inspired militarism which he wants to see purged:
     For the pale light of that provincial town
     Will spread itself, like ink or oil,
     Over the not yet accurate linen
     Map of the world which occupies one wall
     And punish nature in the name of God.
     If only, now, the Maenads, as of right,
     Came smashing crockery, with fire and sword,
     We could sleep easier in our beds at night.
32 Maurice Riordan, 'An Urbane Perspective: The Poetry of Derek Mahon' in M. Harmon (ed), *The Irish Writer and the City*, p 178. Riordan notes that in a review of *Courtyards in Delft* by Séan Dunne (*The Cork Review* II, 3, June 1981, p 12) Mahon is credited with describing the poem as a study of Protestantism.
33 *Lives*, pp 14–16.
34 *Courtyards in Delft*, p 12.
35 Edna Longley, 'Derek Mahon: Extreme Religion of Art' in M Kenneally (ed), *Poetry in Contemporary Irish Literature*, p 299.

36 Seamus Deane, 'Derek Mahon: Freedom from History' in *Celtic Revivals: Essays in Modern Irish Literature*, p 156.
37 *Lives*, p 29.
38 Terence Brown comments on the poem in this context in his essay, 'A Northern Renaissance: Poets from the North of Ireland 1965–1980', *op. cit.*, pp 212–213.
39 *The Hunt by Night*, p 52.
40 *Lives*, pp 30–31. The poem was revised and restructured in *Poems 1962–1978*, Oxford: OUP, p 49.
41 Elmer Andrews has shown that reference to anemones in the closing lines derives from a comment by William James in *Some Problems of Philosophy*: 'Had we no concepts we should live simply "getting" each successive moment of experience, as the sessile sea anemone on its rock receives whatever nourishment the wash of the waves may bring.' See Andrews, 'The Poetry of Derek Mahon: "Places where a thought might grow"', *op. cit.*, p 245.
42 'The Last of the Fire Kings', *The Snow Party*, pp 9–10.
43 *Poems 1962–1978*, pp 66–67. The earlier versions of this poem are 'What Will Remain', *Lives*, pp 26–27, and 'Thammuz', *The Snow Party*, pp 11–12.
44 'The Banished Gods', *The Snow Party*, pp 30–31.
45 *Poems 1962–1978*, pp 72–73. An earlier version, 'The Hermit', appeared as a prose poem in *The Snow Party*, p 26.
46 Kathleen Mullaney, 'Derek Mahon's Poetry' in Tjebbe A. Westendorp and Jane Mallinson (eds), *Politics and the Rhetoric of Poetry – Perspectives on Modern Anglo-Irish Poetry*, p 51.
47 *The Hunt by Night*, pp 55–56.
48 Hugh Haughton, 'Even now there are places where a thought might grow': Place and Displacement in the Poetry of Derek Mahon' in Neil Corcoran (ed), *The Chosen Ground: Essays on Contemporary Poetry of Northern Ireland*, p 111.
49 Tom Paulin, 'Political Verse' in *Writing to the Moment: Selected Critical Essays 1980–1996*, p 137. Paulin's comments are made in the context of a discussion of Mahon's poem, 'A Disused Shed in Co. Wexford' which shares many of the characteristics noted here in relation to 'A Garage in Co. Cork'.
50 Haughton, *op. cit.*, p 93.
51 'An Image from Beckett', *Lives*, pp 8–10.
52 Brendan Kennelly, 'Derek Mahon's Humane Perspective' in A. Persson (ed), *Brendan Kennelly: Journey into Joy: Selected Prose*, p 131. Seamus Heaney, 'Place and Displacement: Reflections on Some Recent Poetry from Northern Ireland' in E. Andrews (ed), *op. cit.*, p 134.
53 All are to be found in *Night Crossing*: 'Grandfather', p 7; 'My Wicked Uncle', pp 8–9; 'Death of a Film-Star', p 10 (called 'The Death of Marilyn Monroe' in *Poems 1962–1978*, p 7); 'As God Is My Judge', p 31 (revised as 'Bruce Ismay's Soliloquy' in *Poems 1962– 1978*, pp 32–33, and called 'After the Titanic' in *Selected Poems*, p 29).
54 'In Carrowdore Churchyard', *Night Crossing*, p 3.
55 'Van Gogh Among the Miners', *Night Crossing*, p 19 (called 'Van Gogh in the Borinage' in *Poems 1962–1978*, p 14 and 'A Portrait of the Artist' in *Selected Poems*, p 20).
56 Bill Tinley, '"Harmonies and Disharmonies": Derek Mahon's Francophile Poetics' in *Irish University Review: Special Issue: Derek Mahon*, p 94.
57 *The Hunt by Night*, p 23.
58 Edna Longley, 'The Singing Line: Form in Derek Mahon's Poetry' in *Poetry in the Wars*, p 184.
59 *Night Crossing*, p 13.
60 *Poems 1962–1978*, p 107.
61 *Lives*, pp 33–38. The poem is revised in *Poems 1962–1978*, pp 51–56.
62 *Poems 1962–1978*, pp 109–114. A revised version appears in *Selected Poems*, pp 113–118.
63 *Selected Poems*, p 117.
64 Terence Brown, 'Derek Mahon: The Poet and Painting', *Irish University Review: Special Issue: Derek Mahon*, p 38.
65 *Night Crossing*, p 28. The poem was slightly revised and retitled 'Thinking of Inishere in Cambridge, Massachusetts' in *Poems 1962–1978*, p 27, and further retitled 'Thinking of Inis Oírr in Cambridge, Mass.' in *Selected Poems*, p 25.

66   John V. Taylor, *The Go-Between God*, p 8.
67   *Lives*, p 4.
68   Terence Brown, *op. cit.*, p 48.
69   *Night Crossing*, pp 20–21.
70   'Girls on the Bridge', *Courtyards in Delft*, pp 24–25.
71   *Courtyards in Delft*, pp 22–23.
72   Terence Brown, *op. cit.*, p 50.
73   Paul Tillich, *Theology and Culture*, p 75.
74   'Four Walks in the Country near Saint Brieuc', *Night Crossing*, p 17. These poems were retitled 'Breton Walks in *Poems 1962–1978*, and then reinstated with the original title in *Selected Poems*.
75   'Auden on St Mark's Place', *The Hudson Letter*, pp 56–57.
76   *Journalism: Derek Mahon*, p 93.
77   W.J. McCormack, 'Edna Longley and the Reaction from Ulster: Fighting or Writing' in *The Battle of the Books*, p 62.
78   Elmer Andrews, 'The Poetry of Derek Mahon: "Places where a thought might grow"', *op. cit.*, pp 252–253.
79   'In the Aran Islands', *Lives*, p 5. Retitled 'Aran' in *Selected Poems*.

CHAPTER NINE

1   Tom Paulin, 'Introduction' to *Minotaur: Poetry and the Nation State*, p 12.
2   Tom Paulin, *A State of Justice*, London: Faber, 1977, p 9. The phrase 'murdering miles of of terrace houses' recalls the 'echoing back streets of this desperate city' in Derek Mahon's 'In Belfast'. Likewise, the first line of stanza two, 'The city is built on mud and wrath' evokes MacNeice's lines in *Autumn Journal* xvi, 'A city built upon mud; / A culture built upon profit', while the reference in stanza three to 'a Judge / Shot in his hallway before his daughter / By a boy who shut his eyes as his hand tightened' bears a resemblance to lines in the second stanza of Michael Longley's poem, 'Wounds'.
3   *Ibid.*, p 10. Other examples which adopt similar language and strategies include 'States', 'Cadaver Politic' and 'A Just Society'.
4   *Ibid.*, p 32.
5   *Ibid.*, p 8.
6   *Ibid.*, p 15.
7   Mr Alwell, whose name is almost Bunyanesque in this context, was reading from II Samuel, ch. 18, the precise reference being to the words of King David who, after learning of the death of his son with whom he had been at war, gives vent to his grief and sense of loss.
8   Tom Paulin, *Walking a Line*, p 10.
9   Tom Paulin, *The Strange Museum*, p 24. In his prefatory essay, 'Political Verse', Paulin shows his impatience with the idea that art exists 'in a timeless vacuum or a soundproof museum', or that poets have 'an ability to hold themselves above history', and insists that this is a mode of thought peculiar to Western democracies. He continues: 'However, in some societies – particularly totalitarian ones – history is a more or less inescapable condition. In these cold, closed societies a liberal belief in the separation of the public from private life is not possible'. (*Writing to the Moment: Selected Critical Essays 1980–1996*, p 103.)
10   *Ibid.*, 'Before History', p 1.
11   *Ibid.*, pp 18–19.
12   *Ibid.*, p 16.
13   *Ibid.*, p 10.
14   *Ibid.*, p 6.
15   *Ibid.*, pp 32–33. The other poem referred to is 'In the Egyptian Gardens', p 24.
16   *Ibid.*, p 34.
17   Tom Paulin, *Ireland and the English Crisis*, p 17.
18   Tom Paulin, *Liberty Tree*, p 46.
19   *Ibid.*, pp 55–56.

20   *Ibid.*, p 13.
21   *Ibid.*, p 20.
22   *Ibid.*, p 22.
23   *Ibid.*, p 23.
24   *Ibid.*, pp 25–27.
25   *Ibid.*, p 32. See also Elmer Andrews, 'Tom Paulin: Underground Resistance Fighter' in M. Kenneally (ed), *Poetry in Contemporary Irish Literature*, p 337.
26   *Liberty Tree*, p 49.
27   A similar sense of loss and decline emerges in 'To the Linen Hall' which regrets the process whereby 'art turns social', and the Whitmanesque 'epic yawp' of uninhibited individual energy is reductively toned down and formalised:

>   . . . now we tell children
>   to shun that original –
>   primal light, soaked green,
>   the slob mud
>   and a salt tang.

   Ibid., p 77.
28   Edna Longley, 'When Did You Last See Your Father?' in *The Living Stream: Literature and Revisionism in Ireland*, p 159. Elmer Andrews, *op. cit.*, p 337.
29   Peter McDonald, 'History and Poetry: Derek Mahon and Tom Paulin', in Elmer Andrews (ed), *Contemporary Irish Poetry: A Collection of Critical Essays*, pp 98–99.
30   Tom Paulin, 'A New Look at the Language Question', in *Ireland and the English Crisis*, p 191. The close relationship between Paulin's essays and poetry is suggested by the way in which certain phrases or words turn up in both. Thus, the 'relished words' in this pamphlet is echoed in the phrase 'relished dialect' in 'Father of History', and other examples occur from time to time.
31   Tom Paulin, 'Observing the Fathers: Christina Rossetti', and 'Writing Beyond Writing: Emily Dickinson' in *Minotaur: Poetry and the Nation State*, p 89 and p 99.
32   *Ibid.*, p 103.
33   *Ibid.*, p 104.
34   *Ibid.*, p 104.
35   *Ibid.*, p 106.
36   Bernard O'Donoghue, 'Involved Imaginings: Tom Paulin' in Neil Corcoran (ed), *The Chosen Ground: Essays on Contemporary Poetry of Northern Ireland*, p 180.
37   *Liberty Tree*, pp 16–17.
38   Gerald Dawe, 'A Gritty Prod Baroque: Tom Paulin and the Northern Politik' in *A Life Elsewhere*, see especially pages 73–74 and 85–86.
39   Clair Wills, *Improprieties: Politics and Sexuality in Northern Irish Poetry*, p 123.
40   The references are to 'Manichean Geography I', p 42, 'Manichean Geography II', p 43, 'A Rum Cove, a Stout Cove', p 34, and 'Local Histories', p 47, all in *Liberty Tree*.
41   *Ibid.*, 'A Written Answer', p 40.
42   Tom Paulin, *Fivemiletown*, London: Faber, 1987, pp 42–43. It is worth remembering how John Hewitt also expressed Protestant feelings of abandonment in 'The Anglo-Irish Accord' (see chapter 6), although his poem adopts a wholly different approach. The impact on Paulin of Harold McCusker's speech in the House of Commons is suggested not only by the allusive reference to it here, but also by his inclusion of it in the section titled 'Northern Protestant Oratory and Writing' which he edited for *The Field Day Anthology of Irish Writing*.
43   'Introduction', *Minotaur: Poetry and the Nation State*, p 14. Paulin includes this passage in context in his selection of 'Northern Protestant Oratory and Writing 1791–1985' for *The Field Day Anthology of Irish Writing*, Derry: Field Day, 1991, Vol 3, p 371.
44   *Ibid.*, p 15. Paulin explains the coded connection between the old story and the contemporary situation as follows: 'Nebuchadnezzar's Babylon was Britain in post-imperial confusion, Daniel was the loyalist imagination which sits "in the gate of the king", identifies with the British sovereign and holds to a British identity.' (p 15).
45   *Ibid.*, p 15.
46   In 'A New Look at the Language Question' (*Ireland and the English Crisis*, p 192), Paulin wrote of the inaccessibility of the platonic ideal of Standard British English to any Irish writer, and continued:

This is because the platonic standard has an actual location – it isn't simply free and transcendental – and that location is the British House of Commons. There in moments of profound crisis, people speak exclusively 'for England'. On such occasions, all dialect words are the subject of an invisible exclusion-order and archaic Anglo-Norman words like 'treason' and 'vouch' are suddenly dunted into a kind of life.

This provides a gloss on the language the disillusioned Unionist listens to in the Strangers' House ('*We vouch*, they swore, / *We deem*, they cried') and reinforces the note of loss and disillusionment on which the poem ends.

47   *Fivemiletown*, p 54.
48   'And Where Do You Stand on the National Question?', *Liberty Tree*, pp 67–69.
49   'Introduction', *Minotaur: Poetry and the Nation State*, p 16.
50   *Fivemiletown*, pp 15–17.
51   Bernard O'Donoghue, *op. cit.*, pp 184–185.
52   '*Fivemiletown*, pp 46–47.
53   'Introduction', *Minotaur: Poetry and the Nation State*, p 13.
54   References are to *The Strange Museum*, pp 42–47, *Liberty Tree*, pp 21–27, and 'Political Verse' in *Writing to the Moment*, p 137 and p 103.
55   Cited in Nadezhda Mandelstam, *Hope Against Hope*, p 262.
56   *Fivemiletown*, p 25.
57   Clair Wills, *op. cit.*, p 149.
58   *Ibid.*, p 151.
59   'The Caravans on Lüneberg Heath', *Fivemiletown*, p 59. Heideigger is subject to renewed attack by Paulin in 'Hegel and the War Criminals', *Walking a Line*, pp 42–43.
60   *Ibid.*, p 65.
61   *Ibid.*, p 66.
62   *Walking a Line*, pp 102–103. Ireland itself has often been metaphorically alluded to as 'four green fields', especially in nationalist writing.
63   *Ibid.*, 'The New Year', pp 8–9.
64   *Ibid.*, pp 33–34.
65   *Writing to the Moment*, p 140 and p 141.
66   'Cadmus and the Dragon', *Walking a Line*, p 93.
67   *Ibid.*, pp 94–95.
68   *Ibid.*, pp 94–95.
69   *Ibid.*, pp 95–96.
70   Jonathan Bardon, *A History of Ulster*, p 711.
71   'Cadmus and the Dragon', p 96.
72   *Ibid.*, p 97.
73   *Ibid.*, p 101.
74   Seamus Heaney, *The Redress of Poetry*, pp 202–203.
75   Tom Paulin cited by Peter McDonald in 'History and Poetry: Derek Mahon and Tom Paulin', p 100. McDonald's source is to be found in *Viewpoints: Poets in Conversation with John Haffenden* (1981).
76   Tom Paulin, 'Hibiscus and Saliva Flowers: D.H. Lawrence' in *Minotaur: Poetry and the Nation State*, p 167, and McDonald, *ibid.*, p 100.
77   Bernard O'Donoghue, *op. cit.*, p 183.
78   Tom Paulin, 'Political Verse' in *Writing to the Moment*, p 116.
79   Tom Paulin, 'Pure Primitive Divinity: The Republican Epic of John Milton' in *Minotaur: Poetry and the Nation State*, p 31.
80   Elmer Andrews, *op. cit.*, p 334.
81   *The Field Day Anthology of Irish Writing*, Vol 3, p 314.
82   *Ibid.*, p 315.
83   Tom Paulin, 'Political Verse' in *Writing to the Moment*, p 117.
84   Elmer Andrews, *op. cit.*, p 323.

CHAPTER TEN

1   John Wilson Foster, *Forces and Themes in Ulster Fiction*, pp 1–10 passim. Despite the passage of time since its publication, and subsequent development in the work of

some of the novelists he discusses as well as the appearance of new names, Foster's book remains indispensable.

2 Leitch, who was born in 1933, belongs to a different generation from Bell (b. 1909) and McNeill (b. 1907). However, he was an admirer of Sam Hanna Bell's writing and, like him, worked for the BBC in Northern Ireland. For many years, Bell was a well-known and distinguished broadcaster and producer and in this capacity knew W.R. Rodgers, John Boyd and Louis MacNeice – all of whom were also employed by the BBC at various times and on some occasions wrote and produced work alongside each other. Janet McNeill's first venture into writing came when she won second prize in a BBC playwriting competition in 1951 with *Gospel Truth* – a drama which focused on the problems of a young Presbyterian clergyman. Thereafter, she produced many radio dramas for BBC Northern Ireland.

3 Sam Hanna Bell, *December Bride*, p 44.
4 *Ibid.*, p 50.
5 *Ibid.*, pp 143–144.
6 *Ibid.*, p 134.
7 *Ibid.*, p 135.
8 *Ibid.*, p 147.
9 W.F. Marshall, *Planted by a River*, p 174.
10 Janet McNeill, *As Strangers Here*, p 116.
11 *Ibid.*, p 189.
12 *Ibid.*, pp 121–122.
13 *Ibid.*, p 101.
14 *Ibid.*, p 9.
15 *Ibid.*, p 12.
16 *Ibid.*, p 79.
17 *Ibid.*, p 81.
18 *Ibid.*, p 25.
19 *Ibid.*, p 82.
20 Susan Manning, *The Puritan-Provincial Vision (Scottish and American Literature in the Nineteenth Century)*, p 9.
21 *As Strangers Here*, p 192.
22 Ruth Hooley, 'A Sculptor in Ivory', (a supplement to *Fortnight*, No 306), March 1992, p 3.
23 *As Strangers Here*, p 140.
24 Maurice Leitch, *Gilchrist*, p 103.
25 *Ibid.*, p 114.
26 *Ibid.*, p 243.
27 *Ibid.*, p 217.
28 *Ibid.*, p 260.
29 *Ibid.*, p 177.
30 *Ibid.*, p 185.
31 *Ibid*, p 309.
32 Robert McLiam Wilson, 'Rhythm Method', *Fortnight*, No 331, Sept 1994, p 46.
33 *Gilchrist*, p 207.
34 See Foster, *op. cit.*, p 274.
35 Anthony C. West, *The Ferret Fancier*, p 33 and p 28.
36 *Ibid.*, p 40
37 *Ibid.*, p 29.
38 *Ibid.*, p 67.
39 *Ibid.*, p 103.
40 *Ibid.*, p 103 and p 104.
41 *Ibid.*, p 179.
42 *Ibid.*, p 98.
43 *Ibid.*, p 149.
44 *Ibid.*, p 134.
45 *Ibid.*, pp 133–134.
46 *Ibid.*, p 76.
47 *Ibid.*, p 77.

48 *Ibid.*
49 *Ibid.*, p 242.
50 *Ibid.*, p 92 and p 93.
51 *Ibid.*, p 254.
52 *Ibid.*, p 255.
53 Julie Mitchell, *Sunday Afternoons*, p 53.
54 *Ibid.*, p 114.
55 *Ibid.*, p 54.
56 *Ibid.*, p 79.
57 *Ibid.*, p 125.
58 *Ibid.*, p 145.
59 *Ibid.*, p 155.
60 *Ibid.*, p 177.
61 *Ibid.*, p 178.
62 Glenn Patterson, *Burning Your Own*, p 167.
63 Eve Patten, 'Fiction in Conflict: Northern Ireland's Prodigal Novelists', in I.A. Bell (ed), *Peripheral Views*, p 140.
64 Glenn Patterson, 'I Am a Northern Irish Novelist', *Ibid.*, p 151.
65 *Burning Your Own*, p 14.
66 *Ibid.*, p 61.
67 *Ibid.*, p 24.
68 *Ibid.*, p 201. It is notable that Ciaran Carson creates an interesting variation on this idea in *The Star Factory*, where he writes: 'Sometimes the city is an exploded diagram of itself, along the lines of a vastly complicated interactive model aircraft kit whose components are connected by sprued plastic latitudes and longitudes'. A little later, he continues: 'Now that I can see the city's microscopic bits transfixed by my attention, I wonder how I might assemble them, for there is no instruction leaflet; I must write it'. (*The Star Factory*, p 15.)
69 *Ibid.*, p 211.
70 Patterson, 'I Am a Northern Irish Novelist', p 150.

CHAPTER ELEVEN

1   This should not be taken to imply that dramatists from Catholic backgrounds have ignored these matters – some of the work of Brian Friel, Martin Lynch and Anne Devlin for example, might be cited – but rather that they receive greater prominence in the work of the dramatists discussed in the course of this chapter.
2   John Boyd, Introduction to *Collected Plays 2*, p vii.
3   St John Ervine, *John Ferguson* in *Selected Plays of St John Ervine*, p 123.
4   *Ibid.*, p 124.
5   *Ibid.*, p 125.
6   Norman Vance, *Irish Literature: A Social History*, p 178.
7   *John Ferguson*, p 127.
8   *Ibid.*, p 157.
9   *Ibid.*, p 168.
10 D.E.S. Maxwell, *A Critical History of Modern Irish Drama 1891–1980*, p 83.
11 *John Ferguson*, p 188.
12 *Ibid.*, p 192 and p 195. Vance, *op. cit.*, p 178, also makes this point about the reading from 2 Samuel, ch 18, vv 32–33.
13 St John Ervine, *The Foolish Lovers* in *The St John Ervine Omnibus*, p 310.
14 St John Ervine, *The Wayward Man*, *ibid.*, p 39.
15 St John Ervine, *Friends and Relations* in *Selected Plays of St John Ervine*, p 352. Norman Vance writes that: 'Pelagius had always been a source of embarrassment for Irish and British church historians. St Augustine had denounced him for being unsound on the total depravity of humankind and for contending that people were capable of self-betterment, able to rely on their own arguments rather than on the grace of God . . . Irish Protestants found Pelagius a particular nuisance because

traditional Protestant polemic tended to caricature Catholic devotion as essentially "Pelagian", a religion of works in which the performance of particular penances accumulated religious merit'. Vance also makes the point that St John Ervine was brought up in a Congregational church in Belfast (in fact, the same church as that attended by John Boyd's father) which 'was even more independent-minded than other Protestant churches such as the locally dominant Presbyterian Church'. The self-reliance which Ervine showed in his own life, and which is celebrated in his plays and fiction, was certainly influenced by this background. As Vance puts it: 'Saving your own soul, taking charge of your own destiny, relying on your own efforts, might be heresy but it is Protestant heresy, the characteristic note of Ervine's Ulster Protestant individualism'. See Norman Vance, 'Catholic and Protestant Literary Visions of "Ulster": Now You See It, Now You Don't', *Religion and Literature*, Vol 28.2–3, Summer/Autumn, 1996, pp 136–139.

16 David Kennedy, 'The Drama in Ulster' in S.H. Bell, N.A. Robb, J. Hewitt (eds), *The Arts in Ulster*, p 62.
17 St John Ervine, *Boyd's Shop* in *Selected Plays of St John Ervine*, p 260.
18 John Boyd, *The Farm* in *Collected Plays 1*, p 89.
19 *Ibid.*, p 91.
20 *Ibid.*, p 156.
21 *Ibid.*, p 126.
22 *Ibid.*, p 163.
23 John Boyd, *Facing North* in *Collected Plays 2*, p 86.
24 *Ibid.*, p 83.
25 *Ibid.*, p 91 and p 95.
26 *Ibid.*, p 142.
27 *Ibid.*, pp 142–143.
28 St John Ervine, *Mixed Marriage* in *Selected Plays of St John Ervine*, p 22.
29 *Ibid.*, p 24 and p 25.
30 *Ibid.*, p 45.
31 *Ibid.*, p 50.
32 *Ibid.*, pp 50–51.
33 *Ibid.*, p 63.
34 D.E.S. Maxwell, *op. cit.*, p 82.
35 St John Ervine, *The Orangeman* in *Four Irish Plays*, p 101.
36 *Ibid.*, p 101.
37 *Ibid.*, p 102.
38 *Ibid.*, p 111 and p 116.
39 *Ibid.*, p 117.
40 *Ibid.*, p 104.
41 *Ibid.*, p 105.
42 John Boyd, *The Flats* in *Collected Plays 1*, p 32.
43 Bill Morrison, *A Love Song for Ulster*, pp 13–14.
44 *Ibid.*, p 54.
45 *Ibid.*, p 145.
46 *Ibid.*, p 174.
47 *Ibid.*, pp 174–175.
48 *Ibid.*, p 175.
49 Sam Thompson, *Over the Bridge*, introd. by Stewart Parker, p 9.
50 *Ibid.*, cited by Parker, p 11.
51 *Ibid.*, p 114.
52 D.E.S. Maxwell, 'Contemporary Drama 1953–1986' in *The Field Day Anthology of Irish Writing*, Vol 3, p 1139.
53 Christina Reid, *Tea in a China Cup* in *Joyriders and Tea in a China Cup*, p 6.
54 *Ibid.*, p 5.
55 *Ibid.*, p 13.
56 Cited in Elizabeth Doyle, 'Men don't cook in West Belfast', *Fortnight*, No 337, March 1995, p 31.
57 *Ibid.*
58 *Tea in a China Cup*, p 13.

59 *Ibid.*, p 14.
60 *Ibid.*, p 33.
61 Stewart Parker, *Northern Star* in *Three Plays for Ireland*, p 17 and p 65.
62 The Seven Ages are Innocence, Idealism, Cleverness, Dialectic, Heroic, Compromise and Knowledge, and the dramatists whose styles are parodied are Farquhar, Boucicault, Wilde, Shaw, Synge, O'Casey and Behan.
63 Csilla Bertha, '"The Ghosts . . . Wrestle and Dance": Irish Drama Haunted by History', in Csilla Bertha and Donald E. Morse, *Worlds Visible and Invisible: Essays on Irish Literature*, p 79.
64 *Northern Star*, p 52.
65 *Ibid.*
66 *Ibid.*, p 36.
67 *Ibid.*, pp 72–73.
68 *Ibid.*, p 57.
69 *Ibid.*, p 75.
70 Terence Brown, 'Awakening from Nightmare: History and Contemporary Literature' in *Ireland's Literature: Selected Essays*, p 249.
71 Stewart Parker, *Pentecost* in *Three Plays for Ireland*, p 147.
72 *Ibid.*, p 156 and p 165.
73 Anthony Roche, *Contemporary Irish Drama from Beckett to McGuinness*, p 221.
74 *Pentecost*, p 196.
75 Roche, *op. cit.*, p 227.
76 *Pentecost*, p 201.
77 *Ibid.*, p 202.
78 *Ibid.*, p 204.
79 *Ibid.*, p 205 and p 206.
80 Norman Vance has suggested that Lenny's speeches in the closing stages of the play have 'a recognisable connection with the liberal Protestant vogue for a Religionless Christianity as it developed in the 1960s from German Protestant sources, especially the *Systematic Theology* of Karl Barth and before that some of the radical possibilities outlined in Dietrich Bonhoeffer's *Letters and Papers from Prison*'. See 'Catholic and Protestant Literary Visions of "Ulster": Now You See It, Now You Don't', pp 139–140.
81 *Pentecost*, p 207.
82 Csilla Bertha, *op. cit.*, p 83.
83 *Pentecost*, p 208.
84 Such a vision is, as Christopher Murray puts it, 'in the optative mood', and 'calls for a change in the form of miracle'. Yet, as he also shows, however unexpectedly, it is 'strangely replicated' in the conclusion to Frank Wright's *Northern Ireland: A Comparative Analysis* (1987) which argues that '"faith" in the "miracle" of the Resurrection provides the only hope of reconciliation'. See Christopher Murray, *Mirror Up to Nature: Twentieth-Century Irish Drama*, p 220.
85 Stewart Parker, *Dramatis Personae* (A John Malone Lecture), 1986, p 15.
86 *Ibid.*, p 15.
87 Robert Johnstone, 'Playing for Ireland', *Honest Ulsterman*, No 86, Spring/Summer 1989, p 62. Elmer Andrews, 'The Will to Freedom: Politics and Play in the Theatre of Stewart Parker' in O. Komesu and M. Sekine (eds), *Irish Writers and Politics*, p 267.
88 Stewart Parker, Introduction to *Three Plays for Ireland*, p 9.
89 Stewart Parker, *Dramatis Personae*, p 3.

Select Bibliography

Acheson, Alan, *A History of the Church of Ireland 1691–1996*, Dublin: Columba Press, 1997.

Adams, J.R.R., *The Printed Word and the Common Man: Popular Culture in Ulster 1700–1900*, Belfast: Institute of Irish Studies, 1987.

Adamson, Ian, *The Cruthin: The Ancient Kindred*, Bangor: Pretani Press, 1974.

— , *The Identity of Ulster*, Bangor: Pretani Press, 1982.

— , *The Ulster People*, Bangor: Pretani Press, 1991.

Amis, Kingsley, 'Ulster Bull: The Case of W.R. Rodgers', *Essays in Criticism*, Vol 3, No 4, Oct 1953.

Andrews, Elmer, (ed.) *Contemporary Irish Poetry: A Collection of Critical Essays*, Basingstoke: Macmillan, 1992.

Armour, W.S., *Armour of Ballymoney*, London: Duckworth, 1934.

Bardon, Jonathan, *A History of Ulster*, Belfast: Blackstaff Press, 1992.

Barkley, John M., *A Short History of the Presbyterian Church in Ireland*, Belfast: Presbyterian Publications Board, 1959.

— , *Blackmouth and Dissenter*, Belfast: Whiterow Press, 1991.

Beattie, Geoffrey, *We Are the People (Journeys through the Heart of Protestant Ulster)*, London: Wm Heinemann, 1992.

Beckett, J.C., *Protestant Dissent in Ireland 1687–1780*, London: Faber and Faber, 1948.

Bell, Desmond, 'Contemporary Cultural Studies in Ireland and the "Problem" of Protestant Ideology', *Crane Bag*, Vol 9, No 2, 1985.

Bell, Geoffrey, *The Protestants of Ulster*, London: Pluto Press, 1976.

Bell, Ian A., (ed.) *Peripheral Views: Images of Nationhood in Contemporary British Fiction*, Cardiff: University of Wales, 1995.

Bell, Sam Hanna, Robb, Nesca A., and Hewitt, John, (eds) *The Arts in Ulster: A Symposium*, London: Harrap, 1951.

Bell, S.H., *December Bride*, 1951; facsimile ed. Belfast: Blackstaff Press, 1974, repr. 1982.

Bertha, Csilla and Morse, Donald E., *Worlds Visible and Invisible: Essays on Irish Literature*, Debrecen: Lajos Kossuth University, 1994.

Birmingham, George A., *The Red Hand of Ulster*, London: Smith Elder, 1912.

— , *The Northern Iron*, 1907; 6th printing, Dublin: Talbot Press, 1946.

— , *An Irishman Looks at his World*, London: Hodder and Stoughton, 1919.

— , *Pleasant Places*, London: Wm Heinemann, 1934.

Blaney, Roger, *Presbyterians and the Irish Language*, Belfast: Ulster Historical Foundation, 1996.

Bowen, Desmond, *The Protestant Crusade in Ireland 1800–1870*, Dublin: Gill and Macmillan, 1978.

— , *History and the Shaping of Irish Protestantism*, New York: Peter Lang, 1995.

Boyce, George, 'Ireland in the First World War', *History Ireland*, Autumn 1994.

Boyd, Andrew, 'The Orange Order 1795–1995', *History Today*, Vol 45 (9), Sept 1995.

Boyd, John, *Collected Plays 1*, Belfast: Blackstaff Press, 1981.

— , *Collected Plays 2*, Belfast: Blackstaff Press, 1982.

— , *Out of My Class*, Belfast: Blackstaff Press, 1985.

— , *The Middle of My Journey*, Belfast: Blackstaff Press, 1990.

Brooke, Peter, *Ulster Presbyterianism: The Historical Perspective 1610–1970*, Dublin: Gill and Macmillan, 1987.

— , *Ireland's Literature: Selected Essays*, Mullingar: Lilliput Press, 1988.

Brown, Terence, *Northern Voices*, Dublin: Gill and Macmillan, 1975

— , *Louis MacNeice: Sceptical Vision*, Dublin: Gill and Macmillan, 1975.

— , *The Whole Protestant Community: The making of a historical myth*, Derry: Field Day, 1985.

— , *Ireland: A Social and Cultural History 1922–1985*, London: Fontana, 1981; 3rd imp. repr. with postscript, 1985.

Brown, Terence and Reid, Alec, (eds) *Time Was Away: The World of Louis MacNeice*, Dublin: Dolmen Press, 1974.

Bruce, Steve, *Firm in the Faith*, Aldershot: Gower, 1984.

— , *God Save Ulster! The Religion and Politics of Paisleyism*, Oxford: Clarendon Press, 1986.

— , *The Edge of the Union: The Ulster Loyalist Political Vision*, Oxford: Oxford University Press, 1994.

— , 'Cultural Traditions: A Double-edged Sword?' *Causeway*, Vol 1, No 4, Autumn 1994.

Bryan, Dominic, 'Interpreting the Twelfth', *History Ireland*, Summer 1994.

Bryan, Mary, *Forrest Reid*, Boston: Twayne, 1976.

Buchanan, George, *Green Seacoast*, London: Gaberbocchus Press, 1959.

— , *Morning Papers*, London: Gaberbocchus Press, 1965.

Buckley, Anthony D., 'Walls Within Walls: Religion and "Rough" Behaviour in an Ulster Community', *Sociology*, Vol 18, No 1, Feb 1984.

— , 'The Chosen Few: Biblical Texts in the Regalia of an Ulster Secret Society', *Folklife*, Vol 24, pt 19, 1985–1986.

Bullock, Shan F., *After Sixty Years*, London: Sampson Low and Marston, 1931.

Burlingham, Russell, *Forrest Reid: A Portrait and a Study*, London: Faber and Faber, 1953.

Calvin, John, *Institutes of the Christian Religion*, 2 Vols, trans, Henry Beveridge, Michigan: Eerdmans Publishing Co., 1983.

— , *Calvin: Theological Treatises*, Trans, introd. and notes J.K.S. Reid, London: SCM Press, 1954.

Campbell, Flann, *The Dissenting Voice: Protestant Democracy in Ulster from Plantation to Partition*, Belfast: Blackstaff Press, 1991.

Carnduff, Thomas, *Poverty Street and Other Belfast Poems*, Belfast: Lapwing Publications, 1993.

— , *Life and Writings*, Selected and introduced by John Gray, Belfast: Lagan Press, 1994.

— , *Carrickfergus and District Historical Journal*, (a Louis MacNeice issue), Vol 17, 1993.

Carson, Ciaran, *The Star Factory*, London: Granta Books, 1997.

Carson, John T., *God's River in Spate: The Story of the Religious Awakening in Ulster in 1859*, Belfast: Presbyterian Church in Ireland, 1958.

Chadwick, Owen, *The Reformation*, London Penguin Books 1964.

Connolly, Sean, *Religion and Society in Nineteenth-Century Ireland*, Dundalk: Dundalgan Press, 1985.

Cooke, Dennis, *Persecuting Zeal: A Portrait of Ian Paisley*, Dingle: Brandon Books, 1996.

Corcoran, Neil, (ed.) *The Chosen Ground: Essays on Contemporary Poetry of Northern Ireland*, Bridgend: Seren, 1992.

Coveney, Peter, *The Image of Childhood*, London: Penguin Books, 1967.

Crawford, Robert G., *Loyal to King Billy: A Portrait of the Ulster Protestants*, London: C. Hurst, 1987.

Crozier, Maurna, (ed.) *Cultural Traditions in Northern Ireland, Belfast: Institute of Irish Studies*, 1989, repr. 1993.

Cupitt, Don, *The Long-Legged Fly*, London: SCM Press, 1987.

Davie, Donald, *A Gathered Church: The Literature of the Dissenting Interest, 1700–1930*, London: RKP, 1978.

Davin, Dan, *Closing Times*, Oxford: Oxford University Press, 1975.

Dawe, Gerald, *How's the Poetry Going? Literary Politics and Ireland Today*, Belfast: Lagan Press, 1991, 2nd ed 1993.

— , *A Real Life Elsewhere*, Belfast: Lagan Press, 1993.

— , *False Faces: Poetry, Politics and Place*, Belfast: Lagan Press, 1994.

— , *Against Piety: Essays in Irish Poetry*, Belfast: Lagan Press, 1995.

— , *The Rest is History*, Newry: Abbey Press, 1998.

Dawe, Gerald and Foster, John Wilson, (eds) *The Poet's Place: Ulster Literature and Society*, Belfast: Institute of Irish Studies, 1991.

Dawe, Gerald and Longley, Edna, (eds) *Across a Roaring Hill.: The Protestant Imagination in Modern Ireland*, Belfast: Blackstaff Press, 1985.

Deane, Seamus, *Celtic Revivals: Essays in Modern Irish Literature*, London: Faber and Faber, 1985.

Dodds, E.R., *Missing Persons: An Autobiography*, Oxford: Clarendon Press, 1977.

Doyle, Elizabeth, 'Men Don't Cook in West Belfast,' *Fortnight*, No 337, March 1995.

Doyle, Lynn, *An Ulster Childhood*, Dublin and London: Maunsel and Roberts, 1921.

Dunlop, John, *A Precarious Belonging: Presbyterians and the Conflict in Ireland*, Belfast: Blackstaff Press, 1995.

Dunn, Douglas, (ed.) *Two Decades of Irish Writing: A Critical Survey*, Cheadle: Carcanet Press, 1975.

Eagleton, Terry, *Heathcliff and the Great Hunger*, London: Verso, 1995.

Edwards, Jonathan, *Basic Writings*, Edited, selected and foreword by Ola Elizabeth Winslow, New York: New American Library, 1966.

Elliott, Marianne, *Watchmen in Sion: The Protestant Idea of Liberty*, Derry: Field Day, 1985.

Elton, G.R., *Reformation Europe 1517–1559*, London: Collins, 1963.

English, Richard and Walker, Graham, (eds) *Unionism in Modern Ireland*, Basingstoke: Macmillan, 1996.

Ervine, St John, *Four Irish Plays*, Dublin: Maunsel, 1914.

— , *The St John Ervine Omnibus*, London: Collins, n.d.

— , *Selected Plays of St John Ervine*, Intro John Cronin, Gerrards Cross: Colin Smythe, 1988.

The Field Day Anthology of Irish Writing, 3 Vols, Derry: Field Day, 1991.

Fitzpatrick, Brendan, *Seventeenth-Century Ireland: The War of Religions*, Dublin: Gill and Macmillan, 1988.

Fitzpatrick, Rory, *God's Frontiersmen: The Scots-Irish Epic*, London: Weidenfeld and Nicholson, 1989.

Foster, John Wilson, *Forces and Themes in Ulster Fiction*, Dublin: Gill and Macmillan, 1974.

— , *Colonial Consequences: Essays in Irish Literature and Culture*, Dublin: Lilliput Press, 1991.

— , (ed.) *The Idea of the Union: Statements and Critiques in Support of the Union of Great Britain and Northern Ireland*, Vancouver: Belcouver Press, 1995.

Foster, R.F., *Modern Ireland 1600–1972*, London: Allen Lane, 1986.

— , *Paddy and Mr Punch: Conversations in Irish and English History*, London: Allen Lane, 1993.

Francis Hutcheson, A supplement to *Fortnight*, No 308, July 1992.

Fulton, John, *The Tragedy of Belief: Division, Politics and Religion in Ireland*, Oxford: Clarendon Press, 1991.

Garratt, Robert F., *Modern Irish Poetry: Tradition and Continuity from Yeats to Heaney*, Berkeley: University of California Press, 1986.

Genet, Jacqueline and Cave, R.A., (eds) *Perspectives of Irish Drama and Theatre*, Gerrards Cross: Colin Smythe, 1991.

Greacen, Robert, *Even Without Irene*, Dublin: Dolmen Press, 1969; rev. and repr. Belfast: Lagan Press, 1995.

— , *Brief Encounters – Literary Dublin and Belfast in the 1940s*, Dublin: Cathair Books, 1991.

— , *Collected Poems 1944–1994*, Belfast: Lagan Press, 1995.

Haire, JLM (ed.) *Challenge and Conflict: Essays in Irish Presbyterian History and Doctrine*, Antrim: W. and G. Baird, 1981.

Hall, Michael, *Beyond the Fife and Drum*. Newtownabbey: Island Publications, 1995.

Harbinson, Robert, *No Surrender: An Ulster Childhood*, London: Faber and Faber, 1960; repr. Belfast: Blackstaff Press, 1987.

— , *Song of Erne*, London: Faber and Faber, 1960.

— , *Up Spake the Cabin Boy*, London: Faber and Faber, 1961.

— , *The Protégé*, London: Faber and Faber, 1963.

— , *Songs Out of Oriel*, London: G.H. and R. Hart, 1974.

Harmon, Maurice, (ed.) *The Irish Writer and the City*, Gerrards Cross: Colin Smythe, 1984.

Heaney, Seamus, *John Hewitt 1907–1987, The Universal Poet*, Belfast: Belfast Workers' Festival Committee, n.d.

— , *The Redress of Poetry*, London: Faber and Faber, 1995.

Hempton, David, *Religion and Political Culture in Britain and Ireland*, Cambridge: Cambridge University Press, 1996.

Hempton, David and Hill, Myrtle, *Evangelical Protestantism in Ulster Society 1740–1890*, London: Routledge, 1992.

Henry, Paul, *An Irish Portrait*, London: B.T. Batsford Ltd, 1951.

— , *Further Reminiscences*, Belfast: Blackstaff Press, 1973.

Herlihy, Kevin, (ed.) *The Irish Dissenting Tradition 1650–1750*, Dublin: Four Courts Press, 1995.

— , *The Religion of Irish Dissent 1650–1800*, Dublin: Four Courts Press, 1996.

Hewitt, John, *Rhyming Weavers and Other Country Poets of Antrim and Down*, Belfast: Blackstaff Press, 1974.

— , *The Selected John Hewitt*, Edited and introduced by Alan Warner, Belfast: Blackstaff Press, 1981.

— , *Ancestral Voices: The Selected Prose of John Hewitt*, Edited by Tom Clyde, Belfast: Blackstaff Press, 1987.

— , *The Collected Poems of John Hewitt*, Edited with an introduction and notes by Frank Ormsby, Belfast: Blackstaff Press, 1991.

Hill, Christopher, *The Collected Essays of Christopher Hill (Vol 3): People and Ideas in Seventeenth-Century England*, Brighton: Harvester, 1986.

Hill, Myrtle and Barber, Sarah, (eds) *Aspects of Irish Studies*, Belfast: Institute of Irish Studies, 1990.

Holmes, Finlay, *Henry Cooke*, Belfast: Christian Journals Ltd., 1981.

— , *Our Irish Presbyterian Heritage*, Belfast: Publications Committee of the Presbyterian Church in Ireland, 1985.

— , *Presbyterianism and Orangeism 1795–1995*, Belfast: Presbyterian Historical Society of Ireland, 1996.

Holmes, Janice and Urquhart, Diane, (eds) *Coming Into the Light: The Work, Politics and Religion of Women in Ulster 1840–1940*, Belfast: Institute of Irish Studies, 1994.

Honest Ulsterman, No 92 – a W.R. Rodgers Special Number, 1991–1992.

Höpfl, Harro, *The Christian Polity of John Calvin*, Cambridge: Cambridge University Press, 1982.

Hughes, Eamonn, (ed.) *Culture and Politics in Northern Ireland*, Buckingham: Open University Press, 1991.

— , 'Ulster of the Senses', Supplement to *Fortnight*, No 306, May 1992.

Hurley, Michael, (ed.) *Irish Anglicanism 1869–1969*, Dublin: Figgis, 1970.

Hurstfield, Joel, (ed.) *The Reformation Crisis*, London: Arnold, 1965.

Ireland, Denis, *An Ulster Protestant Looks at his World*, Belfast: Dorman, 1930.

— , *From the Irish Shore*, London: Rich and Cowen, 1936.

— , *Statues Round the City Hall*, London: Cresset Press, 1939.

— , *From the Jungle of Belfast*, Belfast: Blackstaff Press, 1973.

Ireland's Field Day, (Pamphlets by Tom Paulin, Seamus Heaney, Seamus Deane, Richard Kearney, and Declan Kiberd) London: Hutchinson, 1985.

Irish University Review Special Issue: Derek Mahon, Spring/Summer 1994.

John Hewitt, A supplement to *Fortnight*, No 275, July/August, 1989.

Johnstone, Robert, 'Playing for Ireland', *Honest Ulsterman*, No 86, Spring/Summer, 1989.

— , *Belfast: Portraits of a City*, London: Barrie and Jenkins, 1990.

Johnstone, Robert and Kirk, Bill, *Images of Belfast*, Belfast: Blackstaff Press, 1983.

Kearney, Timothy, 'The Poetry of the North: A Post-Modernist Perspective', *Crane Bag*, Vol 3, No 2, 1979.

Kelly, James, 'Relations between the Protestant Church of Ireland and the Presbyterian Church in Late Eighteenth-Century Ireland', *Éire-Ireland*, Vol xxiii, No 3, Fall, 1988.

Kenneally, Michael, (ed.) *Cultural Contexts and Literary Idioms in Contemporary Irish Literature*, Gerrards Cross: Colin Smythe, 1988.

— , *Poetry in Contemporary Irish Literature*, Gerrards Cross: Colin Smythe, 1995.

Kennelly, Brendan, *Journey Into Joy: Selected Prose*, (ed.) A Persson, Newcastle upon Tyne: Bloodaxe Books, 1994.

Keogh, Dermot and Haltzel, Michael H., (eds) *Northern Ireland and the Politics of Reconciliation*, Cambridge: Cambridge University Press, 1993.

Kiberd, Declan, *Inventing Ireland*, London: Jonathan Cape, 1995.

Killen, W.D., *Reminiscences of a Long Life*, London: Hodder and Stoughton, 1901.

Kinahan, Timothy, *Where Do We Go from Here? Protestants and the Future of Northern Ireland*, Blackrock: Columba Press, 1995.

Kirkland, Richard, *Literature and Culture in Northern Ireland since 1965: Moments of Danger*, London: Longman, 1996.

Komesu, O. and Sekine, M., (eds) *Irish Writers and Politics*, Gerrards Cross: Colin Smythe, 1990.

Kosok, Heinz, (ed.) *Studies in Anglo-Irish Literature*, Bonn: Bouvier, 1982.

Kuyper, Abraham, *Calvinism (Six Stone Lectures given in 1898)*, Amsterdam: Höveker and Wormser, and Edinburgh: T. and T. Clark, n.d.

Leitch, Maurice, *Gilchrist*, London: Secker andWarburg, 1994.

Levine, Ketzel, 'A Tree of Identities and a Tradition of Dissent: John Hewitt at 78,' *Fortnight*, No 213, Feb 1985.

Loftus, Belinda, *Mirrors: William III and Mother Ireland*, Dundrum: Picture Press, 1990.

— , *Mirrors: Orange and Green*, Dundrum: Picture Press, 1994.

Longley, Edna, *Poetry in the Wars*, Newcastle upon Tyne: Bloodaxe Books, 1986.

— , *Louis MacNeice: A Study*, London: Faber and Faber, 1988.

— , *The Living Stream: Literature and Revisionism in Ireland*, Newcastle upon Tyne: Bloodaxe Books, 1994.

— , *Culture in Ireland: Division or Diversity?* Belfast: Institute of Irish Studies, 1991.

Longley, Michael, *Tuppenny Stung*, Belfast: Lagan Press, 1994.

Loughlin, James, *Ulster Unionism and British National Identity since 1885*, London: Pinter, 1995.

Lundy, Jean and Mac Póilin, Aodán, (eds) *Styles of Belonging: The Cultural Identities of Ulster*, Belfast: Lagan Press, 1992.

Lynd, Robert, *Irish and English*, London: Francis Griffiths, 1908.

— , *Home Life in Ireland*, London: Mills and Boon, 1909.

— , *Ireland A Nation*, London: Grant Richards, 1919.

— , *Galway of the Races: Selected Essays*, ed. and introd. Séan McMahon, Dublin: Lilliput Press, 1990.

Lyons, F.S.L., *Culture and Anarchy in Ireland 1890–1939*, Oxford: Clarendon Press, 1979.

McCartney, R.L., *Liberty and Authority in Ireland*, Derry: Field Day, 1985.

McBride, Ian, 'Protestants in the Penal Era', *Bullán*, Vol 1, No 2, Autumn 1994.

— , *The Siege of Derry in Ulster Protestant Mythology*, Dublin: Four Courts Press, 1997.

McCaughey, Terence P., *Memory and Redemption: Church, Politics and Prophetic Theology in Ireland*, Dublin: Gill and Macmillan, 1993.

McClelland, Aiken, *William Johnston of Ballykilbeg*, Belfast: Ulster Society (Pubs) Ltd., 1990.

McCormack, W.J., *The Battle of the Books*, Mullingar: Lilliput Press, 1986.

McDonald, Peter, Louis MacNeice: The Poet in his Contexts, Oxford: Clarendon Press, 1991.

—, 'The Fate of 'Identity': John Hewitt, W.R. Rodgers and Louis MacNeice', *Irish University Review*, No 12, Spring/Summer, 1992.

— , *Mistaken Identities: Poetry and Northern Ireland*, Oxford: Clarendon Press, 1997.

McFague, Sallie, *Metaphorical Language: Models of God in Religious Language*, London: SCM Press, 1983.

McGuinness, Frank, *Observe the Sons of Ulster Marching Towards the Somme*, London: Faber and Faber, 1986.

Mackey, James P., (ed.) *The Cultures of Europe: The Irish Contribution*, Belfast: Institute of Irish Studies, 1994.

McKinnon, William T., *Apollo's Blended Dream: A Study of the Poetry of Louis MacNeice*, Oxford: Oxford University Press, 1971.

McMinn, J.R.B., *Against the Tide: A Calendar of the Papers of Revd J.B. Armour, Irish Presbyterian Minister and Home Ruler 1869–1914*, Belfast: PRONI, 1985.

MacNeice, Louis, *Modern Poetry: A Personal Essay*, 1938; 2nd edn with introd. by Walter Allen, Oxford: Oxford University Press, 1968.

— , *Varieties of Parable*, Cambridge: Cambridge University Press, 1965.

— , *The Strings Are False*, (ed.) E.R. Dodds, London: Faber and Faber, 1966.

— , *Collected Poems*, London: Faber and Faber, 1966.

— , *Selected Literary Criticism of Louis MacNeice*, (ed.) Alan Heuser Oxford: Clarendon Press, 1987.

—, *Selected Prose of Louis MacNeice*, (ed.) Alan Heuser, Oxford: Clarendon Press, 1990.

—, *Selected Plays of Louis MacNeice*, (eds) Alan Heuser and Peter McDonald, Oxford: Clarendon Press, 1993.

McNeill, Janet, *Gospel Truth*, Belfast: H.R. Carter, 1951.

— , *As Strangers Here*, London: Hodder and Stoughton, 1960.

Mahon, Derek, *Night Crossing*, Oxford: Oxford University Press, 1968.

— , *Lives*, Oxford: Oxford University Press, 1972.

— , *The Snow Party*, Oxford: Oxford University Press, 1975.

— , *Poems 1962–1978*, Oxford: Oxford University Press, 1979.

— , *Courtyards in Delft*, Dublin: Gallery Press, 1981.

— , *The Hunt by Night*, Oxford: Oxford University Press, 1982.

— , *Antarctica*, Dublin: Gallery Press, 1985.

— , *Selected Poems*, Harmondsworth: Viking and Meath: Gallery Press, 1991.

— , *The Hudson Letter*, Lough Crew Oldcastle, Co. Meath: Gallery Press, 1995.

— , *Journalism*, Lough Crew Oldcastle, Co. Meath: Gallery Press, 1996.

Moloney, Ed and Pollak, Andy, (eds) *Paisley*, Dublin: Poolbeg Press, 1986.

Manning, Susan, *The Puritan-Provincial Vision (Scottish and American Literature in the Nineteenth Century)*, Cambridge: Cambridge University Press, 1990.

Marsack, Robyn, *The Cave of Making: The Poetry of Louis MacNeice*, Oxford: Clarendon Press, 1982.

Maxwell, D.E.S., *A Critical History of Modern Irish Drama 1891–1980*, Cambridge: Cambridge University Press, 1984.

Mercier, Vivian, *Modern Irish Literature: Sources and Founders*, Oxford: Clarendon Press, 1994.

Miller, David W., *Queen's Rebels: Ulster Loyalism in Historical Perspective*, Dublin: Gill and Macmillan, 1978.

— , 'Presbyterianism and "Modernization" in Ulster,' *Past and Present*, No 80, 1978.

Mistéil, P., (ed.) *The Irish Language and the Unionist Tradition*, Belfast: Ulster People's College/ Ultach Trust, 1994.

Mitchell, Julie, *Sunday Afternoons*, 1988; Harmondsworth: Penguin Books, 1989.

Montague, John, *The Figure in the Cave (and other essays)*, Dublin: Lilliput Press, 1989.

Morrison, Bill, *A Love Song for Ulster*, London: Nick Hern Books, 1994.

Mullett, Michael, *John Calvin*, London: Routledge, 1989.

Murphy, David, *Imagination and Religion in Anglo-Irish Literature 1930–1980*, Blackrock: Irish Academic Press, 1987.

Murphy, Dervla, *A Place Apart*, London: Murray, 1978.

Murray, Christopher, *Twentieth-Century Irish Drama: Mirror Up to Nature*, Manchester: Manchester University Press, 1997.

Nelson, Sarah, *Ulster's Uncertain Defenders*, Belfast: Appletree Press, 1984.

Ní Dhonnchadha, Máirín and Dorgan, Theo, (eds) *Revising the Rising*, Derry: Field Day, 1991.

O'Brien, Darcy, *W.R. Rodgers (1909–1969)*, Lewisburg:Bucknell Univ Press, 1970.

Olney, James, (ed.) *Studies in Autobiography*, Oxford: Oxford University Press, 1988.

Ormsby, Frank, (ed.) *Northern Windows: An Anthology of Ulster Autobiography*, Belfast: Blackstaff Press, 1987.

Orr, Philip, *The Road to the Somme: Men of the Ulster Division Tell Their Story*, Belfast: Blackstaff Press, 1987.

Ó Snodaigh, Pádraig, *Hidden Ulster: Protestants and the Irish Language*, Belfast: Lagan Press, 1995.

Parker, Stewart, *Three Plays for Ireland*, Birmingham: Oberon Books, 1989.

— , *Dramatis Personae* (A John Malone Memorial Lecture), Unpublished.

Patten, Eve, (ed.) *Returning to Ourselves (Second Volume of Papers from the John Hewitt International Summer School)*, Belfast: Lagan Press, 1995.

Patterson, Glenn, *Burning Your Own*, 1988; London: Abacus, 1989.

— , 'Twelfth Nights', *Tribune Magazine*, 9 July, 1995.

Paulin, Tom, *A State of Justice*, London: Faber and Faber, 1977.

— , *The Strange Museum*, London: Faber and Faber, 1980.

— , *Liberty Tree*, London: Faber and Faber, 1983.

— , *Ireland and the English Crisis*, Newcastle upon Tyne: Bloodaxe Books, 1984.

— , *Fivemiletown*, London: Faber and Faber, 1987.

— , *The Hillsborough Script*, London: Faber and Faber, 1987.

— , *Minotaur: Poetry and the Nation State*, London: Faber and Faber, 1992.

— , *Selected Poems 1972–1990*, London: Faber and Faber, 1993.

— , *Walking a Line*, London: Faber and Faber, 1994.

— , *Writing to the Moment: Selected Critical Essays*, London: Faber and Faber, 1996.

Peacock, Alan J. and Devine, Kathleen, (eds) *Louis MacNeice and his Influence*, Gerrards Cross: Colin Smythe, 1998.

Pollak, Andy, (ed.) *A Citizens' Enquiry: The Opsahl Report on Northern Ireland*, Dublin: Lilliput Press, 1993.

Presbyterian Principles and Political Witness in Northern Ireland, Belfast: Presbyterian Church Publications, n.d.

Reid, Christina, *Joyriders and Tea in a China Cup*, London: Methuen, 1987.

Reid, Forrest, *Apostate*, London: Constable, 1926.

— , *Private Road*, London: Faber and Faber, 1940.

— , *Uncle Stephen*, London: Faber and Faber, 1931.

— , *Brian Westby*, London: Faber and Faber, 1934.

— , *The Retreat*, London: Faber and Faber, 1936.

— , *Peter Waring*, London: Faber and Faber, 1939.

— , *Young Tom*, London: Faber and Faber, 1944.

— , *Denis Bracknel*, London: Faber and Faber, 1947.

Reid, James Seaton, *History of the Presbyterian Church in Ireland*, 3 Vols, continued by W.D. Killen, Vol 1, Edinburgh: Waugh and Innes, 1834; Vol 2, London: Whittaker, 1837; Vol 3, London: Whittaker, 1853.

Richtarik, Marilynn J., *Acting Between the Lines: The Field Day Company and Irish Cultural Politics*, Oxford: Clarendon Press, 1994.

Roche, Anthony, *Contemporary Irish Drama (from Beckett to McGuinness)*, Dublin: Gill and Macmillan, 1994.

Rodgers, W.R., 'Balloons and Maggots', *Rann*, No 14,

— , 'Conversation Piece: An Ulster Protestant', *The Bell*, Vol 4, No 5, August 1942.

— , *The Return Room*, BBC Written Archives Centre (unpublished), 1955.

— , *Essex Roundabout*, Colchester: Benham and Co., 1963.

— , *Collected Poems*, London: Oxford University Press, 1971.

— , *Irish Literary Portraits*, London: BBC, 1972.

— , *Poems: W.R. Rodgers*, Selected and introduced by Michael Longley, Lough Crew, Oldcastle, Co. Meath: Gallery Press, 1993.

Rolston, Bill, 'Contemporary Political Wall Murals in the North of Ireland: "Drawing Support"', *Éire-Ireland*, Vol xxiii, No 3, Fall, 1988.

Sekine, Masaru, (ed.) *Irish Writers and the Theatre*, Gerrards Cross: Colin Smythe, 1986.

Smith, Iain Crichton, *Collected Poems*, Manchester: Carcanet Press, 1992 and 1995.

Smyth, Clifford, *Ian Paisley: Voice of Protestant Ulster*, Edinburgh: Scottish Academic Press, 1987.

Smyth, Jim, 'The Men of No Popery: The Origins of the Orange Order', *History Ireland*, Vol 3, No 3, Autumn, 1995.

Stallworthy, Jon, *Louis MacNeice*, London: Faber and Faber, 1995.

Stewart, A.T.Q., *The Narrow Ground*, London: Faber and Faber, 1977, rev. 1989.

Tanner, Tony, *Scenes of Nature, Signs of Men*, Cambridge: Cambridge University Press, 1987.

Taylor, Brian, *The Green Avenue: The Life and Writings of Forrest Reid, 1875–1947*, Cambridge: Cambridge University Press, 1980.

Taylor, John V., *The Go-Between God*, London: SCM Press, 1972.

Thompson, Sam, *Over the Bridge*, Introd. Stewart Parker, Dublin: Gill and Macmillan, 1970.

Tillich, Paul, *Theology of Culture*, New York: Oxford University Press, 1959.

Tonkin, E., McDonald, M., Chapman, M., (eds) *History and Ethnicity*, ASA Monographs 27, London: Routledge, 1989.

Vance, Norman, *Irish Literature: A Social History*, Oxford: Blackwell Publishers, 1990.

— , 'Presbyterian Culture and Revival', *The Bulletin of the Presbyterian Historical Society of Ireland*, Vol 22, 1993.

— , 'Catholic and Protestant Literary Visions of "Ulster": Now You See It,

— , Now You Don't', *Religion and Literature*, Vol 28.2–3, Summer/Autumn, 1996.

Van Til, Henry R., *The Calvinistic Concept of Culture*, Philadelphia: Presbyterian and Reformed Publishing Co., 1959.

Vaughan, W.E., (ed.) *A New History of Ireland*, Vol 5 'Ireland Under the Union 1801–1870', Oxford: Clarendon Press, 1989.

Walker, Brian, '1641, 1689, 1690 And All That: The Unionist Sense of History', *Irish Review*, No 12, Spring/Summer, 1992.

— , *Dancing to History's Tune: History, Myth and Politics in Ireland*, Belfast: Institute of Irish Studies, 1996.

Wendell, F., *Calvin: The Origin and Development of his Religious Thought*, Trans., P. Mairet, London: Collins, 1963; London: Fontana, 1965.

West, Anthony C., *The Ferret Fancier*, 1963; repr. Dublin: O'Brien Press, 1983.

Westendorp, Tjebbe A. and Mallinson, (eds) Jane, *Politics and the Rhetoric of Poetry (Perspectives on Modern Anglo-Irish Poetry)*, Amsterdam: Rodopi, 1995.

Westminster Confession of Faith, 1646; republished Glasgow: Free Presbyterian Publications, 1994.

Wills, Clair, *Improprieties: Politics and Sexuality in Northern Irish Poetry*, Oxford: Clarendon Press, 1993.

Wilson, Robert McLiam, 'Rhythm Method', *Fortnight*, No 331, Sept 1994.

Witherow, Thomas, *The Autobiography of Thomas Witherow 1824–1890*, (eds) Graham Mawhinney and Eull Dunlop, Draperstown: Ballinascreen Historical Society, 1990.

Wright, T.R., *Theology and Literature*, Oxford: Blackwell Publishers, 1988; repr. 1989.

Index